THE ART
OF CURRENCY TRADING

Founded in 1807, John Wiley & Sons is the oldest independent publishing company in the United States. With offices in North America, Europe, Australia, and Asia, Wiley is globally committed to developing and marketing print and electronic products and services for our customers' professional and personal knowledge and understanding.

The Wiley Trading series features books by traders who have survived the market's ever-changing temperament and have prospered—some by reinventing systems, others by getting back to basics. Whether you are a novice trader, professional, or somewhere in between, these books will provide the advice and strategies needed to prosper today and well into the future.

For more on this series, visit our Web site at www.WileyTrading.com.

THE ART OF CURRENCY TRADING

A Professional's Guide to the Foreign Exchange Market

Brent Donnelly

WILEY

Published by John Wiley & Sons, Inc., Hoboken, New Jersey.
Published simultaneously in Canada.

All EBS data provided courtesy of NEX Markets.

For general information on our other products and services or for technical support, please contact our Customer Care Department within the United States at (800) 762–2974, outside the United States at (317) 572–3993, or fax (317) 572–4002.

Wiley publishes in a variety of print and electronic formats and by print-on-demand. Some material included with standard print versions of this book may not be included in e-books or in print-on-demand. If this book refers to media such as a CD or DVD that is not included in the version you purchased, you may download this material at http://booksupport.wiley.com. For more information about Wiley products, visit www.wiley.com.

Library of Congress Cataloging-in-Publication Data:

Names: Donnelly, Brent, 1972- author.
Title: The art of currency trading : a professional's guide to the foreign exchange market / Brent Donnelly.
Description: First Edition. | Hoboken : Wiley, 2019. | Series: Wiley trading | Includes index. |
Identifiers: LCCN 2019001704 (print) | LCCN 2019011822 (ebook) | ISBN 9781119583585 (Adobe PDF) | ISBN 9781119583578 (ePub) | ISBN 9781119583554 (hardback)
Subjects: LCSH: Foreign exchange market. | BISAC: BUSINESS & ECONOMICS / Foreign Exchange.
Classification: LCC HG3851 (ebook) | LCC HG3851 .D66 2019 (print) | DDC 332.4/5—dc23
LC record available at https://lccn.loc.gov/2019001704

Cover Design: Wiley
Graph Image: © AleksOrel/Shutterstock
Background Image: © nartawut/Shutterstock

Printed in the United States of America

SKY10084636_091724

To CnD
Thank you for holding down the fort
11:11

CONTENTS

The title of Brent Donnelly's book is *The <u>Art</u> of Currency Trading*. He did not call it *The Science of Currency Trading*. He also did not call it the *Practice* of currency trading, the *Study* of currency trading, or the *Discipline* of currency trading. Currency trading is an art, much like painting or drawing or playing music. And the people who are really good at it are like artists.

In recent years there have been several attempts to turn trading and investing into a scientific discipline. The proponents of finance as a science call this "evidence-based investing." Get into an argument with one of the evidence-based investing people and they will bury you under an avalanche of data and charts. Thing is, the data and charts are contradicted by the market within a matter of days, and rendered useless. You can pretty much find any piece of data to support your conclusion. They have conferences on this stuff. I am not big on evidence-based investing.

There are no immutable physical laws in finance. No $e=mc^2$. No mathematical certainties. You may learn a technique, it may work for a while, and then it will stop working. The market, as a whole, exhibits a property known as *non-stationarity*, which is the idea that you are playing a game where the rules constantly change. A science can't function under these circumstances, unless it is an adaptive science, which would mean that it isn't really a science. So we're back to square one: trading is an art.

The funny thing about Wall Street is that even though it is filled with the archetypal lax bros from Ivy League schools, the people who really *succeed* on Wall Street for a long period of time are the creative types. People who are out-of-consensus thinkers. One-dimensional linear thinkers don't have a long life expectancy on the Street. Well-rounded people who are also divergent thinkers are survivors. Whenever the tsunami hits, which is usually once every couple of years, they just happen to be halfway up a tree. It's not luck.

I've known Brent since we were both traders at Lehman Brothers, and we have a couple of things in common. We are both creative types with an interest in writing and music, and we both have a curiosity about the financial markets that extends beyond the tiny house that we trade in. Brent says in his book that before 2008 he was the only one on the desk watching things like gold and oil. At the same time, I happened to be the only resident bond market expert on the equity derivatives desk. Cross-asset trading is more common these days, and Brent's work in this area is better than anyone I know. Still, most people are content to live in their silo, wholly ignorant of what is going on around them and oblivious to the macro factors that affect the product that they trade.

A trading book like this has been needed for some time: a book sophisticated enough for professionals to understand, but simple enough for retail investors to take advantage of. Brent is honest about his techniques. He doesn't say that they work all the time for all people; his techniques are what has worked for *him*, someone with a 23-year career who has run a few dealer desks. What many people don't realize is that experience counts for a lot in this business, even though the banks and hedge funds are obsessed with hiring people in their twenties. Outsized returns are what get people's attention, but they should instead care about *risk-adjusted* returns. Brent talks about this. If more people understood Sharpe ratio, the world would be a better place.

I'm glad that Brent devotes a section to behavioral finance. I first started reading about this in 2003, but there was nothing in the popular press at the time. I found myself reading Daniel Kahneman and Amos Tversky's academic papers. We have come a long way since then, and we are now at the point where there are attempts to systematize and profit from cognitive biases—with computer-driven trading strategies. If you're not thinking about these sorts of things, you're at a disadvantage. You're not even in the ballpark.

I have written two books: a memoir, and a very dirty novel. It has never been my aspiration to write a book on trading. Too hard! Even if I sat down to turn my thought process into a rules-based system, there are as many exceptions to the rules as there are rules. There is no methodology. That's trading. Brent doesn't give us *rules*, per se, just guidelines. Best practices. To put an entire career's worth of knowledge into a 100,000-word manuscript is an incredible achievement. There are books on trading stocks, but not quite like this. There are books on trading options, but not quite like this. There are books on trading futures, but not quite like this. There is intellectual rigor in this book, without academic rigor. The goal isn't to teach you what to *do*, it's to teach you how to *think*.

My hope is that this book becomes the industry standard for currency trading. And I think it might.

Jared Dillian
Editor and Publisher, *The Daily Dirtnap*
Author of *Street Freak* and *All the Evil of This World*

ACKNOWLEDGMENTS

Thank you, Mom, for teaching me to take chances. You taught me real risk appetite (and didn't call me weird when I charted stocks on taped-together graph paper and tacked it to the walls of my bedroom at age 15). Thank you, Dad, for teaching me how to turn a double play, for teaching me the difference between wrong and right, and for making me Quaker Oats every day before school when I was 17.

I appreciate my parents' efforts and struggles a lot more now that I have kids.

Thanks to Craig for showing me the wisdom of unconditional happiness and to Steve for the timeless AM/FX logo and for bringing creativity, games, and music to our family. Thank you, Sharon and Barry, for showing me at a young age that it's possible for people to be principled, hardworking, fun loving, and super-successful all at once.

Thanks to SJS for NYC 1997/98 and for showing me how incredibly fun work can be. Thanks to Ed for taking a chance on me after my "sabbatical" and to Joel for bringing me back to the major leagues in 2006. Thank you to Rob for teaching me how to add, and thanks to Pete for imploring me to reduce.

Thank you so much to David Kotok, who has pushed me out of my professional comfort zone and opened up an entire new world to me and my sons. Thank you to Jared for the foreword, for good music and good writing. And for living my dream of one day writing a financial newsletter in South Carolina.

Thank you, Richard and Clyde, for making me feel valued (even when I am losing money) and for backing this book. You are the two best managers I have ever worked for. Thanks to Nick Jonas, Saleh, and Saed for help with the first draft. And to Michael Henton at Wiley for buying into my concept and making things easy and seamless from the start. Thanks Richard Samson and Beula Jaculin at Wiley for your help in editing and preparing the manuscript. Thank you, Tad Crawford, for your encouragement early on, and for suggesting a good title.

Thank you to Gitt for the camaraderie, DFW, and spiritual guidance and for being so crazy good at your job. And thanks to NDWY, NSUV, NJAM, and NSGM for best spot desk performance ever (so far).

The quality of the people we work with determines how much we enjoy the nearly endless string of weekdays behind the screens.

And, of course, I want to give a shout-out to the readers of AM/FX over the past two decades. Thank you so much for your feedback, criticism, and support. I appreciate every single e-mail you send.

Last but foremost: Sideways eight thanks to Adam and Oliver for past and future adventures, like 6 a.m. RPG breakfasts and exploring downhill through the thick forest, past the alien ferns to the frozen stream. And thank you, Christine, for teaching me how to be better at life. And thank you for always believing in me, even those times when I did not believe in myself. None of this would be any fun without you guys. I love you.

Brent Donnelly
Wilton, Connecticut
2019

ACKNOWLEDGMENTS

CHAPTER 1

Introduction

This Book Will Make You a Better Trader

Throughout my career, I have been disappointed with the shortage of quality currency trading books authored by real market professionals. The foreign exchange category is mostly crowded with two types of books:

1. Theoretical textbooks on international finance, the mechanics of the foreign exchange market, and/or the principles of long-term currency valuation.

2. How-to books written by nonprofessionals, usually with the word "forex" in the title. These books tend to rely on a one-dimensional overemphasis of simple, short-term technical patterns while ignoring fundamentals, psychology, positioning, and proper risk management.

I have written this book to fill the void, so you can learn FX trading from a real professional. *The Art of Currency Trading* is a synthesis of everything I have learned in more than twenty years as a professional trader and interbank market maker in FX. This book will give you:

- An insider's deep understanding of what drives currency price movements

- A clear explanation of how to use a fusion of technical analysis, macro fundamentals, behavioral finance, and expert risk management to trade FX successfully

- Specific techniques and setups I use to make money trading foreign exchange

- Specific steps you can take to become a better trader

Trading, like baseball, poker, golf, or any other highly skilled pursuit, can be a game not of inches but of millimeters. Small improvements in your decision-making process can yield large improvements in profitability. This book will give you the insights you need to break through and achieve a higher level of success. Currency trading is like playing the piano. The mechanics are very simple (just press a few keys!) but mastery takes a lifetime.

The book builds in intensity and depth one topic at a time with the goal of enlightening and educating the most experienced, expert FX trader without leaving beginners in the dust. If you are early in your FX trading career, you should find all the building blocks for success here. If you are already an experienced FX trader, you should find a ton of new ideas and inspiration to take your game to the next level.

Most trading books tend to focus on one school of trading thought, whether it's technical analysis, macro fundamentals, behavioral finance, psychology, or risk management. That approach is too one-dimensional. To succeed in FX, you need to master the fusion approach and use multiple types of analysis to reach stronger conclusions and then understand your own psychology and risk management to trade with higher confidence. When every branch of analysis points in the same direction, you have found an extremely high-probability setup: a Five-Star trade.

I have experience trading interest rates, equities, and commodities, so this book will frequently refer to these products. Experienced traders from outside the world of FX will learn a great deal from this book because entire sections (e.g., risk management, trading psychology, the Seven Deadly Setups) apply to trading in any asset class. Please note, however, that my main objective is to increase your expertise specifically in the foreign exchange market.

This book will present a variety of unique approaches and specific trading techniques that I hope will open some new doors in your mind. Every trading book and every hour spent behind the screens is part of an overall trading education. I don't claim to have the holy grail or a simple, foolproof strategy for guaranteed profits in forex. There is no such thing. Trading is a lifelong pursuit and this book should be one step in your ongoing education. Absorb what resonates with you and ignore what does not. Develop your own style. Learn as much as you can from this book, but do not copy my approach or anyone else's. Be an independent thinker.

■ Why I Wrote This Book

When I was in my 20s, I used to greet most trading books with cynicism. I would think something like: "If you're such a great trader, why would you write a book about it? Aren't you giving away all your secrets? And anyway, what do you need money from writing a book for? Shouldn't you be rich already from your superhuman trading skills?"

Let me answer.

First of all, there are no secrets to trading, only knowledge, skill, experience, and psychology. And even if I share all my knowledge, skill, and experience, the psychology bit is by far the hardest part. You can master all the skills, tactics, and strategies and you will still fail if you cannot control yourself. And besides, currency markets are huge. Five trillion dollars a day transact in FX. There is always room for a few more skilled traders. I do not mind sharing what I know at this point. There is no downside for me.

And about the money: You don't get rich writing nonfiction books. The reason I wrote this book is simply because I love to write. And because I love trading. And I think that after more than 20 years of trading, I have something interesting to say about trading generally and currency markets specifically.

I hope you agree.

This book will show you how to come up with intelligent trade ideas using macro fundamental and technical analysis, market psychology, positioning, sentiment, and cross-market correlation. You will learn exactly how to trade the news and economic events. And you will understand the importance of rigorous and systematic risk management.

The book starts with the basics of currency trading and quickly builds to more advanced concepts. While the book works for beginners and quickly brings them up to speed before introducing more advanced topics, my intention is that *The Art of Currency Trading* will appeal to and educate even the most expert and experienced FX trader.

Remember, anyone can learn the rules. Very few can stick to them. Even after more than two decades of trading, I still struggle to stay disciplined and unemotional each day. It is easy to make stupid mistakes, show poor self-control, and go on tilt, no matter how experienced you are.

Each day you walk in to trade the currency market, you battle not just countless algorithms, Ivy league–educated hedge fund professionals, machine learning bots, highly experienced interbank traders, central banks, veteran corporate and real money hedgers, and skilled retail traders. You battle yourself. And even when you win the internal battle and show great self-discipline, every victory is temporary. You must constantly adapt to an ever-changing and highly efficient market.

This book will make you a better currency trader. It will help you understand what moves currency markets, show you how to generate profitable trade ideas, and teach you expert execution methods. This book will help you master foreign exchange trading and achieve sustainable long-term trading success. This book will help you make more money. This book will teach you the art of currency trading.

Thanks for reading.

Good luck ↕ Be nimble.

■　■　■

New York City
8:15PM

The cavernous trading floor is mostly empty, but the foreign exchange sales and trading rows are fully staffed. The trader sits in front of six monitors in the center of the G10 currency trading desk. His pupils flick from various Bloomberg and Reuters headlines to CNN, then to CNBC and foxnews.com. His eyes scan the EURUSD and USDJPY price feeds, and then flick back to CNN. Early presidential election results trickle in. Markets are in a holding pattern still, so he picks at the last few pieces of take-out sashimi.

He is rooting for Hillary Clinton, not for political reasons but because he is positioned for a stronger dollar and the market sees a Clinton win as dollar positive. In contrast, the consensus views a Trump win as bad news for the greenback. For the trader, the event is not about politics, it is about macroeconomic outcomes. He has a big long position in the dollar and he wants a rally.

Just a few weeks ago, a *Washington Post* headline declared, "Trump's path to an electoral college victory isn't narrow. It's nonexistent." And the trader agrees wholeheartedly. It just does not seem possible for Donald Trump to win the US presidential election. The math does not work.

The trader is relaxed and calm as a few Clinton-positive headlines roll by. His heart rate is steady around 85 bpm.

Sweet. Maybe I can get out of here by 10PM and get some sleep.

Live bloggers post compelling anecdotes that point to a possible Hillary Clinton landslide. Early returns look good for the Democrats. The dollar and the trader's profits tick slowly higher. Tick, tick, tick. And then, boom. Everything changes in an instant.

There is a quick, unexplained drop in the dollar. The trader's pulse quickens. His face becomes hot and flushed.

"What's going on?" a sales guy yells over.

"Dude, I have no clue!" the trader hollers back.

A series of headlines scrolls in quick succession. Trump takes the lead in Florida. GOP has a chance in Pennsylvania. Toss-up states lean red. Impossible. Unbelievable.

Over the next twenty minutes, more states lean Republican. Ohio. Wisconsin. Michigan!? The dollar gaps lower as the realization hits the market. Trump has a chance. A good chance. In an instant, gambling odds go from Clinton as a huge favorite to even odds. Nate Silver tweets a nervous mea culpa. Now Trump is the favorite.

Should the trader sell his dollars and get out? Or wait for a turnaround? Frenzied clients sell dollars. Salesmen yell. Markets career lower. Someone spills water on a keyboard. There is no time to think. The dollar lurches lower. Then lower again. The trader feels like he is trapped in a falling elevator. Profits evaporate and losses build.

At 10:53PM, Trump takes Florida and it's pretty much over. Everyone hangs out a few more hours but the result is inevitable. Finally, when Trump takes North Carolina at 1:30AM, election night is over. The dollar has collapsed and everyone on the trading floor is spent. Total exhaustion. Disbelief. The trader has lost more than a million dollars in less than four hours.

The stock market is halted, limit down. Currency markets are pricing in the worst. Fears of trade wars and the end of globalization and … the end of the world? The trader has dumped all his dollars and now he just sits there numb, staring at flickering numbers on a screen.

Finally, he drags himself out of the chair. It has been a marathon 19-hour trading session and he needs sleep, badly. He steps outside into light rain and walks a few blocks, still shell-shocked. He checks into a nearby hotel and falls asleep for a few hours. A quick dream of falling in an elevator. Then, he's awake again. It's 6:00AM. He quickly dresses and heads back out into the dark New York City morning. Back to work.

By 6:30AM, the trader is at his desk and everything has changed. The dollar is exploding off the lows. From a low of 101.19 in USDJPY, the market now trades 103.20. Before he can put down his Starbucks and log in, the phone board lights up. A flurry of customer calls. Something huge is going on. A 180-degree turn in sentiment.

The first phone call picked up by sales is one of the bank's smartest clients and he buys a huge chunk of USDJPY around 103.50.

"It's impossible to buy these!" the USDJPY trader yells.

A full reversal is underway and now the mood is euphoria. Stocks rip higher as the market comes to a brand-new conclusion: Donald Trump is great news for markets. He brings less regulation, lower taxes, and a business-friendly change of pace after the long post–financial crisis economic slog.

Can the trader buy his dollars back and get on board again, even though what is happening is the exact opposite of what he expected? Can he admit that he was wrong and buy dollars on a Trump victory? Of course he can. This is not about politics and it is not about being right. It is about what is the best trade. It's about solving the puzzle.

The trader reloads and makes a big bet on a rising dollar. 104.00 trades USDJPY. 105.00. By 9:00AM he is profitable again. His view that Hillary would win the election was totally wrong. Yet he survived. And now he is back in the black.

Election night 2016 is a microcosm of everything that is fantastic and terrible about currency trading. The hills and valleys. The emotional and financial highs and lows. Currency trading is mentally exhausting and (sometimes) incredibly satisfying. Tiring and exhilarating. Bad decisions can lead to good outcomes and good decisions can lead to bad outcomes. Luck rules on any given day while skill dominates in the long run.

FX trading is hard. But it can be incredibly rewarding.

Trading is a serious intellectual pursuit that is also incredibly fun. The joy of attempting to solve an unsolvable puzzle. A nearly impossible daily test of discipline and self-control. An endless emotional rollercoaster of instant feedback, frequent disappointment, sudden euphoria, and nearly unbearable periods of crushing self-doubt.

Enjoy the ride.

Understand the Foreign Exchange Market (FX 101)

Part One starts with the basics of currency trading and then slowly digs deeper and deeper into specifics about volatility, liquidity, and time-of-day considerations. Even if you are a seasoned FX trading veteran, I suggest you read all of Part One. It starts with simple concepts, but there is substantial advanced knowledge (and cool random factoids) presented as the section progresses.

CHAPTER 2

A Very Brief History of FX

Before we dig into what it takes to become a successful currency trader, I want to take a quick step back and look at some history. I will discuss the history of currency markets first, and then I will give you a brief background on the history of FX trading. Then, we'll talk about some important basics: the mechanics and structure of foreign exchange markets and how currency trading works.

■ A Very Brief History of Currency Markets

Currency trading has existed since ancient times and there are references to money changers right back to biblical times.[1] The Medici family was among the early traders of foreign exchange (1400s).[2] The monetary and currency system as we know it first started to take shape in the early 1800s as various countries like the United Kingdom, Canada, and the United States adopted first a bimetallic standard (gold and silver) and then a straight gold standard. Under a gold standard, a country's paper currency can be converted at will into a fixed amount of gold. A gold-backed system can create high confidence in a country's currency but the system is very inflexible.

An interesting feature of the gold standard is that it required the government to control the entire stock of gold. Therefore, individuals in the United States were prohibited from owning gold (except

---

[1]See, for example, Matthew 21:12–13.

[2]https://www.theguardian.com/artanddesign/jonathanjonesblog/2011/aug/10/medicis-florence-renaissance-art.

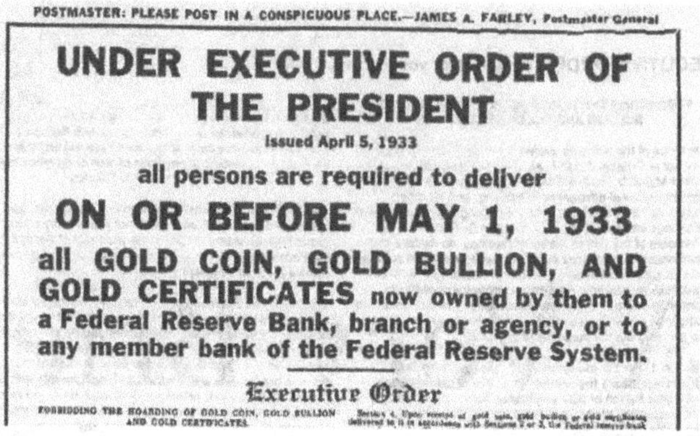

POSTMASTER: PLEASE POST IN A CONSPICUOUS PLACE.—JAMES A. FARLEY, Postmaster General

UNDER EXECUTIVE ORDER OF THE PRESIDENT

Issued April 5, 1933

all persons are required to deliver

ON OR BEFORE MAY 1, 1933

all **GOLD COIN, GOLD BULLION, AND GOLD CERTIFICATES** now owned by them to a Federal Reserve Bank, branch or agency, or to any member bank of the Federal Reserve System.

Executive Order

FORBIDDING THE HOARDING OF GOLD COIN, GOLD BULLION AND GOLD CERTIFICATES

Figure 2.1

https://en.wikipedia.org/wiki/Executive_Order_6102
https://commons.wikimedia.org/wiki/File:Executive_Order_6102.jpg (public domain)

jewelry) while the gold standard was in force.[3] It was a criminal offense for US citizens to own or trade gold from 1933 to 1975. (See Figure 2.1.)

The inflexibility of the gold standard became a problem as early as World War I as countries generated huge imbalances because of war spending while inflation varied dramatically from country to country. In 1944, the Bretton Woods system of monetary management established a fixed gold exchange standard for the major currencies. The IMF and World Bank were also formed at this time and they remain relevant to this day. The end of World War II also marked the end of the British pound as the dominant global reserve currency and the ascent of the US dollar.[4]

Under Bretton Woods, countries kept their currencies fixed to the dollar. International balances were settled in dollars using a fixed conversion rate of $35/ounce for gold. This system was secure and robust as long as money was flowing into the United States, but when money started to flow out because of US balance of payment deficits, the system broke down.

As global trade increased after WWII, then the Vietnam War and OPEC embargoes hit, the pressure on the system became unsustainable. Foreign entities requested more and more conversion out of dollars and into gold. Gold reserves were falling too fast. Recognizing that the situation was unsustainable, Richard Nixon met secretly with 15 advisers, including Fed Chair Arthur Burns and Undersecretary for International Monetary Affairs (and future Fed Chair) Paul Volcker on August 13 and 14, 1971.

---

[3] https://en.wikipedia.org/wiki/Gold_Reserve_Act.

[4] https://sites.hks.harvard.edu/fs/jfrankel/EuroVs$-IFdebateFeb2008.pdf

On August 15, 1971, Richard Nixon addressed the nation, announcing the end of the gold standard and the implementation of new wage and price controls. The next few years were very turbulent for the international monetary system.[5]

By 1973, exchange rates were flexible and currency trading as we know it began.[6] One by one, most countries moved to floating exchange rates, although some countries remain on fixed or managed exchange rate regimes to this day.

The system of floating currencies backed only by faith in the issuing country (and not by gold) is known as a fiat currency system. With no intrinsic backing, the value of currencies floats based on market perceptions of relative value.

The definition of the word *fiat*[7] is:

- A formal authorization or proposition; a decree

- An arbitrary order

In other words, paper money is worth something because the government says so. Since the 1970s, major currency rates have generally been determined by the market but the G7 and G20 monitor markets and intervene verbally or directly by buying or selling when they believe that currencies have become fundamentally misaligned. Examples of coordinated FX intervention include:

- The 1985 Plaza Accord, where nations agreed to intervene to hold down the skyrocketing dollar

- The 1987 Louvre Accord, where the same leaders put a bottom under the dollar after it fell too far, too fast

- 1998 when the Fed, BOJ, and Bundesbank intervened in USDJPY as they believed the move higher had become too speculative in nature

- 2000 when the ECB, BOJ, and Fed intervened to support the euro as the market questioned its viability as a hard currency

- 2011 as the G7 intervened to support USDJPY after the Fukushima earthquake

There are many other instances of currency intervention by individual central banks but the list above covers the major episodes of coordinated intervention since currencies began to float in the 1970s. Generally, the G7 and G20 stance is that currency levels should be

---

[5] http://www.federalreservehistory.org/Events/DetailView/33

[6] https://www.jstor.org/stable/2706594?seq=1#page_scan_tab_contents

[7] https://en.oxforddictionaries.com/definition/fiat

set by markets but extreme volatility or perceived misalignment will sometimes lead to intervention. Here is the official line from the 2013 G7 Statement.[8]

> We, the G7 Ministers and Governors, reaffirm our long-standing commitment to market determined exchange rates and to consult closely in regard to actions in foreign exchange markets. We reaffirm that our fiscal and monetary policies have been and will remain oriented towards meeting our respective domestic objectives using domestic instruments, and that we will not target exchange rates. We are agreed that excessive volatility and disorderly movements in exchange rates can have adverse implications for economic and financial stability. We will continue to consult closely on exchange markets and cooperate as appropriate.

That gives you a quick background on the history of currency markets. Now, let's take a closer look at how currency *trading* has evolved since the 1970s.

■ A Short History of Currency Trading

The business of FX trading has evolved dramatically over the years as technology and regulation have reshaped the landscape many times over. There are four primary eras in the history of FX trading (start and end dates approximate), as explained in the following sections.

■ The Telex Era (1971 to 1981)

In the 1970s and 1980s, currency trading was conducted primarily over telex machines and telephone lines. A small group of bank traders (primarily in London and New York) executed transactions for multinational corporations and high-net-worth individuals. Banks traded with each other direct, asking prices via telex and telephone and using brokers on the telephone to execute trades.

Currency futures were launched on May 16, 1972, as the IMM started trading seven currency futures contracts.[9] This gave

---

[8]http://www.businessinsider.com/g7-statement-on-currency-2013-2

[9]https://en.wikipedia.org/wiki/Currency_future

non-bank players a way to get involved in currency markets. Unlike today, futures trading in the 1970s and 1980s was generally restricted to high-net-worth individuals and sophisticated speculators.

■ The Direct Dealing Era (1981 to 1992)

In 1981, Reuters launched a computerized dealing monitor service that streamlined the FX trading process.[10] Traders still used human brokers (also known as voice brokers) for the majority of transactions but could also call other banks and request a two-way price at any time. These callouts let one bank call 30+ other banks at once for dealable two-way currency rates. This allowed banks to break large trades into smaller chunks and offload risk to their competitors instead of warehousing large deals internally.

For example, if UBS was given 200 million USDJPY by a client, they could call 10 banks and give each bank 20 million USDJPY, thereby distributing the risk. In exchange, UBS promised to show a price to those same banks when they had a large deal to hedge. Voice brokers still played an important role at that time as they still facilitated the majority of interbank FX transactions. (See Figure 2.2.)

Figure 2.2 Legendary voice broker Micky Roberts doing his thing in 1983.

[10]http://thomsonreuters.com/en/about-us/company-history.html

■ The Electronic Era (1992 to 2001)

In 1992, Reuters launched Dealing 2000, an online trading and matching platform that allows banks to show buying and selling interest (bids and offers) to other banks electronically. Around the same time, EBS (Electronic Brokerage Services, now a division of Nex) launched a similar product and the electronic era of FX trading began.

The adoption of electronic brokers was slow at first because traders were used to dealing with human counterparts and valued the information flow from these FX brokers. Over time, though, the superior pricing and execution speed of the electronic systems eclipsed the service offered by the voice brokers and so the electronic platforms relentlessly gained market share. By the late 1990s, EBS dominated EURUSD and USDJPY while Reuters took most of the market share in AUDUSD, USDCAD, and other less-liquid currencies. Only 50 or 60 human voice brokers remain globally, whereas in the 1980s there were more than one thousand.

As electronic platforms increased liquidity and transparency, the direct market between banks closed down because there was no longer a need for banks to trade directly.

■ The Algo Era (2001 to Present)

In the early 2000s, hedge funds developed algorithms (algos) to trade electronically on EBS and Reuters. At first, these algos were specialized and mostly performed arbitrage between platforms. For example, if the futures market showed a 31 bid in EURUSD, while EBS showed a 30 offer, the algos would pay the 30 offer and hit the 31 bid to capture a risk-free profit. Over time, these algos became much more sophisticated and now there are algos running all sorts of strategies. In fact, there is now more volume done by algos than by humans in the FX market.[11] Estimates vary but most put the algo-versus-human share of FX trading volumes around 60/40.

The late 1990s and early 2000s also saw the birth of retail forex trading. Improved computing power, regulatory changes, and the birth of the internet enabled individuals with limited capital to trade FX using leverage. This type of trading has ballooned and now makes up a small but important part of the foreign exchange market, especially in Japan.

Competition among retail FX brokers has led to tighter spreads, better software, and a more even playing field for retail traders.

---

[11]http://www.fxstreet.com/news/forex-news/article.aspx?storyid=f7cece7b-e22f-42e5-9769-16d123085e85

Leverage of up to 100X was once available but many accounts were wiped out in January 2015, when the SNB dropped the 1.20 floor in EURCHF and leverage is now much lower.

The current structure of the FX market is discussed more fully in the next section.

FACTBOX: ALGORITHMIC STRATEGIES

The primary types of algorithms running in today's FX market are:

Data trading: Algos read the economic release data and trade instantaneously based on preprogrammed estimates of how much the market will move.

Market making: Algos show a bid and an offer in the market and attempt to earn a spread and profit from intraday noise.

Correlation: Algos watch other markets and trade FX based on those moves. For example, if oil rallies, an algo might buy Canadian dollars because Canada is a large exporter of crude.

Arbitrage: Systems attempt to profit from disparities in price between venues. If Citibank is willing to buy at 50 and EBS is willing to sell at 49, the arb algos will do both sides and capture a nearly risk-free profit.

Trend following: These systems look for intraday trends and buy pullbacks to a moving average or buy breakouts. The idea is to benefit from trendiness in certain markets.

Mean reversion: This is the opposite of trend following. Algos sell rallies and buy dips in nontrending currencies like USDCAD in an effort to capture mean reversion.

Gamma trading: A system will buy options and then trade the gamma electronically to generate income in excess of the cost of the option.

This list is by no means exhaustive and hedge funds and banks are always developing new strategies and turning off unprofitable strategies.

After reading this chapter, you should fully understand these key concepts:

- The evolution of the global monetary system

- The history of currency markets and currency trading

- What does fiat money represent?
- Many different types of algorithm operate in currency markets

Now that you know a bit about the history of FX trading, let's get into the basics of how currencies trade. While the next chapter is mostly aimed at beginners, even experts should read it because it will strengthen your overall knowledge and touch on some more advanced specifics.

CHAPTER 3

Currency Trading Basics

It is important to have a very solid grasp of the basics when trading foreign exchange. It is surprising how often you will interact with someone who has been in the FX market for years and yet still uses incorrect terminology or does not grasp some basic aspect of market structure, order types, volatility, liquidity, or microstructure. The next two chapters provide a lot of basic information of this sort but also dig deeper in ways that should also enlighten even experienced traders.

Floating foreign exchange rates are a relatively new phenomenon but FX has quickly become the biggest financial market in the world. According to the Bank for International Settlements (BIS), the FX market averaged $5.1 trillion/day of turnover in 2016, up from $4T in 2010 and $3.3T in 2007. Of this volume, $2.0T was spot FX, which is the product discussed in this book. Spot FX is simply foreign exchange traded for immediate settlement (i.e., within 1 or 2 days). FX can also be traded via forwards and futures, which means that the trade is done now but settled at a future date.

The primary difference between spot and forward transactions is that forward rates depend significantly on interest rates in the two countries, whereas spot rates are a pure-vanilla FX transaction and do not depend on forward interest differentials. This book is about spot currency trading. Please note that I use the terms *FX*, *foreign exchange*, and *currency* interchangeably throughout and move randomly between the pronouns *he* and *she* since both men and women trade foreign exchange.

Now let's start with the basics.

Every exchange rate has a numerator and a denominator and therefore involves the currency of two different countries. In theory, any currency pair can be quoted in American terms (with the USD as the denominator, for example, EURUSD) or European terms (with the USD as numerator, like USDJPY) but in reality, there is a standard convention for quoting each currency pair. Always stick to the standard convention when discussing currencies or you will create confusion and sound like a noob. (See Figure 3.1.)

Generally, the currency priority is as shown in the following list, so EUR (as the number 1 ranked currency) will always be the numerator in a currency pair while JPY (lowest-ranked) will always be the denominator. This convention was originally based on the rule of using the strongest currency as the numerator but this practice has evolved with the introduction of the EUR and the passage of time. Here are the currencies, in order of priority:

1. EUR
2. GBP
3. AUD[1]
4. NZD
5. USD
6. CAD
7. CHF
8. JPY

Standard currency pairs always have the higher-ranked currency on top. For example, EURAUD, GBPCHF, NZDCAD, or CADJPY. You buy or sell the numerator currency against the denominator

American Terms	European Terms	Other Conventions
EURUSD	USDJPY	EURNOK
AUDUSD	USDCAD	EURSEK
NZDUSD	USDCHF	USDMXN
GBPUSD	USDSEK	USDZAR
	USDNOK	EURJPY
		EURCHF
		EURGBP

Figure 3.1 Standard quoting convention for major currency pairs.

---

[1] 1 AUD and 1 NZD were worth more than 1 USD when they floated in the 1970s, but their values have fallen significantly since then.

currency but always express a trade by stating both. For example, EURUSD is the rate that euros can be exchanged for US dollars. So if EURUSD is trading at 1.1300, it takes 1.13 USD to buy one euro. If USDJPY is at 100.00, it takes 100 yen to buy a dollar. So if a currency pair is quoted as X/Y, it always takes Y units to buy 1 unit of X.

If you are bullish euro and bearish the dollar, you go long EURUSD.[2] If you are bearish EUR and bullish the US dollar, you go short EURUSD. If you are bullish AUD, you buy AUDUSD.

It is easy when the denominator is USD. But if the denominator is not USD, everything flips. If you are bullish CAD, you sell USDCAD. Therefore, when talking about your position or view, you are always long or short the first (top, numerator) currency. This can be confusing if you are new, but don't worry, it quickly becomes second nature.

To be absolutely clear on this topic: AUDUSD is quoted in AUD terms so trade direction is expressed in AUD terms. You could say any of these to say you went short AUDUSD:

> "I am bearish AUD so I went short AUDUSD."
> "I am bearish Oz so I went short Ozzie/dollar."
> "I am bullish dollar and bearish Oz so I went short Ozzie."

USDCAD is quoted with the USD on top so trade direction is expressed the other way around, in USD terms. When discussing the Canadian dollar, you could logically say the following:

> "I'm bearish USDCAD so I went short USDCAD."
> Or:
> "I'm bullish CAD so I went short USDCAD."

Saying "I'm long CAD" is perfectly logical but can be confusing (even to FX professionals) because the currency is quoted as USD-CAD. Never flip the currencies. For example, never say:

> "I am bullish dollar/euro."
> "I want to sell JPYUSD."

It's unnecessary, confusing, and if you work at a bank, it's amateur. Always think and speak in terms of the standard quoting conventions as described in the list above.

---

[2]In any market, bullish means you think the market will go up and bearish means you think it will go down.

What It Means to Be Long and Short Currencies

In any financial market, long is the position where you own something, betting that its price will rise. Short is a position where you sell something you don't own, expecting it to fall. In FX, every currency trade is both a long and a short—you are always selling one currency and buying another.

For example, if you go long EURUSD, you own euros and owe dollars, hoping that the euro will go up against the dollar. If you are short EURUSD, you make money when the euro goes down. When you cover a position, you are said to be flat or square. If you hold a position past 5PM, you must pay one day's interest on the currency you are short and you earn one day's interest on the currency you are long. This is called the roll and it is explained more fully in a Factbox later in the chapter.

Understand the Different Currency Pairs

In the FX market, 88% of all trades use the USD on one side or the other.[3] The remainder are done in crosses like AUDJPY, EURCAD, NZDJPY, and so on. You can trade any two currencies against each other, but the primary FX market consists of specific pairs.

It is generally best for short-term FX traders to focus on the most-liquid currency pairs. Transaction costs are low in these pairs and they are easiest to learn and trade. Tight spreads and good liquidity mean more profit for you and less for whatever bank or retail platform you trade with. The table below shows the main currency pairs, sorted by liquidity. Stick to the highly liquid pairs unless you are very experienced.

Highly Liquid Pairs

These are the majors. The most important and liquid pairs.

EURUSD	GBPUSD	USDJPY
AUDUSD	EURGBP	USDCAD

Less Liquid Pairs

These pairs are important but less liquid.

EURJPY	USDCHF	USDMXN
NZDUSD	EURCHF	USDZAR

---

[3]https://www.bis.org/publ/rpfx16fx.pdf.

■ Common Crosses

These pairs are created by combining two major pairs. For example, AUDJPY is a combination of AUDUSD and USDJPY. Because they are not truly traded pairs, liquidity is not as good in the crosses. Note that some very popular crosses like AUDJPY and EURCAD do have some direct liquidity on some platforms.

EURAUD	GBPJPY	EURCAD
AUDCAD	GBPCHF	AUDJPY
NZDJPY	CADJPY	CADCHF

■ Illiquid Pairs

These pairs are illiquid and are generally less fun and less profitable to trade because they generate higher transaction costs. As a short-term trader, you should stay away from these pairs.

If you are taking a multiday view, you may find these pairs profitable at times but for most short-term currency traders, 90+% of profits come from the liquid pairs, not these.

USDRUB	USDSGD	EURSEK
EURNOK	EURPLN	USDTRY
USDCNH	AUDNZD	XAUUSD
NOKSEK	EURCZK	

There are other currency pairs out there, but this list covers the ones you need to know about as a trader. Pairs like USDHKD and EURDKK, for example, offer close to zero profit potential because they are managed by central banks and exhibit extremely low volatility.

Any other currency pair can be triangulated from the pairs above. For example, there is no direct market for CHFSEK so if you want to buy that pair, you need to buy EURSEK and sell EURCHF in equal amounts. Some ECNs will offer liquidity in less liquid pairs like CADJPY but this liquidity is generally still triangulated from the primary pairs (in this case USDCAD and USDJPY). So if you trade CADJPY, you are essentially doing a USDCAD and a USDJPY trade.

The reason I outline the primary FX pairs for you is that you should be aware that these pairs are much more liquid than the nontraded pairs. Therefore, you will notice your transaction costs are higher as you move out the spectrum, away from heavily traded primary pairs like EURUSD and USDJPY and towards tertiary, nontraded crosses like GBPNZD or CADNOK.

Again: Stick to the liquid pairs.

Is gold a currency? You may have noticed I included XAUUSD in the illiquid pairs. XAU is the three-letter code for gold.[4] Gold trades on EBS (one of the large electronic FX brokerage systems) and is often considered a currency. There is debate around whether or not it is really a currency but if it is not a currency, it certainly comes close. The debate is mostly semantic. I would say gold is somewhere on the spectrum, a currency/commodity hybrid.

For practical purposes, you can think of gold as an illiquid currency that can be crossed up against other currencies. XAUJPY or EURXAU are perfectly reasonable crosses to think about, although you will generally find that liquidity is so poor that they are not worth trading. I prefer to watch gold as an extremely important indicator but I refrain from trading it because it behaves very differently than most currencies.

Is bitcoin a currency? The short answer is no. Bitcoin is not a currency because it is too volatile and too inefficient to be used as means of exchange. Most merchants do not want to be paid in a currency that regularly moves 10% in a day; it is too risky. While bitcoin could potentially end up as an important store of value in the best-case scenario for crypto-enthusiasts, it is an asset, not a currency.

Most active currency pairs

The currency pairs shown in Figure 3.2 account for most of the volume in FX trading.

These percentages have been fairly stable over the years, although one notable feature in each BIS survey is that CNH volumes are steadily increasing. Many think the Chinese currency could one day rival the EUR or maybe even the USD as a viable reserve currency.

Currency Pair	% of Daily Trading Volume
EURUSD	23.0
USDJPY	17.7
GBPUSD	9.2
AUDUSD	5.2
USDCAD	4.3
USDCNY and USDCNH	3.8
USDCHF	3.5
USDMXN	2.1
USDSGD	1.6
NZDUSD	1.5

Source: BIS 2016 Triennial Survey.

Figure 3.2   Top 10 Currency Pairs by Volume.

[4]For a complete list of currency codes, see https://currencysystem.com/codes/.

■ Quotes, Spreads, Market Structure, and Order Types

The FX market is highly decentralized and divided into two main market segments: retail and wholesale. These markets interact extensively with one another but have some unique characteristics.

Retail tends to consist of individuals dealing in smaller amounts while wholesale FX involves larger transactions, usually between companies, investors, and banks. Wholesale spreads are narrower than retail spreads, although spreads have converged gradually over the years as transparency has increased.

Spreads are expressed as pips. A pip is the smallest normal trading increment in a currency, which for most pairs means 0.0001. So if USDCAD moves from 1.2833 to 1.2834, it has gone up one pip. In JPY pairs, a pip is 0.01. So if USDJPY goes from 110.55 to 110.44, it's down 11 pips.

At one extreme of the retail FX spectrum would be an airport or roadside currency exchange or *bureau de change* booth where spreads could be as wide as 500 pips. At the other extreme, retail also includes day traders accessing 2 or 3 pip spreads via FX platforms on the internet. Wholesale involves all transactions between banks, hedge funds, asset managers, corporations, central banks, and other large users of foreign exchange markets.

FACTBOX: THE ORIGIN OF THE WORD "PIP"

Some corners of the internet say that "pip" stands for "price interest point" but the history of this usage is unclear and I challenge the accuracy of this assertion.

I believe it is much more likely that the word comes from the traditional (especially British) definition: "a very slim margin" or "the smallest possible increment," as in, "One horse pipped the other horse at the finish line to win the Gold Cup." Another definition is that pip refers to one of the spots on dice, dominoes, or playing cards.

All these centuries-old definitions of pip suggest a tiny unit or small increment, just like the usage of pip in foreign exchange. Another reason I strongly doubt the "price interest point" definition is that the word is always written in lower case (pip), not as an acronym (PIP). But I digress.

The spread is the difference between where a dealer (or broker) will buy and sell a currency pair. For example, when you're at the airport, they might buy USDCAD at 1.0100 and sell it at 1.0600. This is a 500-pip spread. At the other end, a bank might show a spread of 1.0355 / 1.0356 in 3 million USDCAD. That spread is 1 pip wide. Quotes are usually displayed like this:

1.0355/56 (pronounced: "one oh three fifty-five, fifty-six")

The 1.03 part of the quotation is called the big figure or simply, the figure. Most professionals will omit the big figure when quoting because it is understood, and it does not change rapidly under normal conditions. So in this case, USDCAD is just 55/56.

If USDCAD is trading 1.0300/05, the bid is 1.03 "the figure" while the offer is 1.0305. You would say or quote this simply as "dollar cad is figure, five," with "figure" being the 00 bid and "five" being the 05 offer. To reiterate, the round number (in this case 1.0300) is called "the figure." All other numbers are referred to normally. So if USDJPY was 102.41/43, you would say "dollar yen is forty-one, forty-three." I will continually emphasize that using the correct terminology is critically important, especially if you work at a hedge fund or in sales and trading at a bank.

At banks, millions are called "bucks" so if someone asks for a price in 15 bucks, that is 15 million US dollars. This shorthand comes in handy because there is rarely a voice trade below 1 million USD at a bank. Average trade size for active clients in the wholesale market is more than ten million dollars and a very large trade could be in excess of a billion dollars. Billions are called "yards" (from the French word *milliard*).

Banks and retail platforms generally compete primarily on price. This is not to say that banks and platforms cannot add value in other ways, such as advisory and research services. This is simply recognizing that currency markets are generally very transparent and highly commoditized. "Price" in the context of foreign exchange trading is the spread, or the difference between the bid and the offer. Very few FX trades are charged a commission. Spread is more difficult to see and measure than the brokerage commission you pay on an equity trade, but it is just as important.

Let's say a day trader does 4 trades of $1 million each in one day. This means 4 buys and 4 sells, so 8 trades total (because a trade involves a round trip, in and out). 1 pip X 8 trades X $1 million = $800. So the difference between a 1-pip and a 2-pip spread would be $800/day for this trader. $800 times 250 trading days is $200,000/year. So you can see that spreads add up fast.

This example is a trader who is not very active (4 trades per day) and is trading on tight spreads, yet transaction costs are huge over the course of a year. Tight spreads are crucially important to minimizing trading friction. Every time you cross a spread, you are paying money to the market. This is why FX trading is a negative-sum, not a zero-sum game. Even though there are no visible transaction costs, you are paying a small but meaningful tax to the market every time you buy and sell.

It is often necessary to cross the spread, but clearly you want to cross the fewest, smallest spreads possible. Note that there are many other features besides price to look at when choosing an FX broker. Never sacrifice reliability, service, or professionalism to get a better spread. Plenty of banks and brokers offer competitive spreads and professional service so you will never need to cut corners and go to a second- or third-tier provider. Stick to the big banks and retail platforms with the best service, technology, and spreads.

Liquidity and trades in the FX market take place in a decentralized manner as banks, brokers, and electronic communication networks (ECNs) interact with one another to set prices. In FX, an ECN is a trading platform or electronic broker that hosts bids and offers and transmits them to users worldwide. The heart of the FX market is made up of two primary ECNs: EBS and Reuters. Although these platforms are slowly losing market share to newer, smaller ECNs, their prices are still considered the primary market. Other ECNs include Hotspot, Currenex, FXALL, FXConnect, ParFX, and many others.

Each ECN broadcasts a price around the world as various participants leave orders to buy and sell (i.e., bids and offers). The prices for a currency pair across different ECNs will necessarily be very similar because algorithms will arbitrage any small differences between them.

For example, if EBS is 32 bid (someone wants to buy at 32) and Reuters is 31 offered (someone wants to sell at 31), an algorithm will do both sides of the trade simultaneously (sell at 32 and buy at 31) and earn the risk-free profit. Trading to earn a risk-free profit is called arbitrage. Once this arbitrage is completed, the two ECNs will no longer have overlapping prices.

Banks provide streaming prices based on what the ECNs are showing, and retail FX platforms stream retail traders a price based on the bank streams. All these price streams are like one huge connected ecosystem. Banks and platforms will often show overlapping prices, but rarely will competing streams cross.

For example, Barcap could show 23/26 in EUR while Deutsche shows 25/28, which is overlapping but not crossed. But if the prices cross (for example, Barcap remains 23/26 while Deutsche goes 27/30), they will be arbitraged and very quickly revert to an uncrossed state. Someone out there will sell to Deutsche at 27 and buy from Barcap at 26 and earn the risk-free one-pip profit. Figure 3.3 shows a diagram outlining how the different nodes in the market network connect.

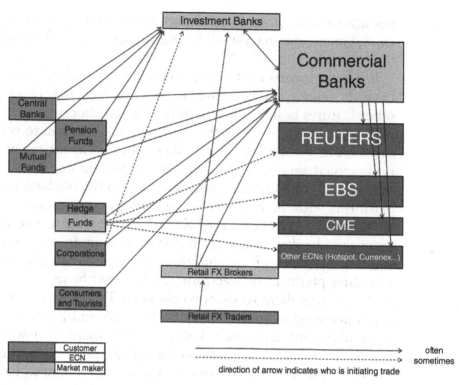

Figure 3.3   The decentralized structure of the currency trading market.

■ Order Types

There are many different order types in the FX market. Many are similar to order types used in the stock market, so if you have traded equities, you will probably have a working knowledge of many of the order types described below. New order types are always in development so be on the lookout for exciting new ways to execute. For now, understand the following order types:

Risk price (also known as crossing the spread or risk transfer) is the most common way to transact FX and is used by customers in retail and wholesale. Also known as "hitting the bid" or "paying the offer," this type of trade immediately gives you the position you want at a known price. If a machine is showing you 1.3817/19 in EURUSD and you pay the offer, you have bought at 19 and you're now long euros. Pay the offer means buy (on the right side of the two-way price). Hit the bid means sell (on the left side of the price).

This type of trade is clean and easy and gets you the position you want right away with no aggravation or delay. In the long run, transacting on risk prices all the time generates profits for the market-maker banks and retail platforms but it is a simple and efficient way to trade, especially for beginners.

The trader taking the other side of a risk price trade is called a market maker. Her ideal scenario is that the market doesn't move and she is hit on the bid and paid on the offer over and over again and thus she captures the spread by buying and selling at slightly different rates. In reality, there is meaningful risk to being a market maker because prices are not static and traders tend to move in herds, creating large imbalances. Trading on a risk price is similar to sending a market order in equities but it differs in that with a risk price you know what your fill will be before you trade—with a market order in the stock market, you don't get your fill until afterward.

Market makers earn a spread when you hit their bid or pay their offer but this is compensation for the fact that they must bear two types of risk. First, market makers take on liquidity risk when you trade with them. This is the notion that only a fixed amount of currency can be dealt on a given price. So if you hit a bank's bid for 50 million EURUSD, the liquidity risk is defined by how far the market moves directly as a result of the bank selling as they try to get out. This is also sometimes called the "footprint" of the trade.

Market makers also bear market risk. This means if you sell to someone at 45 and the market collapses instantly to 25, the market maker takes the loss, not you. The market maker bears the risk of any price movements after a trade.

The next type of order we will discuss is the **limit order** (also called "take profit order"). Limit orders are common in both retail and wholesale FX. A limit order is placed at a specific level and will only be triggered when the market moves to or through your level. For example, EURUSD is 1.3820/22 and you want to buy if it dips to 1.3815. You leave a limit order to buy at 1.3815. This is usually called "leaving a bid." If you are selling, you "leave an offer." The advantage to limit orders is that you do not cross the spread, but the disadvantage is that you are not guaranteed to get filled. In the example described, if EURUSD goes straight up from 1.3820 to 1.3890, you miss the whole move as your 1.3815 limit order would never get filled.

Limit orders are best when you are in no hurry and you don't think the market is going to move much, or if you have a specific entry point in mind. Say EURUSD is 14/16 and you think it's going nowhere for a while. You want to get long but you're in no huge hurry. You can leave a 14 bid and because there is a tremendous amount of random micro movement in FX markets (this is called bid/offer bounce), your probability of getting filled is high. The less liquid the currency, the more important is the decision whether to leave a limit order or simply cross the spread.

You gain more by bidding and offering in illiquid currencies (because the spread is wider) but you are less likely to get filled because there is less bid/offer bounce. There is no right answer when choosing between order types. It is situation-specific and you have to make an assessment of what is the best order type based on your directional market view, your sense of urgency, and current and expected liquidity and volatility. Limit orders are sometimes called take profit orders, even when they are used to initiate a new position.

Two special types of limit orders are **if done orders** and **loop orders**. An "if done" order is simply a limit order that, once executed, creates another order. For example, say I want to sell 20 million AUDUSD at 0.7299, and if that gets done I want to stop loss at 0.7336. I would enter an "if done" order.

A loop order is similar to an "if done" but a loop order creates only new limit orders and it creates them over and over, not just once. Say I want to buy 10 million USDCAD at 1.3125 and if that gets done, I want to sell them out at 1.3165 and repeat this process again if it drops down to 1.3125. I simply enter a loop order as follows: Buy 10,000,000 USDCAD at 1.3125. Loop sell 10,000,000 USDCAD at 1.3165. I will keep buying at 1.3125 and selling at 1.3165 as long as the market cooperates. Loop orders are usually used by traders who own options.

Stop loss orders are used in both retail and wholesale FX markets and are key to proper risk management. A stop loss order is an order to buy higher or sell lower if price moves to a certain level.

For example, I am long euros (positioned for EURUSD to go up) and my entry point is 1.3825. Based on my analysis, EURUSD should not go below 1.3780; if it does, my idea is probably wrong. We will get into detail about position sizing and profit/loss calculations later.

For now, if I am long 10 million euros, my risk is $45,000 on the trade (1.3825 minus 1.3780 is 45 pips. 45 pips X $1,000 per pip = $45,000). If EURUSD goes to 1.3780, I want to sell and exit my position to limit my loss (hence the term "stop loss"). This avoids the risk that I watch EURUSD go lower and lower and suffer huge losses. So I leave an order: Stop loss sell 10 million EURUSD @ 1.3780.

If 1.3780 trades, a market maker will sell my 10 euros for me (or an electronic system will execute on my behalf). The rate is not guaranteed because the stop loss simply becomes a market order when the level is triggered. Standard slippage on most stop losses in the majors is 1 to 3 pips but slippage can vary significantly in fast markets.

Note that stop losses can also be used to enter new positions. For example, a trader thinks that a break below 1.1300 in EURUSD will cause the pair to accelerate lower. He could leave a stop loss (sometimes called a "stop enter") order to initiate a new position, selling to get short when 1.1300 trades. There is a much deeper discussion of stop loss order strategy in Chapter 12.

Quite often, a trader will send her order as an **OCO order** (one cancels the other). This means that the trader sends a take profit and a stop loss for the same position and if one side gets executed, the other side is canceled. Whenever I have an open position and I am off the desk, I pass an OCO order so that my take profit level and stop loss are watched. Once one side trades, the other cancels.

Market orders (also known as "at best") are mostly used for large, wholesale transactions. Customers give a bank an order to execute a large amount in the best way the market maker sees fit. This gives the market maker the ability to judge liquidity and execute the order over time to minimize the market impact as much as possible and achieve the best possible fill for the client. Market orders are an efficient way to deal when you trust the counterparty you are trading with.

No worse than price is a type of order used only in the wholesale market. A customer will ask a bank for their "no worse than" price on a very large FX transaction. For example, a corporation wants to sell 200 million AUDUSD but they are worried about the market moving against them so they do not want to pass a market order. At the same time, they want to be as professional as possible and allow the bank to use its expertise to execute the transaction smoothly.

The bank will provide an "at worst" price and then if the actual execution is substantially better than the at worst price, the bank will share the improvement with the customer. This type of execution is halfway between "risk price" and "at best."

A **two-way price** is when a customer asks a bank to show them both a bid and an offer on a set amount. The bank making the price does not know if the customer is going to buy or sell and so the bank shows both sides and the customer decides whether or not to deal and if so, which side. At any moment in time, there are somewhat standard spreads for two-way quotes in each currency, but spreads change frequently and vary by time of day, market-maker skill, and market conditions. A spread in a fast market will generally be wider than a spread in a quiet market.

Let's look at an example. The market is jumping around and a corporation needs to sell 130 million NZDUSD. The CFO is worried that liquidity is not good and does not want to show his exact interest to a bank. The size of the trade is a bit too big to do on a machine and since the market is volatile, he feels a TWAP (see below) has too much market risk.

He decides to call a bank and ask for a two-way price. The market is currently around 0.6644. In this instance, the market maker at the bank determines that the appropriate spread in 130 million NZDUSD is 10 points wide[5] so he shows the corporation 0.6640/0.6650 without knowing which way the corporation needs to trade.

The CFO thinks 10 points wide is a very fair spread in 130 NZDUSD so he says: "Yours at 0.6640." "Yours" is the FX term for "I sell." And "Mine" means "I buy." So now the corporation has transferred the risk and the bank is long the 130 million NZDUSD at 0.6640. The bank trader then needs to figure out the best way to get out of the risk in a way that makes as much (or loses as little) money as possible.

Personally, I always enjoy making two-way prices as it is the old-school way to deal and is very clean and easy. It puts all the onus on the market maker and instantly puts the customer at ease because the risk is fully passed to the market maker right away.

TWAP stands for time-weighted average price. **VWAP** stands for volume-weighted average price. TWAPs and VWAPs are algorithmic orders used primarily for large, wholesale FX transactions. These orders are managed electronically by slicing a large order up into smaller pieces and executing the trade over a given time frame. Say a corporation wants to buy 100 million USDCAD but doesn't want to leave a big footprint in the market. USDCAD is trading 1.1010/13 (in other words, USDCAD is ten/thirteen). A trader or customer could enter the following variables into a TWAP or VWAP algo and hit GO:

Buy 100 USDCAD over 10 minutes with a limit price of 1.1017.

The system will then start to buy in small slices, 1 million here, 1 million there, buying 10 USDCAD per minute for 10 minutes until it has bought the 100 USDCAD. The TWAP will try to cross the spread as little as possible, although in reality TWAPs and VWAPs tend to pay quite a bit of spread. The TWAP will continue only if USDCAD remains below 1.1017. If the pair rallies, then the TWAP will shut off and wait for USDCAD to come back down. If USDCAD never comes back down, the trade will not happen. The generic format for a TWAP or VWAP order is:

BUY (or SELL) X amount of CURRENCY PAIR over Y minutes with a limit price of Z.

---

[5]This is just an example and I am not making any assertion here about the correct or appropriate two-way spread in 130 NZDUSD.

Z can also be set to "no limit." The advantage of this type of order is that it leaves very little market footprint, but the major disadvantage is that it takes a long time and so the market can move significantly against the execution as time passes. In other words, there is significant market risk and if the market does not cooperate, the order might never get done.

The ideal time for a TWAP order is when the market is not moving or when you expect it to move gradually in favor of the trade. If you need to buy, but you think the market is going to grind lower, a TWAP is a good idea. If you need to buy and expect the market to go higher soon, a TWAP is a bad idea. Get a risk transfer price or do the trade at best.

VWAP is very similar to TWAP but differs in that the amounts executed are sliced into pieces that match the amount of volume being transacted in the market. This allows the algorithm to trade more actively when volumes (and liquidity) are high and less actively when volumes are low. Generally, TWAP and VWAP strategies yield similar results.

Iceberg orders are a type of limit order used only in wholesale FX. An iceberg order shows a small amount to the market but automatically refreshes the order until a larger amount has been filled. For example, let's take the example above where the market maker was given 130 million NZDUSD at 0.6640. The market is now trading 0.6644/46. The trader wants to reduce his risk by selling 50 million NZDUSD at 0.6645. He feels that if he shows an order for 50 million NZD, he might scare the market away because that is a large ticket for an illiquid currency pair. He fears that if he posts a visible order to sell 50 million NZD, traders who are long NZD might get scared and hit the bid, pushing the market lower. He wants to use a little more stealth, or finesse.

He leaves an iceberg order to sell 50 NZD at 0.6645 in clips of 5 NZD at a time. So the market will see a limit order for just 5 million NZD at 0.6645 but as soon as someone trades on that order, it will refresh to show 5 million again. This will continue until the trader has sold his 50 NZD.

Icebergs are popular in less-liquid currencies, although they have been adopted more and more even in deeper markets like EURUSD and USDJPY. The advantage of the iceberg is that you don't show your full size to the market, but the disadvantage is that traders looking for liquidity might not deal on a price that only shows a small amount for fear of moving the market. By showing your full size, you increase the odds that someone with a legitimate interest the other way will transact with you.

Another massive disadvantage of using iceberg orders is that once you sell your initial amount (like the 5 NZD in the example above), anyone else selling at the same level moves ahead of you in the queue. In other words, after each clip of an iceberg, you must go to the back of the line and wait for all other orders at the same rate to be executed before your next clip will transact. This is a very detrimental and often overlooked feature of using iceberg orders.

My belief is that iceberg and similar hiding orders are massively overused and it is generally better practice to show a reasonable market amount instead of tiny slices of an order. When you use icebergs, you are constantly getting sent to the back of the line instead of participating in the full volume at your price.

Dark pools are another type of order available only in the wholesale market. Traders show an interest to buy or sell an amount of currency but do not assign a price to the order. The order goes into the dark pool and waits for someone to match in the opposite direction. When a match occurs, both sides of the trade are filled at midmarket (as derived from a separate primary market price feed). Dark pools have become increasingly popular in recent years because they allow traders to transact without showing their interest to the market.

This completes our discussion of order types. Now let's talk about how to calculate profits and losses in foreign exchange.

■ Understand Profit and Loss

The math involved in calculating profits and losses (P&L) in foreign exchange is simple and you will find as time goes on that you gain an intuitive feel for your P&L. An experienced trader can quickly eyeball a trade idea and size their position appropriately based on a given P&L tolerance without the use of a calculator or spreadsheet. At first, though, you need to be extremely careful as a simple mathematical error can lead to severe loss or ruin.

P&L is calculated in real time according to market prices. If you buy EURUSD at 1.1350 and it rises to 1.1355, you will immediately show a profit even though this profit has not yet been realized and you still hold the position. This real-time mark to market is necessary for proper money management and for calculation of margin. As the market moves, your P&L changes and you know where you stand at all times. This is called real-time mark-to-market P&L accounting.

■ How to Calculate P&L on an FX Trade

Profits and losses on currency trades are reported in the denominator currency. So if you trade EURUSD, your P&L is in USD. If you trade USDJPY, your P&L is in JPY. EURCAD P&L is in CAD. Calculating P&L on currencies with a USD base is very simple. Calculate P&L on an FX trade with a USD denominator (like EURUSD, GBPUSD, etc.) as follows:

$$P\&L = (\text{Position size} \times \text{price change})$$

So if you make 0.0020 (20 pips) on a 1,000,000 position, your P&L is:

$$0.0020 \times 1,000,000 = \$2,000$$

One pip on a position of 1 million EURUSD is $100.

One pip on a position of 10 million EURUSD is $1,000.

When the base is not USD (like, for example, USDJPY), you need to do a two-step calculation. First, calculate how many pips of profit or loss you made. For example, you buy $10,000,000 USDJPY at 109.60 and sell it at 109.65. That's 5 pips profit. 5 pips times $10,000,000 = 0.05 × 10,000,000 = 500,000. That's ¥ 500,000 of profit. Then convert the JPY to USD:

$$500,000 \text{ divided by the USDJPY rate of } 109.65 = \$4,556$$

So 5 pips on 10 million USDJPY in this case works out to $4,556.

Similar math applies to any currency where the denominator is not USD. Let's say I bought 3 million USDCAD at 1.3100 and took profit at 1.3177. P&L is calculated as follows:

$$77 \text{ pips } (0.0077) \text{ times 3 million} = 23,100 \text{ CAD}$$

That is your profit in Canadian dollars, but you want to convert that to US dollars:

$$23,100 \text{ divided by } 1.3177 = \$17,530.55 \text{ USD}$$

Remember, long positions profit when the price of the numerator currency goes up and shorts profit when that price goes down. Note that the P&L of a trade also includes the roll earned or paid if you held the position over more than one trading day. The roll is calculated and paid or earned daily.

As you become more of an expert in FX, you will gain a natural feel for the P&L on various position sizes but when you are starting out, always calculate your target profit and loss for every trade

EURUSD P&L

		\$ Pip move 1		10		50		100
	100k	\$	10	\$	100	\$	500	\$	1,000
Position size	1m	\$	100	\$	1,000	\$	5,000	\$	10,000
	10m	\$	1,000	\$	10,000	\$	50,000	\$	100,000
	100m	\$	10,000	\$	100,000	\$	500,000	\$	1,000,000

USDCAD P&L when USDCAD is at 1.3000

		Pip move 1		10		50		100
	100k	\$	8	\$	77	\$	385	\$	769
Position size	1m	\$	77	\$	769	\$	3,846	\$	7,692
	10m	\$	769	\$	7,692	\$	38,462	\$	76,923
	100m	\$	7,692	\$	76,923	\$	384,615	\$	769,231

Figure 3.4 P&L of various position sizes in FX.

before you initiate. By using a predetermined take profit and stop loss, you will know exactly how many dollars of P&L you have at risk on every trade. I will discuss this more fully in Chapter 12. Figure 3.4 provides a quick table to help you get a feel for different P&L on various position sizes and currency moves.

FACTBOX: UNDERSTAND THE ROLL

The roll (aka, rollover or carry) is the interest you pay or receive each day for holding spot positions overnight. It is the difference in interest earned on the currency you are long versus the interest you must pay on the currency you are short. The concept is very similar to a bank account, with interest calculated daily for spot foreign exchange positions.

If you are long a currency with a high interest rate and short a currency with a lower interest rate, you will earn the roll. You own the currency you are long and you owe the currency you are short (you are borrowing it at the current market rate). The exact amount of the roll is calculated using forward points, which are set by the market but heavily influenced by central bank policy rates. You can look up the roll points on your FX platform or on Bloomberg.

The roll is sometimes called tom/next (short for tomorrow/next) or T/N and is usually quoted in pips. So, for example, if you are long AUDUSD and T/N is 1.2 pips, you will earn 1.2 pips on your AUDUSD notional at 5:00PM New

York time every day. So if you are long 10,000,000 AUD, you will see an extra $1,200 in your account each day once the roll is calculated. If you go long at 4:59PM, you still get the roll: It is simply calculated based on balances at exactly 5:00PM NY time (except NZD, which rolls at 7AM Wellington time, which is generally 1PM or 3PM NY).

If you enter and exit a trade the same day, there is no roll earned or paid.

When there is a weekend or holiday, the roll will cover multiple days so if the daily roll for AUDUSD is 1.2 pips and you are long the weekend roll, you will get three days of roll, or 3.6 pips.

Short-term traders don't need to worry too much about the roll other than to make sure it is calculated and applied correctly. In a world of very low interest rates, the roll is not very important, but before 2007 it sometimes mattered even for short-term traders. I almost never think about the roll because it is just about meaningless for short-term traders.

This concludes our discussion of currency trading basics. Always remember to use correct terminology and stick to market conventions or you will confuse and alienate other participants in the currency market.

After reading this chapter, you should fully understand these key concepts:

- Quote conventions and proper terminology in FX

- What it means to be long and short currencies

- How the FX market is structured

- Order types

- Understanding and calculating FX P&L

Let's move on to some very important and practical aspects of currency market structure, trading, and execution.

CHAPTER 4

Understand Market Structure

Now that you understand the basics of how currencies are traded, let's take a look at the participants and the microstructure of the FX market. Knowledge of the FX players and of the distinguishing similarities and differences that define different currencies will help you better understand and forecast market movements.

This chapter will also delve deep into specifics about currency liquidity and volatility with a detailed discussion of how FX trading activity varies by time of day. This practical information will improve your execution and timing in the foreign exchange market.

■ The Players

Banks. Bank trading floors are the epicenter of the foreign exchange market. Most trades that take place in FX are initiated or facilitated by a bank. Commercial banks dominate the market but investment banks also play an important role. Trading between banks is called the interbank market and this is where price discovery happens. Traders at banks are market makers and also take a substantial amount of directional risk in anticipation of client flow. Figure 4.1 shows the top 10 liquidity providers in foreign exchange by market share in 2018, according to *Euromoney*.

Corporations and hedgers need to buy and sell currencies on a daily basis. There are many reasons corporations transact in FX, but a simple example is an exporter that sells goods to a foreign buyer. Let's say a Japanese car maker sells $6B worth of cars in America.

2018 Rank	Liquidity Provider	Market Share
1	JPMorgan	12.1%
2	UBS	8.3%
3	XTX Markets	7.4%
4	Bank of America	6.2%
5	Citibank	6.2%
6	HSBC	5.6%
7	Goldman Sachs	5.5%
8	Deutsche Bank	5.4%
9	Standard Chartered	4.5%
10	State Street	4.4%

Source: *Euromoney* 2018 survey.

Figure 4.1 Top 10 liquidity providers in foreign exchange (by market share) 2018.

That's a big chunk of dollars coming in as revenue. But they run a balance sheet and pay many of their employees and shareholders in JPY, so at some point they need to sell the dollars and buy yen. They will call banks on a regular basis to sell USD as their dollar balances grow. There are all sorts of corporate transactions involving foreign exchange happening all day, every day as global corporations have diverse and ongoing operational FX conversion needs.

Another type of corporate transaction that leads to very large FX trades is cross-border merger and acquisition (M&A) activity. For example, a large European brewery buys a US beer maker for more than $50B. They will need to buy USD and sell a big chunk of EUR to pay US shareholders. This transaction will involve selling *billions* of EURUSD over the course of many days and might have a dramatic impact on the market. Corporates tend to be more methodical and less active than other segments.

Hedge funds are pools of investor capital put together to trade various asset classes in search of speculative profits. Hedge funds (some of which manage in excess of $10B of capital) are large and important participants in FX. They value the ample liquidity and transparency of currency markets. There are different types of hedge funds that participate in FX:

Discretionary/macro funds try to forecast trends and movements in foreign exchange using macro variables and analysis of the type I describe in this book. In fact, I was a discretionary portfolio manager at a hedge fund for a few years and most of the techniques I describe in this book are techniques I used while trading a pool of investor capital in Connecticut. Macro funds can have different time horizons and the word "macro" is often a misnomer. Many hedge funds trade on a very short time horizon. Short-term hedge funds with a macro approach are known as "fast money."

CTAs (Commodity Trading Advisors), systematic and model funds are hedge funds that make trades and allocate capital based on computer programs, algorithms, pattern recognition, correlation trend following, or states of disequilibrium in the market. While trend-following models were most common from the 1980s until the late 1990s, more sophisticated approaches have emerged and the performance of trend-following strategies has tumbled.

Real money is the term for investors trading FX against an underlying asset. For example, let's say a US-based bond fund has decided to buy EUR 2B worth of Greek bonds. To pay for the bonds, they need euros, but their cash balances are in USD. The real money client calls a bank and buys two billion euros and sells USD. Real money includes pension funds, mutual funds, bond funds, insurance companies, and equity hedgers.

High-frequency trading (HFT) systems attempt to profit from small movements and variations in FX markets. They use different strategies such as arbitrage between markets, market making, economic data trading, and short-term correlation. While HFT is a large part of the volume traded in FX, most HFT activity is extremely back and forth and thus contributes more to noise trading and not directional price movement.

Another important category of FX player is the **central banks**. They operate in FX markets via four separate channels:

1. Central bank monetary policy is a major driver of foreign exchange rates. High and rising interest rates tend to attract capital and make a country's currency appreciate while low and falling interest rates tend to be bad for a currency. This is discussed in Chapter 5.

2. Moral suasion. Central banks attempt to influence currency rates by telling the market their preference. The stronger the preference of the central bank and the more credible the central bank, the more the market will listen. By simply "talking down" or "talking up" its currency, a central bank can often achieve its goal without altering monetary policy or touching the FX market.

3. FX intervention. This is uncommon but very important when it happens. When a central bank strongly believes that its currency is misaligned, volatility is too high, or FX moves are in conflict with monetary policy goals, it can intervene directly in the FX market and buy or sell currency aggressively. This is also discussed in Chapter 5.

4. Diversification. Some countries hold massive foreign currency reserves as a tool either to manage their own currency level or to protect against future crises. Most countries look at their currency reserves the way an investor would look at a portfolio and so they will buy and sell various currencies in the open market in order to diversify risk and capitalize on projected future currency and interest rate moves.

Some countries also operate sovereign wealth funds (SWFs) to help manage their currency reserves and these SWFs trade actively and in large amounts just like the central banks.

While portfolio considerations drive some of the trading decisions made by central banks, the biggest driver of regular currency purchases and sales by central banks is intervention recycling. The mechanics of this intervention and recycling of dollars is covered in Chapter 5.

Retail traders are day traders and speculators trading from home or on their smartphones. FX day trading has become increasingly popular in the past 10 years as equity day trading has plateaued and reliable retail FX platforms have proliferated. Retail is especially important in Japan, where over 1,000,000 active trading accounts exist, in contrast to just over 150,000 in the United States. Japanese retail traders are often women who use FX trading as a way of enhancing the yield on their very substantial pool of savings. They are often collectively referred to as "Mrs. Watanabe."

■ Different Currencies Have Different Personalities

It is important to understand that every currency has its own personality. This section discusses the various ways in which the market places currencies into groups. This can be useful not just for analyzing currencies, but also for hedging, because currencies that have similar personalities will tend to be correlated.

The highest level of categorization is to separate Developed Markets (DM) from Emerging Markets (EM). The currencies in Figure 4.2 are the actively traded DM currencies. Sometimes people will refer to these as G10 FX or G7 currencies, but neither is exactly accurate. Switzerland, for example, is not a member of the G7 and if you include DKK, it's really the G11. But there is no need to be pedantic in this case. If you say G10 FX or G7 currencies, people will know what you are talking about.

Another high-level categorization is the group of currency pairs called: **The Majors.** When someone refers to "The Majors," they are referring to EURUSD, USDJPY, GBPUSD, AUDUSD, USDCHF, and USDCAD.

USD	AUD	CHF
EUR	NZD	SEK
JPY	CAD	NOK
GBP		DKK

Figure 4.2   The G10 currencies.

Next are some other ways to group currencies. The currencies within these groups tend to trade with some degree of correlation to one another.[1] For example, two currencies like EUR and CHF will always be somewhat correlated because of significant economic linkages between the two economies.

European currencies include EUR, CHF, SEK, NOK, and DKK. These currencies are highly correlated and the USD exchange rate against these currencies is determined mostly by EURUSD. For example, while USDSEK is influenced by EURSEK, most of the volatility in USDSEK comes from EURUSD. GBPUSD is also sometimes included when discussing European currencies although its ties and economic links to Europe are not as tight as the others, especially post-Brexit.

Commodity currencies include AUD, CAD, NZD, BRL, ZAR, and CLP. These are commodity-exporting nations whose currencies are somewhat or heavily influenced by commodity prices. There is significant nuance within the group as BRL, ZAR, and CLP are emerging market currencies and each country is reliant on different commodities.

AUD is influenced by copper, gold, and iron ore; CAD is driven by crude oil and natural gas; and NZD is most heavily influenced by the price of soft commodities, especially dairy (Figure 4.3). The sensitivity of the currencies to various commodities logically relates to how much of each commodity each country exports.[2]

Skandies is a catchword for SEK, NOK, and DKK. The Scandinavian economies are grouped as a block, even though in truth the

Country	Top Exports	% of total exports
Australia	Iron Ore	20%
	Coal	15%
	Gold	5%
New Zealand	Milk powder, butter and cheese	25%
	Meat	12%
	Logs and wood	7%
Canada	Energy	24%
	Metals and Minerals	16%
	Motor Vehicles	12%

Figure 4.3 Major commodity exports of Australia, New Zealand, and Canada.

[1]Whenever I write about correlation, it should be understood and emphasized that correlations are not static. They change over time.

[2]Sources: http://www.dfat.gov.au/tradematters/aus-graph.html, https://www.nzte .govt.nz/en/invest/statistics/, http://www.investorsfriend.com/Canadian%20GDP %20Canadian%20imports%20and%20exports.htm

Norwegian and Swedish economies are quite different given the Norwegian focus on crude production. Finland is not included because it is part of the euro. DKK (the Danish krone) is not a free-floating currency; it is managed by the central bank in a very tight band around the euro. Therefore, DKK is not a useful currency for speculation.

Emerging Markets (also known as EMFX) is a huge universe of currencies but the most actively traded EM currencies are shown in Figure 4.4. I sorted them by liquidity/volume/popularity.[3] Currencies in bold are the most liquid and thus are the ones most commonly traded by global speculators.

Note that this is not an exhaustive list; most countries in the world have a currency but most of those currencies are not actively traded. EM currencies are at times categorized by fundamentals into groups such as BRICs, the Fragile Five, and so on, but these groupings tend to be transitory and faddish.

You will often hear people refer to a currency against all others as, for example, "CAD crosses" or "AUD crosses." If someone refers to "the CAD crosses," this is a collective reference to EURCAD, AUDCAD, CADJPY, CADCHF, CADNOK, and so on.

High yield versus low yield is another useful way to categorize currencies. This is because investors and speculators treat high-yielding currencies as a different type of asset than low-yielding currencies. The practical reason that a currency's yield is important is called "carry."

Carry is the amount of interest you earn or pay when you own or short a currency. If Australian yields are 4% per year and US yields are 1%, you will earn 3%/year for holding a long position in AUDUSD. While this is small relative to the volatility in the currency

Asia	Emerging Europe	LATAM
CNH and CNY	**ZAR**	**MXN**
KRW	**TRY**	**BRL**
SGD	**RUB**	CLP
INR	**HUF**	COP
MYR	**PLN**	PEN
PHP	ILS	
TWD	CZK	
THB		
IDR		

Figure 4.4 Important emerging market currencies (actively traded currencies in bold).

---

[3]The rankings are my informed but subjective opinion.

pair, it is still an important consideration for medium- and long-term investors. The higher the carry, the more expensive it is to hold shorts and the more attractive it is to own the currency, especially when volatility is low.

Interest rates go up and down but in recent years the low-yielding currencies have been the EUR, CHF, and JPY. Low-yielding currencies tend to be safe havens. EM currencies, AUD, and NZD have had the highest yields over the years and are known as risky currencies because they usually sell off in times of market stress or fear.[4]

When people refer to yields, they might mean the central bank rate or overnight rate but they could also be referring to 2-year, 5-year, or 10-year yields. Considering that there is a strong relationship between yields all along the curve, a currency that has a high overnight rate will tend to have a relatively high 2-year and 10-year rate anyway so the distinction rarely matters.

The practical way that yields matter is that the market generally has a preference to own high-yielding currencies and sell low-yielders. This leads to structural appreciation and positioning in higher-yielding currencies that can unwind rapidly. In 2006, volatility was low and the yield differential between AUD and JPY was very high (4% to 5%). The NZD versus JPY differential was even higher (5% to 6%). So if you stayed long NZDJPY for a year and it didn't move, you made more than a 5% return. With a bit of leverage, the carry trade can yield very attractive returns.

The combination of low volatility and high carry in 2006 attracted huge pools of money to the long AUDJPY and NZDJPY carry trade and the strategy performed very well. Very well, that is, until the first tremors of the global financial crisis were felt and speculators decided all at once to unwind their carry trades as volatility roofed from abnormally low levels. This resulted in a colossal unwind of all carry trades and saw AUDJPY fall from 107 to 86 in about a month in the Summer of 2007.

In Figure 4.5, you can see the slow, grinding appreciation of AUDJPY from 2005 to mid-2007 and then the brutal unwind. There is a market adage: "Carry trades go up the escalator and down the elevator." The carry trade is also sometimes known as "picking up nickels in front of a steam roller."

The AUDJPY unwind of 2007 was colossal but paled in comparison to what happened next, as the pair dropped all the way from 105.00 to 60.00 in 2008. Check out Figure 4.6, which shows

---

[4]Though in 2018 AUD and NZD rates fell below US interest rates for the first time in recent memory and AUD and NZD are no longer high yielders.

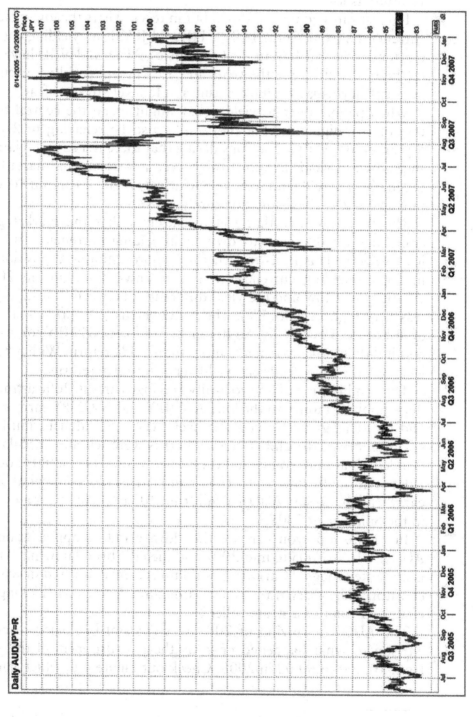

Figure 4.5 Daily AUDJPY 2005 to 2007.

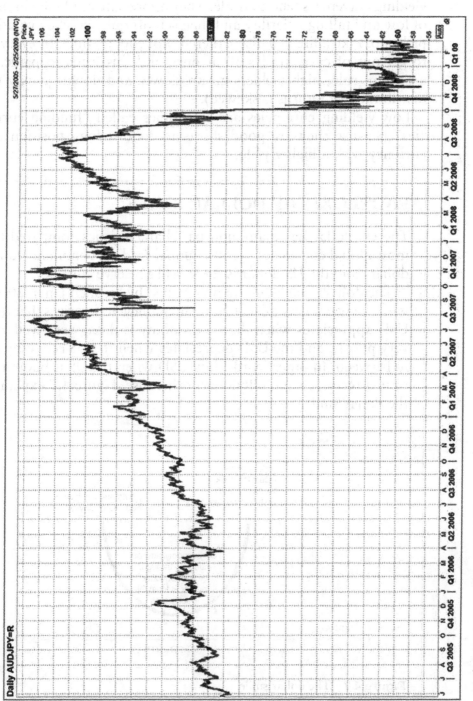

Figure 4.6 Daily AUDJPY 2005 to Q1 2009.

AUDJPY from the same starting point as the previous chart, but with an end point of early 2009 instead of early 2008:

AUDJPY in 2007/2008 is an extreme example of how high-yielding currencies tend to trade. They appreciate gradually in times of low and falling volatility and then sell off quickly when volatility picks up. Like a fire in a disco, there is not enough time for everyone to get out of carry trades all at once and this leads to panic. As a general rule, high yielders go up slowly and down quickly (the distribution of returns is skewed).

Low-yielding currencies are sometimes called "funding currencies" because they are good shorts to fund a long position in a currency with a higher yield.

FACTBOX: THE DOLLAR SMILE

The US dollar has many unusual characteristics compared to most global currencies because global trade is denominated in dollars and the US dollar is the world's reserve currency.

The dollar smile is a term first coined by Stephen Jen in 2001 while he was a strategist at Morgan Stanley. It theorizes that the USD appreciates when the US economy is doing very well, or very poorly, and the USD depreciates when the US economy is in between. In other words, buy USD when the US is booming or in a recession and sell dollars otherwise. Figure 4.7 explains the dollar smile.

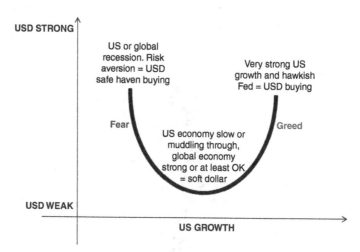

Figure 4.7   The dollar smile.

The dollar smile is a nice (though rather simplistic) model for thinking about US dollar performance. The most important takeaway is that the US dollar tends to rally when the US economy is ripping and the Fed is hiking. And the dollar also rallies during US recessions. On the other hand, the dollar tends to sell off in periods of moderate US growth as long as global growth is decent.

That the dollar tends to rally into US recessions is counterintuitive. It happens because when the US economy goes into recession, investors fear that the global economy will follow. The US dollar is a safe haven, so when a global recession hits, investors buy US treasuries and US dollars to protect their capital.

Furthermore, global trade is financed in US dollars, so less global trade means fewer dollars in circulation globally and hence a possible shortage of dollars. Fears of a USD shortage drive the dollar higher. As with many concepts in financial markets, it is more important to understand the *what* (USD rallies into US recessions) than the *why*. Please note that while the dollar smile is a handy heuristic, the empirical evidence in support of the concept is mixed and one should always keep an open mind when forecasting where the dollar might go next.

Managed currencies are pairs that are not completely free-floating. Examples are CNY, CNH, KRW, SGD, RUB, and CHF (and sometimes the JPY). Managed currencies are somewhat free-floating but the price of these currencies is not 100% set by the free market. Volatility or directional movement is at times restricted by the central bank. This can make these currencies unattractive to macro speculators because a knowledge of the central bank's policy, strategy, and thinking is much more important than any analysis of exogenous macro variables. Domestic investors with inside information have a substantial edge over all other traders.

Currency management can be very active. In China, the PBoC often restrains volatility and directly influences the value of the currency via daily interventions and fixings. Over time, the PBoC have become less active as they allow their currency to float more.

CHF is a different example where the central bank generally allows the currency to float freely but has intervened when the CHF strengthened too much or gained too much momentum because of risk aversion. There was a time when the SNB tried to forcefully weaken the CHF by putting in a EURCHF floor at 1.2000 but this experiment failed miserably and devastated the central bank's credibility for many years to follow. New traders should avoid trading managed currencies and stick to the majors.

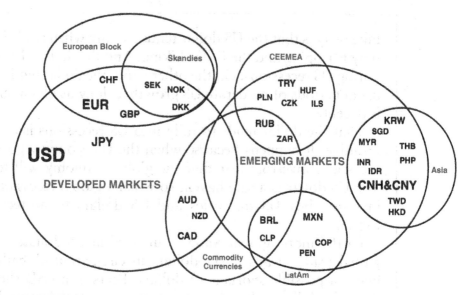

Figure 4.8 Venn diagram of relationships between major global currencies.

The Venn diagram in Figure 4.8 will help you understand how the different currencies relate to one another. (Larger font size indicates a more actively traded currency in that oval.)

■ Understand Volatility and Liquidity

Before you trade any market, you need a good understanding of volatility and liquidity. I am not a huge fan of paper trading in general but one benefit of paper trading is that it allows you to watch a market and get in sync with its ebbs and flows so that you understand how it moves. You should watch a market for at least a month or two before you trade it. This will give you a sense not only of general volatility but also of what constitutes a fast market or a quiet market.

Another important way to familiarize yourself with a market is to analyze the market statistically before trading it. Note that volatility and liquidity are not static; they change over time and therefore historical measures of volatility are by definition backward-looking—the future can be much different than the past (as users of standard VAR models in 2008 found out!).[5]

---

[5]VAR stands for Value at Risk and is a standard risk measurement model that uses historical volatility to estimate future risks for a position of a given size. When volatility stays low for a long time, these models can massively underestimate risk because they only look at recent volatility and therefore a larger and larger position appears to be reasonable as volatility falls. Until at one point (sometimes called the Minsky Moment), volatility mushrooms and risks are much, much higher than suggested by VAR.

Volatility is a statistical measure of how an asset price moves. It uses historical data to analyze the standard deviation of past moves. Assets with higher volatility tend to be riskier by nature. Volatility is usually expressed as an annual percentage. It can also be expressed as a standard deviation or histogram of returns. The higher the number, the more volatile the asset.

The reason that volatility matters is that it relates directly to position sizing. You cannot trade as large a position in an asset that is more volatile, because your risk of ruin is larger. Many experienced traders that I have worked with over the years never fully understood this concept. For example, many bank traders I worked with simply ran 10 lots all the time. In other words, they would tend to be comfortable long or short 10 million NZDUSD or 10 million EURUSD or 10 million USDMXN, completely disregarding the fact that each of these currency pairs has a different volatility and therefore the amount of P&L dollars at risk on each position of 10 million is different. You need to normalize your position size based on volatility. Take smaller positions when volatility is high and larger positions when volatility is low. This is fully explained in Chapter 12, "Understand Position Sizing."

Liquidity is harder to measure than volatility but is essentially the amount of slippage to expect when you transact. If you look at a price in EURUSD, you might see 1 pip wide, whereas the spread in NZDUSD might be 3 pips wide. This means that EURUSD has substantially better liquidity than NZDUSD at that moment. Liquidity is an increasingly important consideration as you increase your transaction size and/or frequency.

The more you cross the spread and the bigger that spread, the more money you are giving to market makers in the long run. The importance of liquidity considerations increases as the amount of capital you manage grows. When you are running a $1B macro fund, for example, managing liquidity and capacity can be as big a challenge as correctly forecasting market direction. The good news is that foreign exchange is the most liquid market in the world.

There is a strong relationship between volume and liquidity: High-volume currencies almost always have better liquidity. Figure 4.9 shows a list of the top 15 currencies by volume[6] along with their volatility[7] and liquidity. The liquidity figure is out of ten and is my best subjective assessment of liquidity as of late 2018. This number varies over time but the numbers provided are a good starting point

---

[6]Source for volume data: https://www.bis.org/publ/rpfx16fx.pdf (page 5).

[7]Figures are implied 1-year volatility for each currency against the USD. Implied volatility is the option market's best estimate of future volatility. You will also see people use Historical Volatility, which is a backward-looking measure of how volatile the asset was in the past.

Volume Rank		1-year volatility	Liquidity
1	USD	8.3	10
2	EUR	7.7	10
3	JPY	8.3	9
4	GBP	9.9	7
5	AUD	9.6	8
6	CAD	7.5	7
7	CHF	7.3	7
8	CNH	6.9	5
9	SEK	9.8	6
10	MXN	14.5	4
11	NZD	9.9	6
12	SGD	5.0	8
13	HKD	1.0	10
14	NOK	9.3	7
15	KRW	9.3	7

Figure 4.9 Volume, volatility, and liquidity for the Top 15 currencies.

for understanding the relative personalities of different currency pairs.

Volatility and Liquidity Vary by Currency

The best currencies to trade have high liquidity and high volatility, but there is often a tradeoff between the two. The majors provide excellent volatility and liquidity while EM currencies are usually volatile but illiquid. Figure 4.10 shows a comparison of approximate liquidity and volatility for the same 15 currencies. It is simply the data from the table above presented in a scatter plot. You can see there is a visible but weak inverse relationship between liquidity and volatility.

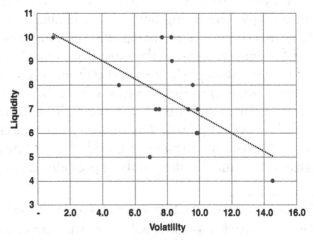

Figure 4.10 The relationship between volatility and liquidity for the Top 15 currencies.

Almost all traders should stick to liquid G10 FX because it is most liquid. There are numerous idiosyncratic issues involved in trading less-liquid currencies. Unless you work at a bank, you will find trading the illiquid currencies difficult and frustrating, and furthermore you generally cannot rely as much on stop losses in those currencies, so risk management is problematic.

■ Volatility and Liquidity Vary by Regime

There are times when volatility across all global asset markets is low (e.g., 2005, 2006, 2014, and 2017) and times when volatility is high (e.g., 1998, 2008, 2011, and parts of 2018). Volatility can change at lightning speed. FX volatility tends to move in sync with global asset market volatility, although there are times when stocks could be volatile while FX markets stay quiet or vice versa. Volatility tends to trend lower in slow motion and then skyrocket when there is a disturbance.

Figure 4.11 shows a 10-year history of FX volatility as defined by the Deutsche Bank FX Volatility Index.

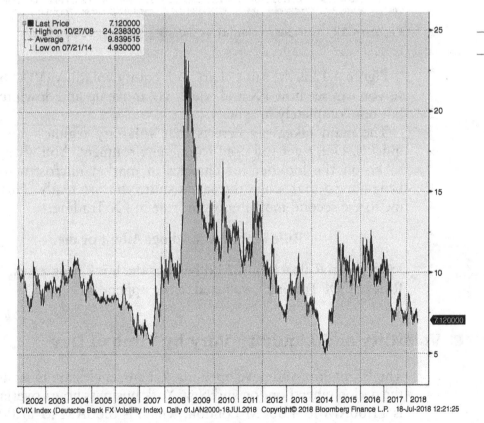

Figure 4.11 Currency volatility, 2002–2018.

Source: CVIX Index (Bloomberg).

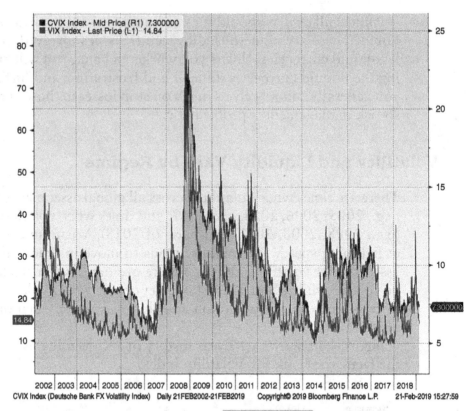

Figure 4.12 Currency volatility vs. equity volatility, 2002–2018.

Figure 4.12 is the same chart with equity volatility (VIX) overlaid so you can see how FX and equity vol move up and down together, but not completely in sync.

The main takeaway here is that volatility regimes can change quickly. Don't get too used to one environment. You always need to be on the lookout for changes in market microstructure and behavior so that when the sands shift, you are ready. This brings me to the second most important rule in FX Trading:

Rule #2 of FX Trading: Adapt or die.

I will get to Rule #1 (and 23 others) as the book progresses. My "25 Rules of FX Trading" are listed in the appendix.

■ Volatility and Liquidity Vary by Time of Day

The FX majors and developed market currencies are most active in the period when London and New York business hours overlap. This is 11:00AM to 4:00PM London, which is 6:00AM to 11:00AM in New York. Some EM currencies are more active and liquid in their home time zone (KRW is more active during Korean business hours,

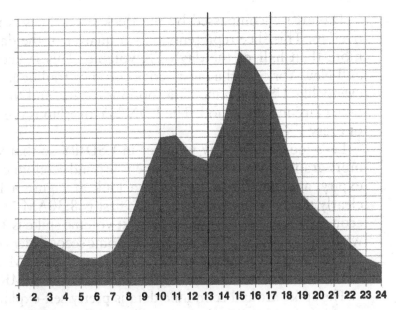

Figure 4.13 Average hourly volumes in EURUSD by time of day (GMT) February–April 2014.

for example) but the NY/LDN overlap is by far the best time to trade currencies in general.

Figure 4.13 shows average EURUSD volumes by time of day for a three-month period in 2014.

Volumes are indexed so there is no y-axis label. This chart simply shows each hour's liquidity relative to the others and it is highly representative of how volume evolves during the day for all major currencies. The numbers along the bottom represent the time in GMT so 12 would be noon GMT, which is 7:00AM NY and noon LDN.[8]

The Key Times to Observe

GMT TIME (chart)	EVENT	LONDON TIME	NEW YORK TIME
7	London Open	7AM	2AM
12	New York Open	Noon	7AM
15	Options Expiry	3PM	10AM
16	WMR Fix	4PM	11AM
17	London Goes Home	5PM	Noon

[8]Note that when the clocks change for daylight savings time, the difference between time zones can change for a few weeks. You can always Google "Current time in London" or "Current time GMT" to make sure you know what the difference is.

The area encompassed by the thick black lines is the LDN/NY overlap. This slice represents only a quarter of the day's hours but more than half of the day's FX volume. This is because London and New York are the most active currency trading hubs and major events like US economic data, options expiry, and the WMR fix all take place in that period. The LDN/NY overlap is the beating heart of every FX day.

Let's look at intraday volumes in USDJPY so that you can see a more granular view of what happens around economic data, options expiry, and the WMR fix. Take a look at Figure 4.14. There are clearly three spikes in volume. The first is 8:30AM NY, when most economic data are released. The next volume spike is 10:00AM NY, when options expire (and also when some second-tier economic data are released). The last volume spike is at 11:00AM NY (4:00PM LDN) and that volume spike coincides with the WMR fix.

The spike around economic data is pretty self-explanatory. When new information is released to the market, traders and investors want to express views about the information and so they trade aggressively on the back of the release. The market speeds up and tries to find equilibrium as players from different time frames all participate at once. The price finds equilibrium and then volumes fall. There are many other key moments in the FX trading day. Let's go through them in detail.

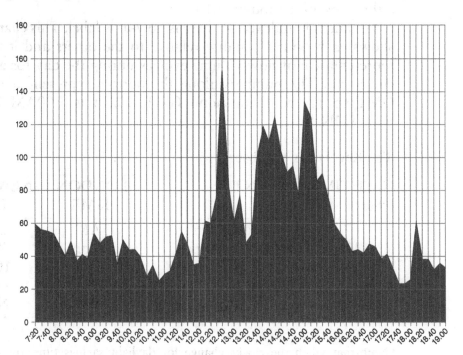

Figure 4.14 Average intraday volumes in USDJPY during London hours 7:00AM LDN to 7:00PM LDN.
Data from Refinitiv.

■ Understand Time of Day

Big bursts of activity and volatility come at predictable times of day in FX markets and you need to understand these key times. In this section I will go all the way around the clock to describe every major time of day effect. To the uninitiated, this might seem like I am getting too far into the weeds, but believe me: This is important. Time of day is a critical consideration for all currency traders.

Figure 4.15 presents a grid of all the major daily intraday events. Here, I will describe each event in some detail.

London Open (7:00AM LDN)

The London open is often an inflection point as big risk takers and market makers sit down and process the information that has filtered into the market since the last daily close. You will often see an aggressive trending move start at this time.

New York Open (7:00AM NY)

The NY open is the beginning of the NY/LDN overlap, the most liquid period for foreign exchange dealing. This 4-hour period tends to be volatile, active, and liquid. Quite often, if there was a big move in London time, the New York traders will hop on that move and extend it, only to watch it reverse later.

The pattern of extension and reversal just after the New York open was especially prevalent during the Eurozone crisis. London would come in and sell euros, then NY would come in and do the same and

Time EST	Time GMT	Event	Notes
2:00	7:00	**London Open**	
7:00	12:00	**New York Open**	
8:15	13:15	ECB fix	
8:30	13:30	Most major US economic data	
10:00	15:00	Option expiry	
		Second tier US economic data	
11:00	16:00	**WMR benchmark fix**	
12:00	17:00	Bank of Canada noon rate fix	
15:00	20:00	CME close	Many CTAs mark to this level
17:00	22:00	**New York Close / Asia Open**	
		Tokyo fix	8:55AM Tokyo
		China Fix	9:15AM Beijing

G10 FX Daily Schedule

FX market closes 5PM NY time Friday and reopens 7AM Wellington time Monday (1PM, 2PM, or 3PM Sunday New York time, depending on the time of year)

Figure 4.15 Key times of day for G10 FX.

then starting around 8:00AM NY time, EURUSD would squeeze and squeeze and squeeze higher for the rest of the day. Watch for intraday patterns like this; they can be surprisingly persistent.

ECB Fix (1:15PM LDN)

Before July 2016, some corporations and central banks used the ECB fixing rate to benchmark their currency positions. These institutions traded very actively around the ECB fix in an attempt to match or beat the fixing rate. This created a big burst of activity, mostly in EURUSD, in the 15 minutes leading up to the fix at 1:15PM London. In July 2016, the ECB changed the methodology around the ECB fix and usage of the fix has dropped off dramatically since then.

US Economic Data (8:30AM and 10:00AM NY, mostly)

US economic data are key for FX direction. This will be discussed in full in Chapter 5: "Understand Fundamental Analysis" and Chapter 10: "Trading the News." Also, don't forget about data that come out at odd times, for example: ADP at 8:15AM NY, Industrial Production at 9:15AM NY and Chicago PMI at 9:42AM NY (released to subscribers) and 9:45AM NY (released to the public).

Option Expiry (10:00AM NY)

Most currency options expire at 10:00AM New York time. This creates a burst of activity as market makers hedge the change in their deltas into 10:00AM and those who were using options as a hedge suddenly find themselves unhedged.

Exotic options (barriers, digitals, etc.) also create hedging needs around 10:00AM as market makers and end users recalculate their net exposure after options expire. Note that OTC options on some currencies expire at times other than 10:00AM NY and CME options expire at 3PM NY time.[9] Examples of nonstandard OTC option expiry times are USDTRY, which expire at 7:00AM NY, and USDMXN, which expire at 12:30PM NY.

4:00PM WMR Benchmark Fix (4:00PM LDN)

The WMR benchmark fix is a rate setting that takes place every day at 4:00PM LDN, 11:00AM NY. WM/Reuters collects data from all trades done in the five-minute window between 3:57:30 and 4:02:30 LDN (10:57:30 to 11:02:30 NY) and calculates a fixing rate bid

---

[9]Note that the CME recently changed its rules so options expiring after June 9, 2019, will expire at 10AM NY just like OTC options.

and ask for each currency. The rate represents an approximate best estimate of the average of where currencies traded during the 5-minute fixing window. Many, many FX players, especially real money, use the WMR fix to value their foreign bond and equity holdings.

Because many FX participants use the WMR fix, there is a large spike in trading activity at this time. Many buyers and sellers converge on the market at the WMR, so there is tremendous liquidity. Fix users are sometimes able to transact massive amounts with minimal impact.

On the other hand, if everyone is the same direction at the WMR fix (everyone is selling or everyone is buying), there can be huge imbalances and outsized market moves in a short time period.

The 4:00PM WMR fix essentially marks the end of the London trading session and the end of best liquidity so many systematic and some discretionary traders use the period leading into that fix to square up or to transact their last large deals of the day. You can see in the previous chart that the WMR fix is the last surge of liquidity of the day and then volumes drop off dramatically into the NY afternoon.

The huge volumes and non-price-sensitive nature of the WMR flow means that there can be incredible opportunities at this time. If you want to buy a currency and it gets absolutely clobbered into the fix, it could provide a great buying opportunity. Quite often when the buying or selling pressure related to the fix abates at 4:02:30PM London (11:02:30AM NY) the currency that was beaten down rebounds or the currency that was on a moonshot comes back down to earth.

Note, however, that it is *not profitable* to go the other way systematically on every large WMR fix movement. In other words, just because a currency moved dramatically higher at the fix does not mean you should automatically sell it.

You should have prior reasons to trade a currency—don't just fade the WMR because there was a big move. Big WMR moves are an opportunity to execute on ideas you had beforehand. I repeat: Don't sell a currency just because it is ripping higher at the fix.

One last observation on the 4:00PM WMR: The month-end fix (the fix on the last business day of the month) is by far the largest fixing each month and you will often see extreme moves in the hours leading up to the month-end WMR fix. This is because most equity funds rebalance their FX exposures at month end, so if there have been large moves in stocks and bonds (most importantly, US equities), then firms will have massive FX rebalancing to do.

Month-end fix activity can be huge and any single bank might at times see upwards of $5 billion in fixes on its book for just that one day. Watch for crazy moves around 4:00PM LDN (11:00AM NY) on the last day of every month. The hours leading up to the month-end fix also see a fair amount of craziness as traders and hedgers try to pre-position for the inevitable flurry in the WMR window.

Bank of Canada Noon Rate (Noon NY)

Some Canadian real money and corporate FX participants bench-mark to the Bank of Canada's noon rate. This creates a small burst of hedging activity in USDCAD (and sometimes CAD crosses) right around noon NY. The use of this fixing has declined over the years but you will still see the odd USDCAD move or volume frenzy around 12 noon NY from time to time.

CME Close (3:00PM NY)

Many hedge funds, systems, and models benchmark to the close of the futures markets at 2:00PM Chicago (3:00PM NY). This leads to a flurry of hedging as 3:00PM NY nears. Most activity at this time comes from models and algorithms that use the 3:00PM CME close as a mark-to-market rate and want to enter or exit positions as close to that rate as possible.

China Fix (9:15AM Shanghai)

At 9:15 Shanghai time, the People's Bank of China (PBoC) sets a daily fixing rate for the US dollar against the yuan (USDCNY). While this fixing generally comes and goes without much fanfare, there are times when this is a critical time of day. In August 2015, when China devalued their currency, the entire market was glued to the screens at 9:15PM every night to see just how aggressively the Chinese planned to devalue. The China Fix influenced not just USDCNY but all of FX, stock, and bond markets at that time. When the Chinese currency is in play, the China Fix is key.

It is important to note that the China Fix (unlike the ECB, WMR, and most other fixes) is not set by a series of transactions in the market; it is set in somewhat arbitrary fashion by the Chinese government using a formula that factors in both G10 FX USD moves and political and strategic considerations.

Tokyo Fix (8:55AM Tokyo)

Many corporate and real money FX traders in Japan use the Tokyo Fix to benchmark their currency trades. Therefore, the Tokyo Fix (which takes place at 8:55AM Tokyo time) is another time of day where you will see a large burst of trading activity and volatility. Most of the activity at the Tokyo Fix takes place in USDJPY,

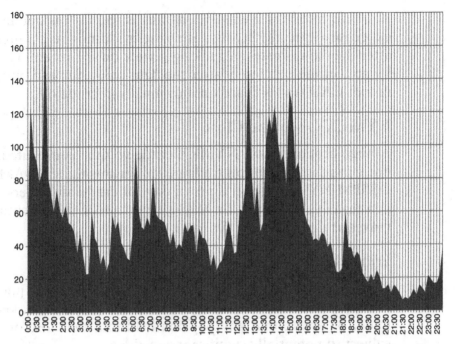

Figure 4.16   Average intraday volumes in USDJPY by time of day (times in GMT).

although you will also see movement in other related pairs like AUDJPY, NZDJPY, and EURJPY. Figure 4.16 is a volume by time of day chart for USDJPY so you can see how important the Tokyo Fix is to that market.

This chart is similar to the previous chart but this one uses the full 24-hour chart of USDJPY, not just 12 hours. Note the large volume spike on the far left. This volume spike is the Tokyo Fix, which takes place daily at 9:55AM Tokyo time. The Tokyo fix is used mostly by Japanese corporates and life insurance companies.

Other times of day you need to know about:

API and Department of Energy Data

Each week, the American Petroleum Institute (API) and the Department of Energy (DoE) announce their estimates of crude oil inventories. These data are extremely important to crude oil traders and often trigger big moves in energy prices. API releases its figure Tuesday at 4:30PM NY and the DoE numbers come out at 10:30AM NY Wednesday. The DoE numbers tend to attract the most attention because the series has been around longer and it is released at a busier time of day.

If you trade currencies correlated to crude oil (Canada and Norway especially), you should be ready for big moves when the API and DoE figures come out. I feel like there is no edge in studying the

API/DoE numbers themselves as this is too far outside my area of expertise (especially because often the crude move is counterintuitive after the data). Instead of taking a view on the inventory numbers, I watch crude oil closely after the data come out and quickly enter or exit CAD trades based on movements in crude oil.

NYMEX Open and Close

A huge proportion of NYMEX crude volume is executed near the open and the close of pit trading. This means that 9:00AM NY and 2:30PM NY are critical times of day for crude oil traders. Again, if you trade CAD, NOK, or MXN, be aware of the potential for big moves at these two key times.

Friday Close

Currency markets close at 5:00PM NY on Friday. Liquidity tends to dry up after 3:00PM so if you have a large position, keep this in mind. Be aware that any position held into the close on Friday is subject to potentially significant gap risk.

Usually FX markets will open on Sunday at a level near where they closed on Friday. But if there is major news over the weekend, FX markets can open at any level. Prudent short-term FX traders reduce risk before the close on Friday. Some of my worst trading memories are when I was offside on a trade and had to sit all weekend worrying about the open. The US downgrade in 2011 (which was announced after the close on Friday) and the capture of Saddam Hussein are two particularly large Sunday gaps I remember.

Sunday Open

Currency markets open Monday morning at 7:00AM Wellington, New Zealand, time. In New York, this is Sunday at 1:00PM or 3:00PM, depending on the time of year (winter or summer). Liquidity is extremely poor for the first few hours of trading until Tokyo and Singapore come in. If there is major news over the weekend, the Sunday open can be very interesting as the market attempts to find a new equilibrium price that incorporates the news. During the Eurozone crisis, there were many large gaps where EURUSD would open 100 pips or even 150 pips higher or lower compared to the Friday close.

NZD Date Change

All currencies roll (change value date) at 5:00PM except the New Zealand dollar. NZD rolls at 7:00AM Wellington time, which is either 1:00PM or 3:00PM NY depending on the time of year. This is not a major deal but keep it in mind when trading NZ in the NY afternoon. Trades done after the date change are called "new value" and trades done before the data change are called "old value."

Equity Open/Close

Depending on the regime, currencies are sometimes correlated to equity markets, so there can be surges of FX volatility around 9:30AM NY and 4:00PM NY, when the New York Stock Exchange opens and closes.

Twilight Zone

Warning: There is a time of day known as the "Twilight Zone." This is the period from 5:00PM NY to 6:00PM NY. Most NY bank desks run minimal staffing at this time (one trader, usually) and Tokyo is not in the office yet so there are very, very few traders active. Most market-making algos are off because bank systems run their end-of-day process at 5PM. Liquidity is at its absolute worst during the Twilight Zone. It is not advisable to trade in this period, regardless of your size.

When news comes out at this time, moves can be dramatic as liquidity is close to nonexistent. The first time the US AAA credit rating was put on negative watch, the announcement came at 5:20PM New York time and it was absolute bedlam!

You will notice that most of the volatility each day is centered around the volume spikes and therefore many good FX traders focus on the 5-hour sweet spot of the LDN/NY overlap and either ignore the rest of the day or try their best not to overtrade when volumes are thin. This is an important skill to learn. Overtrading (especially in the afternoon, when there is no reason to trade most of the time) is one of my greatest weaknesses.

Final Thoughts on the Importance of Time of Day in Currency Trading

When I worked as a hedge fund PM, I graphed my P&L on an intraday basis by recording my intraday P&L every 15 minutes. There was a definitive pattern where I made money from 7:00AM to 11:00AM NY time and then gave back 20% to 40% of my profits from 11:00AM to 5:00PM. I had the same experience when I was day trading equities.

You should actively trade the LDN/NY overlap and do something else when volumes are low. Do research, prepare for upcoming events, exercise, play video games, or write a book about FX trading like I'm doing right now at 1:45PM NY.

Keep your hands off the keys as much as possible during the quiet periods of the day.

When volumes are low, any one transaction can move the market disproportionately because there is not enough volume to take the other side. Therefore, you will find that outside of the LDN/NY overlap there will be a disproportionate number of moves that do not make sense.

During illiquid periods, large corporate or other non-price-sensitive users of FX sometimes still need to transact and so the price will move simply because of that flow. Unless you are the one executing the flow, you have no edge. I cannot stress this enough. Trade the LDN/NY overlap and then put in your stop loss and take profit orders and stop trading.

FACTBOX: WHAT ARE THE BEST CURRENCIES FOR SHORT-TERM TRADING?

An interesting question that I am often asked is: What are the best currencies for short-term trading? Here I answer the question with data.

The ideal currency for short-term trading is both volatile and highly liquid (i.e., moves a lot but is cheap to transact). I carefully estimated spread info (width of the bid/offer) for G10 and EM currencies and found the average daily range for each currency. I then indexed everything and created a list of currencies ranked by their ratio of: (daily range vs. cost to transact). And voilà! (See Figure 4.17.)

ccy	Range/Spread
EURUSD	100
USDJPY	62
GBPUSD	52
AUDUSD	47
EURGBP	44
USDCAD	35
NZDUSD	28
USDCHF	22
EURCHF	16
EURNOK	11
EURSEK	9

(a)

Indexed to EURUSD = 100

ccy	Range/Spread
USDMXN	100
USDZAR	99
USDSGD	97
USDTRY	85
USDRUB	83
EURPLN	41
EURHUF	29
USDILS	25
EURRON	18
EURCZK	10

(b)

Indexed to USDMXN = 100

Figure 4.17 (a) Ranking currencies by daily range compared to spread. In other words: volatility vs. transaction cost. In other words: What currencies are best for short-term trading? G10. (b) Emerging markets. Bid/offer data estimated and liquidity and volatility are not static, so these charts are meant as a rough guide to comparative trading attractiveness, not a definitive and permanent answer.

A Note on Choosing Currencies

Quite often you have a view on a specific currency and you are not sure what other currency to pair it against. For example, you expect the dollar to sell off because of weaker US economic data so you want to go short dollars, but you are not sure which currency to buy against it. Sometimes, a specific currency that you really like will come to mind; then the pairing is obvious. At other times, the prudent strategy is to sell the dollar against a basket of currencies. This avoids the possibility that your dollar view is correct but you lose money because of some idiosyncratic move in the other currency.

Say you express your USD-bearish view by going long AUDUSD (long AUD, short USD); the risk is that your dollar view is correct but some extremely bad news comes out of Australia, and so AUD sells off even more than the USD. If you want to avoid this, put on a basket. Instead of buying one chunk of AUDUSD, do a basket of smaller trades of equal risk: AUDUSD, NZDUSD, GBPUSD, and EURUSD, perhaps. Then you are not subject to the random risk of an event or news in a specific (non-USD) currency.

The other benefit of the basket approach is that it has higher capacity. If you trade large size, that can be helpful. A position of 500 million USD worth of AUDUSD is somewhat difficult to manage because it exceeds the capacity of the short-term market, but 500 million USD split equally or vol-weighted between AUD, NZD, CAD, GBP, EUR, and JPY is easier to get in and out one leg at a time.

■ Understand Jump Risk

For short-term speculators, one attractive feature of the FX market is that it trades continuously from Sunday afternoon New York time until 5:00PM Friday New York. If you leave a stop loss on a small or medium-sized position, you can generally expect minimal slippage on the fill.

That said, you should familiarize yourself with the concept of jump (or gap) risk because most jump risk is known in advance and can be quantified approximately. Jump risk is the size of the move where no trading will take place (the size of the gap) after a news event such as:

- Economic data

- Central bank announcement

- Weekends

Some traders elect simply to avoid all major jump risk by squaring up ahead of major events and weekends. This is a logical strategy.

It is worth noting, though, that research has estimated that jumps account for between 25% and 40% of FX returns on a 1- to 3-month horizon.[10] Further, the jumps can generally be estimated fairly accurately (on average) using information supplied by the options market, so overall it is possible to quantify most gap risk. That said, gap risk can only be estimated; it can never be known for sure in advance, so prudence is never a bad policy.

Figure 4.18 is an example of a jump after a strong Australian jobs data release in December 2015. The market expected a jobs number of −10,000 and the number came in way above expectations at +78,000.

You can see that when the data came out, there was a large jump of 72 pips or 1%. Anyone who left a stop loss between 0.7250 and 0.7300 would most likely be done above 0.7300. So if you sized your position using a stop loss at 0.7250, expecting 3 pips of slippage, you would be in for a major negative surprise and a much bigger loss than expected. Always be aware of jump risk and square up or size your position accordingly ahead of time.

Estimating Jump Risk

There are two ways to estimate jump risk. The first is to look at historical data for a given event and take the average and median moves. The Bloomberg function ECMI is useful for this type of analysis. Looking at how currencies moved over the same event in the past is usually a good way to estimate gap risk but it is, by definition, backward-looking. A more accurate way to estimate jump risk is to use the options market.

The difference between volatility pricing for the day before an event and the day of an event can be used to extract an approximate jump risk for the currency. The calculation is beyond the scope of this book. To be perfectly honest, when I want this information I don't calculate it myself, I just ask an options trader.

If you work at a bank or have an institutional relationship with a bank, you can simply ask, "What is the options market pricing as jump risk for event X?" and they will give you an answer, usually in basis points.

Weekend Gaps

Weekends are a special situation because the FX market closes at 5:00PM New York time and does not reopen until 7:00AM Wellington (1:00PM, 2:00PM, or 3:00PM NY, depending on the time of

[10]https://workspace.imperial.ac.uk/business-school/Public/RiskLab/2%20Jul %2013%20FX/irina.pdf.

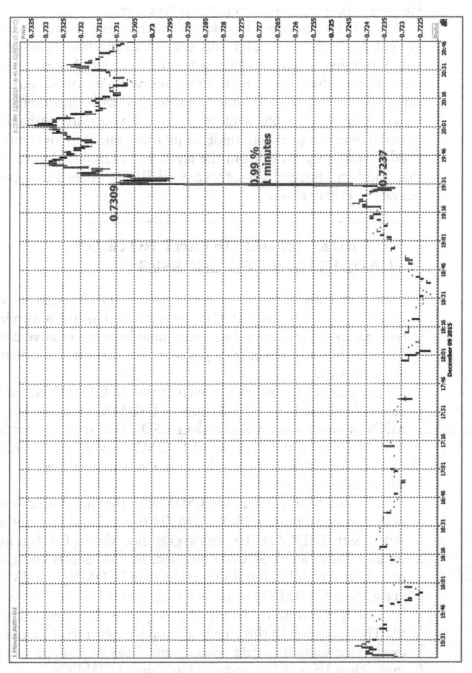

Figure 4.18 1-minute AUDUSD after a strong Australian jobs number, December 9, 2015.

year). This creates meaningful gap risk because news over the weekend can trigger changes in supply and demand for currencies that cannot be reflected until markets reopen. Some weekend gaps can be predicted (elections, Chinese data, etc.) but some cannot (Saddam Hussein captured, China revalues currency, etc.).

Many traders go home flat every weekend and I strongly encourage you to do the same. Not only does this allow you to avoid gap risk, but it gives your mind a rest for the weekend. Instead of worrying about what news might come out Saturday or Sunday, you can have fun with your friends or spend time with your family and recharge for another big week of trading. If you insist on having a position over the weekend, understand that your stop loss could be filled significantly away from the level. For example, the weekend that Saddam Hussein was captured, EURUSD opened 200 points below the Friday close.

FACTBOX: AN IMPORTANT NOTE ON TRADING NON-USD CROSSES

I am frequently asked my view on secondary FX crosses like CADMXN and AUDCAD. Often people think of them as relative macro stories and fail to understand how the relative beta (or volatility) of each currency is often the main factor driving those crosses.

For example, if you ask me what I think of CADMXN, I will generally just tell you what I think of USDMXN because USDMXN is much more volatile than USDCAD. In other words, CADMXN is a main course of USDMXN with a side order of USDCAD. Below I provide some mathematical and visual supporting evidence.

In Figure 4.19, you can see USDMXN (the thin dotted line) ebbs and flows more with CADMXN (black bars) and not as much with USDCAD. The thick gray line shows CAD going up and down, aka USDCAD inverted. In EM selloffs and risk off, USDCAD rallies but it rallies less than USDMXN, and vice versa. So a CADMXN trade is mostly just a USDMXN trade because it is driven by USDMXN, the pair with higher volatility. The exception to this rule is around idiosyncratic Canadian events like Canadian data releases and Bank of Canada meetings, when USDCAD is more volatile than USDMXN.

This is not just true when pairing G10 versus EM. If you look at AUDCAD, the result is similar: Most of the time AUDCAD is just an AUDUSD trade. Using 500 days of data

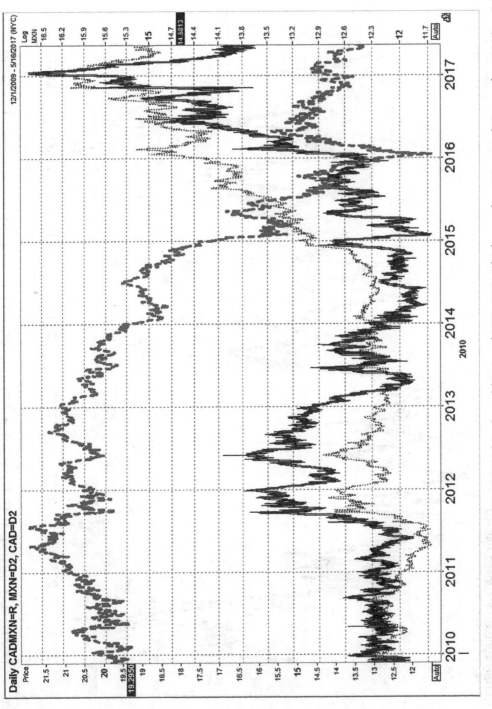

Figure 4.19 CADMXN (black bars) vs. USDMXN (thin dotted line) and USDCAD (thick gray line) (inverted) December 2009 to May 2017.

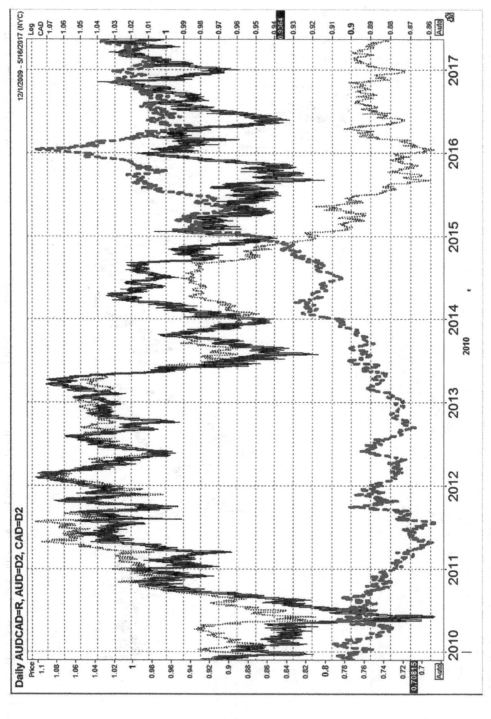

Figure 4.20 AUDCAD (black bars) vs. AUDUSD (thin dotted line) and USDCAD (thick gray line) August 2007 to June 2017.

as of January 2017, here are the correlations between those crosses and their legs:

AUDCAD correlation to: AUDUSD 61.8% / USDCAD 17.5%

CADMXN correlation to: USDCAD −10.2% / USDMXN 76.0%

In addition, look at Figures 4.19 and 4.20, which overlay the cross (in black) with its legs. It does not take 20:20 vision to see that USDMXN is driving CADMXN and AUDUSD is driving AUDCAD.

Note that the tendency of the higher beta currency to drive crosses is just a tendency, not a hard rule. When USDCAD was ripping at the end of 2015, it was so volatile that it was driving AUDCAD for a month or two.

"OK, great," you say, "but who cares?" Well, you should care because any time you construct a cross-trade based on relative fundamentals, you fall into an easily avoidable trap. If you want to trade two countries against each other, you need to weight your exposure by volatility. So instead of going long, for example, 130 CADMXN, do a vol-weighted combo: long 75 USDMXN and short 100 USDCAD.[11] This will deliver returns closer to what you would expect if your macro, relative performance call is correct.

After reading this chapter, you should fully understand these key concepts:

- The players that make up the FX market and their varied roles
- Different currencies have different personalities
- Liquidity and time of day are important in FX
- Volatility varies by currency pair and this is important
- Gap and jump risk

That concludes Chapter 4. Next comes the fun stuff.

Chapter 5 is the first time we start to think about how to come up with trade ideas and how to make money. The chapter will show you how to analyze fundamentals, think about macroeconomics, and start forecasting currency movements.

PART II

Trade the Foreign Exchange Market

"Success is no accident. It is hard work, perseverance, learning, studying, sacrifice and most of all, love of what you are doing or learning to do."

                                                                    Pele

My philosophy is that sustainable long-term success in FX trading is best achieved using a fusion approach. This is a hybrid, adaptive process that combines fundamental and macroeconomic analysis, behavioral finance, technical analysis, and diligent risk management to deliver sustainable long-term trading success.

This book explains trade selection using fundamentals, technicals, correlation, behavioral finance, and news. When all five branches of analysis point in the same direction, you have what I call a Five-Star setup. Five-Stars are trade ideas where every indicator points the same way.

Have the patience to wait for these maximum high-probability trades. Do your best to ignore trades where some indicators are bullish and others are bearish. Put another way: Make sure all planets are in line before you put on a trade.

Understand Fundamental Analysis

"In the short run the market is a voting machine. In the long run it is a weighing machine."

This quote, attributed to Graham Dodd by Warren Buffett, is a useful way of looking at the FX market. It means the market oscillates above and below long-run equilibrium (fair value) because speculators and their emotional trading decisions drive short-term price action. But in the end, fundamentals matter.

This is not a book about macroeconomics or international finance, but you need to understand the macro backdrop no matter how short your trading time horizon. Even day traders should have a strong knowledge of fundamentals or they will inevitably be caught offside by moves they do not fully understand.

"But wait. I trade on pure technicals!" you say.

That's great, but even scalpers need to understand the whole picture. In the long run, you cannot be all trees and no forest. It is fine to specialize in one type of analysis or one trading style but to be a great trader you need to have a complete understanding of the market. And for what it's worth, in my twenty years of trading, I have never worked with a single top-notch FX trader who used only technical analysis.

Fundamental analysis is the study of macroeconomic factors that drive markets (as opposed to other factors like momentum, positioning, and psychology, for example).

■ Long-Run Determinants of Currency Values

Long-term FX valuation is a topic that belongs in finance textbooks; it is mostly useless for trading. That said, it is helpful to understand the concept of long-term fair value in FX because it is frequently discussed and it can provide a better understanding of what determines currency valuations.

The most common methodology used for of FX valuation is called Purchasing Power Parity (PPP). This theory suggests that a basket of goods in one country should cost the same as the same basket of goods in another country and relative currency rates and inflation should be the equalizer. This is sometimes demonstrated by the "Big Mac Index," which compares the price of a Big Mac in various countries to determine if a country's currency is cheap or expensive.

The theory behind PPP is that if an item is cheaper in one country than in another, consumers will buy more of the good in the cheaper locale and less in the more expensive location. But this all rests on the assumption that every good is tradable, transaction costs are zero, and taxes are not important. As is typical with many orthodox economic theories, there are so many faulty assumptions that the theory ends up nearly useless by the time you try to put it into practice. But at least PPP provides a starting point to assess whether a currency is cheap or expensive.

The IMF conducts regular reviews of member country's foreign exchange valuations and you will frequently see a headline like "IMF says New Zealand dollar 5 to 15 percent overvalued." These are long-term assessments, usually filled with caveats and are not important for trading on any time horizon. The reason that fair value measures are not useful for currency traders is that currencies can stay over- or undervalued for years or even decades at a time.

It is useful, though, to understand why a currency is over- (or under-) valued so that you know under what conditions the currency might fall from overvalued back toward PPP or "fair value." For example, this passage appears in the IMF's 2014 report on New Zealand:

> Our estimates suggest that even with the strong terms of trade, the New Zealand dollar is currently stronger than would be consistent with stabilizing net foreign liabilities over the long run, and on this basis appears to be overvalued. There are other factors contributing to the current level of the exchange rate, including the gap between domestic and foreign interest rates, New Zealand's favorable growth outlook, and an appetite for relatively safe New Zealand assets. If any of these factors were to ease, the exchange rate would likely depreciate. The government's ongoing deficit reduction plan should also

ease pressure on the exchange rate by boosting national saving. However, global liquidity could remain ample for some time, and New Zealand's non-agricultural tradable sector will need to continue to adapt by further increasing efficiency to remain competitive. (https://www .imf.org/external/np/ms/2014/033114.htm)

So the fact that a currency is overvalued has little to no importance. It can stay overvalued for longer than you can stay short. However, it *is* useful to know what is driving the overvaluation because those things could change. In this case, the IMF believes that the strength of the NZD is related to high interest rates, a favorable growth outlook, and strong global risk appetite due to plentiful liquidity. This list is a good starting point for what factors to watch when trading NZD. If any of these factors starts to turn negative, you might expect NZD to fall.

This is all extremely big-picture stuff and worth only a few pages of discussion. Some would argue that because in the long run currencies tend to (eventually) revert to PPP, you are better off trading overvalued currencies from the short side and vice versa to get an edge, but this only applies to those trading FX on a multiyear time horizon. For those trading shorter time horizons (i.e., pretty much everyone), you should always be equally comfortable long or short a currency, no matter how cheap or expensive it is on a long-term basis. This flexibility will provide much more edge than any bias toward long-term mean reversion.

It is important to note that drivers of FX markets change as you move from long-term into short-term analysis. Valuation matters in the super-long-term, for example, while positioning and momentum matter much more in the short-term.

■ FX Fundamentals Can Be Domestic or Global

There are four main global drivers of currency values and three primary domestic drivers. The drivers are somewhat interrelated but deserve to be discussed one by one. To give you an idea of how some of the factors interrelate, check out Figure 5.1. I don't expect you to memorize it but it gives you an idea of the interplay and relationships between global and domestic fundamentals.

Let's talk about the **global drivers** of FX first. The four main global currency drivers are:

1. Global growth
2. Commodity prices
3. Risk aversion
4. Geopolitics

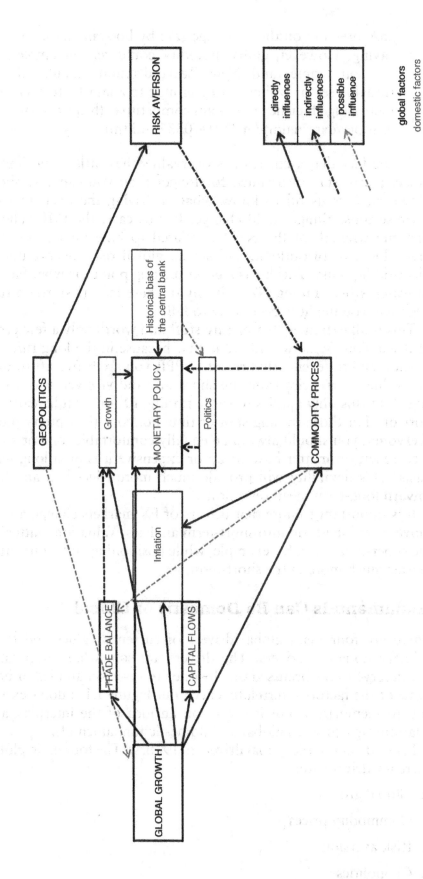

Figure 5.1 How domestic and global factors feed into currency markets.

1. **Global growth** is important because it influences the flow of money around the world. Global growth is a major driver of many currencies. When global growth is strong, exporters like China, Korea, and Brazil tend to do well and when global growth is weak, money tends to flow into safe haven currencies such as JPY and CHF (and often the USD).

2. **Commodity prices and terms of trade** exert a very strong influence on some currencies. Commodities are usually driven by global growth but they also move based on other factors such as climate, supply/production, idiosyncratic demand factors, and the popularity of commodities as an asset class.

Commodity exporters such as Brazil, Canada, and Australia benefit from commodity price strength while importers like Turkey and India are hurt by high commodity prices. Certain countries are known for exporting specific commodities and those commodities tend to influence those currencies more than others. The more a country exports a specific commodity, the more the price of that commodity will influence the currency.

3. **Fluctuations in global risk appetite and risk aversion** often cause FX moves regardless of the underlying domestic fundamentals of individual countries. As you learned earlier, different currencies have different personalities and certain currencies are safe havens. When markets are nervous, traders generally flock to low-yielding safe haven currencies like the JPY and CHF. This was on full display in 2008 when the CHF and JPY (and USD, which was a low-yielder at the time) exploded higher in response to the global financial crisis.

4. **Geopolitics** can influence global risk appetite and can also trigger specific currency moves in affected countries. Instability in Russia will drive selling of RUB, PLN, and TRY, for example, as the market reduces regional risk in an attempt to avoid losses. War, elections, or major policy changes in regions or individual countries can all be sources of geopolitical volatility.

These are the four main global factors that move currencies. Now let's look at domestic drivers of FX rates. As you gain more trading experience, you will notice that the market oscillates back and forth, sometimes focusing mostly on domestic conditions and other times focusing mostly (or only) on global factors.

In times of high-risk aversion or intense focus on China, for example, domestic drivers can become totally irrelevant. On the other hand, when the world is stable, changes in local economies and domestic interest rate policy can be the dominant driver of currencies, to the complete exclusion of global factors.

Let's look at domestic drivers of currency moves.

■ Domestic Drivers

1. Monetary policy
   a. Interest rates
   b. Balance sheet size
   c. Growth
   d. Inflation
   e. Central bank preference for weak or strong currency
2. Capital flows
3. Trade balance

CRITICAL CONCEPT: Understand Change versus Level of the Fundamentals

When you analyze domestic economic data and interest rates, it is critically important that you understand the difference between the absolute level of fundamentals and the delta (change) of those fundamentals. The market trades off the delta, not the level. For example, a country with poor but improving fundamentals is more likely to see its currency appreciate than a country with great but worsening fundamentals.

This is because prices in financial markets are set at the margin. At any given time, there is a momentary equilibrium price where supply meets demand and this gives us the current price of each currency. Then, as new information comes in and time passes, new buyers and sellers emerge and the price changes.

A country that has had poor fundamentals for years probably has a weak currency to reflect this. When information is widely known and prices have moved to reflect this information, the information or news is said to be *priced in*. It's in the price because markets have had plenty of time to absorb it and buy and sell based on the info. Efficient markets should generally factor in all known information.

Prices will change when new information (i.e., information that is *not priced in*) arrives. This is why you will often see a big move in currency markets when economic data come out or central banks make announcements. Economic data and central bank moves are substantial new information that may not have been previously known. The most important aspect of any new information that arrives is not whether it is weak or strong relative to the past but whether it is weak or strong relative to market expectations. This concept will be fully covered in Chapter 10, "Trading the News."

Monetary policy is the number-one domestic driver of currency values most of the time. Monetary policy is most often a reflection of growth and inflation expectations but can also hinge on other economic, political, and sociopolitical considerations. You should read every speech and official release of every central bank whose currency you plan on trading. Every document is publically available and doing the work on monetary policy is the first step toward becoming a professional FX trader.

There are two main monetary policy levers: interest rates and balance sheet size. Interest rates are the main monetary policy lever but because many central banks have hit the zero bound in recent years, they have been forced to resort to quantitative easing and balance sheet management.

For context, it is useful to know that many central banks have a historical bias. The most well-known historical central bank bias is the German Bundesbank's strong preference for tight monetary policy. This is a direct response to the long memory of hyperinflation of Germany's Weimar Republic.[1] On the other hand, the US Federal Reserve has a historical bias toward keeping rates too low for too long as Keynesian values dominate the US economic mainstream.

Much more important than the history, though, is to understand the current monetary policy bias of a central bank. This bias can be described as either neutral, tight (hawkish), or loose (dovish). Hawkish monetary policy is a desire for high or higher rates, while a dovish bias means a central bank is looking for low or lower rates. Central bank bias is often well known and reflected in the central bank's monetary policy pronouncements.

Changes in a central bank's bias are extremely important because the market, being the extremely efficient forward discounting mechanism that it is, often adjusts rapidly in anticipation of future interest rate moves. You will often see a currency react strongly to a central bank's change in bias and then by the time the central bank actually moves rates, the currency barely reacts because the change in rates was fully priced in (expected) by that point.

---

[1]For a fascinating historical account of this period, see Adam Fergusson, *When Money Dies: The Nightmare of Deficit Spending, Devaluation, and Hyperinflation in Weimar Germany* (New York: PublicAffairs, 2010).

Let's take the 2014 New Zealand hiking cycle as an example. People like to trade NZD via AUDNZD because that is the purest NZD play (as opposed to NZDUSD, which is highly dependent on the outlook for the US dollar). As the RBNZ becomes more hawkish (more likely to hike rates), one would expect the NZD to appreciate versus the AUD, sending AUDNZD lower. Take a look at Figure 5.2 and you can see how the RBNZ statements evolved in 2013 to lay the groundwork for their interest rate hike in 2014.

1. **"Although removal of monetary stimulus will likely be needed in the future, we expect to keep the OCR unchanged through the end of the year,"** July 25, 2013.

2. **"OCR increases will likely be required next year,"** September 2013.

3. **"Although we expect to keep the OCR unchanged in 2013, OCR increases will likely be required next year,"** October 2013.

4. **"The Bank will increase the OCR as needed in order to keep future average inflation near the 2 percent target midpoint,"** December 2013.

5. **Hiked on March 13, 2014.**

What you can see is that the market priced in the RBNZ's tightening bias very aggressively starting with point 2 and point 3 on the chart as the central bank switched from neutral to hawkish. As the RBNZ continued to promise hikes (point 4), the market kept selling AUDNZD. When the RBNZ finally hiked (point 5), AUDNZD hit bottom and the market started to buy AUDNZD (sell NZD), taking profit and unwinding positions.

This is an example of a common pattern called "Buy the rumor/Sell the fact," which is covered in Chapter 10. In this case, the change of bias was the driver of stronger NZD and the actual change in interest rates was the end of the story, not the start.

Understanding the bias of a central bank requires an in-depth understanding of what the central bank wants, what data it watches, and what constraints (political or otherwise) might influence the bank's tactics. While face-to-face meetings are the best way to get a full understanding of a central bank, most people cannot get direct access to central bankers on a day-to-day basis and so *you must do the work*.

I cannot emphasize this enough. If you trade NZD, you need to read every speech, every statement, and every interview from the RBNZ and NZ politicians who might influence the dialogue. If you don't do the work, you are at a huge disadvantage compared to more educated and more informed speculators.

Rule #3 of FX Trading: Do the work.

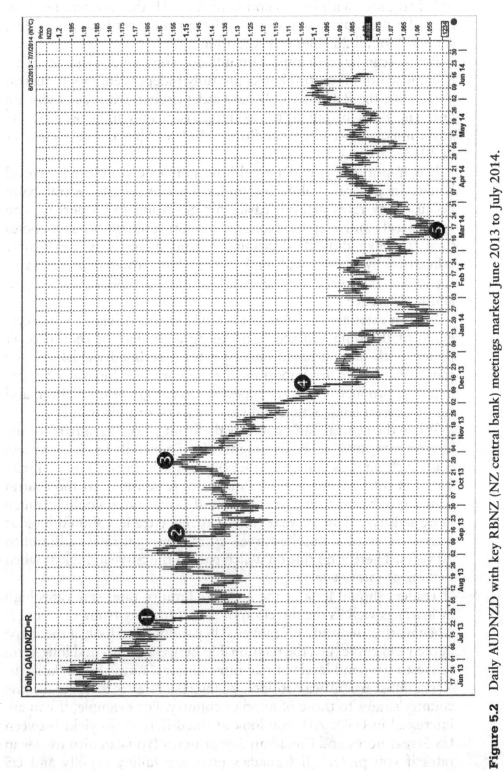

Figure 5.2 Daily AUDNZD with key RBNZ (NZ central bank) meetings marked June 2013 to July 2014.

UNDERSTAND FUNDAMENTAL ANALYSIS

suciety know to those of us daily contact...

Internatio...nal USD... its loss of...ch as... down in between

US Source a... and Cana...an econo... there is ...an to an... increase in

rates if they... d. If Canada's ...rates were ...talling ... and US

rates... belo..., peo...h, mi... would expe... USDC... to ... up (of the

Read the speeches. Listen to the central bankers. Analyze, read, and study.

Throughout this book, I will introduce the most important rules of FX trading. With the exception of Rule #1, they are numbered in the order they appear in the book. The appendix contains a complete summary of all 25 rules of FX trading.

Politics can have an important influence on monetary policy. This is because not all central banks are fully independent. Some central banks, like the RBA or RBNZ, are independent, whereas others are not. The Bank of Japan, for example, is heavily influenced by the government, especially since Prime Minister Shinzo Abe took over in 2013.

It is important to understand how politics can influence central banks. In general, politicians prefer a more dovish central bank because low rates make it easier for governments to borrow and spend freely and keep the economy humming along. When it comes time to make difficult decisions, central banks that are heavily influenced by politics will tend to keep rates lower than necessary for longer than necessary to avoid political problems, discomfort, and interference.

Interest rates are the most important variable driving FX markets much of the time and they tend to be a product of central bank policy. Both market-based interest rates (like bond yields) and the central bank rate are important for the currency. Interest rates are mainly a product of market expectations for growth, inflation, and future central bank action and vary by tenor or time frame.

While the central bank controls the front (short-term part) of the interest rate curve via its overnight rate, it generally has less and less control of rates as you go further out from the curve. For example, 3-month interest rates will be much more sensitive to the central bank's target rate than 2-year rates and 2-year rates would be much more sensitive than 10-year rates. Currency traders should look at interest rates all along the curve—from overnight rates right out to 30 years. There is no rule on which part of the curve to look at when looking at interest rates.

Traders should look at the absolute level of rates (are rates high or low?) as well as the direction of rates (are they rising or falling?) when betting on future FX moves. They should also look at the shape of the yield curve (i.e., the relationship between short- and long-term interest rates) and levels of real rates (interest rates after inflation).

The most useful way to look at interest rates is to compare one country's rates to those of another country. For example, if you are interested in USDCAD, you look at the difference in yield between US 5-year notes and Canadian 5-year notes (you can also use swap rates if you prefer). If Canada's rates are falling rapidly and US rates are rising rapidly, one would expect USDCAD to go up (ceteris

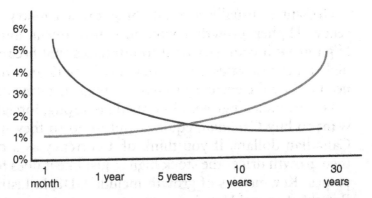

Figure 5.3 Two theoretical yield curves, one positively sloped (gray) and the other inverted (black).

paribus). This is Economics 101 and the holy grail of most of those boring international finance textbooks. For trading purposes, all you need to know is that as a rule, higher rates attract capital and lower rates trigger outflows of capital. This rule works most of the time in developed markets but less often in EM.

Another feature of interest rates that can drive FX is not just the level or direction of rates but the shape of the yield curve. The yield curve is simply a chart showing interest rates at different tenors. Figure 5.3 shows what two different yield curves might look like.

The upward-sloping line shows a normal yield curve where short-term rates are low and rates get higher as you move further out. A normal and steep yield curve is generally bullish for a currency as it implies an accommodative central bank (low short-term rates) and a bullish longer-term economic outlook (high long-term rates).

In contrast, an inverted yield curve suggests that a central bank is holding short-term rates too high and that the future outlook for economic growth is uncertain. Inverted yield curves tend to precede recession. Remember that when you look at interest rates, it is always important to compare one country to another. Rising US rates are good for the US dollar in theory, but if Canadian rates are rising even faster than US rates, one might logically expect USDCAD to fall.

This table shows how currencies generally react to interest rates and gives you a sense of what happens most of the time. But currency markets do not always behave as we expect. If they did, trading would be easy.

Bullish for the currency	Bearish for the currency
High rates	Low rates
Rising rates	Falling rates
Steep yield curve	Flat or inverted yield curve
Steepening yield curve	Flattening yield curve

Growth is usually a good thing for a country and for a currency. Higher growth encourages investment and higher rates. High-growth countries tend to attract capital because they feature higher interest rates and strong stock markets. Outside investors need to buy the currency to pay for their investments.

For example, if growth in Canada is strong, foreign investors will want to buy Canadian equities and to do so they will need to buy Canadian dollars. If you think of a currency as a country's stock, then growth drives the stock higher, just like it does for private companies. Key metrics of growth include GDP, Industrial Production, Retail Sales, and Housing statistics.

Inflation is more ambiguous and can be good or bad for a currency. The impact of inflation on currencies is especially confusing when it comes to emerging markets. It is important to understand the current inflation regime for the currency you are trading because there is no simple relationship between FX and inflation. Some examples of common currency versus inflation regimes are:

Rising inflation is good for a currency when the country's central bank is credible and willing to raise rates in response to inflation. This applies to most G10 countries, most of the time. The same can be said of falling inflation—it is generally bad for currencies in developed nations because it allows the country's central bank to cut rates. Lower interest rates usually mean a lower currency.

Rising inflation can be bad for a country if the market perceives that the central bank is behind the curve and will not respond fast enough with interest rate hikes. This is because lower real rates (real rate = nominal interest rate minus inflation) mean a loss of purchasing power and potential loss of value for the country's currency. At the same time, falling inflation or deflation can be good for a currency if the central bank of that country is perceived to be impotent or unwilling to act. This was the case in Japan until the deflation/strong currency link was broken by Abenomics in 2012.

So there is not always a clear and tradable relationship between inflation and currency values. In order to understand how changes in inflation will affect a currency you are trading, you first need to understand the central bank's reaction function. If inflation falls, what will the central bank do? What if inflation skyrockets? Then you can start to predict the impact of changes in inflation.

An example will help clarify. For many years after the bursting of the Japanese real estate bubble in the late 1980s, Japan was mired in deflation. Investor perception was that since interest rates were already zero, Japanese authorities were powerless to fight this deflation and therefore the yen appreciated for many, many years. As Japan headed from disinflation into outright deflation, the yen rallied more and more.

This all changed in 2012 when the Bank of Japan declared war on deflation and promised to massively expand their balance sheet by printing yen to buy Japanese stocks and bonds. Now, when Japan releases a low inflation number, this is considered bearish JPY (bullish USDJPY) because the central bank's reaction function is well known: More deflation = more printing of yen. By reestablishing central bank (and government) credibility, the BOJ was able to break the deflationary spiral.

Emerging markets are a completely different beast when it comes to inflation. This is because foreigners tend to buy and sell bonds in EM on a currency-hedged basis. High inflation in an emerging market can often lead to a situation where investors need to sell the bonds and the currency of the country at the same time. Inflation is almost always bad for bonds but the currency reaction in EM is difficult to predict because inflation can trigger one of two reactions by investors:

1. Investors liquidate bond positions and sell the currency.

2. Investors are attracted to the currency by high and rising yields.

Trading emerging market inflation requires a strong knowledge of the country's central bank and of investor positioning and preferences. When the market is heavily invested in the long-dated bonds of a country, higher interest rates can be a disaster for a currency but if the market is not heavily invested, higher rates can attract capital to the country and lead to buying of the currency. As a rule, I try to stay away from trading EM currencies after inflation data releases because the moves are often confusing and random.

Central bank currency preference. Does a central bank want its currency stronger or weaker? If so, this is important because central banks can directly and indirectly influence the value of their currency. They do this by raising or lowering interest rates and via two other approaches: direct intervention and signaling.

Direct Intervention

On rare occasions, when circumstances are deemed to be extreme, central banks will intervene directly in the FX market, buying or selling their own currency. The year 2011 provides a vivid example of this as the Swiss National Bank put a floor under EURCHF, promising to sell "unlimited quantities" of Swiss francs (and buy unlimited EUR) to ensure the pair would not fall below 1.2000. As you can see in Figure 5.4, this was a dramatic turn of events in EURCHF.

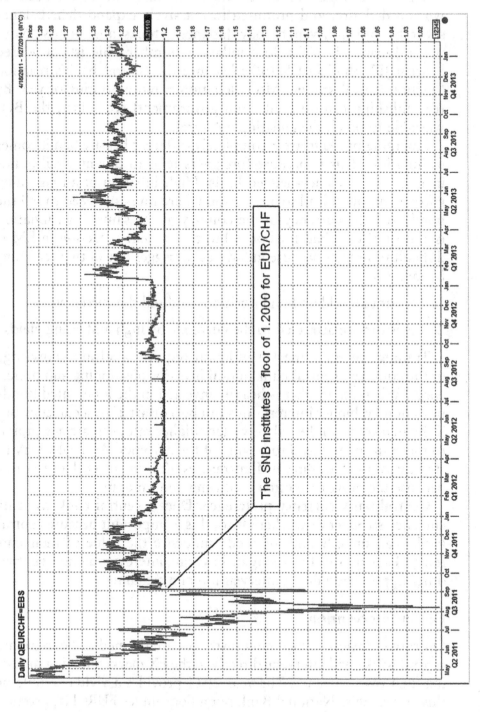

Figure 5.4 Daily EURCHF April 2011 to January 2014.

Signaling

It is expensive and risky for central banks to intervene directly, so a more common approach is for a CB to signal a desire for a stronger or weaker currency to the market and hope the market does the work for them. This approach is sometimes called signaling or moral suasion. It can work if the central bank is credible and the market believes the central bank is willing to change monetary policy or intervene directly to influence the currency if it moves further out of line.

An example of signaling is when the European Central Bank (ECB) noted its preference for a lower EUR at monetary policy meetings in 2014. The market came to believe that if the EUR did not go lower, the ECB would be more likely to announce a program of quantitative easing (which is bearish EUR) and therefore speculators sold EUR, driving it lower. Without changing monetary policy or selling euros directly in the market, the ECB was able to push the euro lower.

Another example of successful moral suasion of this sort was when Bank of Canada governor Stephen Poloz drove down the value of the Canadian dollar via comments in 2013. There are, on the other hand, many examples of central banks failing to persuade the market, including the SNB's famous failure to stimulate a weaker Swiss franc when EURCHF was trading around 1.5000 in 2009.

Central banks like the RBNZ have at times run into a "boy who cried wolf" situation as they complain over and over that their currency is too strong but then fail to take action when the currency keeps rising. When you judge whether a central bank's currency preference matters, first ask whether the central bank is credible. Second, will it be willing to take the necessary action if the market doesn't cooperate? Will they be willing to change interest rates or directly intervene in FX markets? If not, the half-life of the central bank's comments will be short.

As a rule, you do not want to bet against a central bank when it clearly outlines a preference for its currency. There are spectacular examples of speculators taking on central banks and winning, but unless your last name is Soros, I strongly recommend you be careful going against the wishes of a central bank.

■ Understand Intervention and Reserve Recycling

In order to maintain managed or pegged currency regimes, some central banks (most notably China and the other Asian central banks) intervene in currency markets. This intervention has a wide-ranging impact on markets beyond the country's home currency.

Global central banks hold massive reserves of dollars accumulated over recent decades. Most of this accumulation took place since the late 1990s after the Asian Financial Crisis taught global central banks (and especially Asian central banks) the lesson that large foreign exchange reserves can serve as protection during a crisis.

China is the most extreme example of currency reserve accumulation but other countries such as Brazil, Russia, Hong Kong, Singapore, and many others intervene in currency markets. China FX Reserves increased from about $200 billion in 2001 to a peak of almost exactly $4 *trillion* by 2014. Many other countries have increased their reserves in spectacular fashion over the past 20 years.

FX reserves tend to be denominated mostly in USD because currency market interventions are usually against the USD. For example, throughout most of the 2000s, China bought USDCNY in the market to keep its currency (the CNY) weak. As USD reserves ballooned, China needed to sell some USD and buy other other currencies (especially the euro) in order to diversify, so that all of their reserves were not in dollars. Instead of running 100% of their reserves in USD, central banks hold a portfolio of currencies. Figure 5.5 shows the average breakdown of global reserves, by currency.

That is the background, but here's where it gets interesting: As central bank reserves grow and shrink, the central banks need to buy and sell euros and other currencies in order to keep a steady percentage of their reserves diversified.

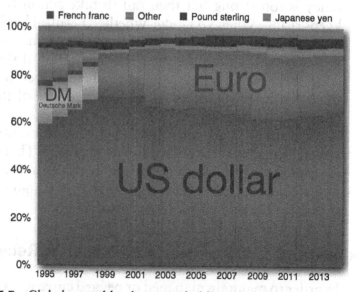

Figure 5.5   Global central bank reserve holdings, by currency.

https://en.wikipedia.org/wiki/Reserve_currency#/media/File:Global_Reserve_Currencies .png.

To take a simple example: If China's reserves drop from $4T to $3T, that's a drop of $1T. If 20% of their reserves are in euros, that means they now have $200B too many euros (one trillion X 20%). So as their reserves shrink, they need to sell EURUSD (and AUDUSD, GBPUSD, etc.) to rebalance. Many reserve managers rebalance quite actively, so you will often see that when there is pressure on EM currencies, G10 currencies will get hit in sympathy.

Whenever a large central bank intervenes in an EM currency, you should be mindful of the potential contagion to G10 currencies. Strong USD versus EM will often lead to a stronger USD versus G10 simply because of the mechanical nature of recycling flows. Quite often, this effect is most visible in the commodity currencies because when EM is weak, commodity currencies suffer under the double whammy of global growth fears (which are usually a big driver of EM weakness) and recycling flows from reserve managers.

Capital flows such as foreign direct investment, mergers and acquisitions (M&A), and equity and bond flows can be important drivers of FX rates. A cross-border transaction can generate massive FX flows in many instances as the foreign company must pay for the acquisition in the domestic company's currency.

While M&A has a short-term, immediate impact on FX, portfolio flows can last months or even years. When Mario Draghi convinced investors that the Eurozone was safe from breakup in 2012 with his "Whatever It Takes" speech, investors spent the next two years frantically accumulating Eurozone assets. This pushed up the euro for two years even as Eurozone economies languished and European rates remained extremely low compared to global peers.

Investment flows are not usually the biggest driver of FX markets but they can have a meaningful influence for extended periods. We saw the same thing in the euro again after Emmanuel Macron won the French presidency in 2017 and fears of a Eurozone breakup receded.

The problem with using capital flows as an input when trying to forecast FX is that these flows are fickle and hard to predict. While you will often see flows as an ex post explanation for currency moves, it is less common to see FX forecasts predicated on future capital flows.

Most of the time, FDI is not an important variable to consider for G10 FX traders but there are times like during and after the Eurozone crisis when investor flows can dominate moves in a currency. Capital flows are much more important in EMFX. Keep an eye on sovereign credit ratings and foreign equity markets for potential shifts in investor preference. While capital flows are rarely the number-one FX driver, it is important to keep them on your radar.

Trade balance and current account balance are important long-run determinants of currency rates but have little influence in the short run. It is often argued that these balances are influenced by FX, not the other way around. Trade and current account balances go in and out of vogue as FX drivers but it cannot be denied that a large percentage of cross-border FX flows are driven by global trade. Every time someone in Japan buys a product from a US technology company, for example, there is a tiny foreign exchange transaction happening as the US tech company receives yen and then needs to sell the yen at some point to buy dollars to fund its operations in the United States.

The sum of all the trillions of transactions taking place in the world leaves various corporations with constant operational FX hedging needs and these needs are a meaningful part of the FX mosaic. Furthermore, during times of rising global and US interest rates, investors may become hyper-focused on current account balances as they are a useful indicator of potential financing pressure on a country.

Finally, **fiscal policy** is a variable that can be important at times and irrelevant at others. It used to be a generally accepted principle that simultaneously loose fiscal and loose monetary policy were the textbook recipe for a lower currency. Over time the market has found the relationship between fiscal policy and FX to be much less reliable than previously thought and so fiscal policy has become less important over time to the point where people barely pay attention to it anymore. Sometimes loose fiscal policy can be good for growth and good for a currency. Other times it can trigger worries about credit quality (more sovereign debt, higher debt-to-GDP ratios, etc.) and debt downgrades.

There is a high degree of interdependence among the fundamental drivers described above; each fundamental can and often does influence the others. There can also be one main variable driving all the others, so when you analyze the drivers of exchange rates, it is always useful to pause and think about what variables are driving the bus and which ones are just along for the ride.

Now that you understand how macro fundamental factors influence currency markets, let's zoom in a bit and take a look at the role of US economic releases in currency trading.

■ Understand US Economic Data Releases

Before you can trade the economic data, you need to understand it. In this section, I will give you a detailed description of the most important US economic numbers and outline specific attributes and features of the data that you need to know before you trade. Non-US economic data will be discussed in the next section while how to trade economic data will be covered in Chapter 10, "Trading the News."

Economic data come and go in terms of market relevance and so it is key to know what matters right now. In this section, I will explain the economic data points one at a time. Remember that I am a trader, not an economist, and this is the lens through which I view the data.

The market tends to focus on three aspects of economic data: timeliness, relevance, and reliability. When data ticks two or three of these boxes, the market (and economists) care about it. US data are much more important to FX markets than data released by other countries, but you also need to understand global economic data so I will cover them separately.

Remember that the importance of various data points changes over time. If the market is focused on a housing-led recovery, for example, housing data gains prominence. Usually car sales don't matter much but if there is huge concern about the health of the US consumer, you might notice an uptick in interest around the auto sales numbers.

The most important thing to understand when it comes to trading economic data is that the only thing the market cares about is how the number compares to expectations. It doesn't matter if it's up, down, or sideways compared to last month or last year. Strong or weak is defined by how the data varies from the median expectation of economists and traders.

This is the concept of "what is priced in?" that I touched on earlier and discuss in detail in Chapter 10. The idea is that the price of a currency before an economic release is an equilibrium price containing all information to that point, including the median expectation for the data release.[2] Therefore, if the number comes out above or below expectations, this is new information and the price of the currency should quickly move to a new higher or lower equilibrium.

You need to get a feel for the size of the average miss so that you can appreciate whether a given release is a major surprise or not. For example: Nonfarm payrolls are expected at +110,000 and come out at +90,000. Is that a major surprise? The standard deviation of (ACTUAL − EXPECTED) for nonfarm payrolls is about 75,000. So the answer is: No, a 20,000 miss on nonfarm payrolls is not a major surprise. Look at a few years of past releases to get an idea of what is a big miss in any specific economic number.

---

[2]It is easy to find the median expectation of economists (check Bloomberg, Reuters, or the internet). Traders' expectations will normally be very close to those of economists, although there can sometimes be differences. The number expected by traders is called the "Whisper Number."

Note that economists tend to cluster around the mean and shy away from extreme forecasts. This means that forecasts tend to be way more tightly clustered around the mean than they should be and therefore there is plenty of room for large surprises on a regular basis.

The number-one reason economists do this is to avoid looking stupid. Say you are an economist and you think the number will come in strong. There is little incentive for you to put in an extremely high forecast. If you put a forecast way above everyone else and the number comes in low, you look really bad. If you submit a forecast just a bit higher than everyone, then no matter how strong the number is, you look smart! And if it's weak, at least you weren't too far away from the crowd. This type of gaming is a way that economists manage their career risk and is why you will notice over time that actual economic data are much more volatile than clustered forecasts suggest they should be.

Let's look at the major economic releases one by one. I will limit my discussion of the economics and econometrics behind the releases as much as possible and try to focus on the information that is most relevant to you as a trader. You need to know the basic underlying mechanics of the major releases so that you understand what is going on immediately after the release and can properly react to nuances, revisions, or idiosyncrasies.

Note that when there are multiple time periods for the same release at the same time (month-on-month, year-on-year), the shorter time period is always the most important. In other words, watch the month-on-month data, not the year-on-year, if both are released at the same time.

Let's go through the important US data while keeping in mind that different data points rise and fall in importance over time.

Indicator	Importance	Released
Nonfarm Payrolls	★★★★☆	First Friday of the month (with a few rare exceptions)

Definition: "Each month the BLS surveys about 145,000 businesses and government agencies, representing approximately 557,000 individual worksites, in order to provide detailed industry data on employment, hours, and earnings of workers on nonfarm payrolls.[3]"

Nonfarm Payrolls has been the mother of all US economic releases for many years. It is considered to be very timely, somewhat accurate,

[3]http://www.bls.gov/ces/.

and it always has an extremely large impact on FX markets. There are three numbers to watch on this release.

The main release is the headline figure, which shows the net number of jobs created. The second number to watch is the Unemployment Rate. The third component of the release that can be important is Average Hourly Earnings.

Here are some statistics about Nonfarm Payrolls and how the market reacts to the release.

NONFARM PAYROLLS STATISTICS (2010 to 2018)

Average Miss: 72,200

1 Standard Deviation Miss: 83,600

Average USDJPY range in 5 minutes after number: 66 pips

Average S&P range in 5 minutes after number: 11 points

The chart in Figure 5.6 shows NFP misses from 2010 to 2018. This should help give you a better idea of what is a big miss and what isn't.

Be ready for the number. Read every preview you can get your hands on. Search the web for "nonfarm payrolls preview" in the days leading up to the release and absorb everything you can. It might get boring after a while as most previews are similar, but you will start to get a good idea of which way economists are leaning and you will pick up details around the idiosyncratic aspects of the month's

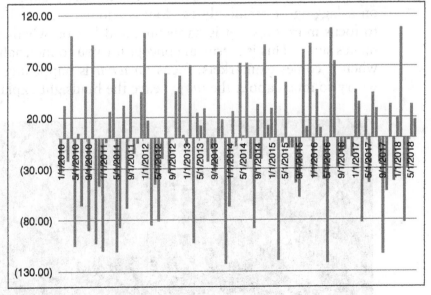

Figure 5.6 US Nonfarm Payrolls (actual vs. expected, 2010–2018).
Data from Bloomberg (000s).

release. You also need to have your trading plan ready before the number comes out, but we will discuss that later.

Indicator	Importance	Released
Initial Claims	★★★	Every Thursday

Initial Claims is a measure of the number of jobless claims filed by individuals seeking to receive state jobless benefits. The Initial Claims release is very important, as it is the timeliest of all major indicators. The series is released weekly (Thursday at 8:30AM NY) and tends to be reliable.

One important thing to remember with Initial Claims is that the release shows the number of new applications for unemployment insurance—so a high number is bad, and a low number is good. This can be confusing because most economic data are traded the other way. To get a better understanding of why Initial Claims is considered so important, take a look at Figure 5.7, which shows Initial Claims overlaid with the Unemployment Rate:

You can see that Initial Claims (the gray line) act as a very good leading indicator for the Unemployment Rate (white line). So why do people still care about the unemployment rate when claims already tell you where it's going? I have no idea! The market trades off all sorts of backward-looking and lagging indicators. My view is that often it is best to know *what* markets care about and not worry too much about *why*.

So many times I have heard traders losing money yelling, "This makes no sense!" or "It's old news!" as the market explodes or tanks on a lagging or seemingly random economic release. I always try to focus more on what is happening and less on whether or not it makes sense. This is a critical concept for you to internalize. Again, when it comes to markets, focus on *what* is happening and don't worry so much about the *why*. Leave the hindsight explanations to

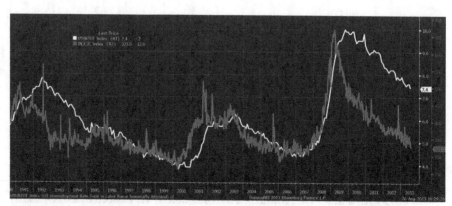

Figure 5.7 Initial Claims (GRAY) vs. US Unemployment Rate (WHITE).

the talking heads on CNBC. The simple fact is that markets don't always make sense.

Continuing Claims are released at the same time as Initial Claims. While Initial Claims is the number of people filing for unemployment benefits for the first time, Continuing Claims is the entire roster of all the individuals who are currently unemployed and receiving benefits. This number is less volatile than Initial Claims and gets less focus from traders.

Indicator	Importance	Released
GDP	☆☆☆☆☆	Quarterly

GDP stands for Gross Domestic Product. It is important to know that there are three releases for US GDP: Advance, Preliminary, and Final. GDP is an estimated figure; the government cannot measure it precisely. The Advance release is least accurate (but most timely) and is followed by the Preliminary and Final releases, which incorporate more information and produce a more accurate report. The Advance report is by far the most important release because it is (by definition) the timeliest but also because it tends to deviate the most from economists' estimates and therefore creates the most volatility. Remember that it's the difference from expectations that drives volatility, not the number itself.

By the time the Final report comes along, not only is it somewhat out of date, but the market has seen most of the inputs and therefore economists are able to more accurately estimate the release. Note that the average miss for Advance GDP is 0.35% while the average miss for the Final release drops to 0.10%. I trade Advance GDP as a release of top importance and I barely pay attention when Final GDP is released. That's how different they are.

Indicator	Importance	Released
Core PCE	☆☆	Same time as GDP

The Core PCE price index is defined as personal consumption expenditures (PCE) prices excluding food and energy prices. The Core PCE price index measures the prices paid by consumers for goods and services, revealing underlying inflation trends without the volatility caused by movements in food and energy prices.[4]

Core PCE has traditionally been the Fed's preferred measure of inflation. The Fed has an inflation target of 2% so when core PCE approaches or breaks 2%, it takes on added importance. Inflation

---

[4]http://www.bea.gov/faq/index.cfm?faq_id=518.

can also matter on the low side because low inflation can lead to deflation, every central bank's greatest fear. Low or falling inflation was one of the main justifications for the endless series of rate cuts and quantitative easing programs since 2009.

Indicator	Importance	Released
Consumer Confidence	☆☆☆1/2	Monthly (mid-month)

> Definition: "The Conference Board *Consumer Confidence Index* (CCI) is a barometer of the health of the U.S. economy from the perspective of the consumer. The index is based on consumers' perceptions of current business and employment conditions, as well as their expectations for six months hence regarding business conditions, employment, and income. The Consumer Confidence Index and its related series are among the earliest sets of economic indicators available each month and are closely watched as leading indicators for the U.S. economy.[5]"

Consumer confidence is among the most important of the survey data. Higher consumer confidence should lead to higher consumer spending (in theory) and consumer spending represents about 70% of GDP.[6] The market tends to buy stocks and USDJPY on a strong Consumer Confidence number and sell when it is weak. Consumer confidence and the stock market tend to move in sync.

Figure 5.8 shows an overlay of Consumer Confidence and the S&P 500 since January 2009.

Indicator	Importance	Released
ISM Manufacturing and Non-Manufacturing	☆☆☆☆	First business day of every month

> Definition: "The ISM Manufacturing Index is a diffusion index based on information submitted by purchasing and supply executives across the United States. The survey is sent out to respondents the first part of each month. Respondents are asked to only report on information

---

[5]http://www.conference-board.org/pdf_free/press/TechnicalPDF_4134_1298367128.pdf.

[6]https://www.stlouisfed.org/publications/regional-economist/january-2012/dont-expect-consumer-spending-to-be-the-engine-of-economic-growth-it-once-was.

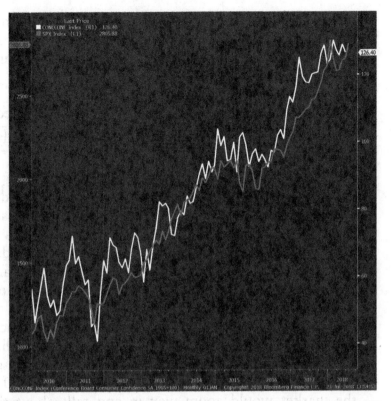

Figure 5.8 Consumer Confidence (WHITE) vs. S&P 500 Index (GRAY), 2010–2018.

for the current month. ISM receives survey responses throughout most of any given month, with the majority of respondents generally waiting until late in the month to submit responses in order to give the most accurate picture of current business activity. ISM then compiles the report for release on the first business day of the following month."[7]

The Non-Manufacturing Index is similar but deals with the services side of the economy. While services (aka non-manufacturing) represent a much larger portion of the US economy than manufacturing, the releases are of roughly equal importance in the mind of the market.

The market focuses most on the headline ISM releases but there are also subcomponents: New Orders, Production, Employment, Supplier Deliveries, Inventories, Customers' Inventories, Prices, Order Backlog, Exports, and Imports. The most-watched subcomponents are New Orders, Prices, and Employment. New Orders tends to be the most forward looking while the Employment

---

[7]http://www.ism.ws/ismreport/mfgrob.cfm.

component is an input into most economists' NFP models because it correlates fairly well with job creation. The ISM releases are of very high importance because they are extremely timely, relevant, and reliable.

Indicator	Importance	Released
CPI	★★★	Monthly (mid-month)

CPI (the Consumer Price Index) is a measure of the change in prices for the average urban consumer. Many pundits expected a surge in inflation following the global QE programs that began in 2008 but this forecast never came to pass as CPI was stable at fairly low levels for most of the 10 years after QE started. When CPI is low and stable, it is easy to forecast and surprises are few and far between. When CPI is volatile, the release is harder to forecast and tends to move the market more.

During 2007–2008 and again in 2018, when prices were rising above 2%, the market was so fixated on CPI that economists would analyze it to extra decimal places to give greater clarity on the potential direction of inflation. Instead of 0.2% or 0.3%, the market would zoom way in and talk about the unrounded number.

For example, a 0.3% release would be discussed as slightly weaker if the unrounded figure was, say, 0.267%. This is a great example of how economic data can gain and lose importance in a short period because for many years, like 2013, 2014, and 2015, the CPI release was all but ignored by the market.

Indicator	Importance	Released
University of Michigan Confidence	★★	Monthly

Definition: "The University of Michigan Consumer Sentiment Index Thomson Reuters/University of Michigan Surveys of Consumers is a consumer confidence index published monthly by the University of Michigan and Thomson Reuters. The index is normalized to have a value of 100 in December 1964. At least 500 telephone interviews are conducted each month of a continental United States sample (Alaska and Hawaii are excluded). Fifty core questions are asked."[8]

---

[8] http://en.wikipedia.org/wiki/University_of_Michigan_Consumer_Sentiment_Index.

There is a preliminary and a final UMich number. This release can move the market at times but it is not as widely followed as the Conference Board figure. The Conference Board's release is more important and extremely highly correlated to the Michigan number. The Michigan number also lost some credibility in the early 2010s as the media caught onto the fact that the figure was sold to subscribers who could see it (and trade off it) before it was released.

Indicator	Importance	Released
Durable Goods Orders (MoM, ex-transportation)	☆☆☆	Monthly

> Definition: "This report is compiled from results of the U.S. Census Bureau's Manufacturers' Shipments, Inventories, and Orders (M3) survey. This survey provides statistics on manufacturers' value of shipments, new orders (net of cancellations), end-of-month order backlog (unfilled orders), end-of-month total inventory (at current cost or market value), and inventories by stage of fabrication (materials and supplies, work-in-process, and finished goods)."[9]

This is a tricky one. The number is very, very volatile. So volatile, in fact, that it looks more like an EKG than an economic data series, as seen in Figure 5.9.

But random-looking series or not, the market trades it, so we need to understand it. The key aspect to understand about Durable Goods is that the headline number is influenced to the extreme by one-off or very large orders. An order for a bunch

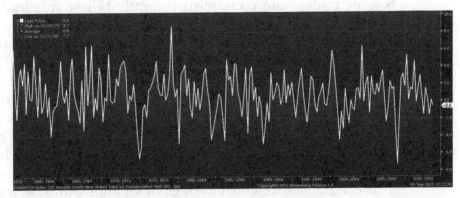

Figure 5.9 Monthly Durable Goods releases 1960–2014.

---

[9]http://www.census.gov/manufacturing/m3/adv/pdf/durgd.pdf.

of Boeing aircraft, for example, will distort the headline figure massively. You should ignore the headline number and focus only on the month-over-month (MoM) change in Durable Goods ex-transportation. This number is still volatile but it tends to be the most important in terms of gauging market direction.

Indicator	Importance	Released
Building Permits	☆☆ to ☆☆☆☆	Monthly
Housing Starts		
Pending Home Sales		
New Home Sales		
NAHB Housing Index		

First off, you need to answer: Is housing a meaningful driver or headwind for the economy right now? If not, housing numbers are ☆ or ☆☆. If the answer is a resounding "Yes!" then housing data can rise all the way up to ☆☆☆☆ importance level. You should focus on month-over-month data in these series.

Building Permits and Housing Starts tend to be considered leading indicators because they are the steps that must be taken before a new home can be built or sold. The relationship is not perfect because some permits are subsequently put on hold, reclassified, or abandoned. The temporal relationship between a permit being granted and the completion of a project can vary according to many factors, including financing, weather, and labor availability.

It is important to understand that many economists will disagree on what is a leading, lagging, or coincident indicator at any given time. Even analyzing the same data, you will see different economists reach different conclusions on what leads and what lags. The most important thing is not the actual truth, but what the market perceives to be the truth. If the market is hyper-focused on building permits because traders and economists currently believe it is leading, you should be hyper-focused on building permits, too.

Note that the NAHB Housing Index is different from the other data listed above because it is a survey, not hard data. Here is a description of the NAHB Index: "The Housing Market Index (HMI) is based on a monthly survey of NAHB members designed to take the pulse of the single-family housing market." The survey asks respondents to rate market conditions for the sale of new homes now and in the next 6 months as well as the traffic of prospective buyers of new homes.

The index is a weighted average of separate diffusion indices for these three key single-family series. The first two series are rated on a scale of Good, Fair, and Poor and the last is rated on a scale of High/Very High, Average, and Low/Very Low. A diffusion index is calculated for each series by applying the formula "(Good-Poor + 100)/2" to the present and future sales series and "(High/Very High – Low/Very Low + 100)/2" to the traffic series. Each resulting index is then seasonally adjusted and weighted to produce the HMI. Based on this calculation, the HMI can range between 0 and 100."[10]

Indicator	Importance	Released
Industrial Production	★★★	Monthly

> Definition: "The Federal Reserve's monthly index of industrial production and the related capacity indexes and capacity utilization rates cover manufacturing, mining, and electric and gas utilities. The industrial sector, together with construction, accounts for the bulk of the variation in national output over the course of the business cycle. The industrial detail provided by these measures helps illuminate structural developments in the economy."[11]

I am surprised the market does not focus more on the Industrial Production (IP) data. It is clean, timely, and relevant but the major gripe against the series is that it does not cover services, which are a large and growing proportion of the US economy. IP is a low three-star or high two-star release.

Indicator	Importance	Released
Retail Sales	★★★ ½	Monthly

Retail Sales are consistently a 3-star or 4-star release year after year. The release is always considered a good measure of the robustness of consumer spending, consumer confidence, and the overall health of the US economy.

> Definition: "The U.S. Census Bureau conducts the Advance Monthly Retail Trade and Food Services Survey (MARTS) to provide an early estimate of monthly sales by kind of business for retail and food service firms located in the United States. Each month, questionnaires are mailed to a probability sample of approximately

[10]http://www.nahb.org/generic.aspx?genericContentID=532.

[11]http://www.federalreserve.gov/releases/g17/About.htm.

5,000 employer firms selected from the larger Monthly Retail Trade Survey (MRTS). Firms responding to MARTS account for approximately 65% of the total national sales estimate."[12]

The most important data point to watch is the month-on-month figure, ex-autos and gas.

Indicator	Importance	Released
Chicago PMI, Philly Fed, and Empire State	★★★	Monthly

These are regional business surveys similar to the ISM surveys released at the start of each month. The numbers are sensitive to the main industries in the respective region so while they are highly correlated to one another, there is still some meaningful deviation in the figures.

It is crucial to note one strange feature of the Chicago PMI release: It is released to subscribers at 9:42AM and then to the general public at 9:45AM. This creates an unusual setup where half the market seems to think the number has been leaked as the USD jumps or dumps at 9:42 and then the move is confirmed by the official release at 9:45AM. "The number is leaked!" Every month. By design. So be aware that whatever moves you see in the market at 9:42AM on Chicago PMI day are not random.

This concludes the rundown of the major economic releases. It is vital to note, however, that the market constantly evolves. A number that I have not even mentioned could jump to prominence at any time. There was a time in my career when M2 was a closely watched figure (released at 4:30PM!) and more recently we have seen TIC data and other data releases enjoy their 15 seconds of fame.

Keep your finger on the pulse of the market by studying as much as you can before the numbers come out. There is no excuse for saying, "Whoa! What just happened?" when a number comes out and the market moves. That's a clown move. You should be ready for every release and if you're not, find a pursuit you are more passionate about. In FX trading, preparation, focus, and passion give you a huge edge.

■ Understand Global Economic Releases

Every country in the world publishes reports on economic growth and inflation along with many, many other economic indicators. The

---

[12]http://www.census.gov/retail/#marts.

importance of different economic releases varies over time as the market focuses on different concerns and pressure points.

Inflation data were especially important in countries such as Australia and Germany in the period from 2010 to 2015, for example, as the central banks there cut interest rates in an attempt to avoid disinflation. At other times, GDP or jobs data are more important. The list of what economic data matters changes over time but there is a fairly consistent group of indicators that usually matter.

Below, I provide a list of important global economic releases. The list is not exhaustive but covers the important releases for each country and currency. As with US releases, it is important to understand what is priced in (expected) before trading any of these events. Also note that the directional impact and half-life of global economic releases tends to be smaller and shorter than the market reaction to US economic numbers.

Important numbers to watch are:

Europe

- Germany ZEW Survey
- Germany IFO Survey
- Germany GDP
- Germany Factory Orders
- Germany IP
- Germany Inflation (core CPI)
- Germany Retail Sales
- Euro Area PMI (Composite and Manufacturing)
- Eurozone Inflation (core CPI)

United Kingdom

- Retail Sales
- CPI
- GDP
- Claimant Count Change (similar to US Initial Claims)
- Manufacturing Production
- Average Earnings
- Manufacturing and Non-Manufacturing PMI
- Exports
- Current Account Balance

Japan

- Tankan Survey
- Trade Balance
- GDP
- Machinery Orders
- Industrial Production
- CPI

Canada

- Net Employment Change and Unemployment
- CPI
- Retail Sales
- GDP
- Ivey PMI
- Building Permits
- Manufacturing Shipments
- Bank of Canada Business Outlook (Future Sales)

Australia

- Net Employment Change
- GDP
- CPI (RBA Trimmed Mean)
- Retail Sales
- Trade Balance

New Zealand

- Employment Change
- Unemployment Rate
- GDP
- Retail Sales
- CPI
- Trade Balance

Norway

- CPI
- GDP
- Retail Sales
- PMI

Sweden

- GDP
- CPI
- Industrial Production
- Retail Sales
- Manufacturing Confidence

Switzerland

- CPI
- GDP
- KOF Leading Indicator
- Manufacturing PMI

After reading this chapter, you should fully understand these key concepts:

- Why fundamental analysis is important, even for short-term traders
- Long-term FX valuation and why it has limited usefulness
- Global currency drivers
- Domestic currency drivers, especially monetary policy
- Understand US and global economic releases

Now that you have a good understanding of fundamentals and how they influence currency markets, it is time to move on to a completely different topic: technical analysis.

CHAPTER 6

Understand Technical Analysis I

■ Introduction

Technical analysis is the study of chart patterns in an attempt to forecast future price movements. The theory is that in a natural system composed of many human beings, price patterns will repeat and echo as humans tend to behave in similar and predictable ways over time. This psychological regularity leads to a series of patterns that can be seen in real time and used as predictors of future market moves.

There are literally hundreds of technical patterns, ranging from generic (support and resistance levels) to very esoteric patterns like the "Abandoned Baby" or the "Three Buddha Bottom." Anything involving charts and pattern recognition usually falls under the heading of technical analysis.

■ Technical Analysis: Does It Work?

Before we spend a whole chapter on technical analysis, it is important to ask an essential question: Does technical analysis work? There is a ton of research on technical analysis out there, but unfortunately no conclusive evidence. There is some modest evidence of persistent trend and tradable patterns in certain markets over time but it is unclear how much of this works in real time. (It could just be hindsight and data snooping.) Trend-following models in FX have performed poorly since the 1990s and the evidence generally suggests that some patterns worked for some periods but profitable technical patterns are arbitraged away over time.

One study of all the literature around technical analysis[1] concluded the following:

> Early studies indicated that technical trading strategies were profitable in foreign exchange markets and futures markets, but not in stock markets before the 1980s. Modern studies indicated that technical trading strategies consistently generated economic profits in a variety of speculative markets at least until the early 1990s. Among a total of 92 modern studies, 58 studies found positive results regarding technical trading strategies, while 24 studies obtained negative results. Ten studies indicated mixed results. Despite the positive evidence on the profitability of technical trading strategies, it appears that most empirical studies are subject to various problems in their testing procedures, e.g., data snooping, ex post selection of trading rules or search technologies, and difficulties in estimation of risk and transaction costs. Future research must address these deficiencies in testing in order to provide conclusive evidence on the profitability of technical trading strategies.

A study by three professors at MIT[2] concluded:

> By comparing the unconditional empirical distribution of daily stock returns to the conditional distribution—conditioned on specific technical indicators such as head-and-shoulders or double-bottoms—we find that over the 31-year sample period, several technical indicators do provide incremental information and may have some practical value.

So there is some evidence that it works, but also plenty of studies showing it does not. Another study[3] came to this conclusion:

> Over 5,000 popular technical trading rules are not consistently profitable in the 49 country indices that comprise the Morgan Stanley Capital Index once data snooping

---

[1] http://chesler.us/resources/academia/AgMAS04_04.pdf.

[2] http://web.mit.edu/people/wangj/pap/LoMamayskyWang00.pdf.

[3] https://papers.ssrn.com/sol3/papers.cfm?abstract_id=1181367.

bias is accounted for. Each market has some rules that are profitable when considered in isolation but these profits are not statistically significant after data snooping bias adjustment.

Some people think technical analysis is useless—a complete joke. Other traders think technical analysis is the only tool you need to trade successfully. My philosophy on technical analysis is somewhere in the middle.

I think technical analysis is a valuable tool but it does not work well as a standalone trade selection or forecasting methodology. The more years I trade, the more strongly I believe that *technical analysis should be used as a tactical and risk-management tool and not as a trade selection tool*. This comes from years of trading experience, from watching many people trade, and from reading volumes of research on the topic.

While I am sure there are examples out there somewhere, in more than 20 years of trading on both the buy side and the sell side, I have never worked with a purely technical trader who made meaningful P&L. Every successful trader I have worked with over the years either trades macro or uses a multifactor approach. And I have seen many traders who use only technical analysis fail miserably. Think of the most successful traders of all time: Soros, Tudor-Jones, Bacon, Druckenmiller. They are macro or hybrid guys, not pure technicians. They supplement their analysis with charts but their ideas come from all over the place.

Most technicians I've seen or worked with always think they are just one tweak away from perfecting their model but can't ever quite produce the profits they just know their system should deliver. There is an entire industry devoted to selling technical analysis tools and systems of questionable (or negative) value. So healthy skepticism is warranted.

Do you really think it passes the commonsense sniff test that you can just look at a chart, see a simple pattern, trade it, and consistently make money? Given the thousands of traders and billions of lines of code you are competing with, probably not. There were systematic funds that profited from simple technical analysis in the 1980s and 1990s, but those days are long gone. Systematic funds now compete on a much more complex playing field and the profitability of simple trend following and other technical systems has converged toward zero.

While it is hard to assess the forecasting value of technical analysis, there is another simple reason that using technical analysis is inherently risky (assuming you are a human being). Humans are designed to see patterns. It's how our biology works. It allows us to simplify and process a complex world. It is called apophenia: the human tendency to perceive meaningful patterns within random data.[4] This image provides an example.

Just a simple socket, right? Face? What face?

If you are bullish some security, I can guarantee that if you look at a chart long enough, you will find a pattern that confirms your bullish view. In other words, another problem with technical analysis is that it is highly subject to confirmation bias. You see what you want to see. A friend of mine once said, "Charts are like clouds. If you stare long enough, you will eventually see something interesting!"

Furthermore, most of the empirical evidence from research shows that if you trade the popular patterns like Head and Shoulders systematically, you do not make money. So I strongly believe that technical analysis is best used for risk management and tactical considerations and not as a primary trade selection tool.

While my belief is that the value of technical analysis as a forecasting tool is limited, I use technical analysis every day. I come up with my trade ideas elsewhere and then go to the technicals to determine optimal tactics such as entry level, stop loss, take profit, and position size.

Without technical analysis skills, you are too often entering trades at midrange with no clear concept of where to get out. Techs give you clear-cut risk management levels and allow you to maximize your leverage and determine the point at which you will admit you are wrong. Note that my approach also meshes with research that shows that portfolio managers who use technical analysis outperform those who do not.[5]

---

[4]https://en.wikipedia.org/wiki/Apophenia.

[5]https://www.cfainstitute.org/learning/products/publications/contributed/Pages/head_and_shoulders_above_the_rest__the_performance_of_institutional_portfolio_managers_who_use_technical_analysis.aspx.

So, to conclude: I strongly advise you to learn about technical analysis and use it as a tool—but consider it a risk management and tactical tool, not a trade selection or forecasting tool. Never do a trade just because a chart looks good or because something is on a big support or Fibonacci level.

The topic of technical analysis is very, very broad. I will explain how I use a few specific technical formations in my trading but there are hundreds if not thousands of entire books on the topic. See a list of my favorite technical analysis books in the "Further Reading" section at the end of this chapter. Now let's get started with the basics.

■ The Need to Know of Technical Analysis

There are three main branches of technical analysis:

1. Traditional technical analysis. This includes trend, breakouts, cycles, retracements, momentum, support, resistance, moving averages, overbought, and oversold.

2. Candlestick charting. This is a Japanese method of charting that is popular globally. It provides a nice, clean, visual way of looking at price charts. While I only know the basics of candlestick charting theory, I use candlestick charts because I like the way they look and the way they transmit information clearly. Figure 6.1 shows the difference between a candlestick chart and a regular Open-High-Low-Close (OHLC) chart.

   The primary difference is simply that on a candlestick chart, up bars are white and down bars are black. Some people use green and red for up and down but the idea is the same. Using candlesticks gives you a better view of the price action and allows you to more clearly identify pivotal days such as dojis (indecision days). I will discuss how I use candlesticks in the section that follows.

3. Elliot Wave and cycle analysis. These are specialized, highly complex systems of analysis used by a limited group of practitioners. They involve looking at the market as a series of waves or cycles and applying specific rules to forecast future price changes. The main criticism of the method is that it can be pseudoscientific and two practitioners will often come up with different forecasts even though they start with the same methodology and the same chart. This makes the method highly subject to confirmation bias.

   In other words, if an Elliott Wave practitioner is biased toward a bullish view, he will most certainly be able to find a bullish wave count for the chart of the security in question, and vice versa. I personally have found the method far too subjective and complicated to have any practical use, and while I am sure there are

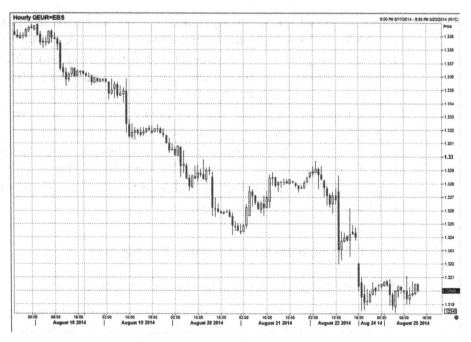

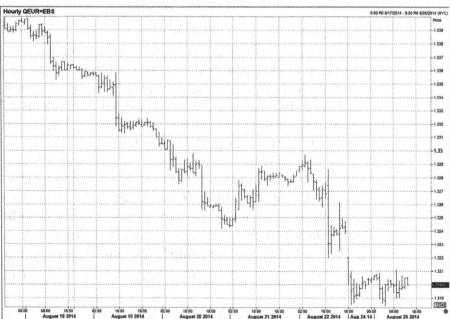

Figure 6.1 The same hourly EURUSD chart presented two ways: candlesticks above and OHLC bar chart below.

some out there, I personally don't know any successful FX traders that actively use Elliott Wave. I subscribed to various Elliott Wave services at various times in my career (including the most famous ones) and found their analysis to be very convincing, highly intelligent, and totally useless.

Choosing Indicators

"Everything should be made as simple as possible, but not simpler."

—Albert Einstein

Occam's Razor states that among competing hypotheses, the one with the fewest assumptions should be selected. Other, more complicated solutions may ultimately prove correct, but—in the absence of certainty—the fewer assumptions that are made, the better.

—Wikipedia

When using technical analysis as a risk management and tactical tool, simpler is always better. First, I will run you through some of the most useful basic indicators and then I will move on to my favorite setups. Use what you like; ignore what you do not.

Basic Indicators

1. Support and resistance

The simplest and most useful concept in technical analysis is support and resistance. This is the idea that price will tend to bounce off the same level more than once. There are four main explanations for the existence of support and resistance:

a. **Large limit orders** create pockets of liquidity that can stop the market. Let's say a corporation needs to buy one billion euros and decides to leave an order to buy them at 1.3335. You might get something like you see in Figure 6.2. The 1.3335 level will act as support until the order is filled.

  Each time the price of EURUSD sells off to 1.3335, all selling is absorbed by demand from the large order as indicated by the up arrows. Then finally, once the order is filled, look what happens at the down arrow—a break through the level and acceleration lower as there is now no demand to satisfy new supply.

b. **Self-fulfilling prophecy.** Another reason support and resistance exist is because many traders use support and resistance to determine entry and stop loss levels. This somewhat circular statement is known as the self-fulfilling prophecy aspect of technical analysis. It works because people think it will work.

  If there is a very obvious support level (like 1.3335 in Figure 6.2) traders will tend to place their bids ahead of this level and their stop loss orders below. So the more times a currency bounces off a given level, the more interest that level will attract from buyers.

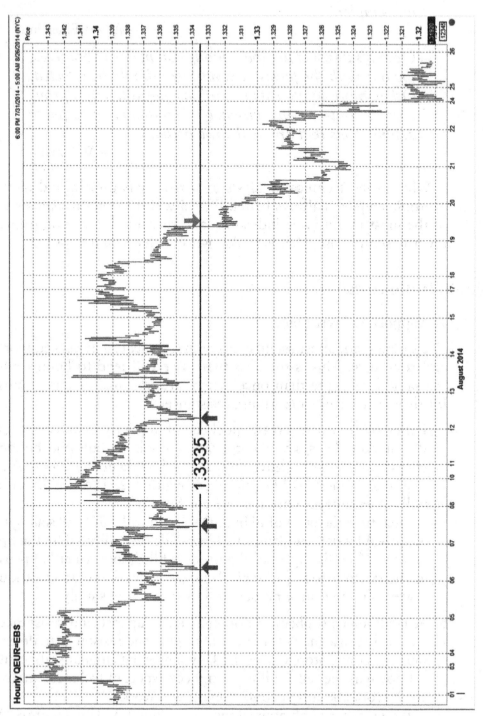

Figure 6.2 Hourly EURUSD, broken support lets the downtrend resume, July–August 2014.

c. **Option-related.** A third reason that support and resistance levels exist is that option strikes and option barriers create certain hedging needs around specific levels. If there is a large option in the market at a given level, there will often be large interest to buy or sell near there. This can create support or resistance.

d. **Round number bias.** Human beings prefer round numbers to non-round numbers—it's a fact! Therefore, traders tend to leave orders at round numbers and tend to attach importance to breaks of round numbers. This has been revealed time and again in myriad studies. This means that highs and lows are more often made on round numbers than on non-round numbers. For example, 50 is more probable as a daily low than 49 or 51. I have studied the data and this is a fact, not speculation.

The implication of round number bias is that if you are a buyer, you should leave your orders just above the round numbers and if you are a seller, you should leave your orders just below the round numbers. For example, an experienced trader will leave a limit buy order at 1.3001, not 1.2999, with the knowledge that 1.3000 has a greater than random chance to hold given it is a major round number. (See "Round Number Bias" in Chapter 9 for more on this phenomenon.)

■ Using Support and Resistance in Your Trading

Say you are bullish EURUSD based on your assessment of fundamentals, positioning, and recent news. Let me emphasize: *You have your view already; you don't come up with your view using technical analysis.* Now you are ready to zoom in via the technicals.

While the concept of support and resistance is simple, it is also powerful. The first step when looking for support and resistance is to simply scan the chart. I use 10-minute, hourly, and daily charts and look for major bottoms and tops. I look for bottoms, double bottoms, triple bottoms, and occasionally more.

The more times a level or zone holds, the more likely the market is focused on it. Keep in mind when using support and resistance that everyone else is looking at the same chart as you. To avoid trading with the herd you need to think a bit outside of the box and leave your orders away from where the herd leaves orders. Let's look at an example.

EURUSD has been falling for two weeks. I'm getting bullish because I think it's come too far too fast and market expectations for next week's ECB meeting are too dovish. Meanwhile, crude oil and the IBEX have rallied like mad the past few days and I think these are good lead indicators for EURUSD direction right now. So I want to go long, but where? Figure 6.3 shows the hourly chart.

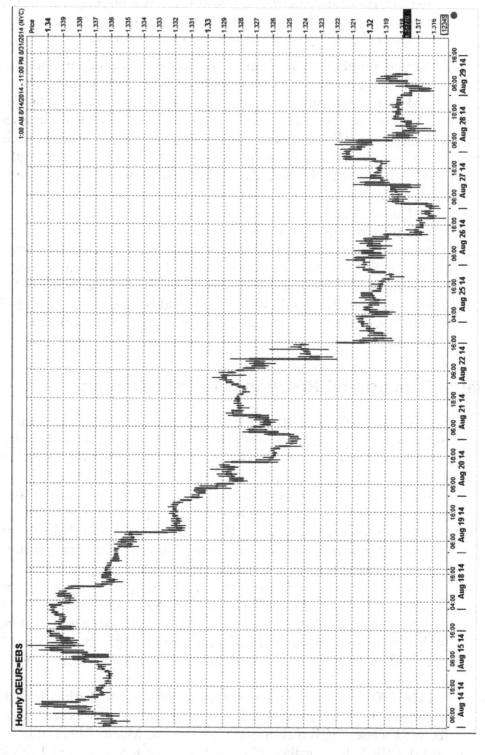

Figure 6.3 Hourly EURUSD, August 14 to 29, 2014.

The market (currently 1.3177) has tested and retested the 1.3150/60 level. It has bounced three or four times now, so people should definitely be focused on the level at this point. Also note the lows are just above the round number (1.3150), which could suggest a barrier is at 1.3150 and someone is protecting that level (i.e., bidding for a chunk of euros so that 1.3150 doesn't trade). Or maybe a patient buyer is on the bid there.

I decide that we are close enough to the support level and I will go long here. Clearly, I want my stop somewhere below 1.3150, but where do I leave it? Knowing that many people will leave their stops just below 1.3150, I will give it some room. 1.3129 is probably reasonable. (I take 1.3149—below the round 1.3150 support—then add 20 pips of additional leeway to avoid a quick bang-bang stop loss run.) So I will go long here (1.3177) with a stop at 1.3129.

Now this is of course a simplistic thought process, but most of the time simple is good. Ideally, you can incorporate other technical concepts to make your thinking more robust and complete.

Something to keep in mind is that if you initiate too far away from a support level, your position needs to be smaller because you are risking more in terms of percent or pips before you hit your stop loss. Therefore, the tighter you can fine-tune your entry point and stop loss, the larger position you can have and the greater the returns you can achieve if you make the correct call and do not get stopped out.

There is always a tension between keeping a tight stop loss, which allows high leverage, and the risk of getting prematurely stopped out by random noise. The tighter your stop, the more likely you are to fall victim to "bad luck." I put bad luck in quotes here because it is not bad luck if you get stopped out on a random move. It means either your idea was wrong, you picked the wrong level for your stop, or you put your stop too close to the market given current volatility.

This balance of trying to find the optimal stop loss distance (not too far and not too close) is discussed further in Chapter 12. For now, just understand that your entry point is a major determinant of how much leverage you have and how big a position you can trade. At the end of the year, your returns will depend on this leverage.

2. Simple and exponential moving averages (plus crossovers)

A simple moving average (SMA) is the average price of a security over the past X number of periods. As time passes, the older prices fall out of the average, to be replaced by newer prices. The shorter the period used for the moving average, the more volatile it will be and the more closely it will track the price of the security itself. The length of the SMA you use depends on your trading time horizon. You can use moving averages on daily or intraday charts.

An exponential moving average (EMA) is similar to an SMA but it puts more weight on recent data versus older data, so the EMA turns up and down faster. Figure 6.4 presents an hourly EURUSD chart with five simple moving averages 20-hour, 55-hour, 100-hour, 200-hour, and 600-hour.

The most obvious feature you should notice right away is that the faster SMA tracks the price of spot much more closely while the slow SMA barely reacts to recent moves. The challenge is to find the SMA that approximately defines the trend without too much noise. Eyeballing this chart, the 200-hour SMA looks like a good approximation of the short-term trend. I generally find the 200-hour to be the best moving average in most currency pairs.

There are many ways to use a moving average (MA) to help your trade entry and risk management. Some of the most common are:

a. Use the moving average as support or resistance. As a general rule, you want to be long when spot is above the MA and short when spot is below. If you are bullish EUR and looking for an entry point, you buy as the market nears one of the fast-moving averages and place your stop loss below a slower one. The ideal bullish scenario is one where spot is above the moving average, plus the slope of the moving average is positive (i.e., the moving average line slopes upward).

My trading strategy is short-term so I use 20-period, 55-period, 100-period, and 200-period moving averages on 10-minute and 1-hour charts. I prefer the 55-hour and 200-hour moving averages as fast and slow indicators for my trading but whether you use 55-hour or 100-hour or 200-hour, the idea and results will be about the same.

You have probably read about backtesting to find optimal moving averages for each currency but my belief and experience is that this is mostly data mining and the optimal length of a moving average that worked in the past is not necessarily the one that will work in the future. It is better to fit your moving averages to your trading time horizon than to obsess over which particular moving average worked best in the past.

b. Use a crossover of two moving averages to trigger buy or sell signals and to define the trend. When the 100-hour crosses up through the 200-hour, that indicates prices are starting an uptrend. There are various nicknames for specific moving average setups, such as the bullish Golden Cross (when the 50-day crosses up through the 200-day) and the bearish Death Cross (when the 50-day crosses below the 200-day). A trader

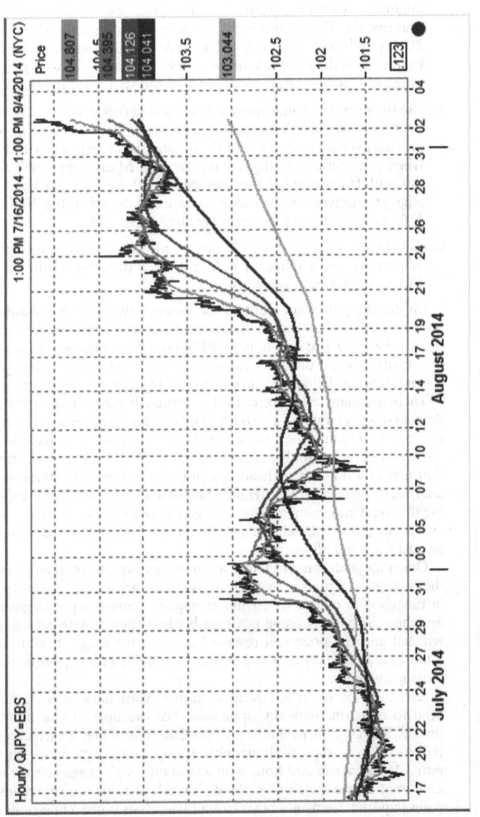

Figure 6.4 Hourly USDJPY, July 16 to September 4, 2014.

might focus on long positions only when, say, the 20-day MA is above the 55-day and focus on short positions only when the 20-day is below the 55-day. This type of thinking will always keep you on the right side of the trend and that is the main point of using moving averages—to identify and stick with the trend.

c. Use the slope of a single moving average together with its location to enter newly forming trends. This strategy waits for a specified moving average to turn up (or down) and then enters a new trade when price returns to the moving average. Many people will do this with faster moving averages like the 20-day MA as a way to align themselves with the short-term trend. So when the 20-day MA turns up, leave a buy order at the 20-day MA.

d. Another strategy is to use closing prices with a moving average. When the close is above the MA, go long. If the close is below the MA, exit longs and get short.

Ultimately, you don't want to use moving averages in isolation, you want to use these tactics to enter and exit trades that you like for other reasons. If you love long EURUSD but you're flat and looking for an entry point, put some moving averages onto a chart and get a sense of what defines the current trend. Then plan your strategy.

There are many advantages to this approach versus a purely fundamental or behavioral approach. The main advantage is that you will not be fighting the market all the time, so you will have less chance of blowing up. If you are bearish EURUSD but you identify that it is in a full-steam-ahead uptrend, you will wait for technical analysis to signal a turn in trend before getting on board. By identifying the trend and using moving averages to fine-tune your entry and exit timing, you will achieve superior results and will avoid sailing against the wind all the time.

One important thing to know when using moving averages is that they give good signals in trending markets and are worse than useless in rangebound markets. Moving average systems will get chopped up when the price is going nowhere because each new trend signal will fail and the price will reverse back into the range. If you are looking at a currency that you expect to trade in a range, ignore the moving averages.

As I mentioned earlier: Keep it simple. Your indicators do not need to be mathematically optimized. For example, if you notice that EURUSD tends to bounce off the 200-hour when it's trending, you can buy at the 200-hour with a stop loss below major support. Or buy at the 100-hour with a stop one day's range below the 200-hour. Those sorts of simple ideas work just fine, no supercomputer required. Remember that technical analysis is just a fine-tuning device. It's one more clue, not the answer.

If you can find a setup where you have a moving average and major support around the same level, this makes your levels much stronger. When multiple technical indicators come together near a single level, it is known as *convergence*.

3. Measuring momentum, overbought and oversold

There are countless indicators used for measuring momentum, overbought and oversold conditions. I find MACD, RSI, Parabolic SAR, and the Deviation to be most useful. I will discuss the first three here and I cover the Deviation in Chapter 7.

Momentum indicators are similar to overbought/oversold indicators as they all generally try to identify moments when price has extended too far, too fast in one direction and could be ready to turn back around. They attempt to identify overshoots, in other words. If price is like a rubber band, there is a point where it becomes overstretched and is primed to snap back. While often dangerous to trade in isolation, these indicators can help you scale in and out of positions at better levels than a purely naïve or random approach.

Take a look at Figure 6.5. It shows USDJPY in black on top with an RSI below that and MACD at the bottom. First, notice that the ebb and flow of the RSI and the MACD are similar. They are based on similar math using the same price series so it stands to reason that there would be a strong link between the two analyses. This is why I prefer to only use one momentum indicator on my charts—it is often redundant to use multiple momentum indicators.

Let's look at the RSI (in the middle). The textbook theory is that when you get below or above certain thresholds (in this case the horizontal lines at 30 and 70), the currency pair is oversold or overbought. Most traders wait for the RSI to go down into oversold territory and then rise back above to get a buy signal, or the opposite for a sell signal.

The reason you wait to sell until the RSI turns back down (instead of just selling when the RSI crosses up through 70) is that a currency can stay overbought for a long time. Often the most dramatic part of a move comes while the currency is in an overbought state. The chart in Figure 6.5 sends a bearish signal for USDJPY because the RSI just broke above and then back below 70.

Another way you can play MACD or RSI is to look for divergence between the price and the indicator in an attempt to determine when the trend is out of steam. For example, in the chart above, price made a new high on the last run up but the MACD did not. This is called "negative divergence" and could indicate that the trend is losing power. Looking at this chart, you therefore see two bearish

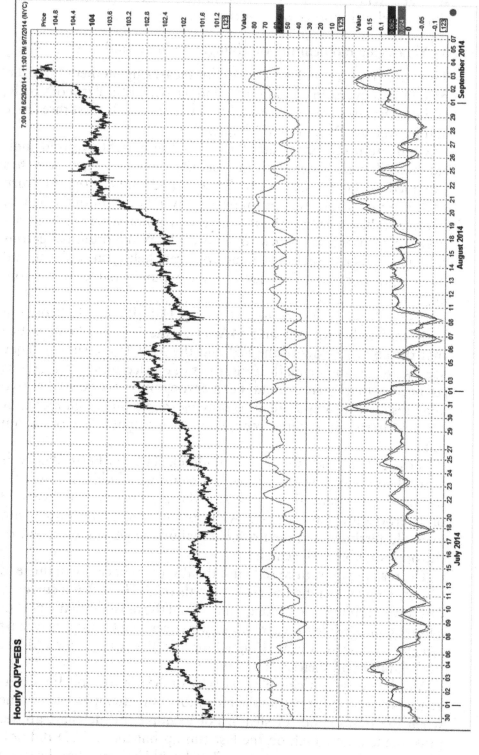

Figure 6.5   Hourly USDJPY with RSI and MACD, June 29 to September 7, 2014.

signals: bearish divergence on the MACD, and an RSI that falls back below 70 after breaking above.

Let's say it is Summer 2014 (the period depicted on the chart) and you are bearish USDJPY for four different fundamental reasons, but you've been waiting patiently to sell because the currency pair is in a raging uptrend. Suddenly, this looks like a juicy setup—it's time to get short.

Given the bearish momentum signals, you decide that if USDJPY breaks to new highs you are probably wrong, so the trade here is to sell and leave a stop loss somewhere above the highs. What you cannot see on this chart is that there is a major double top on the daily chart at 105.40/45. So, the ideal trade is to sell here (104.88) with a stop at 105.66 (which allows 21 pips of leeway for noise above the double top). The first target is the nearby support (103.50/60) and then the next target is the lows around 102.00/20.

Another tool I like is called Parabolic SAR. The beauty of this system is its simplicity. Here is the definition from Wikipedia:

> In stock and securities market technical analysis, Parabolic SAR (Parabolic Stop and Reverse) is a method devised by J. Welles Wilder, Jr., to find potential reversals in market price direction. It is a trend-following (lagging) indicator and may be used to set a trailing stop loss or determine entry or exit points based on prices tending to stay within a parabolic curve during a strong trend.
>
> Similar to option theory's concept of time decay, the concept draws on the idea that "time is the enemy." Thus, unless a security can continue to generate more profits over time, it should be liquidated. The indicator generally works only in trending markets, and creates "whipsaws" during ranging or, sideways phases. Therefore, Wilder recommends first establishing the direction or change in direction of the trend through the use of Parabolic SAR, and then using a different indicator such as the Average Directional Index to determine the strength of the trend.
>
> A parabola below the price is generally bullish, while a parabola above is generally bearish.

The system places dots on the chart in response to the past movements of the price and so you can clearly see if you are in a bull or bear trend. The way I use the Parabolic SAR is mostly as a visual reminder of the current trend and whether I am in harmony with or fighting against the market. Figure 6.6 shows what the Parabolic SAR looks like on that same USDJPY chart. (I've zoomed the timeframe a bit so you can see the dots properly.)

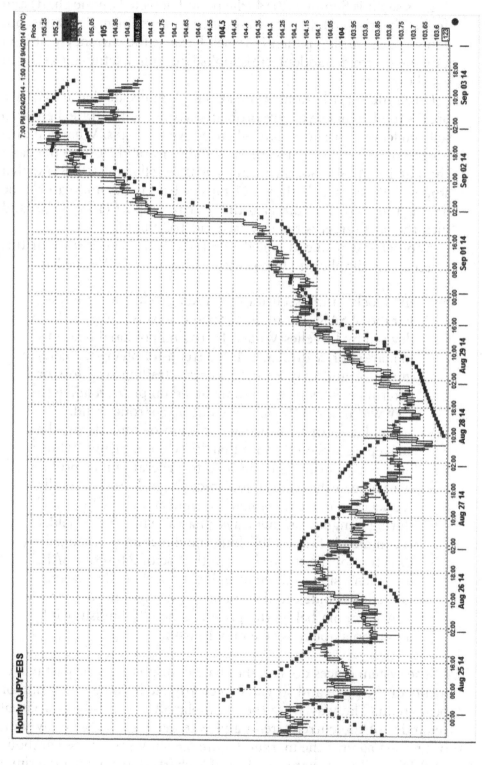

Figure 6.6   Hourly USDJPY with Parabolic SAR, August 24 to September 4, 2014.

The system is nice and simple and that's why I love it. If the dot is above the price, you are in a downtrend.

The other great aspect of parabolic SAR is that it gives you a very clear (and usually rather tight) stop loss level. If you are short USD-JPY here (104.85), you can stop out at 105.12 (the last black dot). And you can see that when USDJPY trends, Parabolic SAR catches a good part of the move. When USDJPY chops around, the signals are not useful.

Note that any trend-following indicator (moving average, Parabolic SAR, MA crossover) will give you approximately the same message, so don't clutter up your chart with too many similar indicators. Pick one or two trend indicators that you like and one or two momentum indicators you like and stop there.

Different traders will swear by different indicators but just be aware that the math underlying each group of indicators is similar. Do an online search for "overbought oversold technical indicators" if you want to learn more ways to find overshoots.

4. Candlestick charts

There is a substantial body of literature outlining various ways to analyze candlestick charts. Countless books describe how to read and trade candlesticks and there is a ton of information online for further research. Let me cover the most important aspects of candlestick charting.

First, the basics of candlestick construction. The difference between the open and the close is called the body of the candlestick. That is the fat part that is black and white (some systems use green and red in place of black and white). The tails outside the body are called the shadow of the candlestick and represent the full range that traded outside of the OPEN/CLOSE range.

When the candle is green or white, it means the currency pair went *up* on the day and if it is red or black the currency pair went *down*. So, to recap, the body is the open to close range, the color defines if the currency pair rose or fell, and the shadows (sometimes called wicks, as in candle wicks) are the intraday extension outside the open-to-close range. The standard up and down candles are shown in Figure 6.7.

Any single candlestick does not have much meaning. Instead, candlestick disciples look at groups of candles in attempt to identify known patterns. Specific candlestick formations have colorful names like gravestone doji and hanging man and shooting star. I find candlestick formations especially useful for identifying reversals. Following are the four candlestick formations I find most useful.

Dojis. A doji is a candle where the open is very similar to the close and therefore the body is tiny and the wicks are long. A series of three consecutive dojis is illustrated in Figure 6.8.

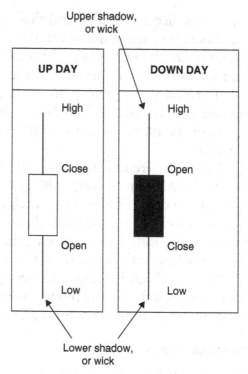

Figure 6.7 Standard up and down candlesticks.

Figure 6.8 Three consecutive dojis on a candlestick chart.

Dojis are important candles because they show market indecision. When you see a doji it means the market went down then up (or up then down) and closed unchanged. So the market tried to move but came back to its opening level and closed near unchanged. It could not choose a direction. These candles are especially important after a long trend. Take Figure 6.9, for example, which shows the ultimate turning point at the lows of the S&P 500 Index (SPX) in early 2009.

You can see the February 2009 downtrend was relentless. And then suddenly, on March 8 the SPX made a doji—the only doji on the whole chart. That doji showed that the market had lost its selling mojo. There was suddenly great indecision. The market tried to push lower that day and could not. Then it tried to recover, but again could not. Then finally it closed flat on the day.

This doji was a powerful signal that the epic financial crisis downtrend in the stock market was out of gas. Stocks never traded at those depressed levels again and quadrupled over the next 10 years.

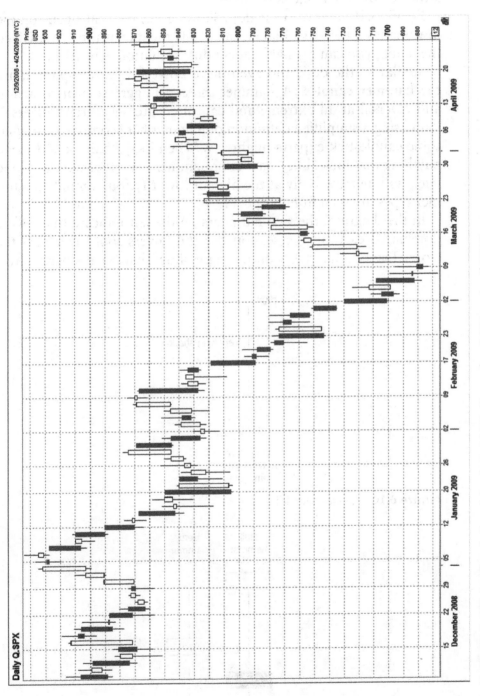

Figure 6.9 Daily S&P 500 (with a doji on March 8, 2009), December 2008 to April 2009.

UNDERSTAND TECHNICAL ANALYSIS I

There are specific types of doji (like the gravestone doji and the spinning top) but in general I think the concept of any doji is similar. Indecision after a long trend should raise your alert level and suggest a turn or trend change is possible.

Figure 6.10, a **gravestone doji**, shows a market that opens on the low, makes a big push higher, then ends the day at the lows. Given the name, you can probably guess this formation is bearish.

Similar to the doji, and even more powerful in my opinion, are the **hammer candles**. A hammer indicates aggressive price action and reversal at an extreme and can often predict a trend reversal. I am using a simplified definition of hammer here compared to what some candlestick experts might say. When I say "hammer," I mean anything that looks like a mallet or hammer—in other words, a long wick with narrow body at the high or low. My four simplified hammer types are seen in Figure 6.11.

In the diagram, the two hammers on the left indicate that sellers dominated early in the session but the buyers took over into the close. The two hammers on the right show that buyers were active

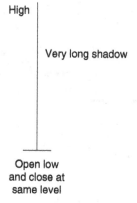

Figure 6.10   Gravestone doji.

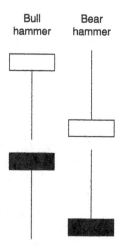

Figure 6.11   Hammer candle formations.

early but sellers took control into the close and prices closed near the low. The two on the left are bullish hammers, while the two on the right are bearish. The size of the hammer head is not especially important but longer wicks make for better hammers because they show larger reversals.

The most important and dramatic hammers hit right at major highs and lows, after a prolonged trend. These hammers have specific names like shooting star but I just call them all hammers for the sake of simplicity. Bear hammer at the highs is bearish. Bull hammer at the lows is bullish.

I especially like trading hammers on the daily chart because they can set up trades with very clear risk/reward. Take a look at Figure 6.12. Let's say it is mid-September and you are bullish USDCAD but the currency pair has been in a downtrend for a while and you don't want to fight it. Then you see that huge bull hammer on September 20. It has extra importance because that same candle is also a major new daily low that could not hold.

That is a great setup to get long USDCAD at the close with a stop below the low. Sure, you didn't catch the exact bottom, but now you have a good trade where you know your exit point and you are buying into a strong market, not a weak one. It took a while, but this USDCAD trade paid off well.

Hammers are especially powerful if your preferred style is to go against the trend. They stop you from trying to top tick or bottom tick the market all the time. Instead, they put you in a position of strength with very clear risk/reward parameters and show you when the uptrend buyers or downtrend sellers are exhausted. Hammers are valid on charts of any time frame.

One more thing I look for when it comes to candlesticks is candles with long wicks. Long wicks indicate uncertainty, and they are of extra interest when you see a few in the same area. This is more common on hourly charts than on daily charts.

Figure 6.13 shows an hourly AUDUSD chart. Note how the rallies on September 4 and September 5 all finish with long wicks. This indicates a quick run higher that was rejected. You can see that after four or five of these failed spikes higher, AUDUSD finally reversed and went lower. Long wicks show that price attempted to enter a new equilibrium zone but was quickly slapped back by more powerful or motivated agents. Finally, note that there is a long wick on that very last candle of the chart, which may indicate that the downtrend is now running out of steam.

5. Ichimoku

Ichimoku charts are a Japanese method of plotting price and time. They are most commonly used when trading USDJPY and JPY crosses. The concept is similar to a moving average crossover but it

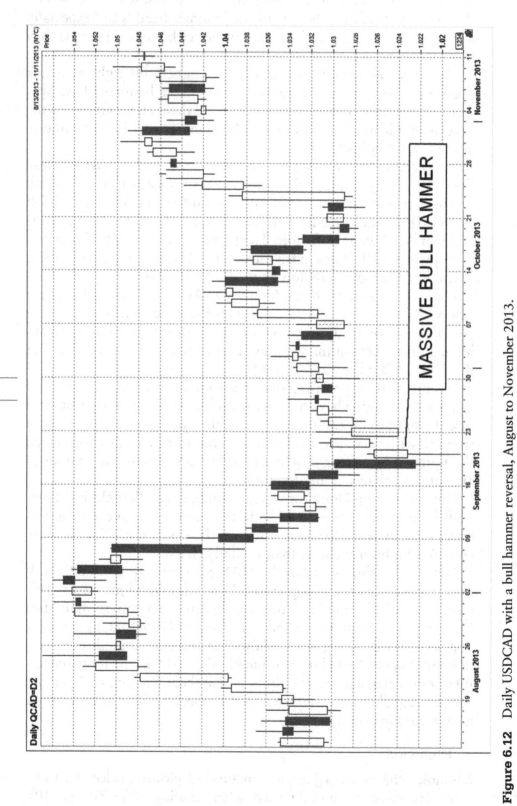

Figure 6.12 Daily USDCAD with a bull hammer reversal, August to November 2013.

Note to self: Resist the urge to make "U Can't Touch This" or "2 Legit 2 Quit" jokes when discussing hammer formations. Readers will not find them funny.

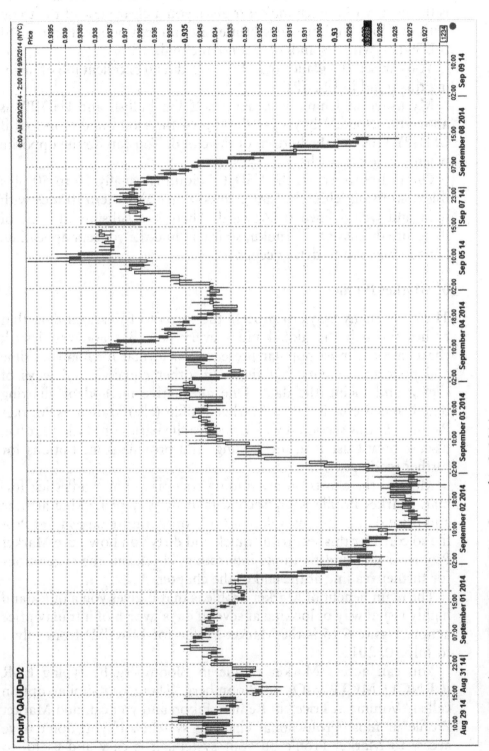

Figure 6.13 Hourly AUDUSD, August 29 to September 9, 2014.

uses a cloud formation, which attempts to define the current and future trend. The Japanese word *ichimoku* means "one look." That is the beauty of the ichimoku: It gives you a clear view of the trend with one look and provides firm entry and exit points. Figure 6.14 is USDJPY with a standard ichimoku cloud.

You can see at a glance that the cloud did an excellent job of defining this trend in USDJPY.

My usage of ichimoku is simple. If I'm bullish and USDJPY is above the cloud, I buy near the top of the cloud and stop loss if USDJPY falls out the bottom of the cloud. You can do the opposite when you are bearish.

On an hourly chart, the USDJPY cloud is usually 10 to 50 pips thick, so using ichimoku can give you nice short-term trades with tight and well-defined risk/reward. There is a substantial body of literature discussing ichimoku, so if you find the concept appealing, I encourage you to delve deeper.

6. Market Profile

There are many ways to process the torrent of financial data that rushes through the global pipes every day. Bar and candlestick charts are the most popular presentation format for financial time and price movements, but there are other equally valid ways of slicing and dicing the data. One alternative method of charting that I find useful is called Market Profile (also known as Market Picture). In this section, I will introduce the basics of Market Profile, discuss how I use it in my trading, and provide some options for further reading.

Most of the charts on my trading cockpit are in candlestick format. Market Profile is my second-favorite way of looking at time and price data. There is a decent body of literature on Market Profile so consider this section a "quick and dirty" on how I use Market Profile. If you find the topic interesting, check out the suggestions for further reading at the end of the chapter.

The main benefit of Market Profile is that it gives you a quick and highly visual way of looking at several days' worth of intraday price action. Figure 6.15 is the Market Profile for EURUSD from July 3 to July 10, 2013.

You can access Market Profile in Bloomberg by typing **EUR {CRNCY} MKTP {GO}** on Bloomberg. There is a similar option called "Volume at Price" in Reuters Eikon and you can find Market Profile in most professional charting systems. If you don't have access to Market Profile on your system, it is easy and useful to create the charts yourself.

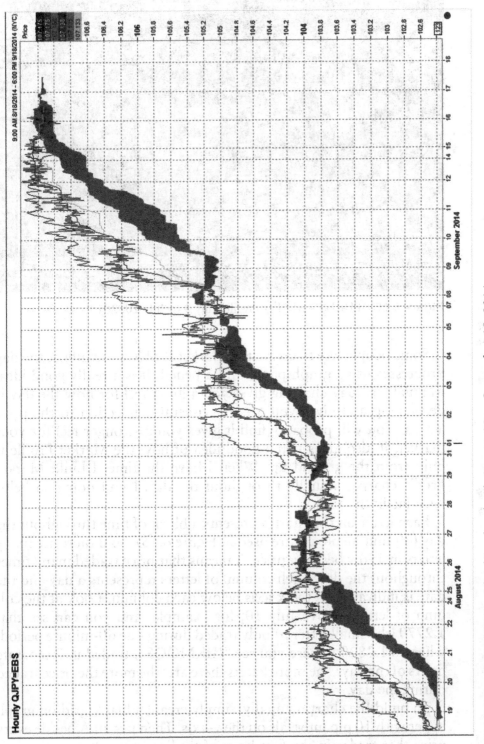

Figure 6.14 Hourly USDJPY with ichimoku cloud, August 18 to September 18, 2014.

UNDERSTAND TECHNICAL ANALYSIS I

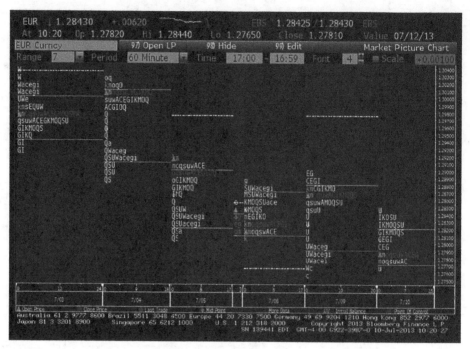

Figure 6.15 EURUSD Market Profile, July 3 to July 10, 2013.

Some people like to create the Market Profile manually as the day progresses using graph paper and a pencil. It is a really good idea. Manual intraday charting gives you a great feel for how the day is developing and gives you a more visceral connection to the price action. You will probably find it gives you a stronger feel for your market. It also gives you a good idea of how the Market Profile is built from the ground up. When I have the time, I build Market Profile charts manually throughout the day. I find doing so helps keep me in the zone.

Each letter on the chart represents a block of time throughout the day (60-minute blocks are used in Figure 6.15). So if there are many letters in a row beside a price, it means that price traded many times throughout the day. Each column of letters represents a day and the date is indicated on the x-axis below each column. Look at the column of letters above July 10, for example, and you can see that 1.2770 (the small letter *u*) only traded during one 60-minute period, whereas 1.2820 (where you see "GIKMOQS") traded in 7 separate hours of the day. The more letters there are, the more the price traded during the day.

To build the chart manually, simply create a blank grid on graph paper with 10 pip intervals on the y-axis. Then put an A beside every price that trades in the first hour of trading, put a B next to every price that trades in the second hour of trading, and so on. I suggest you try this for a few days and see how it feels. If your time horizon is shorter, you can use 30-minute or even 10-minute intervals. This can help with focus and concentration. When people read a suggestion like this in a book, nine times out of ten they just keep reading and forget about it. Don't do that here. *Build your own Market Profile charts during the day!* It is a fantastic exercise that will make you a better trader.

Market Profile gives you the ability to quickly identify equilibrium zones. These are the areas where many letters form large clusters. The longer a row of letters, the more times a given price traded that day. To repeat, areas with many letters show equilibrium zones where a lot of trading took place.

At levels where there are very few letters, on the other hand, the market traded only briefly before more aggressive sellers or buyers came in and quickly pushed the price away. This is all you really need to know to start using Market Picture. The key is to focus on the equilibrium and non-equilibrium zones.

The simplest trading strategy I use with Market Profile looks for what is called a *single print,* which is a point on the market profile where there is only one letter because the price traded there but then moved away before the start of the next time period. When you see a single print, you can clearly see that the market rejected this price point aggressively and therefore this is a price point that you should consider a key pivot.

Let's look at that same Market Profile chart again. On July 4 (07/04, as indicated on the x-axis) there is a series of single prints (all denoted by the letter Q) as EURUSD fell from 1.2990 to 1.2940. This happened after a very dovish ECB statement.[6] The most important thing to know is that price gapped through this level and therefore anyone who wanted to sell in the 1.2940/1.2990 window was unable to do so because the price did not remain there for long.

This means that rallies back toward that zone will likely be sold as players that missed selling on the way down will try to sell when price gets back up there. I would never trade a Market Profile single print (or any technical formation) by itself. Instead, I note the level as an important pivot and use it to maximize leverage and/or determine my stop loss when I come up with a view and take a position in this currency pair.

Let's say now it's July 5 and I am bearish EURUSD because I think yesterday's dovish ECB statement will meaningfully change expectations for the currency going forward. We are trading at 1.2840 and I believe risk/reward in selling here is poor because we are too oversold. So I don't want to get short here; I want to sell a rally.

---

[6]DRAGHI: "RATES WILL REMAIN AT PRESENT OR LOWER LEVELS FOR EXTENDED PERIOD," Bloomberg.

The ideal trade is to wait for the price to get back toward the bottom of the gap down zone from July 4. You can see from the chart that today's high was around 1.2900/20. I would use other charting techniques like moving averages to further zoom in on the optimal entry level but with the information we have here it looks like 1.2900/40 is definitely the sell zone. This is an example of technical convergence as major resistance (today's high 1.2900/20) and the edge of a single print zone (1.2940) are nearly the same. So we want to get short ahead of those two levels. Ideally other indicators also highlight the importance of the 1.2900/40 area and we are closer to a Five-Star trade.

With the information we have here, the optimal trade is to sell EUR just ahead of 1.2900 with a stop loss above the single prints. So in this case we leave a limit order to sell at 1.2898 and a stop loss at 1.2990. This is highly preferable to selling at 1.2840 because it allows us to take a bigger position with much better expected value. You can see the next day the high was 1.2900/10, so we went short and the price soon fell back to 1.2770 over the next day or two.

As mentioned earlier, trading is a game of inches. If you left your sell order at 1.2920 in this example, you missed the move back down.

There are many, many other interesting ways of looking at Market Profile charts. My main objective here was (a) to make you aware of the existence of Market Profile, and (b) to inform you of how I use single prints as key pivots in my trading. As with everything in this book, I encourage you to internalize what you find useful and discard what you don't. You need to develop your own style and your own methods. I'm just here to open some doors. Explore Market Profile and come up with your own ways to use it in your analysis.

FACTBOX

Point and Figure charting is another example of an alternative charting method, but its popularity has waned in recent decades. The main benefit of Point and Figure charts is that they are easy to construct manually. This was important before the computer age but now few traders chart manually. I still have fond memories of manually charting my first stock purchase on pieces of graph paper taped together and stuck on my wall at the age of 15. The chart was about fifteen feet wide by the time I finished and it stretched across three walls of my bedroom. Not exactly the type of activity that attracts high school girls, but it does show the early passion I had for trading and financial markets! Incidentally, that first stock I owned was in a company called Cinram, which manufactured blank audio cassettes and compact discs (CDs). It was a great macro idea at the time (1980-something) as CD sales were about to take off. The company did well for many years but went bankrupt in 2012 as the market for physical CDs (and cassettes!) dried up.

7. Fibonacci numbers

The Fibonacci numbers are the integers in the sequence 1, 1, 2, 3, 5, 8, 13, 21, 34, and so on, where each number is the sum of the two previous numbers. Fibonacci numbers appear frequently in nature—for example, in the relationship between the length of tree branches, in the shapes on the outside of a pineapple or a pine cone, and in the growth and reproduction patterns of many animals, flowers, and plants. Because Fibonacci numbers appear so frequently in nature and many consider financial markets to behave much like a natural organism, there has been significant work done in an attempt to find Fibonacci patterns in financial prices.

The popular Fibonacci (or fibo) ratios in finance are 23.6%, 38.2%, 50%, 61.8%, 76.4%, and 100%. The numbers are used to estimate possible retracements. For example, if a stock falls from $100 to $50, the 50% retracement would be $75 as that is the point where price recoups half its fall. The 61.8% retracement would be ($100 − $50)*0.618 + $50, which is $80.90. In other words, if the stock falls from $100 to $50, the 61.8% retracement would be $80.90. Bearish traders who missed the first sell-off would look to sell around $80.90 with a stop above the $100 level.

I suggest a great deal of caution when using Fibonacci numbers because all too often you will find that traders recognize them and talk about them *after* they hold, not before. The problem with fibos is that there are simply way too many of them. Any given trader might use a different high/low and so if someone says, "Wow, the

50% fibo held perfectly!" keep in mind Figure 6.16, which shows a chart of EURUSD with all the major fibos marked. Obviously, some of them are going to hold! This is why I rarely find fibos useful. There are simply too many of them.

Rule #4 of FX trading: If you look hard enough, you can always a find a tech level to justify a bad trade!

Rule #5 of FX trading: "It's a big level" is not a good enough reason to put on a trade.

Here is a simple real-life example of how I use technicals to fine-tune a trade idea. I am bullish euro for various but I have no position yet. I am keen to pull the trigger but the currency is in no-man's-land around 1.3100, so I am waiting for a better level to get in. A headline comes out:

"German Finance Minister Schaeuble says cannot exclude the possibility of Eurozone breakup"

On the surface, this is a bearish headline and the kneejerk reaction for anyone long euros is to sell immediately. The price gaps lower and the client phone lines trill like crazy. Salespeople yell to the euro trader: Sell! Sell! Sell!

The thing is, Schaeuble has said this exact quote before and so there is no new information here. The kneejerk is for longs to cut their positions, but this headline is not really news[7] so this is my chance to buy euros. But where? And when? If I just stick in a bid arbitrarily, I might buy too early and the price could continue to fall and fall…and fall. If I wait too long, the price will snap back to where it started and then I missed a great opportunity to get long.

Fortunately, this morning I did my technical analysis and I see in my morning notes that the 100-hour MA, the 200-hour MA, and a major support all come in around 1.3050/55. This is a nice tech converge and so I know exactly where to look for a reversal. Remember, other traders also use technicals to enter their positions (and this includes the central banks and the big hedge funds), so big convergence zones can be great entry points as many players all come in to buy around the same area. The more different technical indicators that identify the same level or zone, the better.

I put a bid on my machine at 1.3058 and enter my stop loss at 1.3019. The bid is just ahead of the supports in case others are trying to buy in the same area. I put my stop loss far enough away that there is a bit of leeway in case price modestly overshoots my levels. I try to get my stop loss entered as quickly as possible after entering any position. Think of a stop loss as insurance against both incorrect

---

[7] As discussed, this is a key factor in evaluating and trading headlines. Is this important *new* information? Should it affect the price?

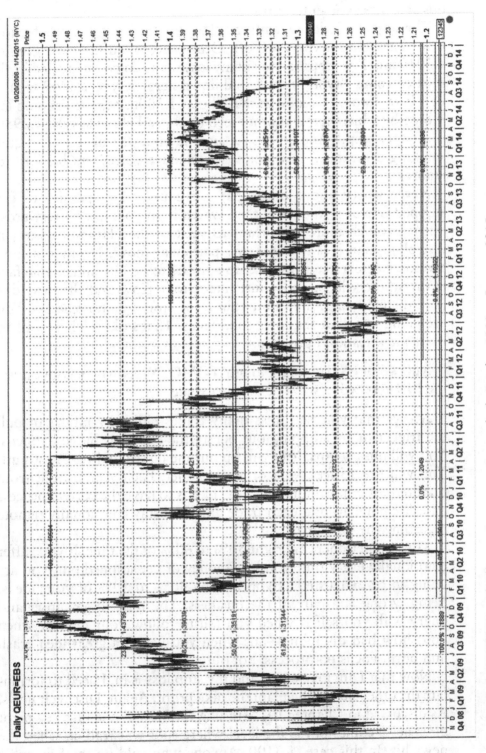

Figure 6.16 Daily EURUSD with Fibonacci retracements marked, October 2008 to January 2015.

trade ideas and poor discipline. You are going to be wrong a lot so it is best to have your risk management plan in place as quickly as possible after you enter a trade.

The stop loss order cements the plan and discourages bad behavior if the euro continues to sell off. Otherwise, when the euro gets to 1.3019 and I'm supposed to cut my losses, the voices in my head will start chirping. "Ooh, it looks bid down here; maybe 1.3009 would be a better stop.... Look at that fibo at 1.3006. Maybe I should let it breathe a bit; there's another tech level just below. Maybe 1.2989 is a better stop." And so on. As anyone on a diet or trying to quit smoking can attest, these counterproductive voices can be hard to ignore.

Never worry about missing it. Of course, it is painful to get stopped out of a trade and then watch it go your way afterwards, but it is much more important to stick to the plan and maintain discipline than it is to catch any particular move. No matter how awesome or perfect a trade setup appears to be, the undeniable fact is that there will be more just like it tomorrow and the next day (and the next day). If you hit your level, stop out and reassess. You are going to sell at the lows sometimes. That's okay. There will be more great trades, I promise.

Rule #6 of FX Trading: No mo' FOMO. Never worry about missing it. There will always be another trade.

Accept that you will miss many trades either by failing to pull the trigger or by stopping out before the expected move happens. You will miss layups. You will lip out the occasional two-foot putt. You will fire 15-feet wide of an open net. Each year is built from hundreds of opportunities and the idea is to have the correct process and discipline around each trade and then stay emotionally remote regarding the outcome.

Most good traders are right 50% to 60% of the time. If you suffer emotionally every time you lose money or get stopped out, you are going to be exhausted as you lose on 40% to 50% of your ideas. Being wrong is a part of the business. The time to get upset and angry with yourself is when you fail to follow your plan or when you show bad discipline—not when you watch a great idea crash and burn. Focus on process, not outcomes.

Now that I am long euros and my stop loss is in, I need to formulate the other side of the plan: the take profit. Again, I use technicals. As discussed in Chapter 10, "Trading the News," the first key pivot after news comes out is the level where spot was trading when the news hit. In this case, 1.3100. Anyone who sold on the Schaeuble headline is by definition short at 1.3100 or lower. If EURUSD goes above 1.3100, shorts are going to feel the pain and start to cover.

On the other hand, anyone who is long and was too slow to hit a bid (or God forbid, was in the bathroom when the headline came out) is thinking they dodged a bullet if we rally back up to 1.3100. Those traders will be happy to sell just ahead of that level. So as the price approaches the original pre-headline level, there is likely to be strong selling that, once exhausted, will be followed by equally heavy buying as shorts stop out on the level breach. If I am extremely bullish, I might add to my long above 1.3100, but for now I am just thinking about my take profit.

I never set my take profit based on how much I have at risk. To say, "I am risking 30 pips so my take profit should be 60 pips" is not the correct approach. The take profit should be based on the market, not an arbitrary ratio. The correct question is not "How much am I risking?" it is "How high do I realistically think euro can go?"

Again, I go to the charts and see the overnight high and yesterday's high, both around 1.3120. This is a logical place to take some profit as the multiple tops at the same level probably indicate the presence of a large seller. I enter my take profit OCO to my stop and now I can relax a little.

Once you have a trade on, the voices in your head will become impatient very quickly. "It's not bouncing very fast! Man, it looks heavy! It shouldn't be taking this long!"

Ignore them. Your ability to interpret price action is dramatically impaired once you are in a position. Your ability to remain impartial is so compromised that once you have a trade on you are almost always better to stick to your original parameters and ignore the price action. Otherwise, you are bound to do something reactionary or stupid.

I believe to some degree in the power of reading the tape (analyzing price action), but I have an equally strong belief that you cannot properly analyze the price action of a currency when you have a trade on. Use tape reading to get into trades but not to get out. If the trade is making you nervous, stop white-knuckling it and go refill your water bottle or do some pushups. The market can be painfully slow when you are in a hurry. In other words, the market doesn't care about your trades or your impatient thoughts. It will go where it wants to go when it is ready. Be patient.

■ Identify the Regime

Zooming out a bit now, you also need to make an assessment of whether the currency pair you are going to trade is in a range or trend regime. This will help you avoid fighting the primary trend all the time and will allow you to forecast better. Identifying the current regime is usually as simple as looking at a chart. Are we in a trend or a range? How long has that trend or range been in force?

But to determine whether or not the current regime will remain in force (trend or range) you need to then overlay your fundamental view. In a trending market, ask yourself: Does the fundamental reasoning for the trend still make sense? In a range trading market ask: Is the uncertainty that has been causing the market to trade in a range about to be resolved? Is a major fundamental catalyst about to break us out of a range? Has the catalyst already happened and the range is about to break?

Your understanding of the fundamentals helps you determine whether the current range or trend regime is likely to expire soon or continue. Here is how rangebound markets differ from trending markets and what you can do to capitalize on each.

1. Rangebound markets are the most difficult to trade. They are characterized (as you might guess) by prices moving within a defined range. Back and forth, back and forth. Bulls and bears both get more and more frustrated as the big move never materializes. Good news pushes the market to the top of the range and everyone gets long for a break that does not come. Bad news drives the price to the bottom of the range but there is not enough momentum to break.

   Lather, rinse, repeat.

   USDJPY in 2014 is a great example of this. All sorts of downside catalysts appeared (lower US yields, Russia invading Crimea) and yet USDJPY could never break the 101.00 area. And whenever good news came out (several strong US economic data prints, for example) USDJPY would pop to around 103/104 and then fail. Figure 6.17 shows the chart.

   Yuck. Note that this rangebound market lasted from January to July, an incredibly long time to be sitting in such a small range. The pain for both the bulls and bears was just about unbearable. Anyone who bought options during this period lost money and anyone who tried to play the breakouts or trade the news was badly hurt. The difficult thing about range markets is that the range is not always perfectly defined, plus you don't really know it's a range until quite a bit of time and rangebound price action has already transpired. So quite often by the time you realize it's a range, the range is ready to break!

   The strategy in rangebound markets is to buy near the bottom of the range and sell near the top of the range. Um, pretty easy, right? But if it was that easy, successful trading wouldn't pay so well. One reason range trading is difficult is that rangebound regimes are characterized by many false breaks. Another is that

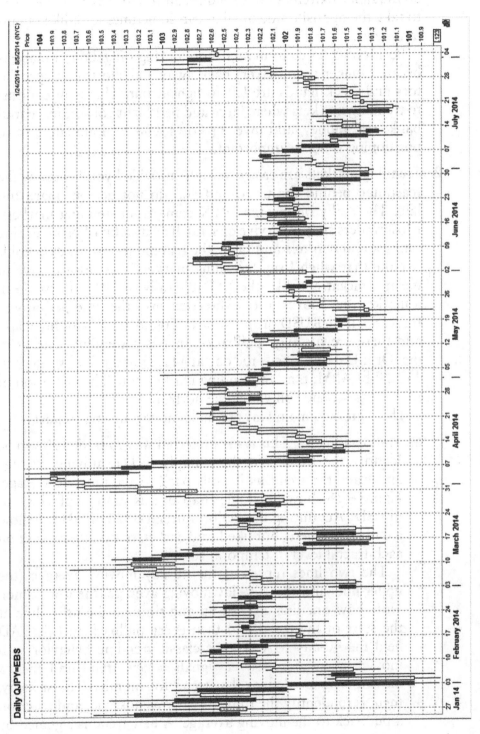

Figure 6.17 Daily USDJPY, January 2014 to August 2014.

usually the bottom of the range touches when bad news comes out and the top of the range touches when good news comes out. So the range extremes are very difficult to fade because you need to take the opposite side of what can sometimes look like important news.

Positioning tends to matter more during rangebound markets because longer-term players back away and short-term speculators and weak hands are left to fight it out. This is in contrast to trending markets where large and persistent corporate, central bank, real money, and investor flows tend to dominate and so positioning is not as important.

2. Trending markets are easier to trade, provided you believe in the reasoning behind the trend and you do not get on board too late. The really big profits in FX come from trending markets. Most traders simply survive or scratch away a bit of profit during rangebound markets and make the real money as trends unfold.

Note that when I say "trending markets" it does not have to mean a megatrend like the USDJPY rally in 2012. I just mean a market that moves in one direction over the time period you trade. So, if EURUSD drops from 1.1500 to 1.1300 in three days and there are no huge pullbacks, that is a trending market to me. Or if USDJPY opens the day at 112.25 and rallies straight to 113.20 by 4PM, that's a trending market, too. The definition of trendiness depends on your time horizon.

There are two main ways to make money during trends:

a. Trade pullbacks. This is my preferred way to trade FX trends. Identify the trend and then simply pick a moving average and trade the trend as it pulls back to the moving average. Figure 6.18 shows a simple chart of this strategy playing out in USDCAD during the major uptrend of 2014/2015. I show a daily trend here, but like I said earlier, trends are present on each fractal level of temporal zoom.

The two lines represent the 40-day moving average (**the upper line**) and the 100-day moving average (**the lower line**). Note how **one** line crossed up and through the **other** line at the start of the trend and then every pullback in USDCAD held the 40-day MA. This is classic trending behavior as a moving average crossover signals a new trend and then a moving average defines that trend for months. The strategy, then, is to identify the trend as early as possible, and enter on a pullback to the moving average. A new trend is signaled by two moving averages when they cross. If the faster MA crosses up through the slower one, that signals a new uptrend. When fast crosses below slow, that signals the start of a downtrend.

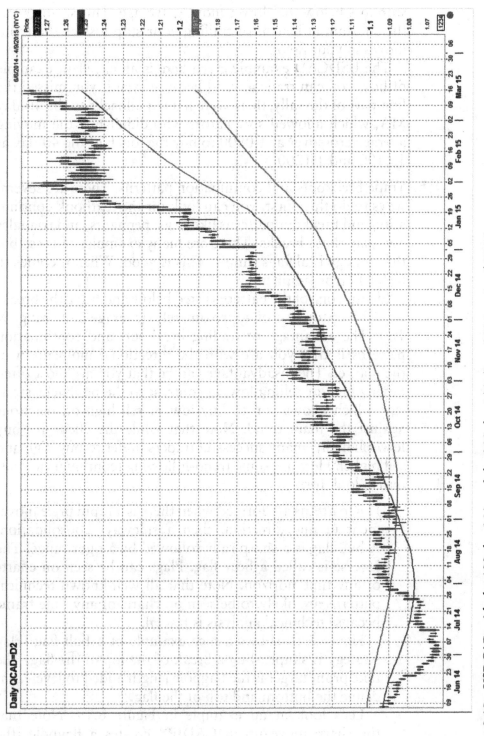

Figure 6.18 USDCAD with the 100-day MA and the 200-day MA, June 2014 to April 2015.

UNDERSTAND TECHNICAL ANALYSIS I

It will not always be the 40-day moving average that defines the trend. Fit the moving average to the trend just as you would fit the angle of a trendline to the trend. Then put your stop loss below the slower moving average. This strategy has the substantial benefit of trailing your stop loss as the trend moves in your favor.

The USDCAD example given here is an excellent example of how you can trade a trend because even if you missed the first part of the rally, there were many pullbacks to the 40-day MA, which allowed speculators who didn't buy the moving average crossover at 1.0900 to buy the touch of the 40-day at 1.1100 and 1.1200.

b. Trade breakouts and continuation patterns. There are several ways to do this. First, you can look for the textbook continuation and breakout patterns like flags, pennants, and triangles and play those breaks. There are many examples of these but the strategy is always simple. This is good. When it comes to techs, I favor simplicity.

Identify one of the patterns listed below and trade the breakout with a stop loss of approximately: (average daily range X 1.5). The advantage of trading breakouts and continuation patterns is that you are with the directional momentum of the market. The disadvantage can be that you are most often buying high or selling low, in contrast to the pullbacks strategy, which allows you to buy low or sell high on reactions against the main trend. Note that while the cliché is "buy low/sell high," many successful traders prefer to buy high and sell higher. Here are some trend-following (continuation) patterns I look for:

i. Flag patterns are formed when there is a rapid price movement in one direction, then a sideways consolidation. A bull flag is a sharp rally followed by a tight range. The inverse is called a bear flag. Flags can be seen on charts of any time horizon. Note that all well-known technical patterns are likely to be seen on charts of any time frame because technical analysis is fractal.

Figure 6.19 shows a nice example of a bull flag. Flag strategy is simple: Buy a break of the top of the flag. The take profit target is the flagpole length added to levels that define the bottom and top of the flag.

Let's look at an example in Figure 6.19. Note that the sharp move up in CADJPY creates a flagpole (the steep vertical line). Then you see a long and frustrating consolidation, which creates the flag (**horizontal** lines).

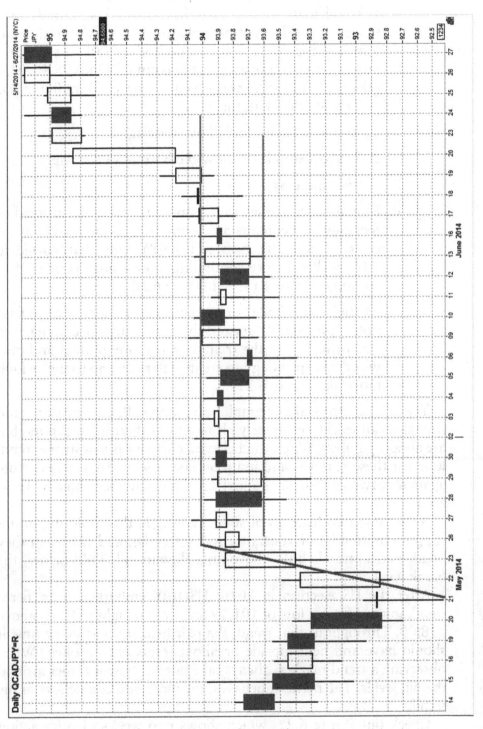

Figure 6.19 Daily CADJPY, a successful bull flag breakout, May to June 2014.

There are many intraday forays outside the flag but each day we close back inside the range until finally there is a break and then CADJPY explodes higher.

To calculate the target for the move in this example, take the length of the flagpole (140 pips) and add it to the bottom and top of the flag (93.60 and 94.00) so you get a target range for the topside breakout of 95.00/95.40. This take profit objective was touched within 10 trading days.

To trade this pattern:

1. Buy on a daily close above the flag.

2. Leave a stop loss below the bottom of the flag.

Nice and easy.

ii. Pennants are similar to flags but are triangular instead of rectangular. Pennants are common and can lead to great trend trades. The massive USDJPY rally that started in 2012 stalled before continuing after a huge pennant formation, as you can see in Figure 6.20.

iii. Triangles are similar to pennants except they have no flagpole. This simply means that price action coming into the formation of the triangle was more gradual and thus wasn't sharp enough to create a flagpole. So triangles look more like Figure 6.21.

You can see from the examples above that flags, pennants, and triangles can lead to extremely clean and profitable breakouts that are almost painless. When you believe a currency is in a strong trend, look for these patterns and jump on board when they break. Note again that two of the charts above are daily and one is hourly. Techs are fractal.

Note these two features of solid trends: (1) they hold important support (uptrends) or resistance (downtrends), and (2) when they break out, uptrends hold above (and downtrends hold below) the break level.

After the US election in 2016, USDJPY embarked on a fierce trend upward from a low of 101.19 on election night to levels above 118.00. Throughout that trend, the pair held support every time it should have and held topside breakout levels once broken. When observing a trend market, always take note of how it trades around the big levels. The better it behaves, the more you can believe in the trend.

Check out Figure 6.22, which shows two weeks of price action in USDJPY a little after the 2016 election. There is a double top at 111.36 on Monday, November 21, and Tuesday, November 22, followed by a big explosion higher on Wednesday. The low a few days

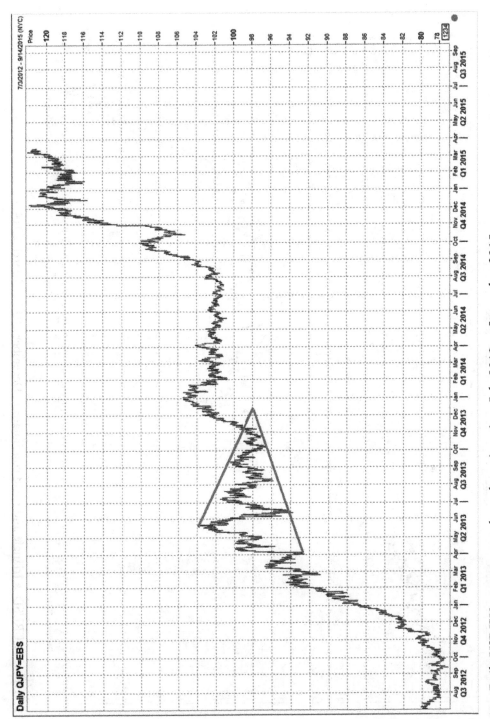

Figure 6.20 Daily USDJPY, a pennant and trend continuation, July 2012 to September 2015.

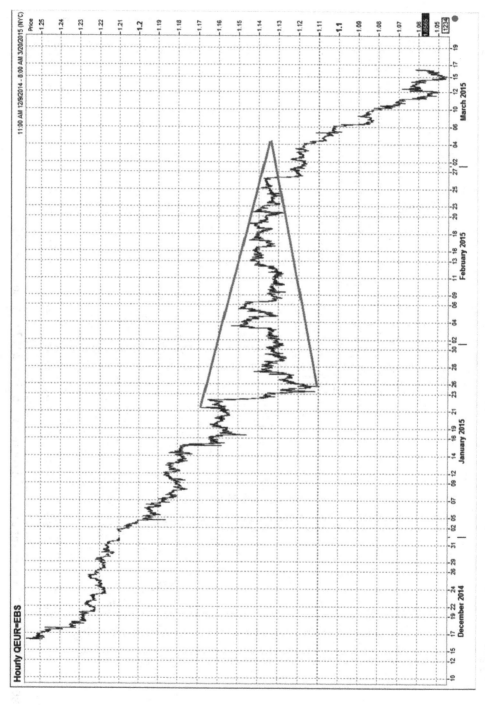

Figure 6.21 Hourly EURUSD, a triangle and trend continuation, December 2013 to March 2014.

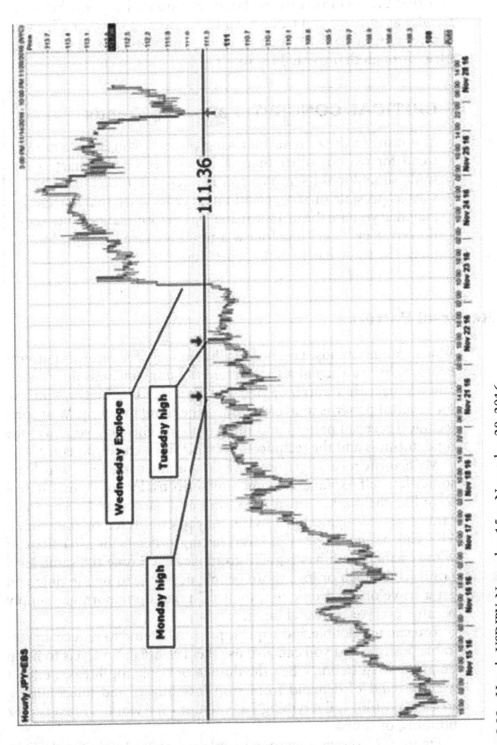

Figure 6.22 Hourly USDJPY, November 15 to November 28, 2016.

later (the up arrow at the right) was 111.355—an incredibly perfect retest and hold—typical of a strong uptrend. The message here was that the trend was strong because important support held. The trend was in force and traders continued to buy USDJPY dips until further notice. USDJPY soon tested a major target at 116 and then blew through that to hit 118.50.

CRITICAL CONCEPT: Following Trends

You only do these trend-following trades if you believe in the trend for reasons other than what you see on the chart. The trade should make sense to you beforehand, for as many reasons as possible (macro, positioning, cross-asset analysis, etc.), and then you use the technical analysis to formulate your execution strategy. Don't just follow a trend because the chart looks nice. The trade has to make sense, too.

◼ Reversal Patterns

When trading trends, you need to be on alert for reversal patterns because they can signal a turn before the fundamentals do. Also, if you are bearish a currency pair but it is trending higher, you can use reversal patterns to avoid fighting the trend too early. Wait for a technical reversal pattern and then jump in. This way you have the fundamentals and the technicals on your side before you enter.

My favorite reversal patterns are double and triple tops, which are somewhat self-explanatory and simple to trade. Sometimes it will seem like the market hits a brick wall at a particular level and just cannot get through. Once, twice, maybe even three or four times. This can be indicative of a large resting order from a participant who is patient and has big size to move. Each time the same level prints as the high or low, more people notice it, so by the time you get a triple or quadruple top, the level takes on importance simply because everyone is watching it.

You can use double and triple tops as an excuse to reduce a profitable position and you can also use them as breakout levels to jump on an existing trend. When the double or triple top breaks, expect a new round of demand from stop loss buyers and longs adding to their positions. Everything I say about tops works in reverse for bottoms, of course.

Figure 6.23 shows a textbook triple top at 1.6280 in GBPUSD in 2012. Note that while the triple top is at 1.6280 on a daily closing basis, there were many intraday stabs through the level, as you can

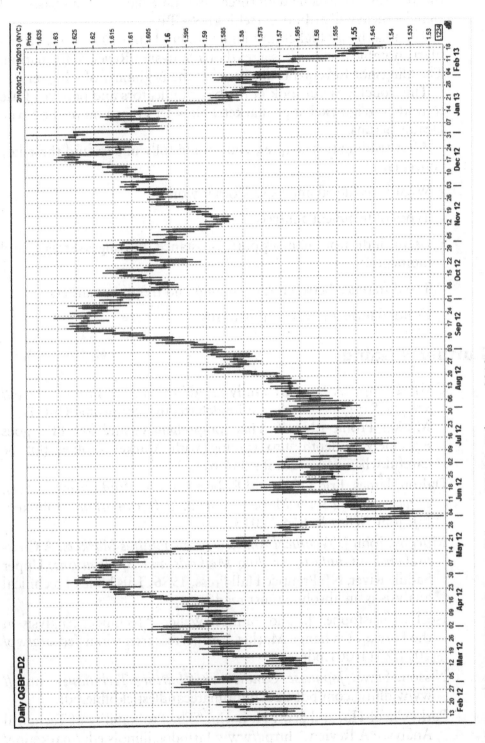

Figure 6.23 Daily GBPUSD triple top, February 2012 to February 2013.

see by long wicks on the daily candles. The spike to 1.6380 at the end of 2012 was particularly aggressive but again you can see that the key 1.6280 level held all three times on a daily closing basis and signaled heavy distribution (selling) of GBP.

The final break higher and failure to hold above 1.6280 is particularly notable because it is a textbook Slingshot Reversal formation. The Slingshot Reversal is discussed at the beginning of Chapter 7.

This concludes our look at the basic indicators and patterns I use to trade foreign exchange markets. Now let's move on to the Seven Deadly Setups.

After reading this chapter, you should fully understand these key concepts:

- What is technical analysis? Does it work?

- Types of technical analysis

- Useful indicators like support, resistance, moving averages, and momentum

- The difference between rangebound and trending markets

- Continuation and reversal patterns

■ Further Reading

CME Group. "A Six-Part Study Guide to Market Profile." http://www.r-5.org/files/books/trading/charts/market-profile/CBOT-Market_Profile-EN.pdf. This comprehensive and free PDF goes extremely in-depth into trading with Market Profile. But be careful when you print: it's 346 pages!

Dalton, James, Eric Jones, and Robert Dalton. *Mind Over Markets: Power Trading with Market Generated Information.* Hoboken, NJ: John Wiley & Sons, 2013.

Murphy, John J. *Technical Analysis of the Futures Markets: A Comprehensive Guide to Trading Methods and Applications.* Upper Saddle River, NJ: Prentice Hall Press, 1986. This bible of technical analysis is an absolute must read.

Neely, Christopher J., and Paul A. Weller. "Technical Analysis in the Foreign Exchange Market." http://research.stlouisfed.org/wp/2011/2011-001.pdf.

Nisson, Steve. *Japanese Candlestick Charting Techniques.* http://www.dlinvt.com/pdf/01ucb/ultimatecandlestickbible.pdf.

Park, Cheol-Ho, and Scott H. Irwin. "The Profitability of Technical Analysis: A Review." http://www.farmdoc.illinois.edu/marketing/agmas/reports/04_04/AgMAS04_04.pdf.

Steidlmeyer, J. Peter. *Steidlmeyer on Markets: Trading with Market Profile.* Hoboken, NJ: John Wiley & Sons, 2002.

CHAPTER 7

Understand Technical Analysis II (The Seven Deadly Setups)

■ Introduction

It is important to research, study, and understand as many trading approaches as possible and then adopt and incorporate the ones that work for you. When it comes to technical analysis, there are seven setups that I find particularly useful. This chapter discusses each setup, provides real-life examples, and explains how and why the setups work.

It is not necessarily that these setups are better than others from a probabilistic point of view; it is just that (1) I recognize them easily, (2) I believe in the underlying logic of why they work, and (3) they fit my trading style. I tend to prefer mean reversion strategies (selling high/buying low) more than breakout and trend strategies but both types are represented in the list. The Seven Deadly Setups are:

1. Slingshot Reversal

2. Shooting stars and hammers

3. Extreme deviation from a moving average, aka the Deviation

4. Volume spike at a price extreme

5. Broken triangles

6. Double and triple top

7. Sunday Gaps

■ 1. Slingshot Reversal

One of my favorite patterns to trade is the false break and reverse, or what I call the Slingshot Reversal pattern. In this section, I will define a Slingshot Reversal, explain why it works, and present an example from the USDJPY market.

A Slingshot Reversal occurs when an important support or resistance level breaks temporarily but then fails to hold. In other words, the market takes out an important support or resistance but then fails to follow through, runs out of momentum, and reverses back into the old range. The key to a Slingshot Reversal is that it must happen around a level of very high importance.

High importance means that many people are watching the level and orders are likely to be clustered around it. When you prepare in the morning, do you notice that everyone is talking about a particular support or resistance level? Keep that level in mind for a potential Slingshot Reversal.

The Slingshot Reversal pattern is effective because when an important support level breaks, it triggers capitulation by longs and encourages shorts to add. It also brings in breakout sellers like models and trend followers and sellers from other time frames who feel they have missed out and must capitulate at lower levels. If price then reverses and recaptures the broken support, the market is suddenly caught offside. Selling is exhausted, stop loss orders are filled, the market is max short, and suddenly there is potential for a very aggressive short squeeze and high-energy upside continuation. Let's look at an example.

From April to early November 2017, USDJPY traded in a 108.00/114.50 range despite raging optimism in US equities on the back of US corporate tax reform. The market expected a topside breakout in USDJPY and the pair rallied up close to 114.50 in the first week of November.

USDJPY shorts and range traders left stop loss orders above 114.50 while longs were ready to add aggressively on the break and corporate and real money hedgers with a natural need to buy USDJPY looked on nervously. On November 7, the pair rallied up and spiked aggressively through 114.50, touching a high of 114.73 before quickly reversing back below 114.50. Figure 7.1 presents the chart.

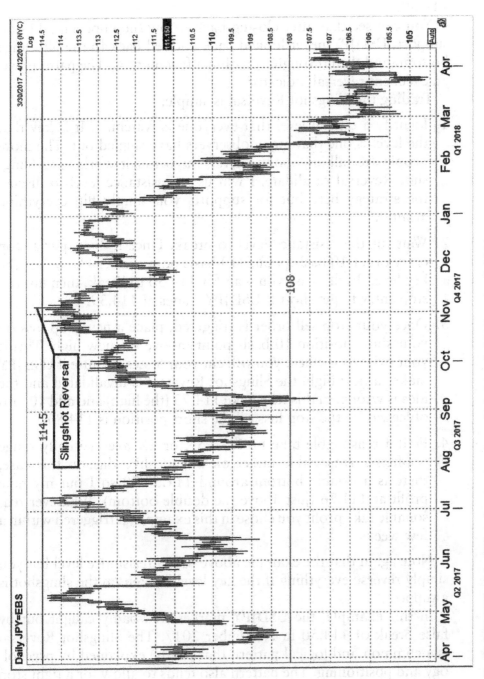

Figure 7.1 Daily USDJPY with a Slingshot Reversal marked, March 2017 to April 2018.

It looks like a blip on the daily chart but that day massive volumes transacted above 114.50. Shorts stopped out, longs added, and those that needed to buy USDJPY bought. But by the end of the day, the buying was exhausted and the market closed well below 114.50.

You can see that after closing back below the important 114.50 support, USDJPY never looked back and fell back to the old range bottom (and then through it) within a few months. The pattern was an excellent reversal indicator.

Trading the Slingshot Reversal is simple:

1. Identify a crucial level that everyone is watching. It is key that the level is one that many observers have singled out. The more people are talking about a level, the better it works as a Slingshot Reversal candidate. I will use a resistance level to discuss the strategy here but for supports you simply flip everything around.

2. Wait for the resistance level to break. Once it does, put a stop entry order 10 basis points (10 basis points is 0.10%) *below* the key level. In this case you wait for 114.50 to break, then insert a stop entry to get short if USDJPY trades at 114.39.[1]

3. Once your stop sell order is triggered, place a new stop loss on your short position 10 basis points above the new high. This is your exit point where you will cut your losses because if USDJPY makes a new high, the Slingshot Reversal is invalidated and the idea is wrong. In this case, take 114.73 (the high) and add 10 pips of leeway so the stop loss on the short position is 114.83.

4. Find a reasonable take profit. 1.5X or 2X average daily range is often a reasonable target on a trade like this. In this case, there is a double bottom around 111.50/70 so I put my take profit at 111.76 (just above the double bottom). Whatever reasonable take profit you chose in this example, it triggered within a few weeks.

Note again that the example above uses a resistance level but you simply reverse everything if the key level broken on the slingshot is a support.

In this example, the USDJPY market was badly caught out by false break of 114.50 in November 2017. The Slingshot Reversal is a common and logical pattern that can be explained by psychology and positioning. The pattern also tends to allow for a tight stop (and therefore significant leverage). Watch for Slingshot Reversals and trade them aggressively.

---

[1]10 basis points is 0.1%. So 114.50 X 0.999 = 114.39.

■ 2. Shooting Stars and Hammers

I touched on shooting stars and hammers in the previous chapter but let me explain why they are so useful. If your bias is bullish but the market is in a downtrend, the risk is that you fight the market and keep buying against the trend all the way down. You can always find another technical level to justify a bad trade (especially if you use Fibonacci levels)!

Instead of picking level after level to buy into a raging downtrend, you are better off waiting for a clear reversal pattern like a shooting star or hammer. These reversal patterns are like the market ringing a bell to tell you it is time to get in. They provide a tradable low to stop loss against and so you can clearly define your risk.

Here is an example. It is early May 2014. I have been bullish USD for the past few weeks because I think the market is misreading the Fed and US rates look set to rise sooner than the market thinks. But the chart looks like what you see in Figure 7.2.

Yuck. Despite the big bottom at 79.00 in October 2013, there is no strong reason to pick a bottom on a chart like this. "There's a major support nearby!" is not a strong thesis. So I wait. Then a few days later the chart looks like Figure 7.3.

Yum. Now you have: (1) a Slingshot Reversal through the October 2013 lows, and (2) a huge bull hammer bottom. This is a nice setup with a clear tradable bottom now in place. I know that if we break to a new low (<78.90), the idea is wrong. If we hold, it looks like we could rally back all the way to the top of the range around 81.20.

Following the hammer bottom, I have a good reason to expect a reversal and so I go long at the close (79.35) with a stop loss at 78.75 (below the low). Figure 7.4 shows what happened next (the chart shows a continuation of the price action from the previous chart):

Kaboom. The dollar exploded higher and never looked back.

Hammers and shooting stars don't always work this well but the point here is that they give you a strong reversal signal and a clear exit point so you can size your position with a decent amount of leverage and know exactly where you're wrong. Look for hammers and shooting stars when you have a strong countertrend view. Again, be patient.

■ 3. Extreme Deviation from a Moving Average (AKA the Deviation)

There are many ways of measuring whether a currency is overbought or oversold. When you look at overbought and oversold, make sure you use a metric that is consistent with your trading time horizon.

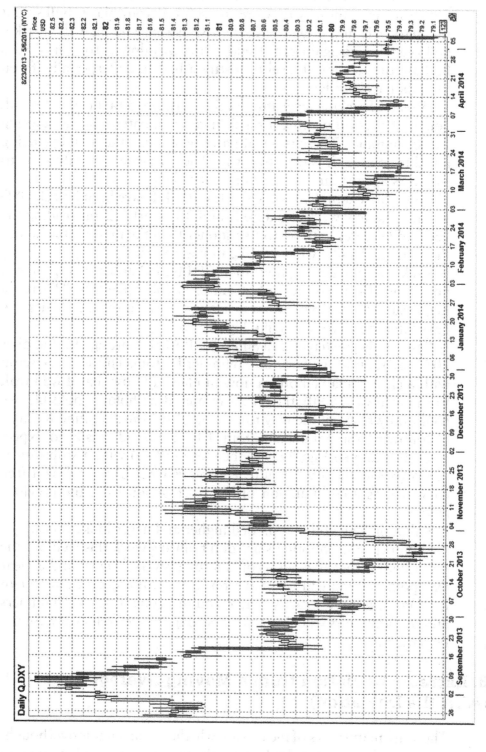

Figure 7.2 Daily Dollar Index, August 2013 to May 2014.

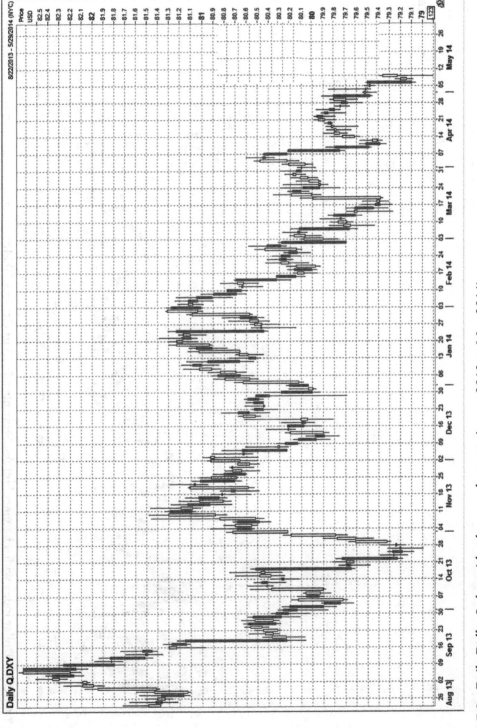

Figure 7.3 Daily Dollar Index with a hammer bottom, August 2013 to May 2014).

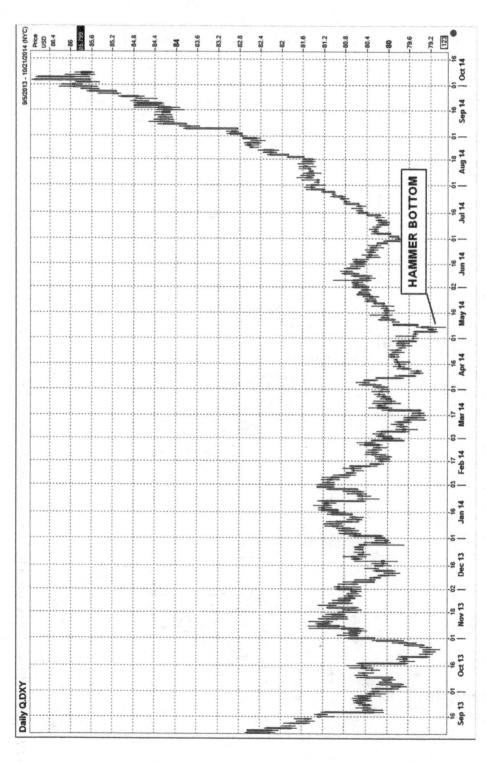

Figure 7.4 Daily Dollar Index with a hammer bottom, September 2013 to October 2014.

For example, if you are a short-term trader, it is not useful to look for overbought and oversold signals on a weekly chart.

To match my time horizon, I look at a simple but effective overbought and oversold measure: How far away is spot from the 100-hour moving average? I call this "deviation from the 100-hour" or just the Deviation and use it as a nice back-of-the-envelope overshoot warning system.

When trading overbought and oversold you must understand that you are, by definition, going against a strong trend. Things that are overbought can get more overbought. Things that are oversold can get more oversold. So no matter how crazy the move is so far, *things can always get crazier.*

As a matter of fact, if things rip way outside of the normal range you are used to for overbought and oversold, the first thing you should ask yourself before reflexively wanting to go the other way is: Why? Sometimes there is a clear reason for the extreme trending behavior and that reason is perfectly valid and should not be ignored. You generally want to fade overbought and oversold markets when there is no strong fundamental reason for the move. Let's look at an example of this using the Deviation as a tool:

USDCAD is a currency pair known for mean reversion. Therefore, it is well-suited to strategies that hunt for conditions of overbought and oversold. When trading USDCAD, I constantly monitor how far it is trading from the 100-hour MA. Take a look at Figure 7.5.

The black bars show USDCAD hourly, the line on the main chart is the 100-hour MA, and the line underneath the main chart shows the difference between the two. The farther spot moves away from the 100-hour, the more stretched it is, like a rubber band. The elastic is eventually more likely to snap back than it is to keep stretching.

You can see in this example that the line below the chart oscillates roughly between −100 pips and +100 pips. The extreme points will depend on overall volatility but I have generally found over the years that anything more than 1% away from the 100-hour means USDCAD is overdone. So with USDCAD at 1.10 that means 110 pips. You can see in the chart that USDCAD generally runs out of steam whenever the deviation touches 100/110 pips on either side.

As with any technical indicator, I will never use the deviation on its own to initiate a trade. However, if I am already looking to get into a short USDCAD trade, I will be on high alert for moments when spot gets more than 100 pips above the 100-hour MA, or I will leave a resting order 100 pips above the 100-hour when I'm out of the office.[2]

---

[2] The 100-hour moves, obviously, so you need to recalibrate your order at times to keep it accurate. I don't change it every hour. That is not necessary because the MA does not move all that fast—once or twice a day is fine.

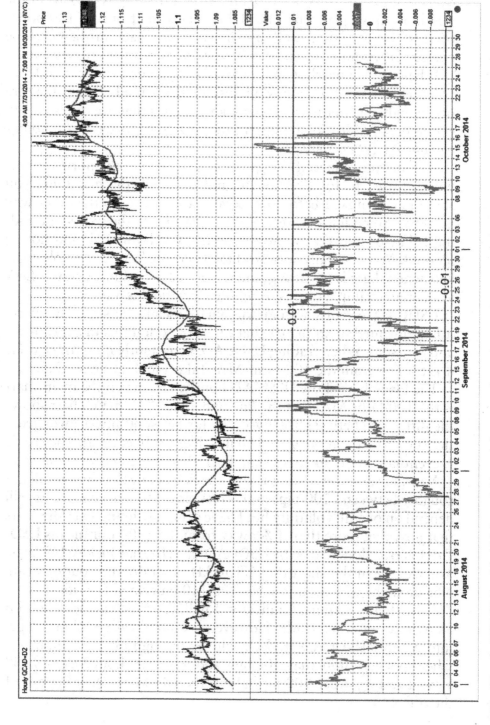

Figure 7.5 Hourly USDCAD with 100-hour MA and deviation from the 100-hour moving average, July 31, 2014 to October 30, 2014.

The chart shows a great example where USDCAD spiked to 1.1400 and took the deviation up to 140 pips before crashing back down to 1.1220 just a few hours later. Understand that when you trade the deviation, you are going against the prevailing short-term trend and so you need to be careful and disciplined. I usually set my position when the deviation touches 1% and then put my stop loss another 0.7% away to give it plenty of extra room to further overshoot.

While my experience is that the deviation tends to close as spot reverts to the mean, there are also instances where the deviation closes as spot goes nowhere and the moving average catches up over time. This relieves the overbought or oversold condition without generating a profitable trade. Note that the deviation is also a good indicator for take profits on winning trades. If you are long USD-CAD and it rallies more than 100 points away from the 100-hour MA, sell some out and buy it back lower.

The deviation from a moving average can be useful on any time frame. A chart that shows how far spot is trading from the 100-day or 200-day moving average, for example, would give a useful reading of bigger picture overbought or oversold conditions. Just make sure you know your time horizon.

■ 4. Volume Spike at a Price Extreme

Not many traders use volume when analyzing FX markets. This is because most FX trading takes place in the interbank or over-the-counter (OTC) market where volume data are not always readily available. FX volume data can be found, however, using futures markets or other sources. While I have always traded in the interbank market, I find futures volumes are an acceptable proxy for overall volume. This is because actual volume is not important; what matters is relative volume.

Some questions I ask when looking at volume: Are volumes high today? Is volume in the latest hour much higher than usual? How does volume in the past 10 minutes compare with volume in other 10-minute periods? Are we seeing a big price move on extreme volume?

There is a large body of theory about how volume and price interact in financial markets and I encourage you to study it and come up with your own strategies on how to combine price and volume in FX. This is a potential source of edge for you because most FX practitioners barely factor in volume.

My favorite volume plus price setup is when you get a large volume spike at a price extreme. This is indicative of capitulation as the market transacts high volumes in a short span. Many positions are transferred very quickly, usually moving risk from weak hands to strong hands.

The next chart is an excellent example. On October 15, 2014, the market was hit by some bad news about Ebola and a weak US Retail Sales report. The market was wearing a large structural short position in fixed income (i.e., the market was short bonds, positioned for higher rates) and there was a massive unwind in the fixed income markets. USDJPY tends to be correlated with US interest rates so when US yields started collapsing,[3] USDJPY started to fall.

As the fall gained momentum, volume started to pick up and the move climaxed with a complete crapout on *massive* volume. You can see the low in price (black bars) coincides with the volume spike (bars below). As volume fell off, USDJPY regained its footing and slowly rallied back.

The way I trade these volume spikes is to stay out of the way until the dust settles. Figure 7.6 shows 30-minute USDJPY bars in black and volume as bars below. When I see a huge volume spike like the one in this chart, I wait until I see two or three bars (60 to 90 minutes) of falling volume. After, say, 90 minutes, you can see that things are settling down so you go long with a stop below the lows.

In this case you go long at 105.70 with a stop at 105.14 looking for a rally back toward the top of the waterfall move (107.40). As I have stated and restated, I would never buy USDJPY just because there was a volume/price spike—I always want to have other reasons for the trade besides a lone technical signal. That said, the volume/price spike is one of the most powerful signals out there and can lead to some spectacular trades.

■ 5. Broken Triangles

Triangles tend to attract attention because they are visually compelling, easy to spot, and logical to trade. The idea is that price consolidations with higher lows and lower highs create triangles on the charts and these triangles, when broken, show the way for either a continuation of the trend or a reversal. Figure 7.7 is a standard triangle formation and breakout.

Notice how USDJPY consolidated from April 2013 to October 2013, making higher lows and lower highs until it finally broke through the top of the triangle and made a run for 100.00. This is a textbook triangle consolidation and breakout.

---

[3]Some interest rate moves exceeded 10 standard deviations that day!

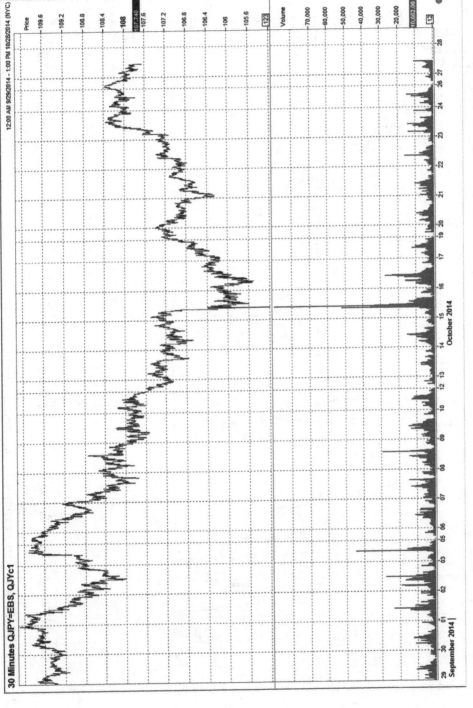

Figure 7.6 30-minute USDJPY candle chart with volume bars below (in gray), September 29, 2014 to October 28, 2014.

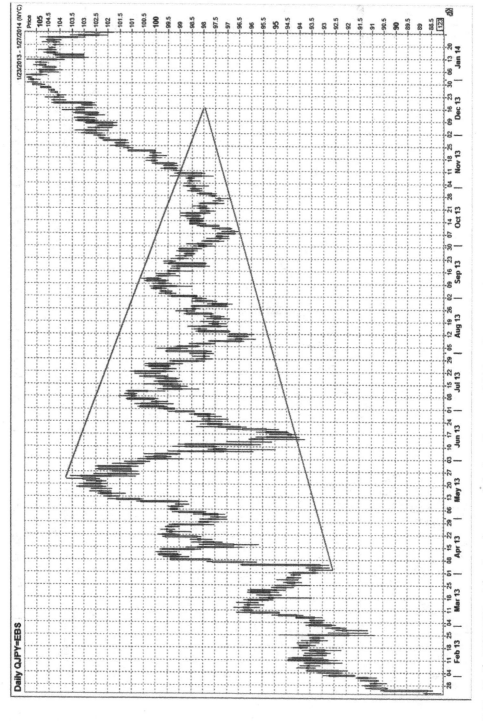

Figure 7.7 Daily USDJPY with triangle consolidation, January 2013 to January 2014.

The broken triangle setup that I like to trade can be equally powerful. It is essentially the second derivative of the triangle breakout and kicks in when a triangle breaks in one direction, then fails and turns back through the triangle the other way. All those people who were patiently waiting for the triangle to break are finally sucked in and they need to stop out when the pattern fails.

The concept is similar to the Slingshot Reversal in that you have a clear pattern and breakout that fails, and then rapid momentum in the other direction. See Figure 7.8 for a nice triangle breakout to the downside in AUDUSD.

But Figure 7.9 is what happened next (the chart is zoomed out so you can see more data).

Oops! That is a textbook triangle break followed by a very impulsive reversal.

If I am bullish AUDUSD and I see this triangle setting up, I will play the breakout to the topside based on the standard triangle breakout concept. But in the case of this chart, the bottom of the triangle breaks, not the top. I am bullish, so there is no trade at first.

Then, when AUDUSD rallies back up inside the triangle (in other words, when it closes above the bottom of the triangle), I go long. I place my stop loss outside the bottom of the triangle. This setup is rare but extremely powerful so I'm always on the lookout for broken triangles on hourly and daily charts. You can see that once AUDUSD reentered the triangle, it rallied way, way higher.

■ 6. Double and Triple Top

This is such a simple set up—simple but effective. You are bearish USDCAD because the pair has just rallied relentlessly, you think oil is going higher for various fundamental reasons, and you think the Bank of Canada is worried about currency weakness. USDCAD has just rallied to the topside 100-hour deviation and the chart looks like Figure 7.10.

The pair is bumping against a major round number resistance (1.4000) and has failed three or four times now. It is a triple or quadruple top. You also remember that USDCAD has rarely sustained moves above 1.4000 in the past (other than around the internet/tech bubble), as you can see in Figure 7.11.

So the beauty of this setup is that you can sell with leverage because you are only risking a little. You simply sell near the double or triple top with a stop above. Here I would sell at the multiple tops (1.3980) and put a stop loss on the other side (at 1.4017).

My stop is far enough away to withstand a minor breach of 1.4000 but not much more. By trading such a tight entry/stop loss,

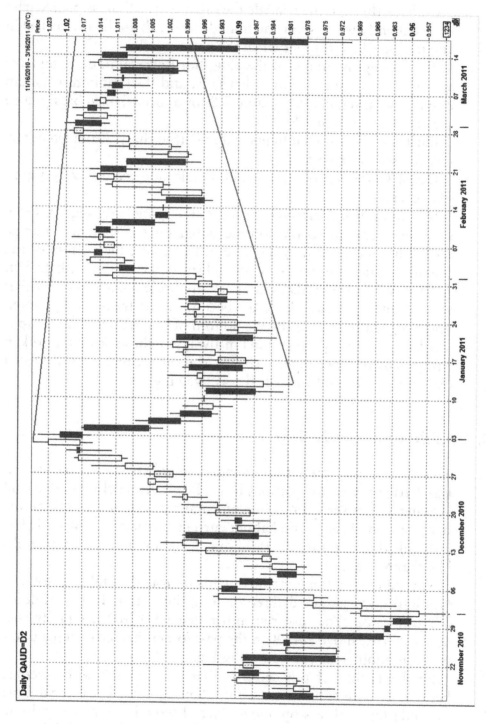

Figure 7.8 Daily AUDUSD with triangle breakout, November 2010 to March 2011.

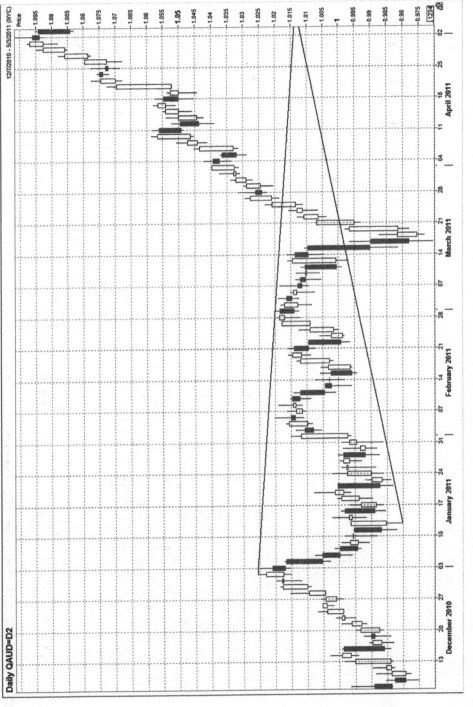

Figure 7.9 Daily AUDUSD with failed triangle reversal, December 2010 to May 2011.

UNDERSTAND TECHNICAL ANALYSIS II (THE SEVEN DEADLY SETUPS)

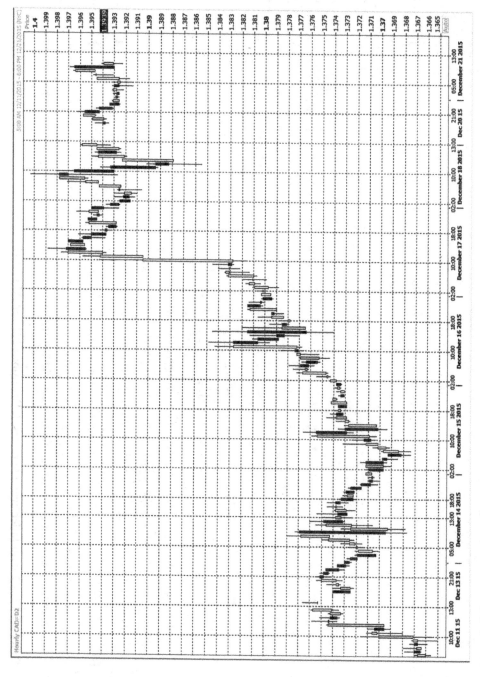

Figure 7.10 Hourly USDCAD, December 11 to December 21, 2015.

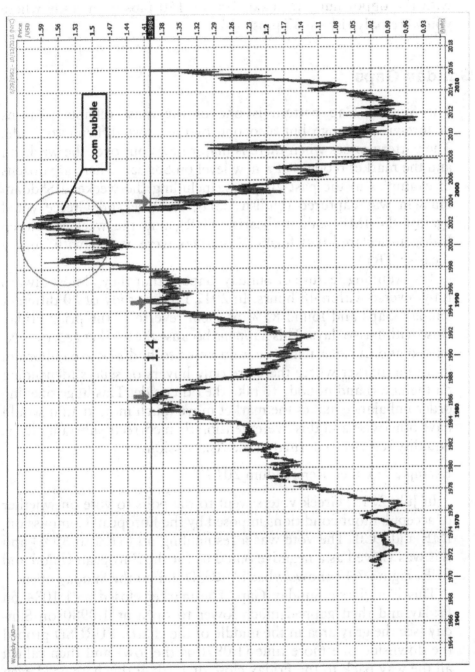

Figure 7.11 Daily USDCAD with dotcom bubble marked 1971 to 2014; USDCAD has trouble staying above 1.40 (other than during the tech bubble).

I can take a big position. That is the best thing about trading near simple support and resistance levels—you can leverage your position aggressively because you are not risking much in percentage terms. In this example, if you catch the turn, you will find yourself with the opportunity to make 100 or 150 pips on a trade where you were only risking 37 pips.

■ 7. Sunday Gaps

The Sunday Gap pattern is one of the most reliable patterns in foreign exchange but also one of the most difficult to trade. The pattern arises when there is major news out over the weekend and the market reopens at a new level on Sunday. There are dozens of examples in the past 20 years, including the weekend Saddam Hussein was captured (bullish USD), the weekend Greece voted against the IMF bailout (bearish EUR), and the weekend Recep Erdogan declared that financial markets were at war with Turkey (bearish TRY).

The stunning feature of Sunday Gaps is that they almost always fully reverse within 48 hours. In 2012 I did a study of 20 different Sunday Gaps and found 85% of them reverse to the prior Friday close within two days. This happens because the market gets overextended and out of balance as it attempts to find a new equilibrium in a thin market where there are only buyers or sellers (depending on the news) and nobody to take the other side. This huge opening order imbalance makes the market move much more than it would have otherwise and this overextension then corrects substantially as liquidity returns to normal in the Asia session.

Example 1: Greek Referendum 2015

In July 2015, Greek voters went to the polls to vote on whether to accept bailout conditions imposed by the European Commission, IMF, and ECB. The vote was a resounding no (61% to 39%) and this was viewed as a negative outcome for the European Union and EUR. Figure 7.12 shows what EURUSD did on the Sunday open.

This is a classic Sunday Gap. The market closed at 1.1084 on Friday and then gapped much lower to open at 1.0980 on Sunday (see the gray area in the middle of the chart). EURUSD probed the downside one more time (1.0970 is the low) and then rallied all the way back to the Friday close of 1.1084; this happened even though the news was unambiguously bad. Let's look at another more recent example. Note that I could fill 25 pages with examples like these—it's a common and powerful pattern.

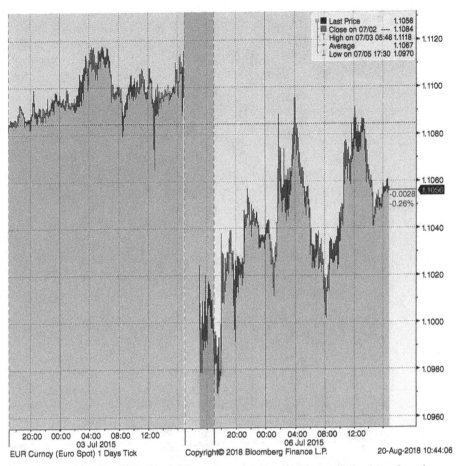

Figure 7.12 Tick chart of EURUSD the Friday before and Sunday after the Greek referendum in 2015, July 3 to 6, 2015.

Example 2: Turkish Lira Crisis 2018

In August 2018, investors were on edge about Turkey's massive current account and corporate financing deficits. The story escalated as President Erdogan refused to allow the central bank to raise interest rates. Friday, the market expected things to get better as President Erdogan was scheduled to speak on Saturday and he would almost certainly make positive remarks to soothe nervous markets.

Instead, Erdogan made a fiery anti-US speech and said that Turkey would not back down from this "Economic War." Investors watched with bated breath as markets opened on Sunday and Figure 7.13 shows what happened.

USD/TRY closed at 6.40 on Friday and then opened more than 10% higher at 7.10 on Sunday afternoon (see white vertical section). Over the next 12 hours, the market proceeded to fill the gap and trade all the way back to 6.40. Once again, even with terrible news (bullish USDTRY news), the Sunday Gap reversed completely.

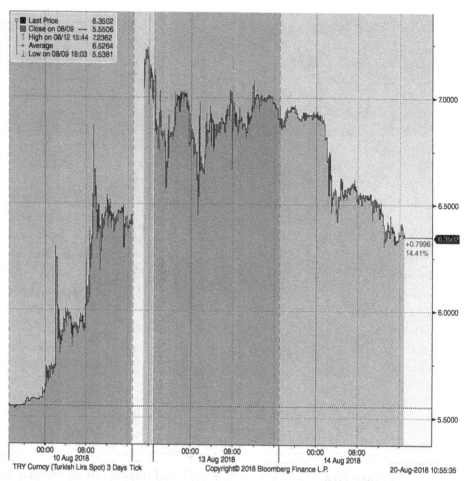

Figure 7.13 Tick chart of USDTRY around the August 10, 2018 weekend gap.

These gaps are *extremely* difficult to trade because in order to fade the gap you need to take the opposite side of what looks like very important news. The strategy is simple: Take the other side of the gap in the opening hour of trading in a position size that makes you feel comfortable. Put a stop loss one average daily range away. Cover (take profit) when the gap is 90% filled.

Precisely because it is so incredibly scary and difficult to trade, the Sunday Gap is one of the most profitable setups in currency trading. Watch for it and take advantage if you dare! This is a double black diamond setup and not for the faint of heart.

■ Combo Setups

A combo setup is a trade setup where you get a bunch of technical indicators all saying the same thing at the same time. A Slingshot Reversal that occurs on extremely high volume at the 100-hour deviation, for example, would be a nice triple play. The more setups that happen simultaneously, the better. This is also true of standard technical and macro analysis. The more good reasons you have to put on a trade, the more likely that trade will make money.

A standard support level on its own would usually have nearly zero meaning to me but if that support level happens to be the year's low and it also coincides with a major trendline and major round number, then I might start to get interested. If I start watching that level and then we get a Slingshot Reversal through the level on record volume, then that is a technical Five-Star. If I am bullish for three different macro reasons, it's time to get aggressively involved.

As you develop your own style of analysis and list of favorite setups, look for moments when you get all sorts of signals at once, ideally not just technical setups like the ones described above, but fundamental, behavioral, positioning, news, and other signals, too. Like I said, the more reasons you can list for a trade, the better the idea. This is a really important concept and with experience you will feel these moments where many reasons come in line at once. These are the moments you summon maximum courage and make the biggest bet possible within your risk management framework.

As you gain experience, you will start to get a good feel for how many indicators need to be in sync or how many planets need to be in line before a trade becomes high conviction. Hunt for Five-Stars and when you find one, bet big.

The opposite of a Five-Star trade is one where you have a bunch of indicators that all look bullish but then when you dig deeper, you find a bunch of stuff that is bearish, too. Do not ignore the bearish stuff just because your initial analysis was bullish! I call these crosswinds trades because some of the winds are blowing one way (bullish) and some are blowing the other way (bearish). This is a recipe for confusion—avoid crosswinds.

That completes our discussion of the Seven Deadly Setups. As you gain experience, keep track of the setups that work for you and look for moments when all your favorite indicators are in sync.

After reading this chapter, you should fully understand these key concepts:

- Slingshot Reversals

- Shooting stars and hammers

- The Deviation

- Volume spike at a price extreme

- Broken triangles

- Double and triple tops

- Sunday Gaps

- Combo setups

CHAPTER 8

Understand Correlation and Intermarket Relationships

■ Introduction

Now that you have some basic technical analysis tactics and strategies, let's look at a more complex topic: correlation between currencies and other asset classes. I believe that my understanding and application of intermarket correlations is one of the primary keys to my success over the past 20 years.[1]

You need many tools to trade FX effectively, but a strong understanding of the links between different markets has kept me ahead of the curve over the years. That said, the world has evolved significantly since I started trading and there is much less edge in correlation trading than there used to be. I remember sitting on the trading floor at Lehman Brothers in 2005–2006 and more than half the FX traders didn't even have a live feed for gold, copper, or oil. My co-workers would ask me, "What's oil doing?" or "Where's gold?" which seemed completely ludicrous to me (because it *was* ludicrous!). How could people trade FX without knowing where other markets are trading?

This all changed in 2007–2008. Correlations between FX and other asset classes jumped toward 1.0 and FX traders suddenly

---

[1] Along with adaptability and a calm demeanor.

understood how important it was to watch other markets. Now there are armies of algorithms that trade FX correlation in real time. There is a phalanx of hedge funds analyzing fair value of currencies using complex quantitative cross-market analysis models. There are fintech startups that will tell you what is driving currencies right now according to their multivariate Granger causality or AI regression or machine learning models. Even with infinitely more competition, though, intermarket correlation is still a great source of understanding and edge for discretionary human FX traders.

■ Understand Correlation

Correlation is a statistical relationship showing the interdependence of two variables. It is used extensively in trading as a way to explain and forecast price movements. I use correlation to look at current movements in one asset price and guess what another price might do in the future, using a historical or theoretical relationship or correlation between the two. This type of trading is called intermarket, lead/lag, cross-market, or cross-asset analysis.

But whenever you see or read about a correlation in financial markets, you need to ask yourself:

1. Does the correlation make any econometric/logical sense? This is the most important question of all. I don't care if the r^2 is 99.9%;[2] if the relationship has no underlying logic, either forget about it or search for a reasonable explanation. Otherwise, it is likely a spurious correlation. Spurious correlation is when people infer a cause–effect relationship between two variables when there is no logical or actual connection between them.

2. Is the correlation likely to continue into the future? Correlations are inherently unstable. You need to make a logical assessment of whether or not a given correlation will continue into the future. This comes mostly from experience. Correlations like interest rates versus currencies have existed pretty much forever and will tend to be reliable most of the time, whereas the correlation between, say, natural gas and CAD might work at times and be completely useless most others.

3. Are there periods of both rising and falling prices in the sample? It is more likely a correlation is spurious if it is simply two prices going straight up or straight down. You can easily find a bunch of price charts that have been rallying steadily for a given time

---

[2]r^2 is a statistical measure of the correlation between two variables and can run from 0 (weak/no correlation) to 100% (perfectly strong correlation).

period and then overlay them to imply some relationship. If prices go up and down together, it's more likely that you haven't simply found two smooth trends that happened at the same time by coincidence.

4. What third variables might be influencing the movement in your two variables? You will hear over and over that correlation does not imply causation. That is certainly true—but it definitely provides a clue![3]

Correlation gives you an idea that you might be looking under the right rocks, at least. Very often, while two financial variables might not be causing each other's variability, they are both influenced by a third variable.

A famous correlation of this type is the finding that as ice cream sales increase in the United States, so do human drowning deaths. Does eating too much ice cream make you more likely to drown? No. This relationship exists because both ice cream sales and drowning go up in warmer weather and go down in cold weather. A third variable (temperature) is influencing both. But even though this correlation is spurious, it is not useless because it is stable and persistent. If you knew nothing about the temperature outside but you knew ice cream sales recently started going up, you could logically infer that drowning deaths are probably going to go up soon, too.

It is not that important whether or not the causality between two variables is real, direct, or determinable. The existence of the correlation is enough, as long as it persists. For example, there is a strong correlation between US and Canadian interest rates, driven by a third variable: changes in the US economic outlook. This is because the US economy is influential in determining not just US interest rates but also Canadian output. Canada's export economy depends on economic growth in the US. Therefore, while correlation does not imply causation (US rates don't cause Canadian rates to move), the relationship is logical and tradable and if you see a big move in US rates, you are probably sane to bet on Canadian rates moving in the same direction.

An important takeaway here is that you don't need one variable to be the cause of movement in the other; you just need them to move together in a semi-reliable fashion. So when someone tells you that correlation doesn't imply causation you can respond, "No, but there is most likely a third explanatory variable driving both asset prices with indeterminate lags and I am trading off those lags."

---

[3]This paraphrases a quote by Edward Tufte, who said: "Correlation is not causation but it sure is a hint."

In other words, the reasons variables are moving (causality) are not as important as the fact that they are moving together in a somewhat predictable fashion. As I have said before, the *what* matters more than the *why*.

The challenge is to be skeptical, but open minded at the same time. It is important to recognize that with thousands of traders constantly blasted by a nearly infinite firehose of global financial market data, spurious correlations are bound to pop up. A spurious correlation for our purposes is when two variables appear to be related but they are in fact just randomly moving in the same direction at the same time.

The more back testing and data mining you do, the more likely you are to find incidents of spurious correlation. Take a look at Figure 8.1, which shows the relationship between wholesale rabbit meat prices and US economic surprises. There appears to be a relationship but logic would suggest that this is probably a spurious and unstable correlation. This is important because spurious correlations are unlikely to persist, while correlations based on real economic relationships are more reliable and persistent. On the other hand, maybe a strong economy means rabbit meat demand outstrips supply? Maybe. I have never bought or sold wholesale rabbit meat.

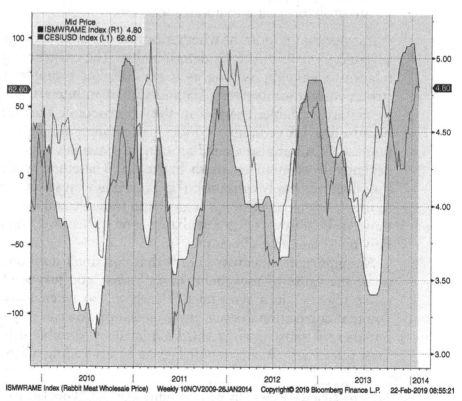

Figure 8.1 Wholesale rabbit meat prices vs. Citi Economic Surprises for the US, 2009 to 2014.

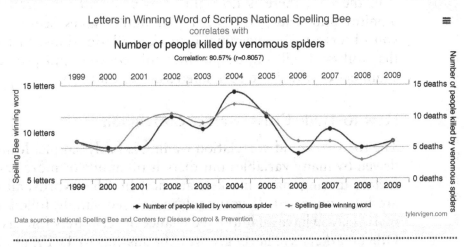

Figure 8.2 Annual data for "Letters in winning word of Scripps National Spelling Bee correlates with number of people killed by venomous spiders."

Some people find spurious correlations very offensive and/or hilarious. There is a website entirely dedicated to spurious correlations: www.tylervigen.com. Figure 8.2 features one I enjoy.

There is no magical way to determine which correlations will remain stable and persistent. As stated earlier, the first step is always to apply a simple logical filter. Does the relationship make sense? If the answer is no, the correlation could well be spurious. You need logic first and regression analysis second. Meaningless correlations can yield high r^2 just by random chance. And at the same time, if there is a lead or lag between two variables, strongly related asset prices that are great to trade lead/lag against each other could yield a low r^2.

Human beings are programmed to look for and interpret patterns—it's part of our DNA—but it can lead to overzealous estimates of correlation and causality, so be careful!

On the other hand, I have had experiences where I felt quite confident about a relationship and many in the market tried to shoot me down. An example of this was in 2006 when I pointed out the relationship between milk prices and the level of NZDUSD in my daily FX commentary for Lehman Brothers. As time passed, the market and most observers eventually came to the same conclusion I had reached early on—milk prices are an important variable in determining the value of the NZD.

The simple fact that New Zealand's most important export is milk products made the relationship logical to me as financial flows in and out of New Zealand and New Zealand's GDP are influenced by the price of milk. But it took a long while before the market bought into the premise.

In the end, there is no right answer for which correlations to monitor and trade—use what you think makes sense and what you observe to be meaningful market relationships. In the pages that follow, I will dig deeper into this concept and provide some examples of how I use correlated asset to trade FX.

How to Trade Cross-Market Correlation

The theory behind correlation trading is fairly simple: Markets are driven by many variables but there is often one or more underlying factors driving many markets at once. In other words, all markets are interconnected. If you analyze or even simply follow non-FX markets, you have an improved chance of accurately forecasting FX. Other markets will never give you the answers to the FX test but they will often give you some great clues.

This is not arbitrage. The currency is not guaranteed to revert to fair value. Think of the correlated variable as one measure of fair value for the currency pair; the currency oscillates around that value. Much like PPP is just an anchor for long-term valuation of currencies, short-term fair value estimates provided by correlated variables are just a starting point, a piece of the puzzle. But unlike PPP, which is completely useless when it comes to trading, correlated variables suggest short-term fair value, not long-term fair value, and so can be exploited profitably.

When correlation trading works, it feels like you know what will happen before it happens. When it is not working properly, it is like watching TV with the audio and video out of sync. It takes significant practice to decipher the messages from other markets, but it is well worth the effort. A good correlation analysis can feel like having tomorrow's newspaper today.

There are macroeconomic reasons for relationships between markets and there are also micro reasons for these relationships. The global economy is a complex system of nearly infinite connections. When one asset price moves, the trigger for the move could be something relevant to other assets as well. Similar to chaos theory where a butterfly flaps its wings in the Amazon and triggers a monsoon in Thailand, every action in the global economy triggers a series of complicated actions and reactions.

Let's look at a simple example of why asset price moves can lead to moves in FX. Gold rallies twenty dollars. A $20 increase in the price of gold represents a marginal increase in prosperity for exporters of gold. Therefore, it is an instant change to the potential future value of Australian exports. This is only a tiny marginal change for an economy as large as Australia's, but all economics and markets operate at the margin.

So, all other things being equal, a $20 rise in gold is good for the Australian economy and thus bullish for the Australian dollar. If not much else is going on, and you see a $20 rally in gold, you should expect the Australian dollar has a greater chance of going up than down in the short term. If you also see copper and Australian 5-year yields going up at the same time, that's even better. Like I explained in the chapter on technical analysis, the more factors you have in favor of a trade idea, the better.

For many different reasons, shifts in commodities, bonds, and equities around the world trigger changes in the perceptions of the value of global currencies. Furthermore, the reasons those other markets are moving are probably somewhat relevant to FX as well.

For example, if there is a story on a Canadian news channel saying that the prime minister might resign, it might take a while for it to hit the US and financial news headlines. A few traders in Toronto might see the story on TV and sell Canadian stocks. Then Canadian bonds might rally a bit in response and then finally, USDCAD might react and go higher five minutes later.

Even if you don't have a Canadian cable subscription, you see the moves in Canadian stocks and bonds and you perk up to the possibility that there might be some CAD-negative news out there. Keenly observe a large universe of asset prices and try to build an understanding of how they interrelate. This will help you win in FX.

There are also micro reasons for FX markets to react to moves in other assets. Suppose a big hedge fund macro trader is having a terrible month. He is so bearish he can't see straight and he thinks the global economy is falling off a cliff. He has expressed this view by going limit short AUDUSD, S&P futures, and copper. It's the last day of the month, and suddenly S&P futures rally 25 handles out of nowhere. The macro trader is scheduled to go on vacation next week and he can't take the pain of his losing positions anymore. He picks up the phone and calls his execution desk.

"Cover all my positions. I'm taking a week off."

The execution desk scrambles to buy AUDUSD, S&P futures, and copper simultaneously and the feedback loops between the products send all three prices skyrocketing higher.

The proliferation of pod-based volatility-targeting macro hedge funds makes scenarios like the one described above very common in today's market as portfolio managers put on positions in baskets of related products and take them off all at once when it comes time to take profits or stop out. Also note that there can at times be a high degree of correlation between what different macro portfolio managers are doing—mutual fund investors and hedge funds can sometimes exhibit herd-like behavior. This can exacerbate feedback loops.

Another reason for correlation among asset classes is that traders and portfolio managers use one asset to hedge another. Say a portfolio manager is long a huge basket of illiquid corporate bonds and she is worried about the global economy; she wants out of her corporate bond portfolio. But the market is too thin; there are no good bids. She decides to hedge the exposure by selling AUDJPY because it tends to be correlated to corporate bonds (or at least global risk appetite). Then she leaves a bunch of limit orders to sell the bonds if they rally.

As the corporate bond markets rally, she is filled on some of her limit orders. Now her AUDJPY hedge is too big so she will then buy back some of the AUDJPY. This is how a rally in corporate bonds can lead to a move higher in AUDJPY or another correlated asset price. You will see similar activity in other pairs. A trader who is nervously long oil might buy USDCAD to hedge if he feels he can get more liquidity there. When oil rallies back and he takes profit, he will sell the USDCAD.

Think of the entire global capital markets as an infinitely complex super-organism where action in one part has potential implications for activity in another. Like a crazy Rube Goldberg machine, activity in one sector or asset class can echo and rebound and ricochet into others.

As correlation rises, there is also a positive feedback mechanism that leads to even more correlation. Hundreds of systematic algorithmic hedge funds detect correlations in real time and trade on them. So when the correlation between, say, AUDUSD and the S&P 500 is very high (as is sometimes the case), these algos will reinforce the correlation by trading it in real time.

If S&P futures rally 3 or 4 handles, you will see algos getting on the bid in AUD and if the S&P turns around, they will move off the bid and get on the offer. As correlation rises, more and more algos deploy to capitalize on the correlation, so strong correlation leads to stronger correlation until there is a regime shift and the correlation breaks down.

Now let's go through the most reliable correlations and get into some more detail about how to trade them. The most reliable correlations in FX are (in order of reliability):

1. FX vs. other currencies (one currency vs. another)

2. FX vs. interest rates

3. FX vs. commodities (especially gold, oil, and copper)

4. FX vs. equity indices

5. FX vs. single name equities and ETFs

Understand that even the strongest correlations are dynamic and unstable. Correlations come and go, but interest rate and commodity correlations tend to be most persistent. Understanding current correlations and how they might evolve is critical to your success in short-term FX trading. I will now discuss each of the five types of cross-market correlation listed above.

■ Correlation of One Currency Pair versus Another Currency Pair

The simplest correlation in FX is the relationship between one currency pair and another. For example, EURUSD is the most liquid and important currency pair in the world. Many speculators will use it to express their view on the dollar. If EURUSD moves significantly, it is most likely that other USD pairs such as AUDUSD and GBPUSD will move in sympathy.

There was once a time when you could make money trading AUDUSD simply by watching EURUSD and doing trades with the expectation that AUDUSD would catch up to the move in EURUSD. Those days are gone now as algorithms capture the small deviations in one currency pair and effectively arbitrage away gains before a human being can capitalize on them.

It is still important to understand, though, that all USD-based currencies have a strong tendency to move together. If EURUSD, GBPUSD, and NZDUSD rally (and other pairs have not moved), the odds are greater that the next short-term move in AUDUSD is up and USDCAD is down as the overall momentum of the dollar dominates. Get a feel for general dollar direction and identify which currencies are leading or lagging. If nothing is going on and USDCAD suddenly moves 30 points higher, you can bet that the short-term weak side in AUDUSD will be lower as the USDCAD move hints at dollar strength.

Some traders believe so strongly in the power of USDCAD to predict the rest of the dollar pairs that it has earned the nickname "The Truth."

Correlation of a currency pair versus interest rates in each country. During my career (1995 to present), the most consistent driver of currencies has been changes in relative interest rates. This is because investors tend to favor currencies that pay a higher rate of interest (high-yielders) and avoid or short currencies that pay low or negative rates. Furthermore, most of the reasons that interest rates rise in a country (higher growth, higher inflation, confidence) support the currency. If things are going well somewhere, you will tend to see both the currency and interest rates (yields) go up. So a move higher in rates is often a good predictor of an upcoming move higher in the currency.

This is important to understand as it is the reason that currencies react so violently to unexpected moves in interest rates. If a central bank becomes hawkish (i.e. signals a greater intention to raise rates) or dovish (i.e. signals a greater intention to lower rates), the currency of that country will react in a predictable fashion. Here is an example of how a currency reacts when there is an unexpected move in rates:

On November 1, 2010, the market expected the Reserve Bank of Australia (RBA) to hold rates steady at its board meeting. Instead, the RBA hiked their cash rate by 0.25% (25 basis points). Figure 8.3 is a 5-minute chart of AUDUSD around the announcement.

The jump from 0.9880 to 0.9990 occurred instantaneously at the moment the RBA announced the rate hike. This is a very micro example of how interest rates directly impact the exchange rate. Now let's zoom out and take a look at the bigger picture. Figure 8.4 shows AUDUSD versus the 10-year spread between Australian and US rates from 2006 to 2012.

As you can see, the ebb and flow of the interest rate gap tends to be similar to the ebb and flow of the currency. It is important to note, however, that while direction of moves tends to match, magnitude does not. Furthermore, there are leads and lags. These features of magnitude differential and lead/lag are true of most FX correlations, no matter how strong and persistent.

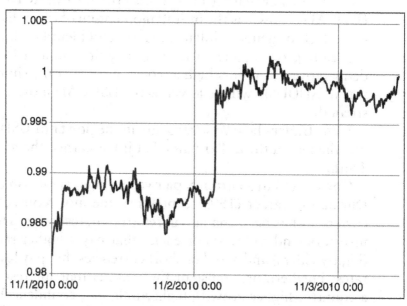

Figure 8.3 5-minute AUDUSD through an unexpected RBA rate hike, November 1–3, 2010.

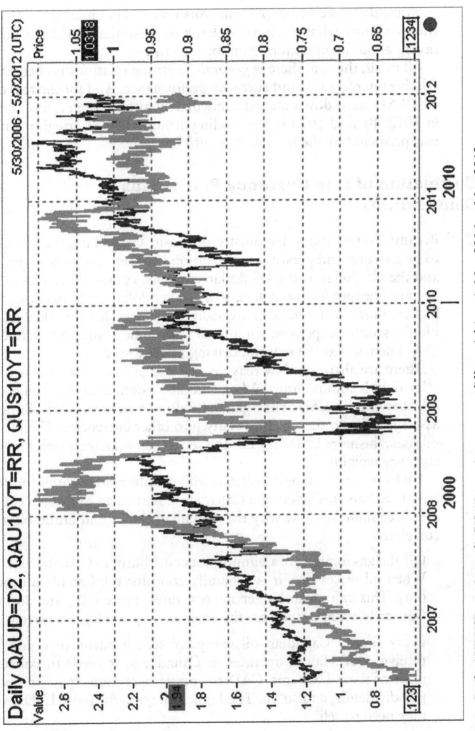

Figure 8.4 Daily AUDUSD vs. Australia/US 10-year interest rate differential (gray), May 2006 to May 2012.

UNDERSTAND CORRELATION AND INTERMARKET RELATIONSHIPS

Astute readers may be thinking that AUDUSD is a sell based on this chart. If I had nothing else to trade based on, I would agree. But, of course, in real life I want to see other variables, like Chinese equities, the price of copper, and Australian economic data. And I want to know what the Reserve Bank of Australia (RBA) has been saying about its intention to cut or hike rates.

All in all, though, there is *generally* a strong relationship between relative interest rates and currency performance. And for the record, AUDUSD went down almost immediately after I clipped this chart in 2012. By mid-2013 it was trading around 0.9000, roughly what was predicted by the interest rate differential.

■ Correlation of One Currency Pair versus Commodities

Because commodities are mostly priced in US dollars, there tends to be a strong and persistent correlation between commodity prices and the US dollar. If the US dollar weakens, commodities instantly become cheaper for foreigners, so a weaker dollar tends to equate to higher commodity prices. Conversely, a stronger dollar makes commodities more expensive for non-US consumers and thus reduces global demand at the margin, driving prices lower.

There are also cash flow reasons that explain why the USD is correlated with commodities. When Middle Eastern countries sell their oil, they receive USD. They generally do not want to hold all their assets in USD so they will diversify into other currencies. The more oil rises, the more USD they need to sell to maintain their benchmark currency weights.

Each currency can be correlated with specific commodities for different reasons. Let's take the Canadian dollar as an example. There are three main reasons why the Canadian dollar and crude oil are correlated:

- Oil and gas mining are an important contributor to Canadian GDP. When oil prices rise, it is generally good for the Canadian economy. This can mean higher interest rates, more jobs, and so on. Generally, what is good for the economy is good for the currency.

- Every time a Canadian oil company sells a barrel of crude, it receives USD. But it operates in Canada, so it needs to convert most of these USD into CAD to run its operations, pay its staff, pay its dividends, and so on. The higher oil goes, the more USDCAD they need to sell.

- Canada is a reliable, geopolitically stable supplier of crude. So if crude prices rise on global geopolitical fears, people will buy Canadian dollars as a safe haven. This is why CAD and NOK are often known as "petrocurrencies." In the past, the Dutch guilder and British pound traded as petrocurrencies because of their abundant North Sea oil supplies but the Netherlands joined the euro and North Sea production has fallen, so Canada and Norway are the major oil currencies today. This is an example of how correlations change over time.

Generally, a rise in the value of a country's exports is good for the currency and vice versa. Higher gold and copper prices tend to benefit Australia and Chile (for example) while higher milk prices tend to benefit New Zealand. These are important relationships founded on the macroeconomics and terms of trade of each nation. Because of this strong macroeconomic relationship, these correlations tend to be sticky. Figure 8.5 shows the price of milk against NZDUSD from 2006 to 2012.

You can see that there appears to be a strong relationship here. Anyone who deals in correlations and overlays will inevitably be told that correlation does not equal causation. It is a common cliché and like most clichés, it is true. The snarky implication is often that most correlations are bogus—but that is simply not the case.

If you see something that appears to have a strong connection visually and you can support the connection with reasonable fundamental arguments, you are probably onto something. Don't worry so much about the correlation coefficients and r-squared; they can be less important than the inherent logic and economic linkages between the two time series. Remember, we are using correlation between assets as just one input into our process here. We are not building a systematic correlation trading algorithm.

Building systems to profit from correlation between markets is certainly possible and there are many funds that do so. It has become a crowded part of the quant universe, though, and is beyond the scope of this book.

Understanding not just correlation trading but how the correlations themselves come and go can be an important source of edge. If everyone is talking about oil and stories about crude oil are on the front page of every finance website like in 2014–2015, the correlation between oil and other assets will tend to be high. As oil finds a base and starts to range trade, you should expect the market's focus on oil, and the correlation between FX and oil, to fade. Whatever is top of mind in the market is the first place to look for correlations.

◼ Correlation of One Currency Pair versus an Equity Index

In the late 1990s, the US internet bubble was in full swing and when equities rallied, it was seen as a sign of strength for the dollar because

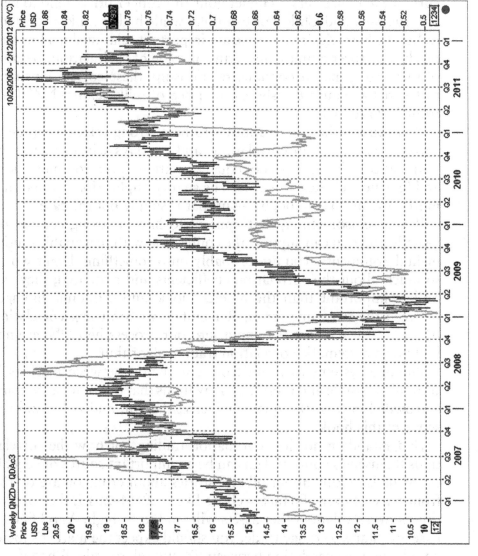

Figure 8.5 Daily NZDUSD vs. Dairy futures prices (gray line), October 2006 to February 2012.

it signaled money flowing into US technology stocks. The correlation between the US dollar and US equities was strongly positive. Equities up = dollar up.

Then, from 2003 to 2010, the relationship ran the other way. There was a strong relationship between risky high-yielding currencies and equity performance. This was called the "Risk-On, Risk-Off" or the RORO regime, where a large group of highly correlated risky assets moved together in sync like a school of fish. When equities went up, the USD sold off and commodities and risky currencies like AUD, NZD, and CAD rallied.

However, the US economy started to outperform its global peers around 2012, and the correlation flipped again. Stronger US equities were a sign of US strength while global economies flagged. So once again, rallies in equities meant a stronger dollar.

As computers detect rising correlation, they contribute to accelerating feedback loops between assets with potentially different fundamentals. It is crucial to keep in mind that correlations rise and fall in unpredictable ways. They can remain important for years at a time or come and go in weeks.

Figure 8.6 shows the inverse relationship between the NASDAQ and AUD during the dotcom bubble.

Now take a look at Figure 8.7, AUDUSD vs. the NASDAQ during the heat of the RORO period from 2007 to 2010.

It is crucial to know what regime you are in when analyzing potential correlations between equities and currencies. There is usually some correlation between equity and currency markets but these relationships are unstable and thus you must always be on the lookout for changes in direction and magnitude of correlation.

One of the most reliable equity index-versus-FX correlations in my career has been the Nikkei versus USDJPY. This is because Japanese citizens hold the largest pool of savings in the world. When things look good, they buy foreign assets and sell JPY, seeking higher returns. When things look bad, they repatriate money (bring it home), which triggers yen buying (lower USDJPY).

Next, Figure 8.8 is a daily chart of USDJPY versus Nikkei futures. You can see that this correlation was strong throughout almost all of the 10-year period.

Another way to look at currency versus equity correlation is to use the relative performance of two equity indices to determine possible direction for those two currencies. I like doing this with AUDCAD versus the ratio of Australian to Canadian equities.

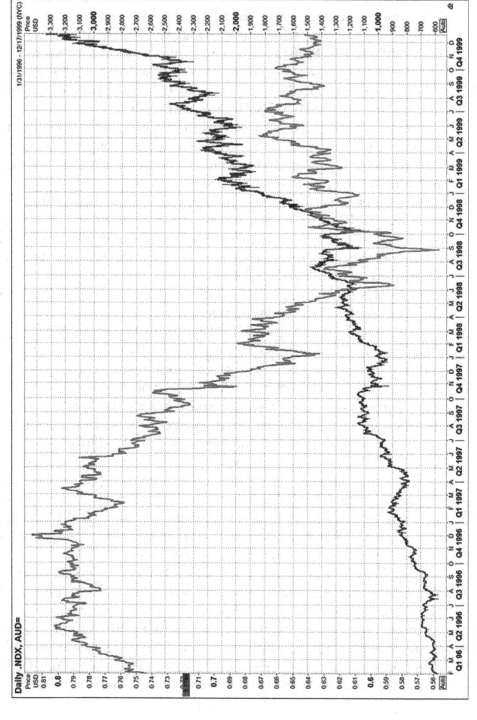

Figure 8.6   Daily NASDAQ vs. AUDUSD (gray line), January 1996 to December 1999.

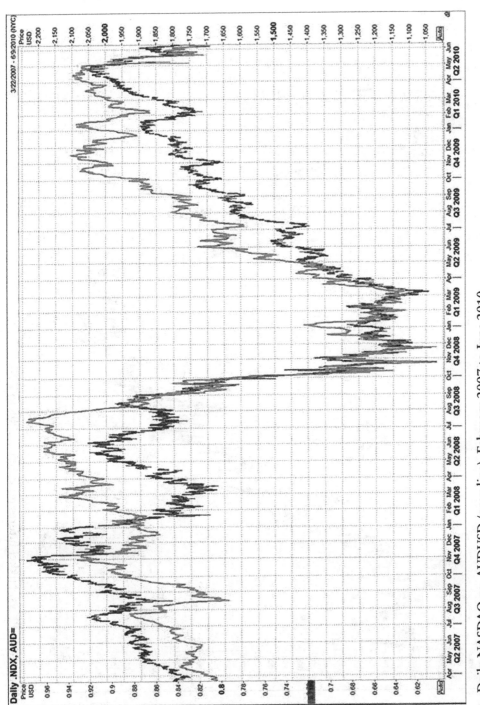

Figure 8.7 Daily NASDAQ vs. AUDUSD (gray line), February 2007 to June 2010.

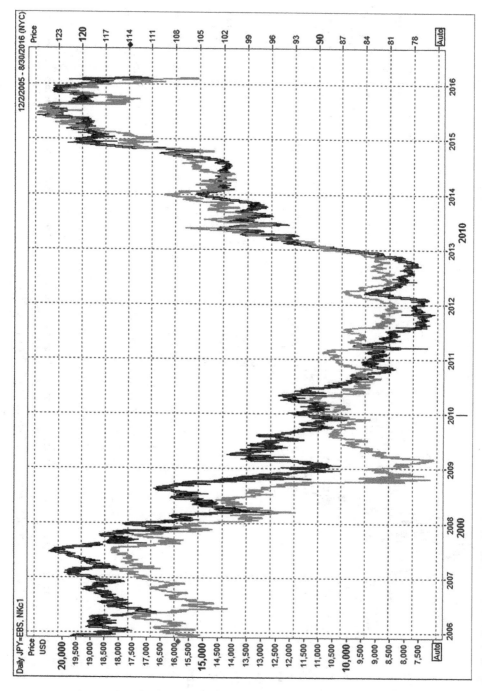

Figure 8.8   Daily USDJPY vs. Nikkei futures (gray line), 2006 to 2016

■ Correlation of a Currency Pair versus Single Name Equities or ETFs

A smart way to monitor equities is to look at individual stocks and ETFs that relate to the currency you are trading. In the case of Canada that would mean crude producers like Suncor, Encana, and Cenovus. With Australia, you might watch BHP or Freeport (mining stocks) and the China A-Shares ETF (FXI). Using ETFs helps you focus on what is happening in specific sectors relevant to the currency you are trading. Keep in mind that these equities will be correlated to the related commodities (Suncor is correlated to crude oil, for example) but still provide a slightly different lens through which to look.

One particularly powerful use for single names and ETFs is when looking for divergence or confirmation. For example, if I see a big divergence between AUD and copper, the first thing I will do is check how BHP and Freeport are trading. Do the mining stocks confirm the copper move (and thus give a stronger AUD signal)? Or do they suggest caution?

■ Trading the Correlations

"Okay, great," you say. "So there are correlations. But how do I trade them?"

First, the ideal setup is to create a group of overlay charts if you have the software to do so. This can be done on Reuters Eikon or Bloomberg or other high-quality charting software. Once you have 15 or 20 overlay charts of FX versus correlated assets, scan for divergences. In my cockpit, I have every major currency pair overlaid with every one of its key drivers on a series of separate charts.

In Figure 8.9 you will see a comprehensive table of the asset prices I was watching for each currency as of January 2019. The table is a starting point to help you understand the important drivers of each currency pair. As I have made clear a few times, drivers change over time.

I usually run 50 or 60 overlays at a time with maybe 5 or 10 new ones added each year and 5 or 10 dropped. Many overlays stay the same year after year (e.g. USDCAD versus crude oil, AUDUSD versus interest rate differentials, etc.) but I add and remove new overlay charts as time goes on and correlations evolve, appear, and disappear.

Let's say I sit down at my desk in the morning and have no view and no position. The first thing I will do is flip through my overlays to look for major dislocations. Most of the charts will show a market somewhat close to equilibrium like that seen in Figure 8.10.

	Driver1	Driver2	Driver3	Driver4
USD	US 2, 5, and 10-year interest rates	US equities	Gold	ISM/consumer confidence
EURUSD	US/Germany rate differential	Gold	Italy 2-year and 10-year yield	Crude oil
USDJPY	Nikkei	US 2, 5 and 10-year interest rates	Gold	S&P
USDCHF	US 2, 5, and 10-year interest rates	Gold		
EURCHF	German interest rates	Global risk appetite	Italy 2-year and 10-year yield	European bank stocks
GBPUSD	UK/US rate differential	Crude oil		
EURGBP	Germany/UK rate differential			
AUDUSD	AU/US rate differential	Gold	Copper and iron ore	BHP, FCX, FXI (equity)
AUDNZD	AU/NZ rate differential	Australia vs. New Zealand equity price ratio		
NZDUSD	NZ / US rate differential	Dairy prices (MMRA on Bloomberg)		
USDCAD	Crude Oil	US/Canada rate differential	Canadian Oil Equities (SU etc.)	Gold
EURNOK	Crude Oil	Germany/Norway rate differential		
EURSEK	Germany/Sweden rate differential	Sweden equities (OMX)		

Figure 8.9   Some important currency drivers as of January 2019.

That chart shows that USDJPY and Nikkei futures are moving in tandem and a simple glance at the chart suggests that USDJPY is not out of line at current levels. Then I might scroll across to a chart like Figure 8.11.

Now my interest is piqued. Note that here I am looking at crude oil inverted so that the overlay is logical (lower crude = weaker CAD = higher USDCAD). At this moment there is weakness in crude (the **gray** line is going higher) and USDCAD has not responded much. Crude is in the bottom third of its range on this chart (remember the **gray** line going up means crude is going down). Meanwhile USDCAD is still near the lows. All other things being equal, if crude is near the lows, USDCAD should be near the highs, not the lows. So on this chart both lines should be moving together so USDCAD looks low.

This is a basic but effective way to find trade ideas. Look for currencies that have diverged from their current driver variables as a starting point and then drill deeper via other methodologies (technicals, fundamentals, positioning, etc.).

This looks at first glance like a decent setup to buy USDCAD, playing for a catch-up move to oil. USDCAD is already more than 150 points off the lows, though, so if you want to go long here, you need a wide stop loss.

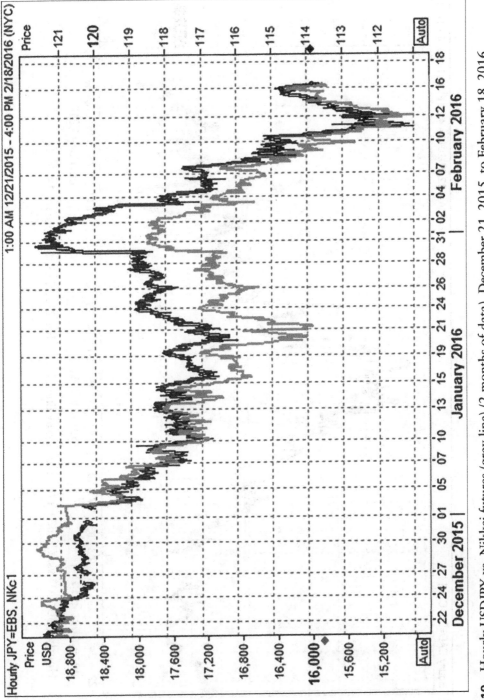

Figure 8.10 Hourly USDJPY vs. Nikkei futures (gray line) (2 months of data), December 21, 2015, to February 18, 2016.

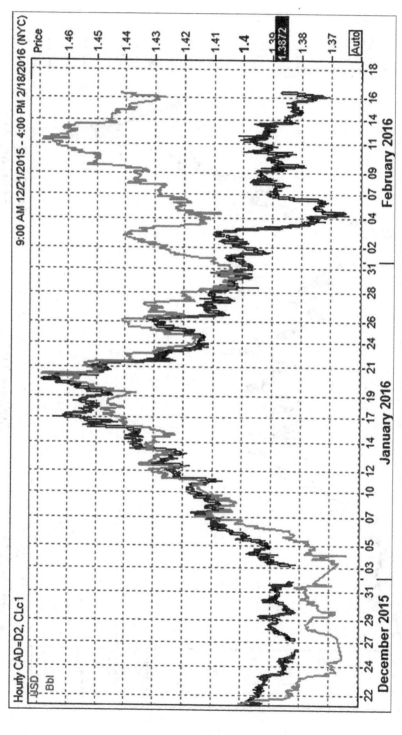

Figure 8.11 Hourly USDCAD vs. Crude oil (inverted, gray line), December 21, 2015 to February 18, 2018.

Once I see this CAD chart, I flip to my other CAD correlation overlays and see what the other variables say. The first place I turn is Canadian interest rates and then Canadian equities and then gold. If the other indicators support the trade idea, it gets stronger. If they are neutral, that is fine, but my excitement level drops. If they point the other way (lower USDCAD), then I'll stay away. Remember to stay away from trades where different variables point different directions. Avoid crosswinds. You want strong winds at your back when you put on a trade.

If rates, gold, and Canadian equities support the idea, I'll dig deeper. What are the fundamentals in Canada and what are upcoming catalysts? How is the market positioned? And so on. If I like the idea, then it's time to put on the trade.

I look at the technicals as a guide to where to place my stop loss. In this case, a lot of other planets lined up so I went long USDCAD spot and placed my stop loss order below the lows, at 1.3689.

Technicals and the fair value level suggested by the correlated variable (in this case oil) will both factor into my take profit objective. In this case I saw the major high in early February at 1.4100 and put my take profit just below there at 1.4089. Check out the technicals section and the position sizing section for more on my thought process when putting on and taking off positions.

I have focused here on the correlation piece, but good trade ideas involve more planets in line than just a correlation overlay. Perhaps the Bank of Canada meeting is coming up soon and I expect the market to sell CAD into it on rate cut expectations. That would be a nice catalyst to throw in the mix. If I knew from either statistical or anecdotal evidence that the market was limit short USDCAD—that would add to my conviction. As you read this book, understand that each form of analysis helps build the picture and the goal is to fill in as many blanks as possible to *find trades where everything points the same way.*

So the objective when you are watching other assets for direction in FX is to find large divergences between the correlated asset and the currency, then trade the currency as it catches up to where it "should be." This is why the strategy is sometimes called "lead/lag"—you are watching one variable lead and expecting the other to move in the same direction, with a lag. Let's take a look at an example of a classic lead/lag setup.

In 2010/2012, markets were embroiled in the heat of the Eurozone crisis as it looked like Greece might default and other members might be forced out of the euro single currency. A disintegration of the euro would be catastrophic for the economies (and corporations and stock markets) of Europe. This created a regime where moves in European equities had a strong positive correlation to moves in

EURUSD. Good news on Europe meant buy DAX (the German stock market index) and buy EURUSD. Bad news meant existential risk in the Eurozone and lower DAX and lower EURUSD.

The Setup

January 2, 2012, was a holiday in the United States but not in Europe. The DAX futures opened up 3% but most US traders were still at home. Take a look at the next chart (Figure 8.12). The **gray** line is the ratio of DAX to DJIA (German stock market versus US stock market) and the black bars are EURUSD. US stock markets were closed for the holiday so any movements in the **gray** line on January 2 were driven solely by moves in the DAX.

You can see that the equity ratio and EURUSD had been moving together faithfully throughout November and December, but then EURUSD did not react to the January 2 rally in the DAX. This is a nice setup because there is a logical explanation for the divergence: Most traders were on holidays, so the market is less efficient.

The Trade

The trade was to buy EURUSD on the view that it would catch up to the move in DAX at some point (see Figure 8.12). In this case, the early short-term low was 1.2870 so I went long and put my stop loss order at 1.2839. This put my stop below the low and below the round 1.2850 level. An eyeball take profit would be the point DAX suggests as fair value; this looks like about 1.3170. This would imply a perfect relationship between the two variables at this exact level of scaling (which is not reasonable) but it's a good starting point for estimating the potential size of the move higher if it happens.

The Result

Now look at the bottom right corner of Figure 8.13 and you can see what happened next. EURUSD went up 150 pips in a straight line the next day. At this point, I noted major resistance just below 1.3100 (the place where EURUSD broke down from on December 28) and thought about taking profit or at least cutting half and letting the other half ride.

This was a profitable lead/lag trade with limited risk and attractive upside. Risking 100 points to make 150 is nice here because the big move up in the DAX suggested to me the implied theoretical odds of a EURUSD rally were better than 50/50. In other words, this trade had a high expected value with a payout of 1.5:1 and a probability of success greater than 50%.

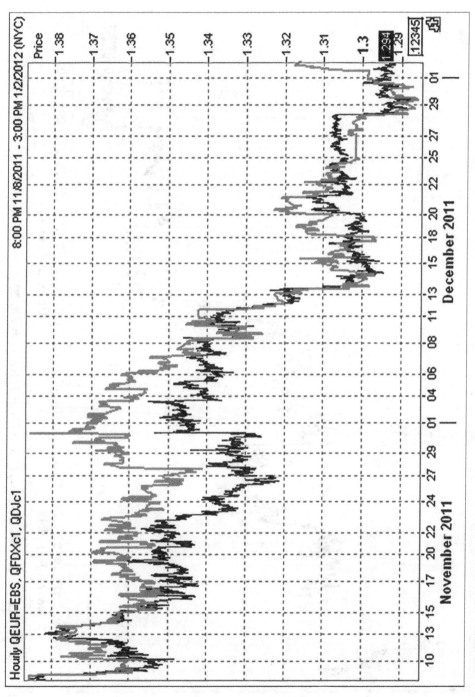

Figure 8.12 Hourly EURUSD vs. DAX/DJI ratio (gray): Chart 1, November 8, 2011, to January 2, 2012.

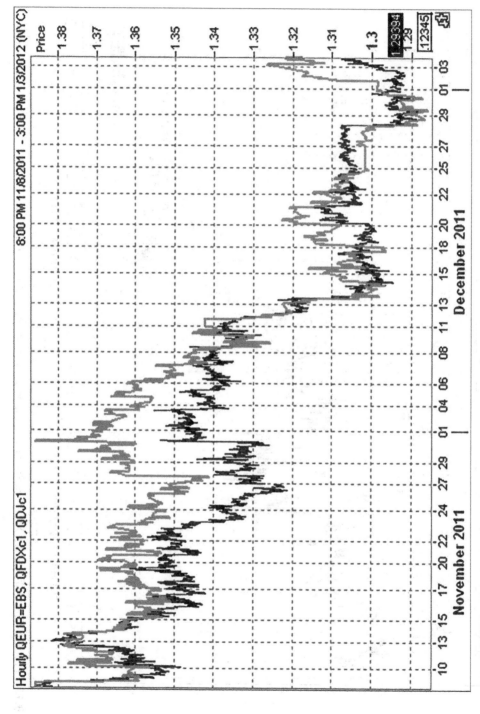

Figure 8.13   Hourly EURUSD vs. DAX/DJI ratio (gray): Chart 2, November 8, 2011, to January 3, 2012.

Another Example: The Setup and the Trade

Let's look at another example of how to trade FX versus exogenous (outside) variables. Remember, good trade ideas are built with multiple inputs, not just one correlation. Let's look at another example using USDCAD.

A dislocation between the Canadian dollar and the price of oil is often a good place to start with USDCAD, but ideally you want other confirming factors to support your view. What is the macroeconomic backdrop? What are Canadian interest rates doing? What direction is the trend of Canadian economic surprises? How is US economic performance? These should all factor into your decision to trade (or not trade) the Canadian dollar.

The analysis from my January 2012 trading journal captures what I'm getting at.

■ January 2012

USDCAD looks extremely elevated as crude oil is very strong (see Figure 8.14). While this weakness in CAD could theoretically be attributed to the weaker run of Canadian economic data lately, Canadian interest rate futures disagree as they trade near multi-month lows (see Figure 8.15).

The dollar index (DXY) has made yet another top at 81.50, while Chinese equities have put in an explosive and impulsive 2.5% reversal rally, nearly engulfing the previous 15 sessions of losses (see Figures 8.16 and 8.17). A return of confidence at the margin in China plus high and rising confidence around the US cyclical story suggest to me that USDCAD should be closer to 1.0150 (not 1.0278 where it currently trades).

I will go short here (1.0278) with a 1.0326 stop loss and take profit at 1.0156.

■ The Result

By incorporating much more than just the oil correlation, I was able to generate a nice trade idea with many factors all working together. Figure 8.18 shows what happened.

Nice trade. Oil did nothing and USDCAD went straight down. I also considered some other factors with this trade, beyond those listed above. I was watching Canadian resource stocks and US homebuilders as well. Canadian resource stocks are a major part of the

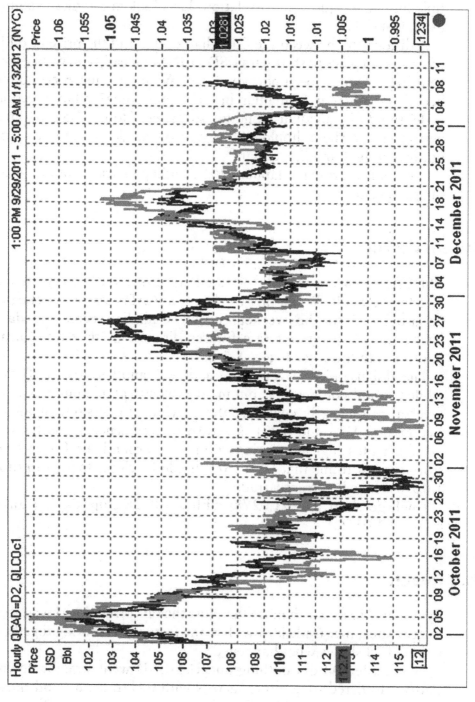

Figure 8.14 Hourly USDCAD vs. Crude Oil (inverted, in gray), September 29, 2011, to January 13, 2012.

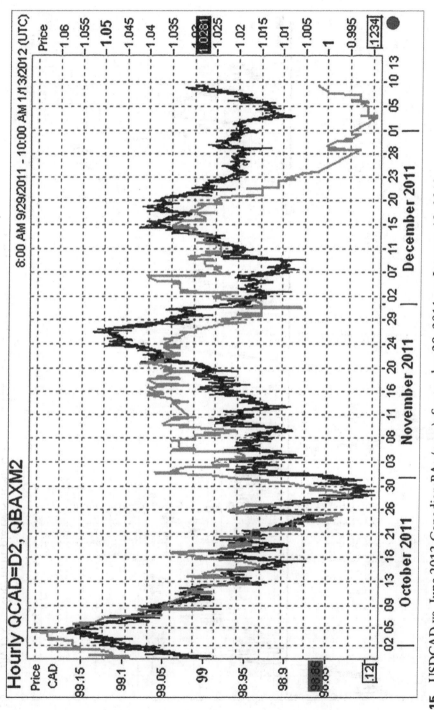

Figure 8.15 USDCAD vs. June 2012 Canadian BAs (gray), September 29, 2011, to January 13, 2012.

BA is short for "Banker's Acceptance" and is the actively-traded interest futures product in Canada. All other things being equal:
Lower BA prices = higher interest rates = stronger CAD = lower USDCAD.

UNDERSTAND CORRELATION AND INTERMARKET RELATIONSHIPS

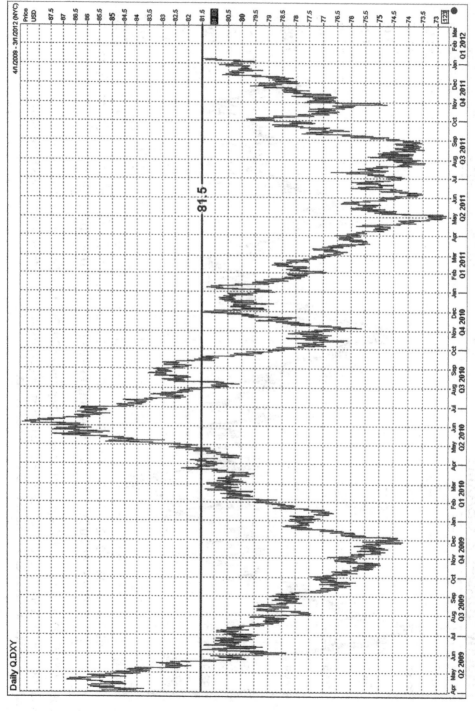

Figure 8.16   Daily DXY: Note multiple tops around 81.50 in late 2010, April 2009 to January 2012.

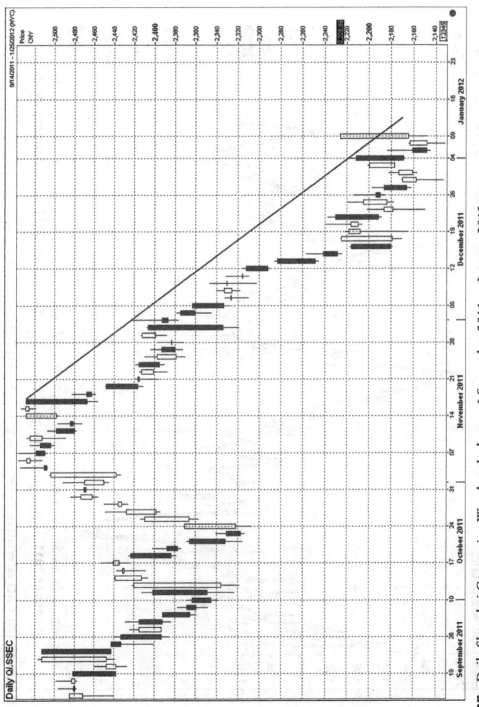

Figure 8.17 Daily Shanghai Composite: Was that the bottom? September 2011 to January 2012.

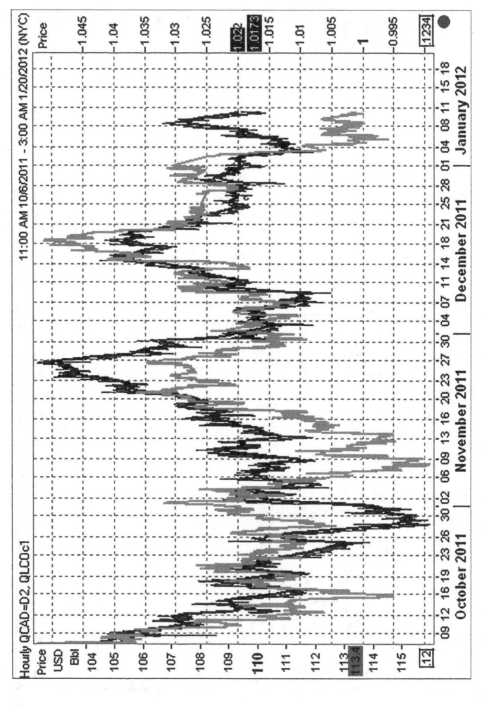

Figure 8.18   Hourly USDCAD vs. crude oil (inverted, in gray), October 2011 to January 2012.

Canadian economy while US homebuilding is a major source of future demand for commodities like lumber and copper. By watching these specific sectors, you can also get an advance read on what CAD should be doing.

This USDCAD trade is an excellent example of how you bring as many factors as possible into your analysis and act when everything points the same way.

■ Understand the Regime and Relevant Correlations

It is important to understand that regimes come and go and correlations that work today might not work tomorrow. Correlations can flip without notice or just fade to irrelevance. The best way to understand what correlations matter right now is to listen. Listen to traders around you. Listen to the news. Read the Reuters and Bloomberg stories about FX. What are traders worried about, excited about, looking forward to?

Very often perception is just as important as reality so you need to know what other traders care about on any given day. There are correlations that remain stable over time and there are correlations that will work for a week and then disappear forever. If you see a correlation developing in real time, try to figure out why it is happening. Most real, sustainable correlations have a logical fundamental underpinning.

■ A Note on Stop Losses and Discipline

One pitfall when trading divergences and correlation is that the larger the divergence, the more attractive the trade. So if you enter a trade based on a divergence and that divergence widens, you are tempted to add. This is a recipe for disaster, similar to the stock trader who likes a stock at $10, buys some, and then watches it go to $5 and simply *loves* it at $5. Then it goes to $2 and he simply *must* buy more! It's so cheap! If you liked it at 10, you gotta love it at 2, right? The key to avoiding this trap is that part of your plan when you initiate a trade is to decide on a firm stop loss level and stick to it.

If I am playing the divergence between USDCAD and crude oil and I enter long USDCAD at 1.3740, I will immediately decide on a stop loss level. Say I pick 1.3639 as my stop. Then no matter what crude and USDCAD do from that point on, my stop loss remains the same. Even if crude falls another $10 (which makes USDCAD longs more attractive), I will still stop out of the position if USDCAD goes to 1.3639. By setting a stop when you get in and then sticking to it, you acknowledge the reality that trading divergences is only meant to increase your odds of winning—it doesn't work every time! Always employ stop losses on every position you trade. Always.

■ FAQ about Correlation Trading

Lead/lag, correlation, or cross-market correlation trading is one piece of the puzzle for me—it's not the be-all and the end-all. I use divergences between correlated variables and FX as one clue in a bigger puzzle that also includes analysis of macro, behavioral, technical, and other factors. While I rank cross-market moves as one of my most important trade selection tools, there are many challenges to trading this way. I am frequently asked about various limitations and hurdles to this style of trading and I will try to address these in the following FAQ.

1. **What causes these divergences?**

   The main reason that a series of variables might move one way and FX might not is that large flows in FX can distort prices. Taking the simplest possible example, imagine a scenario where Australian interest rates and Chinese equities start ripping higher as there is news out and the market suddenly expects a Chinese fiscal stimulus package. You see this and then notice that AUDUSD is still at the lows, hovering around 0.7500; it hasn't moved at all. Why might this be?

   The simplest explanation is often that there is a large, non-price-sensitive player doing something in AUDUSD. Say an Australian company is buying a US company for $1.5 billion; they need to buy USD and sell AUD to complete the transaction. They might have a certain FX rate budgeted and they don't really care what Aussie interest rates or Chinese stocks are doing. They just need to sell their AUD and buy USD. In this case, they might leave an order with a bank to sell 2 billion AUDUSD (buy $1.5B USD) at 0.7500 or better. This is a big order so the selling will weigh on the AUD for a while, no matter what is going on with other asset prices.

   Astute traders will see other proxy assets rising and buy AUD, but until the 2 billion AUD sell order is gone, the price will not move. Eventually, if the China story continues to look good, the AUD sell order will get chipped away. When it is finally filled, AUDUSD will jump higher toward a new, more representative equilibrium.

FX flows and orders are often executed for players who are trading a completely different set of variables and different time horizon than short-term speculators and this creates the frequent divergences and dislocations between correlated variables and FX.

2. **Isn't it possible the variable is wrong, not the currency? In other words, maybe the currency doesn't move to narrow the divergence but instead the variable turns back the other way?**

This question generally is most valid when running a single variable against a currency pair. If copper is ripping higher but AUDUSD hasn't moved: How do you know if AUDUSD is wrong, or copper? It could be a big, non-price-sensitive flow in copper, right?

There are two things to consider here. First, if you have multiple variables all pointing in one direction as described in Question 1, you have a better trade because then it is most likely that FX is wrong.

Second, I generally find that the variable with the most momentum wins. Let's say copper and AUDUSD are both trading a quiet range and then copper breaks out to the topside. I would favor the direction of copper (higher) versus AUDUSD in that case so I would go long AUD, expecting it to catch up to copper.

On the other hand, if AUD breaks higher and copper continues to flounder near the bottom of the range, I would do nothing. This is because AUD has the momentum and what you are looking for are divergences where FX is doing nothing and correlated variables are moving with momentum in a specified direction. When one variable is rallying hard and the associated FX pair is selling off aggressively, that is the most confusing of all—do not touch.

Essentially, what you are looking for are moments when the FX market is out of line or half asleep and other variables are suggesting it should wake up soon.

3. **Why don't you just do a relative value trade (buy the low one and sell the high one), instead of only trading one side via the FX?**

I am a directional short-term FX trader, not a relative value (RV) trader. RV trading is a different skill set and a different kettle of fish completely. There are all sorts of subtleties to RV trading, including position sizing, risk management, when to stop out or add as the divergence grows, and so on. It is a completely different style of trading. RV trading between FX and correlated variables is feasible but it's a completely different skill set and thought process.

I use external variables to give me clues as to future FX direction and then I incorporate these clues as part of a larger holistic process. Trading RV between FX and other variables is a completely different business model. Most successful RV traders put on many, many RV trades in small size in an attempt to place multiple uncorrelated bets. Directional FX traders put on a few concentrated and levered trades looking for directional profits.

4. **Doesn't the magnitude of the move and (sometimes) the direction of the divergence depend on how the chart is scaled?**

Yes! This is a smart observation and you need to be careful about how you scale your charts. I use hourly charts and overlays and usually scale them between 21 and 42 days (one to two months or approximately 500 to 1000 hours) of data. If you use daily charts and look at 5 years of data, you might get completely different results.

The key is to be consistent with your choice of scales because otherwise you can fall prey to confirmation bias as you scale your charts to different dimensions in an attempt to find the answer you want. Your scaling should fit your time horizon. If you trade short-term, you should look at three months of data or less and if you are a bigger-picture trader, then scale up the charts to reflect that.

Most short-term and day traders use 10-minute, 30-minute, or hourly charts looking back one to three months. Anything less than a month gets noisy and anything more is too zoomed out to see short-term dislocations. The ideal scenario is when a divergence appears on all scales of a chart, but this is not always the case.

One other way of scaling your charts is to capture a specific regime period. For example, let's say the market doesn't care about Portuguese yields at all. Then news comes out and suddenly there are fears that Portugal might default on its debt; so EURUSD starts trading tick for tick with Portuguese yields. You look at a chart and see that Portugal yields started ripping on August 1. Now it's September 14. It makes more sense to scale your chart from August 1 to September 14 than to go back a full three months because you want to look at the correlation only over the period where it meant something to the market.

Note that I never think of the divergence and implied fair value suggested by overlay charts as definitive. When you overlay a currency pair and a correlated variable, you are getting a rough sense of how the two relate and interact but it is a combination of art and science, not just pure math. I have tried to go more systematic with this stuff and I find that it doesn't work very well because lead/lag relationships are unstable, imperfect, and hard to measure and because I use many other types of analysis to make my trading decisions, not just lead/lag.

5. **Are there any other ways to trade cross-market correlations?**

Yes! This section has focused on trading commodities, rates, and equities against FX but I also use cross-market analysis to help forecast equities. The stock market can be such an important driver of overall risk sentiment and currency movement that I tend to have a view on stocks most of the time. There are a few ways I forecast stocks using lead/lag:

a. Use leaders to forecast the index. In other words, overlay a volatile, widely followed stock like Apple over the NASDAQ and take views on the index based on leadership from Apple.

b. Use sub-indices to predict moves in the main index. The most useful analysis of this type is to watch the Transports Index as a leader for the broader market. Here are some notes from my February 2016 trading journal that show my thought process on this topic:

■ February 2016

Transports are ripping and could be showing the way for the broader indices. This reminds me of how the Transports showed the way throughout 2015. Thinking back, I remember July 2015, the Transports started to diverge aggressively lower even as the S&P was at the all-time highs. The first chart (Figure 8.19) shows the Transports (**gray** line) heading lower while the SPX (in black) stayed pinned to the highs.

Then the broader market cratered, catching up with the Transports. They moved together after that, too, with Transports continuing to show the way in both directions (see Figure 8.20).

Now Transports are ripping. This move in Transports makes me bullish equities (Figure 8.21).

For the record, February 2016 was a great time to turn bullish equities!

Be creative and find other ways to trade lead/lag. Wheat versus milk prices? Brent crude versus NYMEX crude? USDCAD against natural gas futures? Keep an open mind and logical correlations and relationships will come to you as you gain trading experience. But always remember that correlations are just one piece of the puzzle, not the Holy Grail.

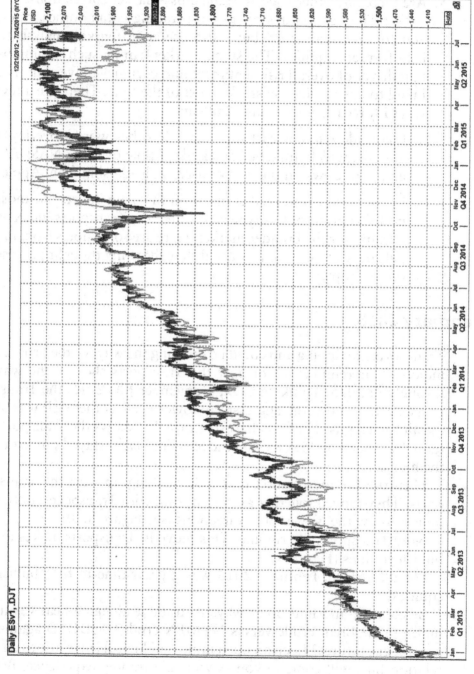

Figure 8.19 Daily SPX vs. Transports (gray), December 2013 to July 2015.

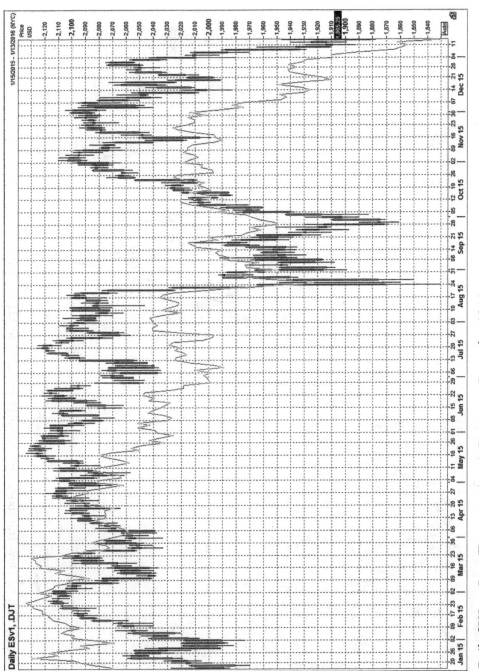

Figure 8.20 Daily SPX vs. Dow Transports (gray), January to December 2015.

UNDERSTAND CORRELATION AND INTERMARKET RELATIONSHIPS

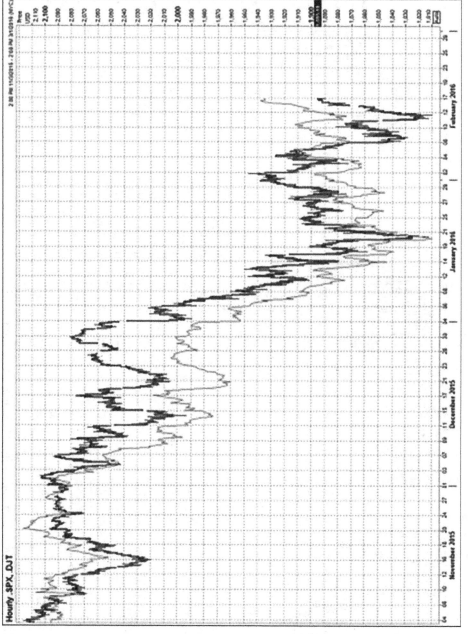

Figure 8.21 Hourly SPX vs. Dow Transports (gray), November 2015 to March 2016.

This completes our discussion of trading FX via correlation. Add lead/lag analysis to your toolbox and combine it with other techniques and tactics to find new and interesting trade ideas. Keep an open but simultaneously skeptical mind.

After reading this chapter, you should fully understand these key concepts:

- What is lead/lag trading and how does it work?

- What is correlation?

- How to find sensible cross-market relationships

- Coming up with your own ideas for correlation trades

- What are some limitations and problems with correlation trading?

Next up, we take on my favorite trading subject: behavioral finance.

CHAPTER 9

Understand Behavioral Finance

"Wouldn't economics make a lot more sense if it were based on how people actually behave, instead of how they should behave?"

Dan Ariely, *Predictably Irrational: The Hidden Forces That Shape Our Decisions*

■ Introduction

Until fairly recently, the study of finance was dominated by the view that in aggregate, rational self-interested humans make utility-maximizing decisions and this is the best explanation for how economies and markets work. This fit with the theory of efficient markets where price discovery is primarily the result of many well-informed, unemotional actors incorporating all available information and acting collectively to maximize their own utility and move prices toward equilibrium.

There is just one problem with this view: It does not reflect how humans behave on planet Earth. Anyone who has spent time on a trading floor or traded in real-life financial markets knows that the idea of rational, unemotional actors moving prices judiciously toward equilibrium is not how markets function in the short run.

In recent decades, many traders, economists, and academics have focused more on the irrational aspects of human behavior and how those irrational behaviors influence markets and create disequilibrium and opportunities for profit. This branch of study, called behavioral economics, helps bridge the gap between academic theory about financial markets and the practice of real-life trading.

Most non-academics understand that there is a significant behavioral element to price action on all but the longest time horizons. It is important for you to integrate an understanding of human behavior into your market analysis. Behavioral finance studies how human behavior and cognitive bias interacts with financial market pricing and leads investors to act in irrational (but potentially predictable) ways. Understanding and then anticipating this irrational behavior is an important way that traders can outperform in all financial markets, including FX.

Behavioral finance is a large, important, and relatively new field in economics and many, many works have been published on the subject in recent years. See the Further Reading section for some must-reads. For the purposes of this book, behavioral finance includes human psychology, market positioning, market sentiment, cognitive bias, feedback loops, and other individual human and group behavior characteristics that lead to price moves that cannot be explained by rational macro factors.

If you want to trade FX successfully on any time horizon, you need to understand behavioral finance. Please understand that behavioral finance is a large and expanding academic universe. I am boiling it down to one chapter of what I believe are the essential need-to-know elements for FX traders. I will inevitably leave out a lot of juicy detail. There are two sections laid out as follows:

1. Positioning and sentiment

2. Some important cognitive biases

■ Positioning and Sentiment

> *"You can't escape the madness of crowds by dogmatically rejecting them ... The most contrarian thing of all is not to oppose the crowd but to think for yourself."*
> – Peter Thiel, *Zero to One*

First of all, let me lead off by saying that it is key to understand that positioning and sentiment are part of the picture, *not the whole picture*. I emphasize this early on because I find that positioning and sentiment tend to be overrated in FX. Traders generally spend way too much time thinking about positioning and treat it like some sort of be-all and end-all.

It does not pay to be a reflexive contrarian all the time.

You will miss almost every major trend and you will find yourself fighting the fundamentals way too often. You analyze sentiment and positioning only to identify selective extremes when excessive positioning or sentiment pose outsized risks to the prevailing trend and justify taking a countertrend position.

Before we start on positioning and sentiment, it is important to understand the difference between the two. Many traders and analysts use the two terms interchangeably but they are not the same thing. Sentiment is how people view the market. If you take a poll of traders, you will get a sentiment reading. An example of this sort of reading is the Daily Sentiment Index (DSI) published by Jake Bernstein, which is a daily survey of retail futures traders.

On the other hand, positioning is a metric that measures *actual positions*. An example of this type of data is the Commitment of Traders report, which comes out every Friday and summarizes futures positions held by commercial and noncommercial traders.

You can have a market that is extremely bearish, but not heavily positioned and this is different from a market that is extremely bearish and extremely short. The difference is that the skew of future moves is completely different in the two situations. The reason is simple: A market that is bearish but not yet positioned is primed to go down as people take new positions to reflect their bearish view. On the other hand, a market that is bearish but heavily positioned short is more at risk of a short squeeze or reversal because there could be nobody left to sell.

Why would a market see extreme sentiment but no extreme positioning? There are many possible reasons. For example:

1. **The theme is new.** It takes a while for positions in one direction to become extreme. Sentiment moves faster than positioning. Many traders will build into a position as their conviction rises and as new information substantiates their view. As a general rule, sentiment leads positioning because it is faster and easier for a trader to get bearish than it is for her to put on a sizeable bearish trade.

2. **Major event risk upcoming.** This is one of the most common and highly profitable setups. Let's say the market is extremely bearish EURUSD but there is an ECB meeting or nonfarm payrolls coming up. Nobody wants to go into nonfarm payrolls short EURUSD because there is gap risk or event risk if the number is weak.[1]

   The moment the number comes out (assuming it is not extremely weak), the EUR will drop aggressively as traders

---

[1] Weak US data tend to lead to selling of USD, which is bullish for EURUSD.

put on the trade they wanted to have all along. Traders were just waiting for the event to get out of the way and did not really care about the outcome of the event. This can lead to surprising moves where you get, for example, a slightly weak US number (which should be bullish EURUSD) and EURUSD drops aggressively because traders care less about the number itself and more about the fact that the event risk is out of the way and now it's safer to get short EURUSD.

If you can identify moments where the market has a very strong view but does not have the position yet because they are waiting for an upcoming event to pass, you can often profit by simply putting on the position faster than others once the event is out of the way.

3. **Time of year.** A trader's risk appetite varies depending on her profitability and the time of year. For example, as we get close to the end of the year, traders like to reduce risk and book profits to start the new year with a clean slate. Therefore, you might see a situation at the end of the year where the market is extremely bullish USDJPY but flat because of an unwillingness to commit. In this case, the turn of the year could trigger substantial USDJPY buying even though nothing macro has changed between December 31 and January 1.

4. **Positioning clear-outs.** From time to time, crowded positions will get rinsed by sharp counter-moves. The market might hit a point where traders cannot take any more pain and the majority cut their losses. While they still hold the macro view, they cannot afford to hold the position any longer and so they cut it. This is called a stop loss run.

A good example of this is the price action in interest rate and FX markets in Fall 2014. Throughout 2014, the market was heavily positioned for higher US interest rates and a stronger dollar. In mid-October, however, the market started to lose faith in the interest rate trade as global and US inflation fell.

This reached a tipping point on October 15 as a weak US Retail Sales release was the final straw and the market stopped out of most of its dollar and interest rate positions all at once. In the weeks following this positioning wipeout, the market came to the conclusion that while US rates were not set to rise, the dollar should continue to benefit as the ECB and BOJ embarked on quantitative easing (QE) programs.

This led to a situation a few weeks later where the market was very bullish USD (sentiment) but flat (positioning) as they simply could not bring themselves to get long USD again as they were scarred by the pain of October 15. Once new catalysts pointed to further USD gains, the market went from extremely bullish and lightly positioned back to extremely bullish and extremely long USD and the dollar shot higher.

While sentiment and positioning move together, it is important to remember that they are not always the same thing. Most of the time sentiment and positioning will match fairly closely but it is the times when they do not match that can be most important.

Positioning

In FX, there are many proprietary positioning indicators published by the major banks and there is the Commitment of Traders (COT) report from the Chicago Mercantile Exchange (CME).

The COT report shows the positions for commercial and noncommercial currency traders as measured by reported positions in the futures markets. Futures markets represent a fairly small proportion of the FX market (around 10% of interbank volumes +/- depending on the estimate) but usually provide a decent snapshot of overall market positioning. Commercial traders are those using futures markets to hedge while noncommercial traders are usually speculators.

There are many potential sampling issues with the COT data (for example, it overrepresents carry, trend-following, and momentum traders) but it is still generally regarded as the best aggregate measure of FX positioning available. Have a look at how positioning and price move together (see Figure 9.1).

A few observations here:

1. Positions and price normally trend in the same direction. The market tends to follow the trend and tends to add to winning positions and reduce losing positions.

2. Positioning often leads price at turning points. If you look at the lows in mid-2012, for example, you can see that positioning (the gray line) led the move off the lows in spot (the black line). This is worth noting because you should always keep on the lookout for moments when price and positioning diverge. This is an early warning that a long-running and crowded trend is ready to turn.

3. Positioning can trend for a long time. The market took more than a year to get from the highs in positioning (and price) to the lows between May 2011 and June 2012.

4. Absolute levels of positioning mean less than the rate of change of positioning. In May 2010, you can see that short EUR positioning reached what was then an extreme level of more than 100,000 contracts. This then led to a very aggressive reversal

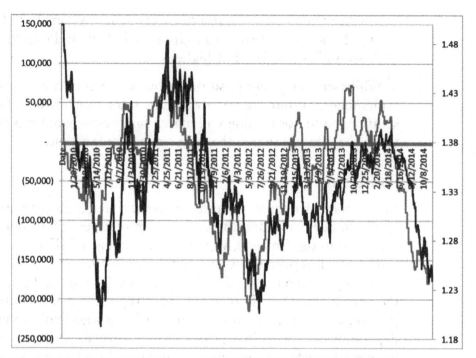

Figure 9.1 Daily EURUSD vs. COT NON-COMMERCIAL NET EUR
POSITION (gray), 2009 to 2014.

from 1.18 to 1.48 in EURUSD. The next time positioning reached
short 100,000 contracts (early 2012), many traders took that as
an indication that positioning again could go no further.

Positions then went from short 100,000 to more than 200,000
contracts and EURUSD kept going down from 1.28 to 1.22
before it bottomed. The overall size of FX markets varies
over time and positioning size can depend on many variables,
especially volatility. In less volatile markets, positions will tend
to get larger and when a theme is very popular and has a strong
macro logic, positions will get very large.

When you hear someone say that positioning is extreme, don't get
too excited. Usually all that means is that the market is in a strong
trend. Ask more questions: Can positioning get more extreme? How
long has it been extreme? Is the price continuing to go in favor of
those who are positioned with the trend (i.e., do price and positioning confirm each other?) Are the variables and narrative that led to
the big position still in play? Or are the fundamentals changing?
What upcoming catalysts could lead to a turn in positioning?

Simplistic views of positioning will always suggest that you take
the other side, but rarely is that approach profitable because trends
can last many months or even years. Most research shows that it
is generally more profitable to go *with* COT positioning, not go
against it.

While positioning data are important, my experience over the years is that well-informed observation can be more useful than any quantitative analysis of positioning. As a market maker, I have often noticed that you can get a good read on positioning by the number of enquiries you get as the market moves. You can get the same vibe on Twitter.

If people are generally asking "what the...?" about a move, or saying the move is "stupid" or "dumb" or "ridiculous," you can assume they are *not* on the winning side of the move. Similarly, if you are at a hedge fund and you get 11 different "BUY USDCAD!" recommendations in your inbox; you should probably hit a bid. The deeper your involvement in the market and the greater your experience level, the better your sense of positioning and sentiment.

As outlined in the example above, the most useful trading signals come when sentiment and positioning are both extreme and at a turning point. This is an important distinction because sentiment and positioning can remain extreme for a long time and it is often when they are pinned to an extreme that you get the juiciest and most aggressive part of a trending move.

If you're going to trade sentiment and positioning successfully, you need to identify moments when sentiment and positioning are both extreme and then wait for signs that they are starting to turn. In other words, when price is going up and sentiment is becoming less bullish, there could be an outstanding opportunity to take the other side.

As a general rule, FX pairs tend to be in one of the following six states:

SENTIMENT	BULL MARKET	BEAR MARKET
HIGH and STABLE	Bullish	
HIGH and RISING	Very bullish	
HIGH but FALLING	BEARISH	
LOW and STABLE		Bearish
LOW and FALLING		Very bearish
LOW but RISING		BULLISH

You will rarely see, for example, a situation with falling prices and bullish sentiment because sentiment almost always follows price. If you are looking to use sentiment to take the other side of a trend, your best bet is to look for the conditions marked in bold all caps in the table above: situations where sentiment diverges from the price action.

Ideally, you get a sense of this not just from the data but also from talking to other traders and reading blogs and media reports about the FX market. If you are a professional FX trader with access to direct market information, quite often you can feel a turn in sentiment before it shows up in the data; this will help you get ahead of the crowd.

Another way to pick a top or bottom in price is to identify situations where sentiment readings are extreme and then wait for a reversal formation such as a shooting star or bear hammer. This is a great way to trade sentiment because you remain very patient, recognizing that high sentiment readings are a standard part of a bull market; then when you see a bearish technical setup, you pounce.

The theory is that the elevated sentiment and positioning readings will fuel the correction that you have been waiting for. I must emphasize once again, though: *Never* sell just because "the market's long." That is a recipe for failure in trading and will constantly put you at odds with the prevailing trend. Look for points when positioning is extreme *and* fundamentals are turning *and* positioning is turning *and* there is a clear technical reversal pattern. Then you have a Five-Star setup.

■ Cognitive Bias

Many academics and market practitioners believe that the main source of inefficiency in financial markets is irrational human behavior. I agree. The idea of markets populated by totally rational actors trying to maximize their wealth is complete nonsense to anyone who has ever traded real financial markets.

There are many, many explanations for how and why investors act irrationally. It is important to understand these types of bias for two reasons: (1) so that you can see others acting irrationally and capitalize on it and (2) so that you can recognize yourself acting irrationally and stop it.

Here is a list of important cognitive biases that influence trader and market behavior:

- Confirmation

- Overconfidence

- Extrapolation

- Asymmetric loss aversion

- Greed and fear

- Anchoring

- Round number

- Favorite/longshot

- Herding

Confirmation Bias

Confirmation bias is the single most important bias to understand because it can distort and impair your decision making at crucial moments. This bias is the phenomenon where humans tend to absorb and internalize information that confirms their beliefs and ignore or discount information that contradicts their beliefs or hypothesis.

Confirmation bias is prevalent both in financial markets and in the outside world but I focus here on confirmation bias as it pertains to trading. Confirmation bias generally means that if you are bullish, you will be very open to good news but you will tend to downplay, question, or ignore bearish information. I have seen this many, many times in my own trading and in the trading of others. *You believe what you want to believe.* Check out this quote from Charles Darwin:

> "I had, also, during many years, followed a golden rule, namely, that whenever a published fact, a new observation or thought came across me, which was opposed to my general results, to make a memorandum of it without fail and at once; for I had found by experience that such facts and thoughts were far more apt to escape from memory than favorable ones."
> – Charles Darwin, *The Life and Letters of Charles Darwin*

Confirmation bias can often be seen clearly when economic data are released. Economic releases often consist of a headline number plus a bunch of details. The monthly nonfarm payrolls release (for example) is made up of a headline number (net change in nonfarm payrolls) and a bunch of details (unemployment rate, hours worked, average hourly earnings). I have often seen traders go into the release hoping for a strong number, and when the headline number comes out weak you hear:

"But wait! Look at the details! The details are strong! Ignore the weak headline!"

And then the next month they are looking for a strong number again and the headline is strong and the details are weak and the trader can't stop hollering about how strong the headline is... while completely ignoring the details! This is classic confirmation bias.

Another way that confirmation bias plays out is when traders go searching for information that supports a weak starting hypothesis. A trader might be bullish AUD in her gut but she has no good thesis yet. So she starts scanning through charts to support the idea. "Wow, this chart looks super-bullish!" is usually the eventual result as she keeps changing time horizons and rescaling overlays and drawing trendlines and Fibonacci levels until she finds a chart that supports her view.

The only true antidote to confirmation bias is to get flat. It is critically important to understand the *power of flat*. Only when you are totally flat can you process incoming information with zero bias. It is important to truly understand and believe that. No matter how smart you are, no matter how self-aware, everyone is subject to confirmation bias. Do not think you are exempt. Flat is a position. A good position.

When you see incoming news, be aware of your own thought process. Is everybody interpreting the news as bullish and you see it as bearish? That is a sign you may be falling victim to confirmation bias. Clearly, it is good to be an independent thinker, so just because everyone disagrees with you that doesn't mean you are wrong. It just means you need to be careful. When there are conflicting views flying around, somebody is wrong. Is it you?

If you are confused ... get flat.

Rule #7 of FX Trading: Flat is the strongest position. When in doubt, get out.

Overconfidence Bias

There is one simple stat that explains overconfidence bias perfectly: Studies show that *70% to 90% of all Americans think they are above-average drivers*. Overconfidence bias exists in many areas, including investing.

I ran a survey in AM/FX in 2014 and 70% of my readers responded that they are "better than average" or "way better than average" traders while just 5% said they were "below average." A 2006 study by James Montier showed that 74% of fund managers believe they are above average. Reading these studies makes me 120% sure that you are sometimes overconfident, too.

Overconfidence bias is important because if you are overconfident, you are probably blind to your weaknesses and overestimate your edge. This can lead to all sorts of faulty behaviors such as overtrading, confirmation bias, and improper position sizing.

Recognize that you are not the only smart person in the world and be alert to signs that you may be overconfident in your view. Consider alternative hypotheses. Be confident in your view but remain open to other viewpoints. Remember that you are human.

Extrapolation Bias (or Recency Bias)

One could write an entire book on the topic of extrapolation bias but the gist of it is that people tend to assume that whatever is happening right now will continue to happen in the future. Traders overemphasize recent price action and the current theme and fail to see new themes that could be just around the corner. Forecasters are guiltiest of this but traders fall victim as well. A great example of this was seen in the crude oil market in 2013–2015. Here's what a leading investment bank had to say in August 2013 with oil trading around $110:

> "The disruptions in Libyan oil supplies have lasted far longer than we initially thought with no near-term resolution in sight, which was further complicated by the involvement of the military late last week," said [the analyst] in a new note to clients. "Combined with the ongoing problems in Iraq which we see extending into the autumn, OPEC outages since the beginning of the summer have taken 33 million barrels off the market, which was further exacerbated by a 32 million barrel downward revision to total OECD petroleum inventories by the IEA."
>
> "In our view, these developments will likely lend support to Brent prices around the $115.00/bbl level in the very near term," he said.

And then as you might be aware, in 2014 oil collapsed from $110 to $50. Here's an update from early 2015 as the same analyst then confidently justifies a lower forecast:

> "To accommodate the substantial expected first half inventory build and using the storage arbitrage to the one-year ahead swap, we are revising down our 3-, 6- and 12-month price forecasts for Brent to $42, $43 and $70 respectively, from $80, $85 and $90," the bank said in a report by [the same analyst].
>
> "While history would suggest that a storage blow-out would push spot prices below $35, we believe that by avoiding breaching storage capacity, the market will hover around $40, potentially dipping at times into the high $30s which we see as the likely lows of this cycle," the report said.

Figure 9.2 presents this in a chart.

The point here isn't to say that this analyst or investment bank is bad at forecasting. The point is that humans in general are bad at forecasting. We tend to overweight recent information and assume that whatever is going on right now will continue into the future. When oil is collapsing, it is very hard to imagine a scenario where it turns back around.

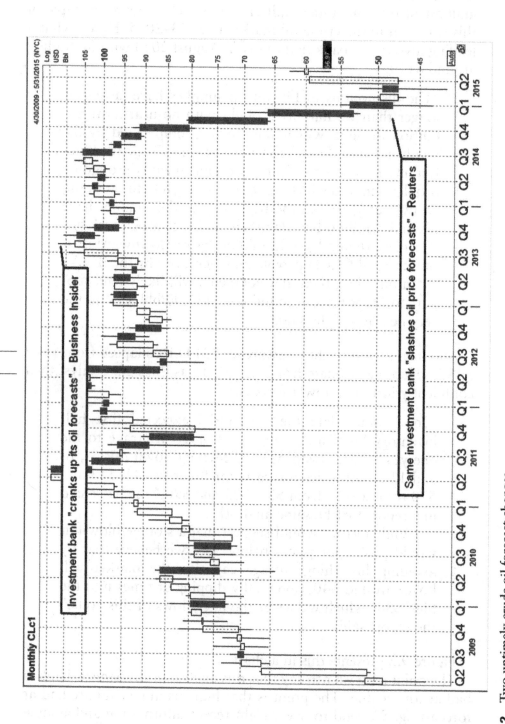

Figure 9.2 Two untimely crude oil forecast changes.

http://www.businessinsider.com/goldman-raises-oil-price-target-2013-8 http://www.reuters.com/article/2015/01/12/us-research-goldmansachs-crude-idUSKBN0KL0RR20150112

Extrapolation bias leads to all sorts of bad trading behaviors and provides an important part of the overall explanation for why individual investors consistently underperform the market.[2] When individual stocks or the overall market are up, investors buy on the belief that the rally will continue. When stocks are selling off, investors sell on the assumption that the moves will continue.

The antidote to extrapolation bias is an open mind. Think independently and question whether a continuation of the current trend and economic narrative makes sense. Is it fully priced in? Has the market overshot? If the market has been talking about the same theme for six months and a currency pair has moved 20% on the back of that theme, maybe it's time to be wary?

It is easy to get caught up in a theme for too long, especially when the price action supports it. Think for yourself. Read everything you can but trade your own view, not someone else's. Ignore professional forecasters as much as possible as they will constantly adjust their forecast as spot moves. As my friend Jared Dillian once put it: Read many, respect few.

A classic example of extrapolation bias in the FX market is when USDJPY rallied from 75 to 120 in the 2012/2014 period. The BOJ started a massive quantitative easing program in 2012 and this pushed the yen down (and USDJPY up) steadily for 2+ years. When the move started, most forecasters correctly predicted yen weakness on the back of BOJ action and set targets for 2015 of 100 or 105. When USDJPY reached 100, however, instead of declaring mission accomplished, almost every forecaster then raised their forecast for USDJPY to 105 or 110. When USDJPY hit 110, they raised their forecast to 120. At 120 they wheeled out a 130 forecast. The higher USDJPY goes, the higher the forecasts go so the forecasts tend to have no meaning or predictive power whatsoever.

The direction of the forecast and the underlying logic often have some use but the point estimates are meaningless and subject to constant revision. You can see in Figure 9.3 that if you simply took USDJPY spot and multiplied it by 1.08, you would get a good estimate of where the professional forecasters saw USDJPY ending 2015.

The inverse of extrapolation bias is the Gambler's Fallacy. This is the assumption that many gamblers make where they see a roulette wheel land on red 10 straight times and thus expect the next spin to land on black. This is wrong because each spin of the roulette wheel is an independent (mutually exclusive) event. You will sometimes hear arguments like "Euro is down seven days in a row, you have

[2]https://www.qidllc.com/wp-content/uploads/2016/02/2016-Dalbar-QAIB-Report.pdf.

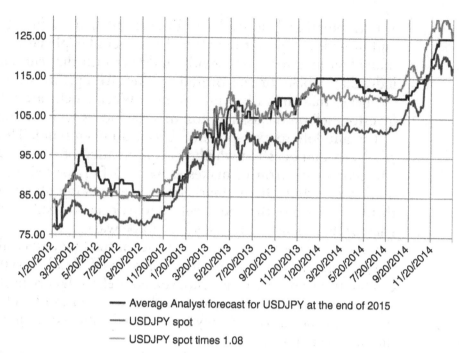

Figure 9.3   USDJPY spot vs. forecast, 2012 to 2014.

to be long!" Umm, no. No you don't. Extrapolation is much more common than the Gambler's Fallacy in FX markets.

Asymmetric Loss Aversion

A significant body of research shows that humans feel more pain from losses than they feel joy from wins in a ratio of about 2:1. We will go out of our way to avoid losses whenever possible. Humans will also take more risk to avoid a loss than they will take in pursuit of gains. If you are a human, it is important that you understand this fundamental quirk in the human psyche as it leads to all sorts of suboptimal behavior.

The most important behavioral issue that arises from loss aversion is that traders find it hard to exit losing positions because once they exit the position the loss becomes crystallized and thus real and irreversible. If you hold onto (or double down) on a position, you might get back to flat or even make money on the trade, but once you cut out, the trade is over. You're a loser. Nobody likes a loser.

But the thing is: Most successful traders take many, many small losses and achieve fewer but larger gains. So you need to turn off this instinctive loss aversion and embrace the idea of taking frequent but small losses. You need to ride your profitable trades and get out of your losers as quickly as possible. When you take a loss after hitting a predetermined stop loss level, try to pat yourself on the back. Say, "Good, another small loss. I am sticking to my plan and showing

The chart legend reads:
— Average Analyst forecast for USDJPY at the end of 2015
— USDJPY spot
— USDJPY spot times 1.08

solid discipline." We will discuss this concept more in Chapter 14, "Common Weaknesses in Trading."

Loss aversion also leads to a strange psychological asymmetry where you will find that the joy you feel on your up days is half as strong as the pain you feel on your down days. Over the course of many years, this can lead to trader burnout. Let yourself to be happy. It is simply too exhausting to be either (a) bummed out because you lost money or (b) afraid to be happy when you're making money because you don't want to jinx it.

It is okay to be happy when you are making money (just not too happy)!

If you are interested in reading more about loss aversion, check out the classic 1984 paper from Kahneman and Tversky or *Thinking Fast and Slow* by Daniel Kahneman (http://dirkbergemann .commons.yale.edu/files/kahnemann-1984-choices-values-frames .pdf).

Emotions: Greed and Fear

Emotional decision making leads to suboptimal outcomes and creates frequent periods of extreme inefficiency in the market. Greed and fear are such powerful forces that they can be the primary (or only) market driver at times. Economics and fundamentals can go completely out the window when people hit extreme levels of greed or fear. You need to recognize these moments and take the other side.

A strong battery of quantitative measures for evaluating prices can be a key tool for avoiding greed and fear extremes. For example, the large price move on volume spike discussed in Chapter 7 is an example of using quantitative analysis to identify peak moments of fear or greed.

Professional traders with experience can sometimes feel these extremes by observing the behavior of those around them, from watching price action, and from the overall electricity in the market. I remember in 2008 there were many moments when the guano was hitting the fan and everyone on the trading floor was freaking out. You could feel these frenzies reach a fever pitch and then when the volume and electricity started to subside, just a little, it was always a fantastic short-term buying opportunity.

One piece of advice when you are taking the other side of a market that is gripped by extreme fear or greed: Make sure your position is not too big. Smaller positions allow you to ride out the extra volatility that usually accompanies highly emotional market moves.

As the mother of all bias, emotion leads to many interesting market tendencies and helps explain why there are many, many times when you will hear a trader screaming "THIS MAKES NO SENSE!"

Remember: It doesn't have to make sense; quite often, it won't! Markets are driven by much, much more than economic fundamentals or logic.

Greed and fear can create feedback loops between news and price as news causes price to move and then price moves cause new behavior as traders react not to the news but to the move in the price itself. As prices fall, other sellers come into the market either willingly (as they fear prices will fall even lower) or unwillingly (because of margin calls or a shoulder tap from their boss).

Feedback loops are endogenous drivers of price action and can drive markets in one direction for much longer than anyone would rationally expect.[3] This leads to what is known as overshooting. This type of overextension is common and FX rates are notorious for overshooting on all time horizons.

Warren Buffett said it best: "Be fearful when others are greedy and greedy when others are fearful." The only thing I would add is: Make sure your position is sized correctly or you will be adding to the feedback loop when your stop loss order is triggered. There is much more on position sizing and risk management in Part Three.

Anchoring

Anchoring is another behavioral bias that is hard to avoid. Quite often, even when I know I am anchoring, I have trouble ignoring the anchor and behaving rationally. The concept of anchoring says that once a human being is given an initial starting number for something that they are trying to estimate or value, they have a hard time moving away from that starting point. Here's an excerpt from the Wikipedia entry on anchoring:

> The anchoring and adjustment heuristic was first theorized by Amos Tversky and Daniel Kahneman. In one of their first studies, participants were asked to compute, within 5 seconds, the product of the numbers one through eight, either as $1 \times 2 \times 3 \times 4 \times 5 \times 6 \times 7 \times 8$ or reversed as $8 \times 7 \times 6 \times 5 \times 4 \times 3 \times 2 \times 1$. Because participants did not have enough time to calculate the full answer, they had to make an estimate after their first few multiplications. When these first multiplications gave a small answer—because the sequence started with small numbers—the median estimate was 512; when the

---

[3] *Endogenous* means "from within" and so endogenous drivers like feedback loops are different from exogenous (aka external) drivers like economic data or central bank actions and often much more difficult to identify or understand.

sequence started with the larger numbers, the median estimate was 2,250. (The correct answer was 40,320.) In another study by Tversky and Kahneman, participants observed a roulette wheel that was predetermined to stop on either 10 or 65. Participants were then asked to guess the percentage of the United Nations that were African nations. Participants whose wheel stopped on 10 guessed lower values (25% on average) than participants whose wheel stopped at 65 (45% on average).[4] The pattern has held in other experiments for a wide variety of different subjects of estimation.

Anchoring influences many areas of economics, especially finance and marketing. In investing, anchoring makes it difficult for traders and investors to sell an asset below the price they initially paid for it. For example, you buy EURUSD at 1.1633 and then two minutes later, you change your mind. If it's trading at 1.1638, you probably just hit a bid, but if EURUSD is trading 1.1631, your first instinct will probably be to try to get out at 1.1633 or better on a small bounce. This is not rational. The market doesn't care where you got in, and neither should you.

You will see this bias again and again as it infects both short-term traders and long-term investors. How many times have you heard yourself or another trader say something like: "I'll just wait 'til I get back to flat. Then I'll cut this position for sure. I promise!" Be aware that just because you bought EURUSD at 1.1633 doesn't mean the market will go back there when you change your mind. If you change your mind on a position, get out. Do not wait for it to get back to your entry level. Just get out.

Round Number Bias

Round number bias is less important than other types of bias outlined above but it is nevertheless interesting and worth knowing about. Humans behave as though round numbers are more important than non-round numbers. If you don't believe me, next time you are meeting someone tell them, "I'll be there in 19 minutes!" It sounds weird even though it is not appreciably different in any way from the normal-sounding "I'll be there in 20 minutes!" Humans just prefer round numbers.

Round number bias shows up frequently in financial markets. In FX markets, for example, most hedgers and investors will naturally leave their orders on the round numbers, preferring 50 to 49

---

[4]http://www.its.caltech.edu/~camerer/Ec101/JudgementUncertainty.pdf.

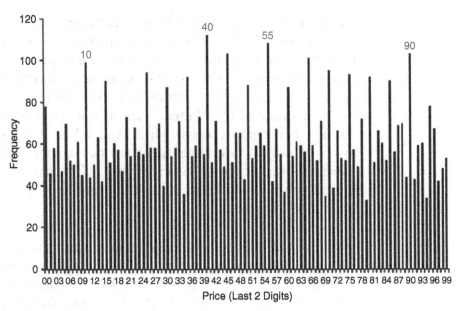

Figure 9.4 Last two digits of the highs and lows in EURUSD since inception.
I only used data from 1999 to 2011 because EBS went to half pips after that.

or 00 to 99 for no rational reason. Going through all the daily highs and lows in EURUSD from 1999 to 2011, you get the distribution seen in Figure 9.4.

If you analyze any other currency, the distribution looks about the same, with clustering of highs and lows on the round numbers.

Why are round numbers more likely to be highs and lows? There are two reasons: (1) Less sophisticated market players tend to leave take profit orders on the round numbers just because of human nature. It feels kind of weird to leave a bid at 52 so customers just generally leave the bid at 50 instead. (2) Barriers and option strikes are usually on round numbers and so bids and offers tend to cluster there.

The takeaway for short-term FX traders is that you should assume extra stickiness at the round numbers and put your orders on the appropriate side. If you are trying to buy the dip, for example, put your bids at 03 or 01, not 99 or 97. On the other hand, if you are leaving a sell stop, put it below 00, not just above. If you find this topic interesting, here are some links for additional reading on round number bias:

http://www.michiganjb.org/issues/62/text62b.pdf
http://faculty.chicagobooth.edu/devin.pope/research/pdf/Website_Round%20Numbers.pdf
http://www.newyorkfed.org/research/staff_reports/sr150.pdf
http://www.psyfitec.com/2010/02/irrational-numbers-price-clustering.html

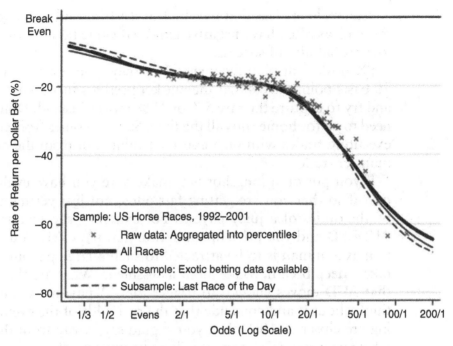

Figure 9.5 Rate of return of horse racing win bets, by odds.

https://www.jstor.org/stable/10.1086/655844?seq=1#page_scan_tab_contents

Favorite/Longshot Bias

Favorite/longshot bias is another human trait that you need to be aware of when trading, especially when trading options. Human beings overvalue longshots and undervalue favorites because:

a. The perceived asymmetry provided by the respective payouts makes the longshot look good.

b. Humans tend to overweight small probabilities.

In other words, longshots are tempting because of the high pay-off odds but are generally bad value because people systematically overpay for them and overestimate the chance they will pay off. Figure 9.5 shows what this bias looks like in horse racing, where betting on favorites is expected to cost you about 10% of your money in the long run while betting on longshots gives you expected losses closer to 80%!

One way this bias manifests in financial markets is through a consistent bias to overpay for tail options and tail trades that offer high leverage. Tail options also tend to be overpriced because there is no natural seller, but always plenty of natural buyers. So not only are out-of-the-money options more expensive than in-the-money options, the more out of the money you get, the more you have to pay in transaction costs and skew to get the trade done. Another way of saying this is that the market loves to buy lottery tickets and hates selling them.

Traders love ideas that pay 10:1 or 20:1 but fail to recognize that those ideas often have negative expected value because of their very low probability of success.

FX traders display this bias when they ignore the routine 50 to 70 basis point moves that the market presents just about every day and try to capture the rare 5% or 10% moves instead. Don't feel the need to go for home runs all the time. Success comes from repeatedly executing trades with high expected value, not from the occasional monster trade.

If you put on a longshot bet, make sure you have evaluated the payoff so that you are getting fair odds, not just getting sucked in by the optics of a juicy payout. For example, say you are bearish AUDUSD and you price up an option that pays 7:1. Your gut reaction as a human is to be attracted to such a large payout ratio. But take a deep breath. Make a fair assessment. What are the true odds that AUD moves enough to trigger the 7:1 payout? Clearly if you think about it and conclude that the real odds of the event happening are closer to 10:1, then you should stay away from the option, whether or not a 7:1 payout will make your year!

Herding Bias

Herding bias directly impacts economists, investors, and traders on all time horizons. The simple explanation of this form of bias is that for most people it is safer to be wrong with everyone else than to try to be right on your own.

If every other trader you work with is long dollars, can you be comfortable short dollars? Most traders (if they were being honest) would say no. It's easier to run with the pack. If everyone is wrong and loses money, you can easily justify your poor performance but if everyone has the big trade on and you miss it, you feel like a donut.

In a world of perfectly rational economic actors, there would be no need to worry about what your boss will think of your positions or whether your investors will think you are an idiot for going against a long-running and supposedly logical market trend. But in the real world, there are plenty of non-economic reasons that people trade, and a big one is to manage career risk by staying with the crowd.

You see the same phenomenon with economists. If every big-name economist on Wall Street is predicting higher US interest rates, an economist needs to have extremely high conviction to publicly predict lower rates. Yes, if he's right, he might be celebrated, but if he's wrong, he looks bad and his job could be in jeopardy. And he probably has a wife and kids and a mortgage payment to worry about!

There are examples of this type of behavior everywhere in FX but a great one is 2010–2011 when every investor in the world dumped their Eurozone assets. Yes, it was a scary time for Eurozone assets as the Greek and PIIGS crisis sent shockwaves around the world. But the selling of European assets was greatly exacerbated because investors figured: "If I hold onto my European assets and they bounce back, I will outperform the index and get paid a little more" versus "If I hold onto my European assets and the Eurozone breaks up, I will be fired for not protecting my investors against a known risk."

Even if a money manager felt that the market was overreacting to the European crisis and felt European assets were discounted to unrealistic or cheap levels, they made the personal calculation to manage their career risk. They decided it was better to sell like everyone else rather than risk a career-ending loss in the unlikely event that Mario Draghi failed to do whatever it takes.

Another important instance of herding occurs when economists forecast economic data. Let's say you are an economist and your job is to predict next month's US Retail Sales figure. You have been looking at your handy-dandy models and you see that all signs point to a very strong number next month. A normal month's release for Retail Sales is in the range of –1.0% to +1.0% but your model is saying a good estimate for this month's release might be closer to +2.5%. You have a peek at other economist forecasts and see that the highest forecast is +1.1%. Suddenly, you feel like your +2.5% estimate might be a tad extreme. Why bother going so far away from the rest of the forecasts? Might as well just submit a forecast of 1.2%. Maybe 1.3%. You are still the highest forecast but you don't look too stupid if the number comes in weak.

Evidence supports the idea that economic forecasters herd around the mean and fail to forecast large economic surprises in either direction despite the fact these surprises are common. Figure 9.6 shows the distribution of economists' estimates for Retail Sales from 2010 to 2014 versus the actual distribution of the data releases. You can see that in general, forecasts are clustered in a tighter range than the real data and economists don't forecast extremes very often compared to reality.

This is rational behavior if you are an economist who does not want to look stupid or get fired, but as a trader you need to be aware that economic data are distributed in a less normal way than economists' forecasts would imply. Economic numbers, like financial market returns, are not normally distributed—they have fat tails. A lack of imagination can catch you by surprise and so you should always remember that anything can happen, even if nobody is forecasting it!

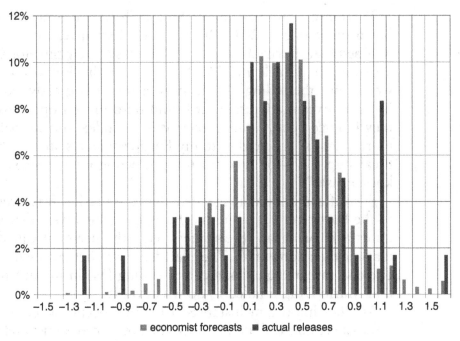

Figure 9.6 Distribution of economist forecasts and actual releases of US Retail Sales, 2010 to 2014.

■ Conclusion

In the end, many of the types of bias that I describe are similar or interrelated and come down to one fact: From time to time, individual humans act in a way that is not rational. And as a group, humans can sometimes act in totally insane ways.

Markets are made up of fallible, irrational human beings with imperfect information. These human beings are emotional and constantly scrambling to maximize their wealth, protect their families from ruin, and avoid getting fired. Investors pivot frequently from emphasizing return on capital to worrying about return *of* capital and these oscillations between fear and greed are punctuated by short and temporary periods of sane equilibrium.

This leads to all manner of wild, herd-like, and irrational behaviors and these behaviors create all sorts of price distortions, dislocations, and overshooting in the market. If you understand behavioral FX, you will sometimes find yourself on the winning side of these dislocations. Instead of acting as part of the feedback loop problem, you will be greedy when others are fearful and take the other side. You will be a strong hand, not a weak one.

Good trading takes courage.

UNDERSTAND BEHAVIORAL FINANCE

Anecdotal Evidence

Anecdotal evidence is any information you gather by personal observation or from one-off stories. It is fun, but also usually unscientific and often unreliable. There is a wide range of anecdotal evidence you can incorporate into your analysis of the financial markets and use to confirm existing views or establish new conclusions.

There is a saying that the plural of *anecdote* is not *data* and like most sayings, it contains some truth. The risk with anecdotal evidence is that it is fraught with the potential for sample size issues, confirmation bias, and other types of prejudice. This is because the anecdotes you choose to focus on could be biased either by your preexisting views, by regional idiosyncrasies,[5] or by other factors. The advantage of anecdotal evidence is that it can be observed in real time and can be easy to understand, logical, intuitive, and sometimes obvious proof of sentiment extremes.

First, let's look at the Magazine Cover Indicator, an anecdotal indicator that is well known, logical, and effective. The indicator says that when a financial story or market theme is displayed on the cover of a magazine, that theme or the related trend is near exhaustion. In other words, magazine covers are reverse indicators.

Two famous examples of this phenomenon are when the cover of *Business Week* hollered: "The Death of Equities," right as the stock market made a major bottom in August 1979 (Figure 9.7) and when the *Economist* proclaimed the world to be "Drowning in Oil" just as oil bottomed in 1999 (Figure 9.8).

Two other well-known examples of the Magazine Cover Indicator are the appearance of Jeff Bezos as *Time* magazine's Person of the Year in 2000 just before the tech bubble burst (Figure 9.9) and Russian President Vladimir Putin as Person of the Year in 2007 right before the collapse of oil brought down the Russian economy.

The premise behind the indicator is that when a journalist or editor finally devotes a cover to a market trend, company, country, or person, the story or theme has been in the market for some time and is likely past its peak. Positioning and sentiment should already fully reflect the story on the cover of the publication. In other words, by the time a magazine features a trend, it is not news. The story is priced in.

---

[5] An example of the regional issue is that many people living in New York City observed the bustling restaurants and packed shops and concluded that the US economy was on the mend in 2010. On the contrary, it was probably foreign shoppers, a rebound in the finance industry, and worsening income inequality that caused the economic boom in New York while the rest of the United States languished, underemployed in the new normal.

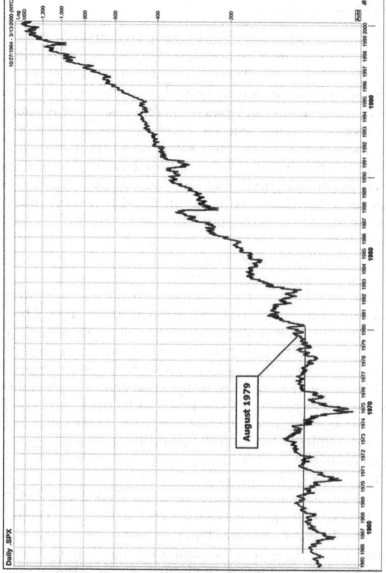

Figure 9.7 S&P 500, 1965 to 2000.

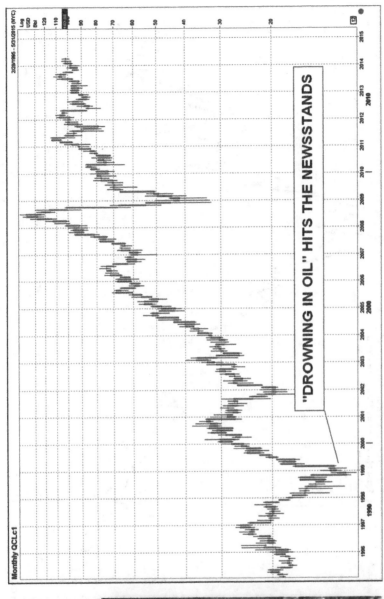

Figure 9.8   Crude oil, 1990 to 2016.

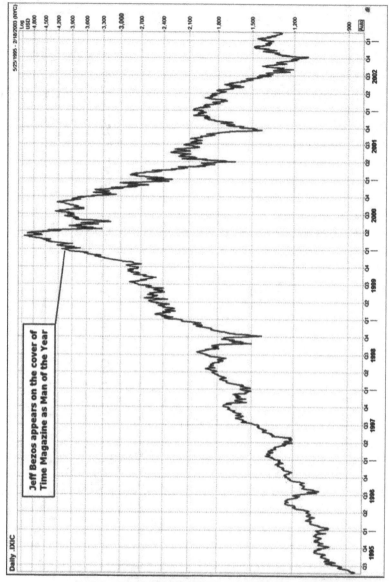

Figure 9.9 Daily NASDAQ Composite 1995 to 2003.

My former colleague Greg Marks and I researched this phenomenon and found that there does tend to be a major reversal in a market after it is featured on the cover of the *Economist*. We found that *Economist* covers that express a strong bias toward an asset or asset class are a reverse indicator one year later about 68% of the time.[6]

■ The Skyscraper Indicator

The Skyscraper Indicator suggests that when a country builds the world's tallest skyscraper, it is a sign of overconfidence and a potentially imminent financial crisis. Countries build world-record-setting skyscrapers only during bull markets when credit is plentiful, and thus historically there have been many instances where the country building the world's tallest skyscraper subsequently fell upon hard times.

Some salient examples are 1929, The Empire State Building (followed by Great Depression); 1972, the World Trade Center and Sears Tower (1970s stagflation); 1997, the Petronas Tower (Asian Financial Crisis); and 2005, the Burj Dubai (real estate collapse and financial crisis). The indicator doesn't produce many signals, of course, but it has an impressive track record. An interesting academic paper on the topic can be found at http://mises.org/journals/qjae/pdf/qjae8_1_4.pdf.

Instead of focusing on a single anecdotal indicator, you can also observe extremes in sentiment when many anecdotes come together at once. A good example of this was in 2007, when fears of a dollar collapse raged because of the twin US deficits (trade deficit and budget deficit) and massive dollar selling by central banks like China and Saudi Arabia. The following three anecdotes appeared around the same time:

1. November 6, 2007: Supermodel Gisele Bunchen asks for her contracts to be modified and paid in euros instead of dollars.

2. November 17, 2007: In his new rap video, Jay-Z is featured making it rain euro notes instead of the traditional Benjamins (US dollars).

3. November 2007: This meme goes viral:

The EUR hit an all-time high shortly after these three anecdotes circulated. The weak dollar was part of the mainstream narrative

---

[6]https://www.economist.com/buttonwoods-notebook/2016/10/26/are-magazine-covers-a-contrarian-indicator.

and these anecdotes were evidence that the theme was popular, well known, priced in, and at risk of turning stale. The dollar peaked four months later and the EUR never traded higher again.

One major caveat here (and a recurring theme when dealing with anecdotal evidence) is that EURUSD was 1.4800 in November 2007 and went all the way to 1.6040 before it finally peaked. It then sold off aggressively to close 2008 around 1.2500.

In this case, the anecdotal evidence provided an accurate but not timely signal of excessive bullish EURUSD sentiment (see Figure 9.10). The pair went 12 big figures higher over six months before finally crashing, so anyone who went short on the anecdotal evidence had to endure a lot of pain. This is typical. Quite often the last wave of euphoria is the most violent and the most obviously extreme sentiment period with the most anecdotal evidence of euphoria or despair.

Overall, anecdotal evidence is interesting and fun and can be a useful input into your big-picture macro analysis. Just be aware that anecdotal evidence is unscientific and fraught with pitfalls. The power of contrarian anecdotes tends to be evident in hindsight but my experience is that people are constantly pointing out anecdotal evidence to support their contrary view during strong trends and some of it works, and some of it doesn't.

Don't get too excited about anecdotes. Treat them as one extremely fascinating but not very predictive input into your process. Those with experience will recognize when history repeats or rhymes and anecdotes from the present market will match past anecdotes and help the experienced trader to see patterns that may have some forecasting value. If you find yourself thinking, "I've seen this movie before," you probably have.

A good example of anecdotal evidence successfully calling a top was the bitcoin bubble in December 2017. The anecdotal evidence of the bitcoin bubble was so obvious and so similar to the crazy stories I lived through in 1999 that it became obvious at that point the bitcoin story was set to pop. This is not a hindsight call; I (and many others) identified the absurdity of the cryptobubble in December 2017 using mostly anecdotal evidence.

A more robust approach to anecdotal evidence collects data in various ways (by adding up the number of bullish articles on the front page of the WSJ versus the number of bearish articles, for example) to avoid sample size and confirmation bias pitfalls. This approach is sensible and many natural language approaches are currently in use to extract sentiment from Twitter and other newsfeeds.

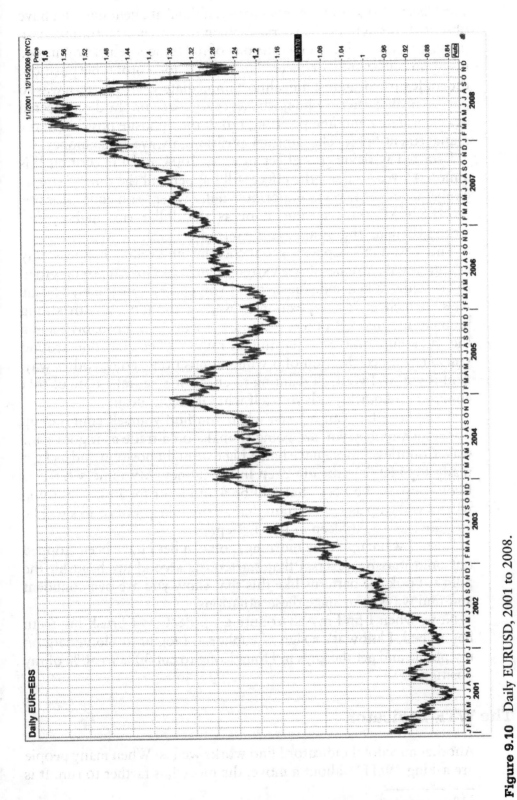

Figure 9.10 Daily EURUSD, 2001 to 2008.

Anecdotal evidence of extreme bullish sentiment was piling up by November 2007 but the high came 6 months and 12 big figures later.

UNDERSTAND BEHAVIORAL FINANCE

The Cheer Hedge

The Cheer Hedge is an interesting psychological phenomenon I have observed throughout the years. Early in my career as a trading desk manager, I noticed that any time one of my traders yelled or pumped his fist in celebration, or cheered in any way for a profitable position, the trade turned against him almost immediately. This pattern was so persistent that after a while, whenever someone on the desk cheered or celebrated a winning position, I took the opposite position in my management book. The contrary positions always made money.

I started noticing this effect in early 2004 and I'm writing this almost 15 years later—the effect still happens all the time. Extreme exuberance is a very important tell. When someone screams "AMERICA!" on a trading floor as the dollar rips higher after strong US data, that is always the intraday high!

The reason this happens is that cheering and yelling happens only at emotional extremes. Price extremes and emotional extremes tend to coincide. When someone around you cheers, most likely (1) she feels invincible as her position is well in the money with strong momentum, and (2) others around the world are probably feeling the same euphoria. So keep this in mind: When someone around you cheers in celebration of a winning position—go the other way. And if you feel yourself wanting to cheer or sing, take note of that emotion and quickly ask yourself what it might mean.

A similar effect can be seen when you find yourself counting up how much money you are going to make on a trade as it goes your way. Countless times I have had a big overnight position and as I get ready for bed, it's already deep in the money. My mind whirrs as I count up all the P&L that will be waiting for me in the morning when I wake up as I am certain that all my take profit orders will be executed while I'm deep in REM sleep.

When I wake up in the morning, you can bet I have been stopped out on a massive reversal that started the second my head hit the pillow. Look for patterns like this that show you are overconfident and find ways to manage these situations.

Now, when I find myself counting up P&L as I brush my teeth before bed, I know it's a sign of euphoria. I log in to Bloomberg on my phone and get the guys in Hong Kong to cut 30% to 50% of my positions.

The WTF Indicator

Another anecdotal indicator I find works well is: When many people are asking "WTF"[7] about a move, the move has farther to run. It is

---

[7] What the fudge!

easiest to observe this if you work at a bank because you receive incoming calls from clients, but if you trade from home, this can be surmised via Twitter.

People asking WTF about a market move are almost certainly on the wrong side of that move; that's why it's a good sentiment indicator. When traders are frustrated or confused by a move, it is a strong signal. If I'm long a currency and it's going up, I am not asking WTF. When a position goes my way, it makes perfect sense every time!

Watch for moments when the market is angry and confused about a move. Expect that move to continue. The stock market rally from 2014 to 2016 is a good example of this. If a move is making people viscerally angry, it probably has further to run.

■ The IPO Indicator

A massive IPO[8] can be another indicator to watch for as the sign of a top in a specific industry or for the stock market as a whole. By definition, the only time the market will absorb a very large IPO is when sentiment is bullish and the market is trading extremely well. Companies will never go public in a weak market because they want to sell shares in their company for the highest price possible.

IPOs tend to be plentiful in the late stages of a bull market as owners of companies see their market value rise and decide to cash out. IPOs are often seen as smart money selling out to dumb money. After all, if you strongly believed that your stock was cheap and your company was set to grow dramatically, why would you sell?

A great example of the IPO indicator is when Glencore sold its initial public offering in 2011. Glencore is one of the largest commodity producers in the world and in 2011 the world was in the midst of the second wave of an extreme bull run in commodities known as the Commodity Supercycle. Chinese and speculative demand had pushed commodity prices to new peaks and investor appetite for anything commodity-related was insatiable.

The insiders at Glencore were smart and realized that if they ever wanted to sell their company (which was massive at the time, valued at about $60B), this was a great time to do so. It is not hindsight to talk about how they sold the top—many observers and analysts (including me) pointed out at the time that the IPO could be a textbook sign of a top for commodities.

Take a look at Figure 9.11, which shows the Glencore IPO marked on a chart of the CRB. The CRB is the benchmark commodities

---

[8]*IPO* stands for "Initial Public Offering" and is the process where a private company sells stock to the public. Often called "going public," it is an extremely important one-time event in the life of a company. Cynics say IPO stands for "It's Probably Overpriced."

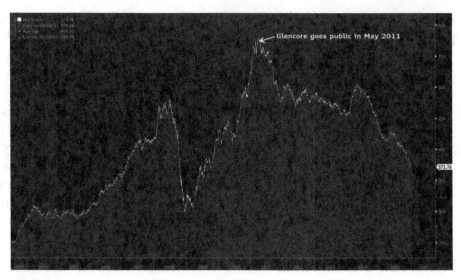

Figure 9.11 Daily CRB Index, 2003 to 2015.

index. Note how the Glencore IPO marked the exact top tick for commodity markets.

Monster IPOs do not happen often but the signals are so powerful that it is worth keeping this indicator in the back of your mind in case you see something similar in the future.

While behavioral finance is a huge topic, I hope this chapter has given you a solid introduction to the topic and opened your mind to some new ways of looking at positioning, sentiment, and behavioral bias. I strongly encourage you to read all five books in the Further Reading section. All these books are fantastic and should be on every trader's must-read list.

After reading this chapter, you should fully understand these key concepts:

- Markets are not always efficient and humans are not always rational.

- Understand the difference between positioning and sentiment.

- Understand cognitive bias, especially confirmation bias and overconfidence.

- Anecdotal evidence is fun but unscientific.

- The Cheer Hedge

- The WTF indicator

■ Further Reading

Dorsey, Woody. *Behavioral Trading: Methods for Measuring Investor Confidence and Expectations and Market Trends.* New York: Texere Publishing.

Kahneman, Daniel. *Thinking Fast and Slow*. New York: Farrar, Straus and Giroux, 2011.

Montier, James. *Behavioural Finance*. Hoboken, NJ: John Wiley & Sons, 2007.

Shiller, Robert J. *Irrational Exuberance*. Princeton, NJ: Princeton University Press, 2015.

Silver, Nate. *The Signal and the Noise*. New York: Penguin Press, 2012.

CHAPTER 10

Trading the News

■ Introduction

Once you have a solid understanding of the fundamentals that drive your currencies and you have a good handle on the current narratives in the market, you are ready to trade the news. With your knowledge of current themes along with positioning and sentiment, you are ready to figure out how new information will move prices. Remember that the current price is the sum total of all the known information in the world.

When news comes out (e.g. economic data, monetary policy announcements, or unscheduled headlines) the price zigs and zags as it looks for a new equilibrium level. This search for equilibrium is sometimes said to be guided by an "invisible hand"[1] because it is uncanny how price rapidly incorporates new information and adjusts to the new outlook.

When news hits, there is significant opportunity for profit. Traders who have the best understanding of the fundamental backstory going into an event will have the best chance of coming out the other side in the black. Before you trade the news, you need to have a solid understanding of what is driving the FX pairs you trade and any correlated markets.

The prevailing economic and fundamental landscape has a massive influence on how the market interprets new information.

---

[1] "Every individual ... neither intends to promote the public interest, nor knows how much he is promoting it ... he intends only his own security; and by directing that industry in such a manner as its produce may be of the greatest value, he intends only his own gain, and he is in this, as in many other cases, led by an invisible hand to promote an end which was no part of his intention." Adam Smith, *The Theory of Moral Sentiments*.

For example, during the 2010–2012 period, the stock market consistently rallied on bad economic news because it was perceived that bad economic news meant the Fed would announce more quantitative easing (QE), and more QE usually means higher stock prices.

Traders who weren't fully cognizant of the macroeconomic landscape in those days were always complaining, "This price action makes no sense! Why are we rallying on bad news?!" Those who were focused and did their homework understood the reaction function perfectly. A nuanced understanding of the market gives you a huge edge when trading the news.

There are many types of news and events that can generate profitable trading opportunities. In this section I will discuss the following:

a. Economic data

Trading economic data using NewsPivots

Beat the algos! When the headline number is not the whole story

b. Central bank meetings

FOMC

ECB

Other

c. Central bank speeches and comments

d. Other headlines and news events

CRITICAL CONCEPT: Understand What Is Priced In

Before you can trade a data release, central bank meeting, or other event in the FX market, you need to understand what is priced in. This is an absolutely critical concept for anyone who trades any financial market. If you trade or you are ever planning on trading any security in any market, you need to fully and completely grok the concept of "priced in." If you read this section and still don't really get it, ask someone to explain it more fully. Do not trade the news until you are completely comfortable with the concept of what is priced into a market.

Financial market prices are generally set by the sum total of all the buying and selling done by every human and computer market participant. Different buyers and sellers will decide to buy or sell depending on the price, and as prices move different actors with different time frames will enter or exit the market.

Decisions to buy and sell are generally driven by the market's assessment of fair value for the security and this assessment should (in theory) be composed of all the available information that relates to that security. As new information comes in, prices move in real-time and should reflect and anticipate all available information, often before the information itself is released. Let's look at an example.

Currencies are highly sensitive to interest rate movements. Therefore, it makes sense that currencies should move when central banks adjust their primary interest rate. Figure 10.1 shows an example of how a currency can move when a central bank unexpectedly changes interest rates.

When something unexpected like this happens, it is *not priced in*. This move higher is what you would anticipate because an unexpected rate cut makes holding Canadian dollars less attractive given the lower yield. The market sells CAD and buys USD, driving USDCAD higher.

All other things being equal, would you rather hold something that yields 1% or something that yields 0.75%? Obviously, the higher yield is more attractive and so when the Bank of Canada cut rates, the market sold CAD to reflect the news. This, again, was *not priced in*. Let's look at an interest rate move that *was* priced in. You may remember this story from Chapter 5 when we looked at how a central bank changes its bias.

In 2008, the Reserve Bank of New Zealand (RBNZ) cut rates dramatically in response to the global financial crisis and then they cut rates again after the 2011 Christchurch earthquake. By 2013, economic activity had rebounded significantly and it was clear to the RBNZ that rates were too low. Inflation was starting to pick up and so the RBNZ felt it would become appropriate to start raising rates at some juncture, but not right away. The story plays out as shown in Figure 10.2. The first hint that the RBNZ wanted to hike rates was delivered on July 25, 2013, and it is marked by point 1 on the chart.

You might recognize this chart from earlier discussions. I have used AUDNZD to show the evolution of the story because AUDNZD is the purest play on the New Zealand dollar. Take a look at the chart and the comments marked. You can see that the RBNZ slowly prepared the market for the interest rate hike over a period of 8 months and the NZD gradually appreciated over this time period (lower AUD, higher NZD). Finally, the RBNZ hiked in March 2014 but it was completely expected—fully priced in. The market priced in the hike over the course of many months and when the hike finally arrived, NZD *sold off* in response.

This reaction is counterintuitive to someone who is not following the NZD closely. "They hiked and the currency sold off? What the ...?" But any professional following the NZD would know that the hike was fully priced in and so the reaction in the currency market is perfectly understandable. There is no need for NZD to rally after a rate hike that is fully priced in.

In fact, quite often the reaction to an event that was priced in is the opposite of what the macroeconomic textbooks might suggest because those who had been buying the NZD in anticipation of the rate hike sell (take profit) on the day of the event.

1. "Although removal of monetary stimulus will likely be needed in the future, we expect to keep the OCR unchanged through the end of the year." – July 25, 2013

2. "OCR increases will likely be required next year." – September 2013

3. "Although we expect to keep the OCR unchanged in 2013, OCR increases will likely be required next year." – October 2013

4. "The Bank will increase the OCR as needed in order to keep future average inflation near the 2 percent target midpoint." – December 2013

5. RBNZ hiked on March 13, 2014.

This concept of a market pricing in an event and then reversing (somewhat counterintuitively) after the event is known as "buy the rumor/sell the fact."

CRITICAL CONCEPT: Buy the Rumor/Sell the Fact

Buy the rumor/sell the fact is a common trading pattern. The market prices in an event in advance and then reverses after the anticipated event takes place. The AUDNZD story above is a good example. Let's look at one more using GBPUSD in September 2014.

Currencies are often sensitive to political noise and prefer stability over instability. For example, when Quebec voted on

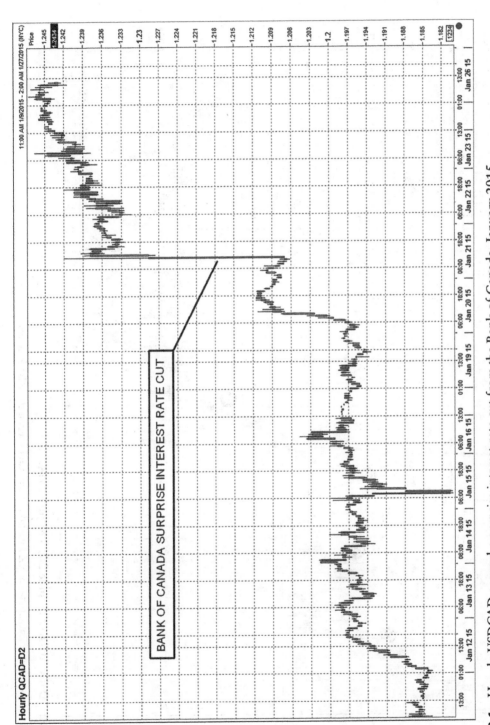

Figure 10.1 Hourly USDCAD around a surprise interest rate cut from the Bank of Canada, January 2015.

Note USDCAD higher = weaker CAD, stronger USD.

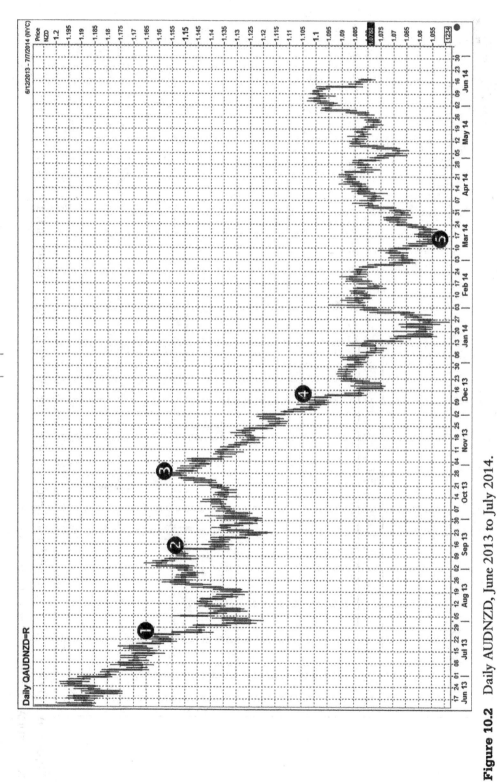

Figure 10.2 Daily AUDNZD, June 2013 to July 2014.

The pair falls as the market anticipates a NZ rate hike, then rallies when the RBNZ hikes.

whether to separate from Canada in 1995, investors sold Canadian dollars in the lead-up to the event in order to hedge the risk that Quebec might leave.

In 2014, there was a similar situation in the United Kingdom as Scotland called a referendum on whether to stay in or leave the United Kingdom. Initially, GBP barely moved because there was an overwhelming view in the market that the Scots would vote NO. The way the ballot was worded, a NO vote was a vote to *stay* in the UK. So a NO vote was bullish for GBP.

As the referendum drew near, however, the polls moved from a clear NO majority to a near 50/50 split between YES and NO. This triggered several rounds of GBP selling as each new poll suggested the vote would be closer and closer. When referendum night came, the market was on edge as results came in one council area at a time.[2] I stayed in the office past midnight (on my birthday!) to trade the event.

You can see in Figure 10.3 how GBP rallied gradually throughout the day and evening of the referendum as good news trickled in council area by council area. Odds of a Scottish NO vote (remember NO = stay in the UK = good news) rose with each exit poll released. GBP rallied gradually and then finally the currency peaked on one last push higher right as the official result (bullish GBP) was announced.

Then the market spent the next 12 hours selling GBP in a classic buy the rumor/sell the fact pattern. Quite often, the exact moment of a news release is the absolute apex of sentiment.

Let's look at one more example of buy the rumor/sell the fact because this is an important and counterintuitive pattern that you need to fully understand.

In August 2018, tension was high as Donald Trump threatened to withdraw from the North America Free Trade Agreement. Over the weekend of August 26–28, news came out that suggested the United States and Mexico had just about agreed on a new Mexico–US trade pact. This was viewed as positive for Mexico and so USDMXN opened lower on Monday. But the news was not yet official. As more details of the announcement leaked to the media, USDMXN slowly pushed lower. Then (see Figure 10.4), the moment Donald Trump appeared on TV to formally announce the pact, USDMXN made one last hard push lower.

---

[2]A council area is similar to a county. They have awesomely Scottish names like Clackmannanshire, Dumfries, Aberdeenshire, and Nah-Eileanan Siar, to name a few.

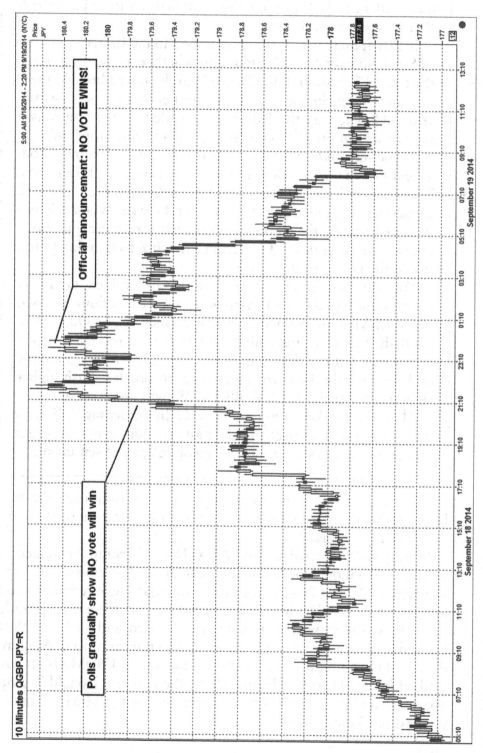

Figure 10.3   Hourly GBPUSD around the Scottish Referendum September 18 and 19, 2014.

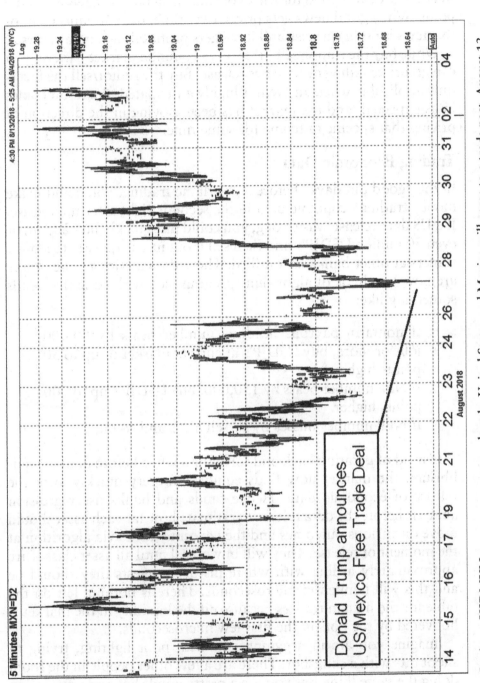

Figure 10.4 5-minute USDMXN as news comes out that the United States and Mexico will agree to a trade pact, August 13 to September 4, 2018.

The news is bearish USDMXN but the market reverses (buy the rumor/sell the fact).

The chart is labeled:

- 5 Minutes MXN=D2
- 4:30 PM 8/13/2018 - 5:25 AM 9/4/2018 (NYC)
- Log
- Donald Trump announces US/Mexico Free Trade Deal
- August 2018

With the news out, the market subsequently scrambled to take profit and with buyers substantially outnumbering sellers, USD-MXN exploded higher. Traders were screaming "This makes no sense! The deal is good for Mexico!" and such but the news is not the point. When good news gets priced over time, the announcement of the news is not a surprise and it triggers profit taking and a reversal.

While buy the rumor/sell the fact is a common market pattern, you can go broke fading every news release. Buy the rumor/sell the fact is only applicable when an event is highly anticipated, the result comes in as expected, and the market has been moving in the direction of pricing that specific outcome for some time.

Trading Economic Data

In the "good old days" before algorithmic trading, you could make money trading economic data in the seconds right after the release. If a US data release was strong, you could just quickly buy 20, 30, or even 50 million USDJPY and then sell it out just as quickly to slower traders at other banks as it rallied. Those days are long gone. There are now hundreds of algorithms programmed with code that reads something like:

> If nonfarm payrolls headline number beats by 80,000 jobs or more, buy USDJPY at current market or up to 50 points higher.
> If NFP number beats by 150,000, buy USDJPY up to 100 points higher.
> If NFP number misses by X, sell Y ... and so on.

Instead of gyrating back and forth for a while before finding equilibrium, the market now finds equilibrium very quickly after the release of economic data. Hedge funds and banks use regression analysis before the data release to estimate how far each asset should move on various outcomes and they execute trades via algorithm at the moment of release. They will buy or sell until all asset classes are approximately in line with where history suggests they should be and this will happen in microseconds. There is nothing left on the table for the human traders because all the liquidity in the market is hoovered by the bots in the first few microseconds.

Imagine you are in a gymnasium with poor lighting, trying to shoot rats with a slingshot. There are a few other people in the room doing the same thing but you are a pretty good shot and your vision is good. You are doing okay. You are hitting your fair share of rats.

Suddenly, a cyborg marches into the gym. He is equipped with infrared night vision and a fully automatic laser gun with motion-sensitive targeting. He shoots 50 rats in 10 seconds without missing. You and the other human rat hunters stand there, jaws on the floor.

That is what trading economic data is like now that algos are programmed to trade every economic release. With hundreds of electronic players all using similar algos, competition is at the microsecond level and humans are shut out. Pre-2005 or so, you could just about make your year trading economic data alone. Now there is far less money to be made by humans after data releases. This is one of many examples of how you need to adapt to changing market conditions over time. Remember Rule #2 of FX trading: Adapt or die.[3]

Despite the depressing scenario laid out above, there are still many profitable ways to trade FX around economic releases. Here are the best ones:

■ Trade the Extreme Data

Algos will take out the first pocket of liquidity when economic data are released, but there are still opportunities for profit when important data come in extremely strong or extremely weak. This is because the bots can only buy or sell so much (they have risk limits too!). The first wave of algo trades can be followed by more waves of macro and hedge fund trades in the same direction and you can get in after the algos but before everyone else. Let's look at the US Retail Sales release in April 2015 as an example.

The Setup

The US economy is performing well, job growth is strong, and oil prices have recently collapsed. There is an expectation that some of the money saved on gasoline will be spent on other items; that should boost Retail Sales. Despite positive momentum in the economy, Retail Sales have been consistently weak over the past 12 months, so there is expectation for a catch-up. Adding up the 12-month cumulative difference between Actual and Expected Retail Sales over time you get the chart seen in Figure 10.5.

The chart shows that on average, Retail Sales have missed significantly month after month since mid-2014. Thus, the market expects a rebound (mean reversion) in the data because the weakness in Retail Sales doesn't appear to match the strength in the rest of the economy.

Important reminder (as explained in the section on "What's Priced In"): The only thing that matters when you are trading economic data is the *actual release* compared to *what was expected*. A strong number compared to last month means nothing; the key is always whether data come in better or worse *than expected* this month.

---

[3]http://uk.reuters.com/article/2012/05/02/uk-markets-forex-ranges-idUKBRE8410YN20120502.

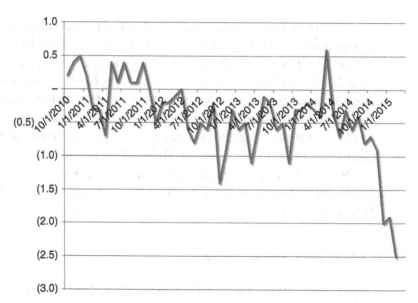

Figure 10.5 12-month cumulative miss in US Retail Sales (ex-autos and gas), October 2010 to March 2015.

You can find economist forecasts for economic data on the web, Bloomberg, or Reuters.

Economists look for Retail Sales ex-Autos and Gas to come in at +0.6% but traders are thinking that this estimate is probably low and the whisper number[4] is closer to 0.8% or 0.9%. The market is structurally long dollars and has been adding to longs ahead of the release on the assumption the data will be strong.

Traders wait patiently for the news. How strong will the number be? Heart rates rise across global trading floors and dreams of a skyrocketing dollar percolate inside the mind of every FX trader on the street. The question is not whether to be long dollars, but how many dollars to be long!

The Result

Ouch. The number comes in weak. The actual release is +0.5% with negative revisions to prior months. The market is caught wrong-footed.

Look at the 1-minute USDJPY chart in Figure 10.6 and focus on the moments labeled 1, 2, and 3. The first gap move at Point 1 is the moment immediately upon release as the algos sell whatever dollars are available on the bid. This takes USDJPY from 119.92 pre-release

---

[4]The whisper number is the number expected by the market, as opposed to the number predicted by economists. Usually those two numbers are similar but sometimes traders will expect something different. The whisper is the most important as it best defines how the market will react.

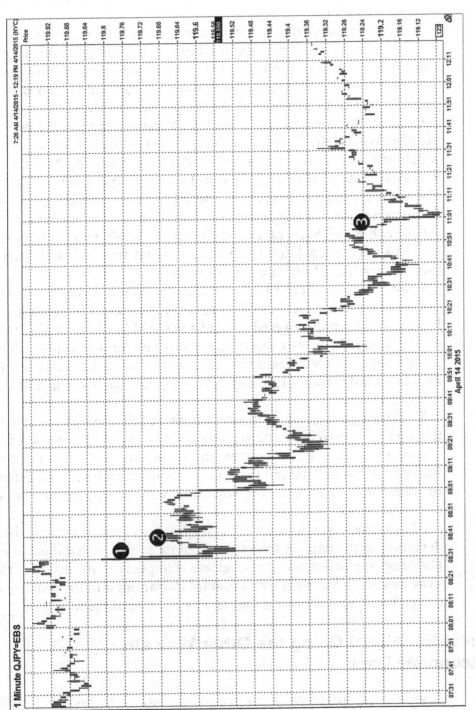

Figure 10.6 1-minute USDJPY, April 14, 2015.

TRADING THE NEWS

to 119.57. Then, the market consolidates for a few minutes, rallying back to 119.68/70 (Point 2). Somewhere in this small rally is the place where human traders should sell, knowing the market has not yet found equilibrium.

It is not prudent to "go with" every economic data release, but in this case you know that the market was heavily positioned long dollars for a strong number and therefore there is more downside for USDJPY. So on this day, I went short USDJPY at 119.66 with a stop loss at 120.03 (10 pips above the pre-release level).

I call the level where a currency was trading the instant before the news release the NewsPivot. NewsPivots are important levels to watch after any release; how price behaves around the NewsPivot is critical. 120.03 is a sensible stop loss because if USDJPY rallies above the NewsPivot (119.92—where USDJPY was trading before the number came out) it means the market has completely rejected the bearish Retail Sales news and there is something bigger happening. This is a concept known as bad news/good price. We will discuss this concept more fully later in this section.

Point 3 shows where I took profit on the trade. Usually I would use some basic technical analysis to determine my take-profit level. In this case, I simply covered around 11:00AM because the FX trading day is mostly over by this time and most major buyers and sellers should have done whatever they were going to do. Expect momentum to dwindle after 11:00AM NY as London goes home and liquidity dries up.

The strategy of going with an economic release works best when the number is extremely counter to expectations and the market has a strong bias and a big position the wrong way into the number. Make sure you understand the specific economic release well before the number comes out so that you know what is an extreme release and what is not.

The simplest way to measure extremes is to look at the standard deviation of the data. A miss or beat of more than 2 standard deviations on any major economic release is important. In this case, the miss was much less than two standard deviations and the move was driven more by positioning and less by the size of the miss.

■ Beat the Algos! Going the Other Way after Economic Data

Another way to profit from economic data is to take the other side (or fade) the initial kneejerk move. The term "fade" means to take the other side of a big move or view in the market. Sell a rally or buy a dip. Quite often on a trading floor you will hear someone say, "This move is a fade" or "This move is baloney; I'm fading it."

Fading economic data is a scary strategy because you are going against short-term momentum and against the theoretically logical direction dictated by the economic release. That said, with the proliferation of algos trading the initial headline, quite often the fade strategy is most profitable.

The reason fading the kneejerk move often works is that algos and humans pile in based on the initial reading but there are quite often times when the details are not as strong as the headline or the headline is not really all that strong in the first place. Then you often see a rapid turnaround in the market because the algos are risk-averse and so they hit or pay almost any price to get out of a trade that is not instantly in the money. As usual, it pays to know the setup going in. Which way is the market leaning? What is the asymmetry?

A key skill in trading is to identify asymmetries. Always be on the lookout for moments when the market looks much more likely to go a particular direction after an event due to positioning or some other bias in the market.

As a human trader, there is sometimes a profitable opportunity to take the other side of a move if the headline is not representative of the full story. For example, say the headline jobs number is extremely strong but the details of the report (unemployment rate, average hourly earnings) are weak. You can sell the spike in USD-JPY because the bots will be long too many USD and will need to sell. The best way to be ready for this type of reaction is to listen to the immediate reaction and commentary from economists and strategists.

This is easiest if you work at a bank or hedge fund because you can hear your economist's reaction almost immediately, but there is also real-time reaction on CNBC, Twitter, Reuters, Bloomberg, and so on. If the headline is very strong but the details are weak, the dollar will often fail to hold initial gains as the market views the knee jerk as incorrect or exaggerated and fades it.

Remember that the last trade before the release (the NewsPivot) is a simple but effective reference point for trading economic data and other news releases. Make a note of where each of the majors is trading before any major release and consider those levels to be the critical pivots for each pair for the rest of the day. This works because the reaction to the news is often just as important as the news itself.

If very good news comes out and the currency goes back through the level it was trading before the news, that's bearish price action. This is a concept known as good news/bad price. The opposite situation (bad news/good price) is bullish.

Why would a currency rally on bad news? There are all sorts of reasons for counterintuitive moves in FX after news and economic releases but the two main ones are (1) the underlying details of the release are not consistent with the headline release (strong headline/weak details) and (2) supply and demand, not news, determine FX rates. Let's look at these two situations separately.

■ Reversal for a Good Reason (Headline and Details Do Not Match)

In this situation, the reversal makes sense. The initial headline looks extremely bullish (or bearish) but then there are details or mitigating factors that offset the headline release. Here's an example.

The Setup

September 10, 2014. Traders wait nervously for the Australian jobs release. The market has been expecting a big fall in AUDUSD for months but the currency is extremely resilient. Any sign of economic weakness is likely to open the door for the sellers while longs are praying for strong data to keep their P&L afloat. AUDUSD is trading at 0.9160. The market expects the Australian economy to add 15,000 jobs and economist forecasts range from −5k to +35k.

Traders in New York are eating dinner with one eye on the conversation at the table and another eye on their smartphone FX app while traders in Singapore, Sydney, Hong Kong, and Tokyo hunch over their keyboards. Everyone watches the seconds tick off until the number is finally set to come out: 3 . . . 2 . . . 1 . . . . The number hits the screens:

The Result

KABOOM! . . . +122,000 jobs! The strongest jobs number in the history of Australia! AUDUSD spikes 60 pips instantly from 0.9160 to 0.9220 and shorts cover in a panic, paying any offer they can. Algos go limit long AUD to capitalize on their calculations that show such a huge beat means AUD should go up at least 1%.

Buyers are frantic and AUD trades wildly back and forth between 0.9200 and 0.9220 for 90 seconds or so, trying to find equilibrium. Then, after about three minutes. . . . Wait! What's this!? Full panic on the trading floor as a new red headline hits the wires.

AUSTRALIAN BUREAU OF STATISTICS SAYS METHODOLOGY CHANGE HAS DISTORTED JOBS DATA

In other words, the release is meaningless. Most of the shorts have already been obliterated and anyone who is long is now badly caught. Traders in a position of strength see an incredible opportunity to get short as AUDUSD goes down, down, down.... Check out the chart in Figure 10.7.

This type of scenario provides a tremendous opportunity for profit to anyone who is paying attention and is ready to act quickly and forcefully. Look at how AUDUSD went straight down after the spike, falling 1.5% over the next few hours.

■ Reversal for No Reason

The other type of reversal on news is more confusing. It occurs when the news is unambiguously bullish (or bearish) and the market goes the logical way at first but then reverses for no understandable macro reason. Perhaps large buyers were waiting on the sidelines and want to use the selloff following bad news to buy at attractive levels.

When price reverses after big news, the "what?" is much more important than the "why?" If a currency is rallying hard after bad news, don't worry too much about trying to figure out why it's rallying. The fact that it is rallying on bad news is all the information you need. Counterintuitive reactions to data can give you important information about underlying supply and demand.

Rule #8 of FX Trading: It doesn't always have to make sense.

The media's job it is to tell a story around every market move, and even the best journalists cannot always come up with a coherent narrative. It doesn't always have to make sense.

Let's look at an example of a big reversal after a data release:

The Setup

September 19, 2014. The market has been long USDCAD since 1.00 and now the pair is trading around 1.10. Spot traders and hedge funds are keen to add to long USD positions but Canadian CPI is out today and traders are nervous. A strong number could increase the odds of an interest rate hike by the Bank of Canada and so a strong CPI is bearish USDCAD. The median economist forecast for Core CPI is 1.8% with the lowest estimate at 1.5% and the highest at 1.9%. Anything above 1.9% is big and above 2.0% is a blockbuster.

NY traders put their Starbucks somewhere safe so it won't get knocked over when they lunge for the BUY and SELL buttons while Canadian traders do the same with their Tim Hortons. USDCAD traders around the world count down the seconds as they wait for the data to hit the screens: 3, 2, 1 ...

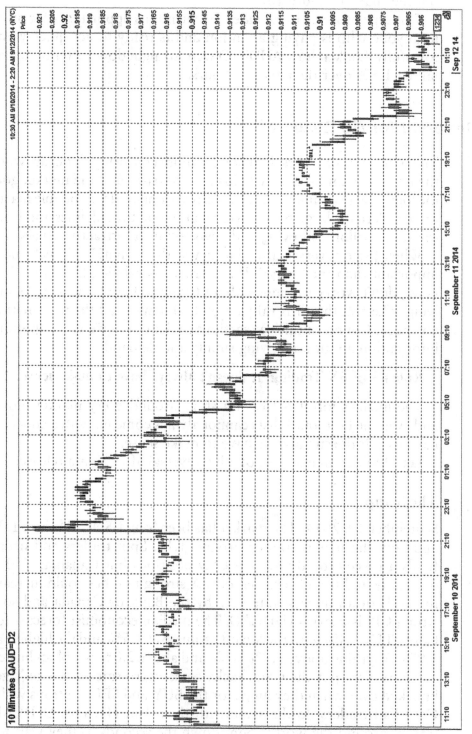

Figure 10.7 10-minute AUDUSD around the Australian employment report, September 10 and 11, 2014.

The Result

BLAMMO! The number comes out... 2.1%! Higher than the highest forecast. USDCAD immediately plummets from 1.0980 to 1.0895. But then suddenly, there is one wave of buying. And then another wave... and another... and less than four hours later, USD-CAD is all the way back to unchanged. Figure 10.8 shows the chart.

There was no fundamental or macro reason for this reversal in price. This is a classic bad news/good price setup. There was very bad news for USDCAD but it could not hold onto losses and reversed nearly immediately for no known reason. This is bullish price action.

Now look at Figure 10.9 to see what happened after. You can see in the first chart that USDCAD rallied right back to the NewsPivot level (1.0980). The NewsPivot became resistance for a few hours and then when it broke, zoom-zoom, USDCAD trended higher to 1.1070.

Always be on the lookout for moments when things don't move the way you would expect them to. This counterintuitive price action can provide clues as to future direction.

Economic data releases are just one type of news trading opportunity. Now, let's look at another: central bank meetings. Central banks are the biggest drivers of currencies as they set interest rate and currency policy in most developed countries. While in theory central banks are independent, there are various levels of political interference in different countries and so this section will also touch on the political aspects of central banking.

Understand Central Banks

There is a skill to understanding central banks; it comes mostly from doing the work. I cannot emphasize this enough: If you want to trade FX, you need to do the work on the central banks. Yes, the speeches and official statements are usually pretty boring... but *yes*, you need to read every one of them if you want to be a serious FX trader. The evolution of a central bank's thinking is mostly communicated via speeches and official statements and therefore you need to read every single one. Don't be lazy! The longer you follow a central bank, the more of a feel you get for their bias, tactics, and communication strategy.

Central Bank Meetings

Central bank meetings can have a dramatic impact on currencies as central banks use regular official meetings to communicate their most important policies such as the level of official interest rates

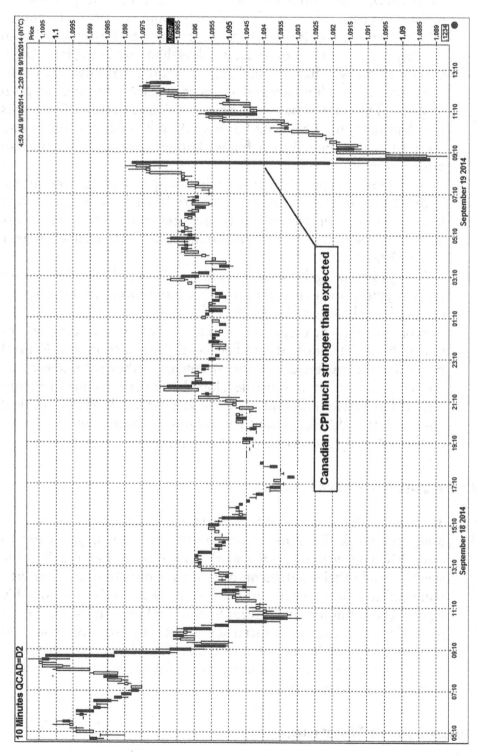

Figure 10.8 10-minute USDCAD chart around the release of the CPI number, September 18 and 19, 2014.

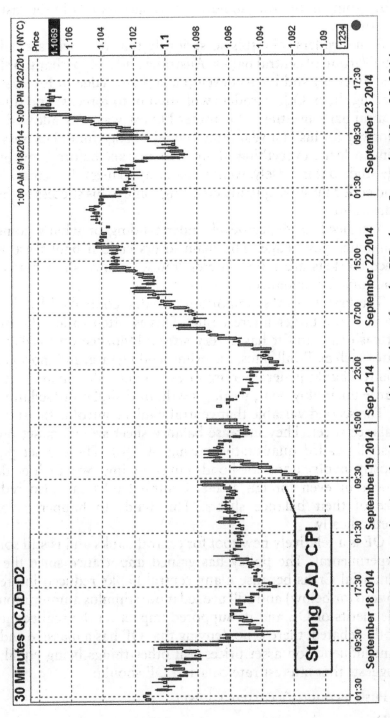

Figure 10.9 30-minute USDCAD chart showing what happened in the days after the CPI release, September 18 to 23, 2014.

and the size of quantitative easing programs. To make money on central bank meetings, you need to be prepared. I cannot overstate this enough. You need to fully understand all the subtleties of the story going in or you can never trade successfully in the fast market aftermath.

Some traders take this so seriously that they will specialize in a small group of central banks (Australia and NZ, perhaps, or Norway and Sweden) and try to develop a superior edge in forecasting and trading them. Other traders will attempt to forecast and trade every central bank meeting. One trader I know was only allowed to trade Norway for his first year after joining a hedge fund. His boss wanted him to learn everything about that market before branching out. He studied it intensely, went to Norway to meet the central bankers, and ended up subsequently crediting some of his success to this initial constraint.

You need an expert-level understanding of what's going on to maximize your edge. The main levers central banks use to influence markets are target interest rates, balance sheet management, and forward guidance.

The first and most important variable controlled by the central bank is the target interest rate. This is often called the overnight or cash rate and it has a very strong influence on market interest rates such as T-Bill rates, the prime lending rate, and mortgage rates. Central banks generally raise rates to fight inflation and cut rates to battle unemployment, weak growth, or disinflation/deflation.

The second variable that central banks control is the size of their balance sheet. They increase balance sheet size via asset purchases (usually called quantitative easing or QE). These asset purchases mostly involve domestic bonds but sometimes will include domestic stocks or even foreign assets. Central banks can also reduce the size of their balance sheets. This tends to happen slowly and methodically.

QE is a relatively new tool for central banks and is still somewhat experimental. The policy has gained importance since the Global Financial Crisis because many central banks reduced interest rates to zero (or below) and still needed more stimulus ammunition. While the merits of QE and its supposed impact on the real economy are hotly debated, there is no denying that QE has a massive and important influence on asset prices. All other things being equal, theory suggests that interest rate cuts and QE should:

- Push a country's currency lower
- Drive bond yields lower
- Drive its stock market higher
- Increase inflation

In practice, results have been extremely mixed and as more empirical evidence builds, more questions pile up about the unintended consequences of QE and sub-zero interest rates. Like a drug, loose monetary policy creates dependence and also has many side effects. These side effects can outweigh the benefits as the dosage increases and the years go by.

Side effects of prolonged QE include greater wealth inequality and risks to financial stability. Note that the textbooks say that rate cuts and QE are bad for a currency, but in reality this is not always true. When the Bank of Japan cut interest rates below zero in January 2016, the yen sold off for just one day.... Then it rallied for a year!

The third tool a central bank uses to influence markets is forward guidance. By telling participants what it plans to do in advance, the central bank can guide behavior (in theory) and influence markets without actually doing anything. An example of this is when the Federal Reserve promised to keep rates at extremely low levels throughout 2012 and 2013.

By making this promise, the Fed encouraged market participants to buy riskier assets with higher yields and this pushed the stock market higher. The Fed hoped that a higher US stock market would generate a wealth effect. The wealth effect posits that people feel richer as stocks rally and so they spend more. The evidence for a wealth effect is mixed.

Like every news trade, the most important thing for you to understand going into central bank meetings is: What is priced in? In other words: What is expected to happen at the meeting? If everyone expects the central bank to hike rates and they hike rates, financial markets should not move much. On the other hand, if nobody expects the central bank to hike rates and they hike rates, you can expect a massive market reaction.

■ Positioning into a Central Bank Meeting

The key factor when positioning into a central bank meeting is that you need to have a view that differs from the market. If the odds of a rate cut are priced at 50/50 and you believe the true odds are 50/50, there is nothing to do. On the other hand, the ideal setup is when you have a view that strongly differs from the market.

Say you think the RBA will hike interest rates but the odds of a hike are only priced at 20%. The expected value of going into the meeting long AUD is very high. I usually construct a simple expected value (EV) diagram to see if a central bank trade is worthwhile. Here is an example of how I approach a central bank meeting, estimate EV, and then take a position before the meeting.

The Setup

June 18, 2015. The Norges Bank (Central Bank of Norway) meets this week and the market is split on whether or not they will cut rates. The pricing is about 40/60 for a cut versus no cut. But reading all the Norges Bank speeches this year, I have the strong impression that the plan is to cut rates once in the first half of the year. It's June and they have not cut yet so it is about time!

In fact, after the last meeting where the Norges Bank stayed on hold, the governor said this: "Following an overall assessment of new information and the risk outlook, the Executive Board decided to keep the key policy rate unchanged at this meeting. At the same time, there are still prospects that the key policy rate will be lowered in June."

My base case is always to take what the central bankers say at face value. The Norges Bank has been saying they want to cut in the first half of the year and the statement above is clear. This meeting is the last meeting in the first half of the year.

Next, I go through all the recent economic data to see if there is any compelling reason for a change of course. In this case, the recent economic data are mixed to weak since the Olsen speech and so there is no reason to expect a change of direction or bias from prior statements.

The interesting part of this setup is that the market is 40/60 on whether the Norges bank will cut rates while I think the odds are closer to 65/35. I have a different view than the market so I want to bet on a Norges Bank rate cut.

To assess the possible outcomes for this trade, I need to estimate how much EURNOK will move under each scenario (cut and no cut). Note that EURNOK is always the best way to play Norway monetary policy because it is the most liquid and purest play on NOK.

I can look at past reactions to Norges Bank moves (and non-moves) plus use past experience and the options market to estimate potential volatility. Overnight option breakeven prices will give you a decent estimate of how much FX will move on any given event. I then assign probabilities to each outcome and come up with a standard expected value grid (see Figure 10.10).[5]

This grid tells me based on my probabilities that positioning for a rate cut has a very high expected value. The probabilities you insert and the estimates of where you think spot will go allow you to make an informed wager on the outcome of the central bank

---

[5]You need to have a clear understanding of the concept of expected value to be a good trader. If you don't, read this: https://en.wikipedia.org/wiki/Expected_value.

	Estimated Probability [p]	Spot Level Estimate [e]	p*e	P&L on 10 EUR
spot rate now	8.7300			
Norges cuts	65%	8.8500	5.7525	98,712
Norges does not cut	35%	8.6500	3.0275	(35,435)
	expected value of long 10 EURNOK			63,277

Figure 10.10 Expected value calculation for a theoretical EURNOK trade.

meeting. This grid also allows you to play around with the inputs so that you can take a look at where your breakeven expected value lands. If you only need a 50% chance of a cut to generate breakeven EV (for example) and you think the real probability is 65%, then clearly you have a good trade.

This goes back to the concept of a strong process. If you do this type of analysis and then the Norges Bank does not cut rates, you can file it under "good decision/bad outcome" and move on. But if you go in unprepared and have no idea where spot will end up under various scenarios—that's just bad trading.

The Result

I went in long 15 EURNOK, risking $175,000 on the idea. This estimate of dollars at risk was calculated using an entry point of 8.7300 and a worst-case stop loss level of 8.6400.[6] Here is what happened.

The Norges Bank cut rates by 25bps, just as I hoped. Check out Figure 10.11. The huge spike in the middle of the chart is where the Norges Bank announcement hit. NOK was clobbered and so EURNOK ripped higher. My estimate was good and I sold the EURNOK between 8.83 and 8.85. Total P&L was almost $200,000. Nice trade!

Let's look at another example of how you do the work and then profit from a central bank meeting.

The Setup

It is late October 2016 and there is an RBA meeting tonight. The RBA have cut rates twice this year and there is an outside shot at a

---

[6](8.7300 – 8.6400) * 15 million / 7.8000 = $175,000; note: 7.8000 is the USD-NOK rate, which is used because profits in EURNOK are earned in the denominator currency (NOK) and so you have to convert the NOK back to USD.

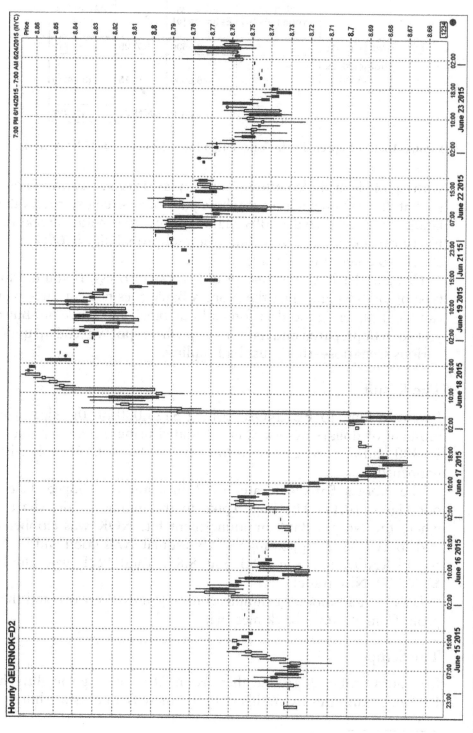

Figure 10.11 Hourly EURNOK around a Norges Bank meeting, June 14 to June 24, 2015.

cut tonight. While most traders are calling for no move, some analysts are calling for a cut and others are expecting a strong easing bias to send the currency lower. There is a new head of the RBA as Glenn Stevens has retired and Philip Lowe is in charge. Conveniently, Lowe just gave a detailed speech on monetary policy less than two weeks ago, so there is an opportunity to do the work and come up with my own conclusions. After reading the speech and thinking about the global macro story, I wrote out the following trading thoughts:

Six out of 28 economists are calling for a cut tonight. Many others are expecting a dovish outcome even if the RBA does not cut rates. I carefully read through Philip Lowe's October 18 speech on Inflation and Monetary Policy and my conclusion is different; I do not expect a cut, and I do not expect a dovish outcome. Here is how I dissect the speech. Philip Lowe's text is centered in italics and my comments are in a normal font.

Recent Decisions

Over the course of this year the Board has lowered the cash rate twice, in May and August. These reductions followed inflation outcomes early in the year that were lower than expected as well as an assessment that inflation was likely to remain quite low for some time, for the reasons that I have discussed. The easing in policy was not in response to concerns about economic growth. If anything, the growth outcomes over the past year, as measured by real GDP or the trend in unemployment, have been a bit better than expected.

My takeaway: The RBA's focus is on inflation, not growth.

We have continued to carefully examine the incoming flow of data. On balance these data suggest that the economy is continuing to adjust reasonably well to the downswing in mining investment. This downswing still has some way to go, but the end is now in sight. And recently, commodity prices have picked up, which is a marked change from the large declines in prices we have seen for some years. Measures of business and consumer sentiment are also slightly above average.

Commodity prices and the Aussie terms of trade have rebounded dramatically in recent months. Business confidence is stable near the highs.

In terms of inflation, we have been looking carefully at the various measures of inflation expectations, which have clearly declined, although not to unprecedented levels. The experience elsewhere suggests that we do need to guard against inflation expectations falling too far, for if this were to occur it would be more difficult to achieve the inflation target. Of course, one of the key influences on inflation expectations is the actual outcomes for inflation. We will get an important update next week, with the release of the September quarter CPI.

The Australian CPI update he refers to came out with a strong headline and weak details. RBA inflation policy is a:

...flexible medium-term inflation target, with the objective of delivering an average rate of inflation over time of between 2 and 3 per cent...

This is not a mechanical framework set to react to current inflation readings.

With the recent rise in Chinese inflation, the rally in oil, the improvement in Australia's terms of trade, and two rate cuts this year yet to fully pass through to the Australian economy, I doubt there would be much alarm right now as the RBA assesses the future path of inflation. Inflation is currently low but the mania around global deflation has passed its peak. The RBA will see the same turn in global inflation momentum that I see.

In terms of the labour market, as I said earlier, the picture is mixed. The unemployment rate has drifted down, but growth in hours worked is weak and many part-time workers would like to work longer hours. Wage pressures remain weak, although there are some signs that the downward pressure on average wages from workers moving out of high-paying mining-related jobs might be coming to an end.

Labor markets are sending a neutral picture and downward wage pressure might be coming to an end.

My expectation for tonight is a relaxed RBA that shows little desire to cut rates further. Global deflationary psychology is reversing and the RBA will view monetary policy as appropriate for now given this reversal, especially with two cuts already in the pipe. Downward momentum in wages and CPI looks like it has waned.

I included this write-up to give you a sense of how you can go through a central banker's speech and then figure out what matters to that central bank and what does not. Then you add in your own assessment of the global macro picture (and ideally your best guess of how the central bank sees the global macro picture) and come up with a prediction for the outcome. Think about what is expected and compare it to the outcome you expect. If there is a divergence, there is an opportunity.

As the day rolled on, I spoke to many other traders and I noticed that absolutely everyone I talked to expected either a rate cut or a dovish result. This was very different from my interpretation, which was a relaxed and neutral RBA that thinks the worst is over. Therefore, I decided to go into the meeting long AUDUSD with a 75-point stop, thinking there would be a meaningful short squeeze if the outcome resembled my forecast.

I chose 75 pips, or 1% for my stop loss because I figured no matter how much noise there was around the RBA meeting, the only way I would be stopped out of the position was if the meeting was extremely dovish or the RBA cut rates. You want to make sure your stop loss is far enough away to survive the noise before and after the event; otherwise, you might be right and still lose money as you are stopped out before the event or on pre-release noise.

I considered the idea a 3.5-star trade—a good trading setup but not worthy of huge sizing. I decided to risk $200,000. I will discuss position sizing later but for now the math is simple: Because I am risking 75 pips, my position should be ($200,000 divided by 0.0075). Remember in USD-based currency pairs that 0.0075 = 75 pips; $200k / 0.0075 is $26.7 million so I go long 27 million AUDUSD at 0.7620 with a stop at 0.7545

The Result

The RBA was neutral and my assessment was correct as they elevated their concern about Sydney housing and showed new optimism on global growth. They upgraded their language on China and reduced their concern about the jobs market. Overall, the statement was balanced but the market was expecting something much more dovish so relative to expectations it was a hawkish statement.

Figure 10.12 is a chart of the price action.

Given that I was not expecting a home run here, I took profit when I woke up the next morning with spot at 0.7670 for a profit of 50 pips or $135,000. Note here the risk/reward was worse than 1:1. I am fine with that once in a while.

Here I thought there was a much better than 50/50 chance of a neutral/hawkish outcome and I viewed the odds of losing the full

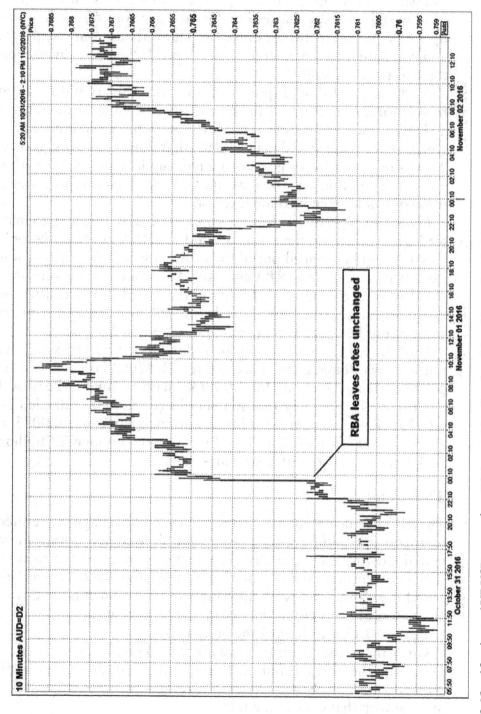

Figure 10.12 10-minute AUDUSD around an RBA meeting, October 31 to November 2, 2016.

75 pips as sub-20%. So this trade was clearly positive EV despite risking 75 pips to make 50. As a general rule, though, this type of risk/reward ratio is not the path to long-run success.

■ Trading the Outcome of a Central Bank Meeting

If you do not see any edge in taking a position beforehand, you can often make money trading the outcome of a central bank meeting afterward, especially when the outcome is a major surprise. This is a similar concept to trading economic data, although central bank surprises are often easier to trade because they are unambiguously important whereas economic data matter on some days and don't matter on others. The key to remember is that unexpected central bank moves are a go with, not a fade.

Rule #9 of FX Trading: Never fade unexpected central bank moves. Jump on them!

Let's take a look at an example.

The Setup

January 21, 2015. Oil prices are in freefall, down from $120 in June to a current level of $50. The market is starting to freak out because in the past ten years the relationship has been "oil down = global demand crumbling." The pace of the drop in oil is so extreme that economists cannot forecast the short-term or long-term impact.

The regularly scheduled Bank of Canada meeting is at 10:00AM today and while it is clear that the drop in oil is bad for Canada, no change is expected from Bank of Canada Governor Stephen Poloz at today's meeting. Up until very recently, most market participants had expected the next move by the Bank of Canada to be a *hike* in interest rates, not a cut. But with the drop in oil, the market now expects the Bank of Canada will switch into neutral for the foreseeable future. USDCAD is 1.2070.

The Result

Wait! What?

BANK OF CANADA CUTS KEY OVERNIGHT LEND-
ING RATE BY 25 BASIS POINTS

The 1-minute chart in Figure 10.13 says it all.

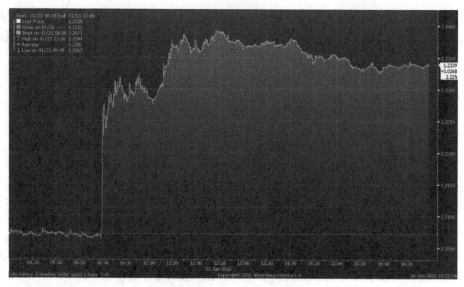

Figure 10.13 1-minute USDCAD, January 21, 2015.

Governor Poloz made a surprise move; he cut rates by 25 basis points and shocked the world. USDCAD was 1.2070 one second and 1.2230 the next. Note that any USDCAD you bought in the minutes after the cut were deep in the money by the end of the day as USDCAD closed around 1.2340. When a central bank moves like this, it is a huge opportunity. Jump on it. Be fast and be aggressive. Figure 10.14 shows what happened in the following days (with the surprise cut at the far left of the chart).

You can see the first move after the interest rate cut at the very far left of the chart and then USDCAD continued to rally, trending

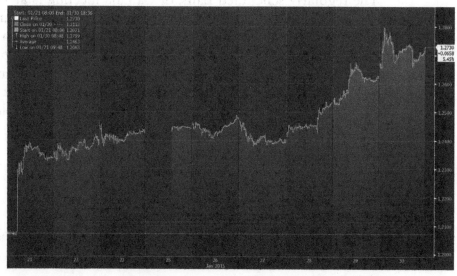

Figure 10.14 Intraday USDCAD, January 21 to January 30, 2015.

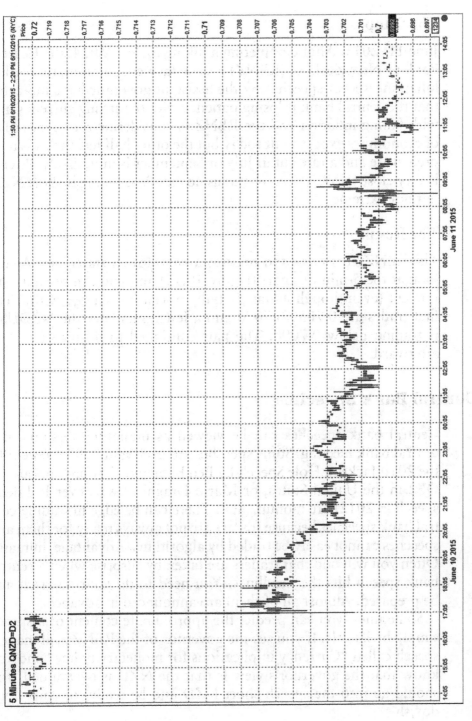

Figure 10.15 5-minute NZDUSD, June 10 to June 11, 2015.

all the way up to 1.2800. A totally unexpected move like this comes infrequently and so this is a time to go *all in*.

Now let's look at a less extreme example:

The Setup

June 11, 2015. After completing a hiking cycle in 2014, the Reserve Bank of New Zealand (RBNZ) is now facing a stunning reversal in inflation. Recent speeches by the assistant governor have indicated that the central bank is losing patience with the strong currency and with falling inflation and the RBNZ is considering a rate cut. Half of economists expect a cut today but the other half feel that it is a bit premature and a rate cut in July or September is more likely. Pricing is very close to 50/50 for cut versus no cut. Positioning is short NZD but not extreme.

The Result

The RBNZ cuts rates and releases a very dovish statement. Again, look at the 5-minute chart (Figure 10.15) and you can see that this rate cut (even though it was partially priced in) is a "go with." The first trades are 0.7050/0.7070 and a few hours later the NZDUSD is trading below 0.7000. The pair continued to drop in the days afterward.

■ Central Bank Speeches

Central bank speeches can be viewed as miniature versions of a central bank meeting. Some speeches are irrelevant, while some (like the 2010 Jackson Hole Speech by Ben Bernanke that pre-announced QE2 in the United States, or Mario Draghi's "Whatever It Takes" speech in 2012) are monumental. There can be edge in trading central bank speeches because traders are not always ready for them and speeches cannot easily be traded by algorithms. Advantage, humans! Often you will find that traders are taken by surprise when a central bank speech hits the headlines. You need to do your research and be prepared. Almost all of them are announced in advance.

Sometimes, you can predict the approximate content of a speech simply by its title. If you see the governor of the RBNZ will make a speech called "Currency implications for monetary policy" and you know that the governor's view is that the NZD is overvalued, you should go into the speech short NZD and be ready for something dovish.

Usually central bankers talk down their currency more when speaking to exporters so the audience for the speech matters, too. Also know the bias of the speaker: Is she always dovish? Always hawkish? Flexible and pragmatic? You can often put a bunch of clues together and hazard a good guess as to whether a speech will be bullish or bearish for the currency.

Trade central bank speeches just like you trade central bank meetings but because the market impact is usually less pronounced, you need to be careful not to get too excited. The moves will tend to be smaller. That said, stay on high alert for the occasional game changer.

■ Other Headlines and News Events

There are countless other opportunities to trade headlines and news events. Examples include:

- **Unscheduled central bank actions.** These are similar to normal central bank moves but have a much larger impact because they are completely unexpected. The element of surprise makes these actions epic because no one is positioned for them. There was a flurry of surprise actions in the 2008–2009 financial crisis but there are other examples of central banks acting between meetings since then. Any unscheduled central bank action is a "go with." Jump on it and do not get out unless the market goes back through the initial NewsPivot.

- **Correlated news releases.** If USDCAD is highly correlated to oil prices and there is an OPEC meeting today, you can trade the result of the OPEC meeting via USDCAD. Let's say OPEC is expected to announce production cuts (less production is bullish crude) and they do not. When the headline hits, OPEC ANNOUNCES NO CHANGE TO PRODUCTION, you can bet that oil will sell off dramatically and so you can buy USDCAD before it moves much.

  These can be very profitable trades because the market is not always ready to jump on the correlated product the way they would be ready to trade the primary one. The Department of Energy (DoE) inventory data (released every Wednesday at 1030AM) is another example of a news release that will influence crude prices and therefore will move USDCAD. New Zealand milk auctions are another good example. The price of milk is extremely important to the NZ economy and so the biweekly milk auctions sometimes impact NZDUSD.

- **Sympathy plays.** Global central banks often move in the same direction at approximately the same time as they react to global conditions in similar ways. This implies that if one central bank starts to move aggressively in one direction, the probability of other central banks doing the same rises. This can result in sympathy moves.

A good example of this is when the Bank of Canada cut rates unexpectedly in January 2015. There was a very aggressive move lower in AUDUSD as the market (correctly) figured that the odds of a cut from the RBA were instantly higher than previously estimated. Traders that were smart and focused that day made money by selling AUDUSD in the hectic moments after the Bank of Canada cut rates.

- **Geopolitical events.** Wars, invasions, attacks, and geopolitical instability can often have an important impact on markets. Obviously, news of war is generally bad for a currency but it can also have big effects on bond markets and commodities (especially oil). When a geopolitical story hits, you can put yourself in a strong position by staying as informed as possible. Information gives you the power to understand events as they unfold and react to news as it happens. You need to be smarter and faster than the competition.

This is in keeping with the idea of staying as informed as possible on all current themes. You don't need to be an expert on global geopolitics but if there is a major geopolitical event going on you should read as much as possible relating to that event. This will keep you in a position of strength. The trader who has to ask, "What does that headline mean?" or "Is that bullish or bearish?" hasn't done the work and doesn't deserve to make money. Do not rely on other people. Do the work yourself.

- **Natural disasters.** Occasionally a major natural disaster will have a big impact on foreign exchange markets. The Christchurch earthquake in New Zealand in 2010 and the Fukushima earthquake and subsequent nuclear disaster in Japan in 2011 are good examples of market-moving natural disasters. While these are exceedingly rare, they are important to be aware of because they can generate massive market moves out of nowhere.

FACTBOX: STEPS TOWARD BECOMING AN EXPERT IN YOUR CURRENCY

- Read everything on the central bank's website.

- Read all the central bank speeches.

- Watch the currency all day and chart the market profile manually on graph paper to get a feel for the texture and price action.

- Always be completely on top of what strategists and technical analysts are saying about your currencies by reading Reuters, Bloomberg, and other articles.

- Have a list of all major support and resistance levels on hand for any currency you are trading.
- Make a list of what drives your currencies and learn as much as you can about those correlated markets, especially:
  - Interest rates
  - Commodities
- Read the press of the country you are trading:
  - Canada: the *Financial Post* and the *Globe and Mail*
  - Australia: *AFR*
  - UK: *Telegraph* and the *Guardian*
- List the central bankers and outline some bullet points on their recent views/comments. This allows you to interpret headlines quickly. You will instantly know if a central banker's comments are news or just repeats of comments they made in the past. For the major central bankers, you should know his or her:
  - Interest rate view (dove/hawk)
  - Currency view
  - Most recent comments
- Make a list of the strong and weak parts of the economy:
  - Jobs
  - Manufacturing
  - Trade/import/export
  - Housing
  - Inflation (How does it relate to official target? Do you understand the central bank's target? Do they target core or headline, etc.?)
- Understand what is priced into interest rate markets.
- Learn as much as possible about what moves the drivers of your currency.
  - For example, if you trade a commodity currency:
    - What are the main commodities that matter?
    - What is the major narrative for those commodities right now?
    - What is the supply/demand dynamic?

Trading news and events can be a huge source of edge for skilled traders. By understanding initial conditions and how new information impacts the equilibrium, you can move faster and trade smarter than your competitors. Do the work and then be fast and courageous when news comes out. Trust your instincts and capitalize before the invisible hand finds a new equilibrium.

After reading this chapter, you should fully understand these key concepts:

- When news comes out, whether it is economic data, monetary policy announcements, or unscheduled headlines, the price moves quickly to find a new equilibrium. This process presents significant opportunities for profit.

- Critical concept 1: What is priced in?

- Critical concept 2: Buy the rumor / Sell the fact

- How to trade economic data using NewsPivots

- How to trade central meetings and speeches and other events

PART III

Understand Risk Management

"Yes, risk-taking is inherently failure-prone. Otherwise, it would be called 'sure-thing-taking.'"

Jim McMahon

For every 100 books on trade selection, there is one great book on risk management. This is why so many traders spend so much time coming up with the perfect trade idea, only to blow up their trading accounts thanks to poor risk management.

You cannot trade successfully without a proper risk management framework and I would strongly suggest to you that risk management is much, much more important than trade selection when it comes to long-run trading success. You need a clear risk management plan before you do a single trade. The smartest guys in the room can still blow up. Priority number one is to avoid ruin.

Spend time thinking about risk management. Create a formal plan of action so that when the market starts flying around, you know what your parameters are supposed to be. Ideally, your framework should be flexible but systematic so that you reduce your volatility and risk when things are going poorly and increase risk in a controlled way as your P&L builds.

In Part Three we will look at risk management and investigate the role of stop losses and how to properly size your trades. Understand that there are very few correct answers or absolutes when it comes to risk management. I will explain how I think about risk, and then it is up to you to develop a framework that works for you.

CHAPTER 11

Understand Free Capital

There are many different ways that banks, hedge funds, and individuals define "capital" but it all comes down to one question: How much money can you afford to lose? That is your *free capital*. Make sure you understand this section before moving on.

If you have $150,000 in your FX trading account but you have 10X leverage, is your free capital $1,500,000? No. It is $150,000.

Let's say you are at a hedge fund and you have $100 million of capital to manage. Is that your free capital? No. Your contract probably includes a maximum drawdown or stop loss. Your contract might say that if you lose more than 10% of the $100m, you are out of a job. So in that case, your free capital is $10 million.

This is not just a matter of semantics; it is an important concept to internalize. In the hedge fund example, sure you have $100 million of trading capital; but you can only lose $10 million before you're going to have to update your LinkedIn profile. So $10 million is your free capital—that is the number that matters.

■ Set Goals

What are you trying to accomplish? Without a clear set of goals, it is hard to create a sensible risk management plan. You need targets for returns and volatility because these targets, plus your amount of free capital, will determine how much risk you can take any day, month, or year and how much money you can lose before you have a problem.

These targets vary, depending on where you work. They could be:

- Your budget or revenue target if you work at a bank
- Your absolute return target (in % or bps), volatility target, and target Sharpe ratio if you work at a hedge fund
- Monthly USD P&L goal or % return goal if you are a retail FX trader

Once you have determined your free capital and your P&L target(s), you have set the approximate boundaries for your downside and upside performance. Free capital and P&L targets are the two critical support beams in any risk management framework and you should spend a good chunk of time coming up with numbers that make sense.

It is important to use manageable chunks of time when thinking about your P&L. I always have a yearly goal, which I set in January, but I manage my risk and P&L on a monthly basis. I have tried various approaches but this is the method that works best for me. I break the year into monthly chunks and set objectives and stop loss limits for each month.

I have tried daily and yearly chunking but I find that daily limits fail to recognize that the opportunity set varies dramatically from one day to the next (so it doesn't make sense to allocate the same amount of capital to each day) while thinking only about yearly goals is just not granular enough. A year is simply too long a period to manage—and it is too exhausting to focus on the same YTD number for 12 full months.

Weekly or monthly chunking of goals and risk makes the most sense for short-term traders. It gives you a regular mental reset, too, which is extremely useful whether you are trading well or trading badly. You can also ignore the chunking suggestion and portion your risk management on a trade-by-trade basis. I will discuss that later.

Monthly chunking means this: Every month I reset my P&L target and risk limits to zero and start over. I have a new stop loss limit and a new goal. This goal is not static; it goes up or down depending on my year-to-date P&L. As my YTD P&L goes up, my monthly risk goes up. As my YTD goes down, my monthly risk goes down.

There is no correct formula for how to determine your monthly target and stop loss, but here is how I do it. Let's say I'm trying to make $10 million in a year and my max drawdown limit (peak to trough) is $5 million. That is a pretty standard setup if you work at a bank or if you manage around $100 million of hedge fund capital. In this scenario, my free capital (money I can afford to lose) is $5m.

My January stop loss will be 10% of my year's free capital ($500k) and my January P&L target will be 2X my stop loss ($1 million).

Depending on my YTD going into a new month, I will adjust my goal and stop loss for the following month so that my goals (and thus my risk appetite and position size) reflect how I am doing. As I make money, my risk increases, and when I lose money I take less risk in the following month.

When you reset your risk on a monthly basis, you get a fresh outlook for the new month and you are not bogged down by emotions related to your performance or specific trades from prior periods. Another benefit of this approach is that you increase risk throughout the year when you are doing well and you reduce risk if you are trading poorly.

Let's look at a realistic example using the criteria described above. Say I make $2 million in January. Now my free capital for the rest of the year is $7m (the original $5m plus the $2m I just made in January). So now I can risk $700k in February (10% of $7m) and aim for a target P&L of $1.4m (2 X $700,000). As the year progresses, I take more and more risk when I'm doing well and less and less risk if I am losing money. Each month I reset my parameters and go from there.

To be clear. In January:

Free capital X 10% = January stop loss

Stop loss × 2 = Take profit objective

In each subsequent month:

(Free capital at start of month) X 10% = Stop loss for the month

Note (Free capital at start of month) = (Free capital at start of year + YTD P&L)

Stop loss X 2 = Take profit objective

What happens if I hit my stop loss for the month? I stop trading completely and wait for the calendar to roll over. This allows a mental reset and forces me to take my foot off the gas when things are not going well. When I hit my P&L target for the month, on the other hand, I do not stop trading but I do my very best to slow down and protect the successful month.

Rule #10 of FX Trading: Making money is hard. Keeping it is harder.

When I found myself in a trading slump one time, my manager said to me, "You don't have a money-making problem, you have a money-keeping problem!" Which sounds funny; but it's funny because it's true. Many traders become sloppy when they are doing well because they subconsciously feel like they are playing with house money. The purpose of the P&L target for the month is to remind you that at a certain point you have done a good job and thus it's time to book profits, not increase leverage.

This is also a nod to the fact that trading P&L tends to mean revert. If you are overearning for a period, there is a point where you want to reduce risk in anticipation of a pullback. Some model funds do this systematically. As P&L gets too far above trend, the models will reduce risk in anticipation of some mean reversion in the performance of the model.

Many people (logically) ask: Doesn't a monthly chunking approach create arbitrary breaks in your risk management? You are potentially taking different risk on the 31st of the month than you will take on the 1st of the following month even though the opportunity set might not have changed.

The answer is yes, it does create an arbitrary break in your risk management. I believe, however, that the psychological and process-related benefits of a fresh start every month substantially outweigh the negative of using arbitrary time period breaks to frame your risk. Furthermore, the turn of the month is not completely arbitrary because opportunities tend to cluster near the start and end of the month for most traders, given the distribution of economic data and central bank meetings.

The monthly chunking approach I have described is not for everyone. I am sharing what has worked for me over the past twenty years. It is up to you to take what makes sense and discard what does not as you build your own risk management framework.

Now let's look at other strategies I use to manage risk effectively.

■ Track and Analyze Your P&L

There are many metrics you can use to track your trading P&L. A simple framework is best. If you track too many statistics, you will find yourself inundated with data and find it very difficult to draw useful conclusions. Every trader should track the following statistics:

■ Daily P&L

This is the most basic unit of P&L tracking. Create a spreadsheet with OPEN, HIGH, LOW, and CLOSE P&L for each trading day. OPEN is your overnight P&L. That is, how much money you are up or down when you sit down in the morning. If you go home with no positions overnight, your OPEN figure the next day will be zero.

HIGH and LOW allow you to track the volatility of your intraday P&L and can provide important insights. CLOSE is your total end-of-day P&L.

If you trade many different products, you should also set up columns in your P&L spreadsheet to track performance by product or product type. I do not track my P&L by currency but I like to keep separate columns for options, commodity, and interest rate P&L so that I know if I am making money when I move away from my core product (G10 spot FX).

Every six months or so, I sit down and look at my daily data and ask questions like:

How does the HIGH compare to the LOW? I want my upside volatility higher than my downside volatility. Are there many days where I am down significantly and recover back to flat? This might signal that I'm starting too aggressively in the morning instead of waiting for better opportunities later in the day. Or is it the opposite pattern, where my CLOSE is often way below my HIGH? This might signal that I trade too loose after I'm up money on the day.

Is there a level where my HIGH tends to peak? Personally, I have had the experience many times over the years where I tend to hit a specific P&L number (say $1M on the day) before reversing and closing lower on the day over and over. In my case, there are two reasons this happens. The first is that markets often tend to mean revert intraday. This means that if I catch a big intraday trend, my peak in P&L will coincide with a peak or trough in a specific market. As the move reverts, my P&L reverts.

The second reason you might regularly peak near a specific P&L level is that your position size combines with average daily volatility to create rough limits on how much you can make on most days. If you are trading an average position size of $100M and intraday moves tend to max out around 1%, you will notice many days where you peak around $1M P&L.

If you consistently trade the same risk units intraday, you will probably find that there is a specific level where your P&L tends to peak and only on extremely volatile days will you ever exceed that level. If you tend to hit the same HIGH all the time and then finish significantly below by the CLOSE, this can be a useful signal. This tells you that going forward, you should reduce risk as you near what is typically your intraday high-water mark.

■ Create a Chart of Your Daily and YTD Data

Figure 11.1 is a sample P&L chart showing daily bars and YTD P&L.

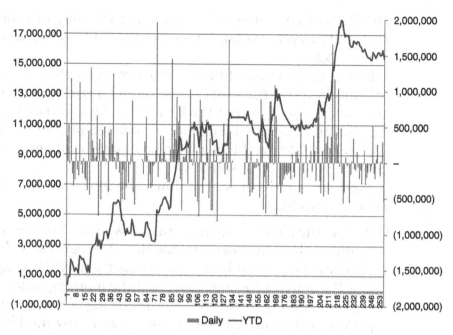

Figure 11.1 Sample P&L chart showing daily and year-to-date P&L.

Left y-axis is YTD P&L (**rising** line) and right y-axis is daily P&L (gray bars).

Some takeaways from this chart, which is a realistic representation of the P&L for a solid trader at a bank (stylized, not real data):

1. Note the skew in the gray bars. A good day is up $1.5 million, while a bad day is down $750,000 (right-hand y-axis). This is how you achieve very strong performance while making money on only 50% of days. The trader shown above made more than $15 million dollars of P&L while putting up a winning percentage of just 46%. This is because his average up day was $411,000 while his average down day was $273,000.

2. Note the big bursts in P&L followed by flat line and consolidation. This is what my P&L looks like when I am trading well. It is symptomatic of small position sizes and small losses while dabbling and then big positions on high-conviction ideas. The result is that a few bursts of "in the zone" trading account for most of the year's P&L. Some traders are more consistent than this and others are less consistent. There is no correct profile, although the relationship between good periods and bad periods obviously determines the end result so you need to make hay while the sun shines. Extract as much money as possible from the market when things are going well.

3. If you look very closely, you will see that there are a few periods where the P&L doesn't move at all for 5 or 10 straight days. This shows the trader took some time off and was perfectly flat while

on holiday. This is a healthy practice that keeps you fresh all year and extends your career longevity.

Month-to-Date P&L

Monthly P&L increments are the most important units for your long-term success. Can you make money most months? Are your good months substantially better than your bad months? Obviously, each month is made up of many days but there is huge randomness in daily performance. Luck will have a significant influence on daily P&L, whereas monthly and yearly performance is primarily determined by skill, not luck.

A month is a big enough unit to eliminate some of the noise and allow many good trading opportunities to play out. Most successful traders will record mostly positive months throughout the year, even if they only win 50% of the days.

Rarely will you find a successful trader who doesn't make money at least 7 or 8 months of the year, although it is possible. Your best months should be much larger than your worst months.

Year-to-Date P&L

This is the ultimate measure of your long-run performance and most people cannot survive more than two or three bad years before running out of capital or losing their job. Ideally, you want to behave like a call option. This means that your bad years are flat or down small and your good years are up and potentially up big.

This is the payoff profile that management is looking for when they hire hedge fund or bank traders and it is the payoff profile you need as an individual trader if you want to succeed long term. This payoff profile (down small or up big) is achieved through a risk management system that increases risk when things are going well and reduces risk when they are not.

Win%

This is the number of days you make money divided by the number of days you trade. Most traders are in the 45% to 60% win% area, while bank traders with good franchise books can hit a win percentage as high as 80%. Win% depends on your trading style. Those who chip away and trade very tactically will have high win%, while those who go all in on big opportunities and stay flat much of the time will have a lower win%.

■ Average Gain/Loss

Your ultimate success will depend on a combination of your win% and your average gain/loss ratio. Generally, traders with higher win% have shorter holding periods and lower gain/loss ratios. There is no right answer when it comes to these ratios but the important thing to understand is how your ratios are evolving.

If you see, for example, your average gain/loss ratio is falling month after month, then it probably means you are cutting your winners too early or riding your losing days for too long. Big up days and small down days are the key to success in trading. It sounds simple but I present it here so that you take time to think about how you can increase that ratio. It is the most important ratio in your P&L spreadsheet.

Rule #11 of FX Trading: Successful traders make more money on up days than they lose on down days.

A good strategy once you have a decent amount of P&L data is to zoom in on one particular metric and think about how you can improve it. For example, I noticed in the past that very often I would not stick to my original plan on winning trades and would tend to book profits before the intended take profit level hit. For example, if I went long at AUDUSD at 0.7710 with a take profit of 0.7880, I would often take profit at, say, 0.7840 as the price action stalled, instead of riding out the trade and extracting the maximum P&L as originally planned.

It is always a tricky situation when you have made 70% or 80% of your planned profits on a trade because the risk/reward at that point looks bad if you hold on all the way back to your original stop loss. On the other hand, if you consistently take profit too early, then the risk/reward you had originally planned for is not realized. In addition, if you trail your stop loss up too much, you are frequently stopped out by noise.

Once I analyzed the metric, I decided from that point on to simply stick to my original plan and stop changing my parameters once a trade moved deep in the money. By discovering and fixing this leak, I made a meaningful improvement in my average gain/loss ratio.

■ Sharpe Ratio

The Sharpe Ratio is a commonly used measure of trading performance that measures the relationship between volatility and returns. It is the idea that if an investor receives the same return from two investments, she will prefer the investment with lower volatility.

Let's look at a simplified example. Trader A made $320,000 this week and Trader B made $300,000. Who did a better job? With only that information, the answer is Trader A. But now let me give you some more information. Here is the daily P&L for Trader A:

+250,000 +120,000 − 500,000 + 400,000 +50,000 = $320,000

And here's the P&L for Trader B:

+50,000 +100,000 +100,000 +0   +50,000 = $300,000

Now who did a better job? I pick Trader B because I would expect from this distribution of P&L that there is a much better chance that Trader B performs well going forward while Trader A was probably lucky and has too much volatility/variance/randomness to his revenue stream to validate the tiny difference in absolute returns.[1] Obviously, the data set provided is too small to make sweeping generalizations; this is just a stylized example.

The formula for Sharpe Ratio is: (Return minus risk-free rate / Standard deviation).

Higher Sharpe ratios are almost always better as they represent higher returns relative to volatility. In the example above, you have Trader A with a Sharpe Ratio around 1.0 for the week while Trader B comes in with a Sharpe Ratio of about 7.0. Almost every investor would prefer the lower returns of Trader B because his Sharpe is so much higher.

For most strategies and traders, a Sharpe above 1.0 is good and a Sharpe above 2.0 is outstanding. Some traders can maintain Sharpes as high as 4.0 for certain periods but most humans find it hard to sustain a Sharpe above 2.0 for long. Sharpe ratios can be very stable or extremely erratic and so a Sharpe is just one measure of performance and not the be-all and end-all.

It is very important to note that Sharpe ratios can be meaningless if a trader or strategy has very non-normal returns. For example, a trader who sells S&P 500 puts or VIX futures will have a very good Sharpe Ratio for extended periods but this high Sharpe Ratio will obscure the fact that the trader will almost certainly blow up one day when volatility spikes (like it did in February 2018, for example). Especially in small samples, the Sharpe Ratio can hide the non-normal distribution of a strategy's returns.

The more years of data, the more informative the Sharpe Ratio. Sharpe ratios are most useful when comparing traders and strategies

---

[1] Clearly a sample size of 5 is not good enough to make a truly accurate assessment. This is a simplified example for explanatory purposes. When analyzing real P&L figures, larger data samples are necessary and anything less than 30 to 50 data points would make any analysis meaningless. The more data points, the better.

in similar asset classes. Hedge funds often focus on Sharpe Ratio while banks focus much more on absolute returns because market making distorts the Sharpe Ratio and renders it somewhat meaningless.

Regardless of where you work, better P&L analysis leads to better risk management.

■ Fat Tails and Risk of Ruin

Good returns and even a good Sharpe can hide some types of risk. A key risk that is not always captured by Sharpe ratios is tail risk. This is an absolutely key type of risk because tail risk can lead to ruin. Risk of ruin is the premise that if you lose a certain amount of money, you are done. Out. Fired. The first consideration for every trader should be to avoid risk of ruin. Live to fight another day.

Tail risk can come from one specific trade or from an overall trading style. A famous example of tail risk is the 2015 SNB CHF trade. In 2011, the Swiss National Bank announced a currency floor at 1.2000 in EURCHF as a way to stop the relentless buying of CHF (selling of EURCHF) triggered by the Eurozone crisis. The SNB committed to sell unlimited CHF and buy unlimited EUR in order to protect the floor. The floor held successfully for several years despite a few tests and more and more speculators viewed long EURCHF positions as nearly risk-free because everyone knew the SNB had their back at 1.2000.

Then, in early 2015, concerns about Greek finances and expectations of a huge quantitative easing program from the ECB unleashed relentless supply of EURCHF. The SNB was there on the bid, buying billions and billions of euros around 1.2010 in order to enforce their commitment to the 1.2000 floor. Various SNB board members continually reiterated their commitment to the floor, saying they would sell unlimited CHF to protect it. This statement, made on January 12, 2015, is a good example of the message consistently delivered by the SNB:

> "We took stock of the situation less than a month ago, we looked again at all the parameters and we are convinced that the minimum exchange rate must remain the cornerstone of our monetary policy."
> – SNB Vice Chairman Jean-Pierre Danthine

There appeared to be a nearly risk-free trade from 2011 to 2015. Simply buy EURCHF every time it gets close to 1.2000 and sell any rally. Figure 11.2 shows the chart.

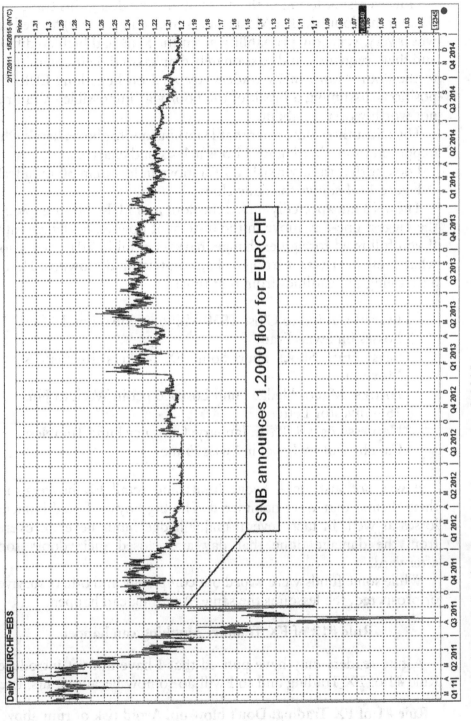

Figure 11.2 Daily EURCHF February 17, 2011, to January 5, 2015.

You can see it was an extremely profitable trade to simply buy EURCHF every time it went near 1.2000 and wait for the rally. What could possibly go wrong?

However, simmering in the mind of anyone doing this trade was: What if the floor breaks? Most traders (including myself) figured this was a very, very low probability given the SNB had high credibility and they frequently and passionately emphasized their commitment to the floor. Many, many traders strapped on huge long EURCHF positions, assuming a break of the floor was impossible. A tail risk not worth worrying about.

Then, just three days after that Danthine quote above, here's what happened (note that Figure 11.3 is a 1-second chart!).

Look at that right y-axis! A 30% move in less than 30 minutes!

Figure 11.4 shows the daily chart.

The SNB unexpectedly pulled the floor and EURCHF collapsed in the biggest one-day move in the history of floating exchange rates. If you followed foreign exchange markets at all in 2015 you know what came next was a string of bankruptcies and blowups. Here is a sampling of headlines from that time:

> Everest Capital to Close $830 Million Global Fund After Losses on Swiss Franc
> Swiss Franc Shock Shuts Some FX Brokers; Regulators Move In
> Fortress Macro Hedge Fund Lost 7.6 pct in Week to Jan. 16 – Investor Letter
> Harness Loses 8.8% in January: Currency Fund Tumbles; Caught Out by Spike in Swiss Franc

It was not just small hedge funds and retail FX brokers (and their clients) that were hammered. The big boys suffered immense losses as well. In fact, several major hedge funds never recovered from the damage done that day and closed their doors soon afterward.

While some funds were wiped out completely and others survived or prospered, the lesson is the same. Anything can happen.

Rule #12 of FX Trading: Anything can happen.

Astute readers may have noticed that I have not yet introduced Rule #1 of FX Trading and so I will do so now because it fits here.

Rule #1 of FX Trading: Don't blow up. Avoid risk of ruin above all else.

If you blow up, none of the other rules of FX trading will matter because you will be bankrupt or unemployed.

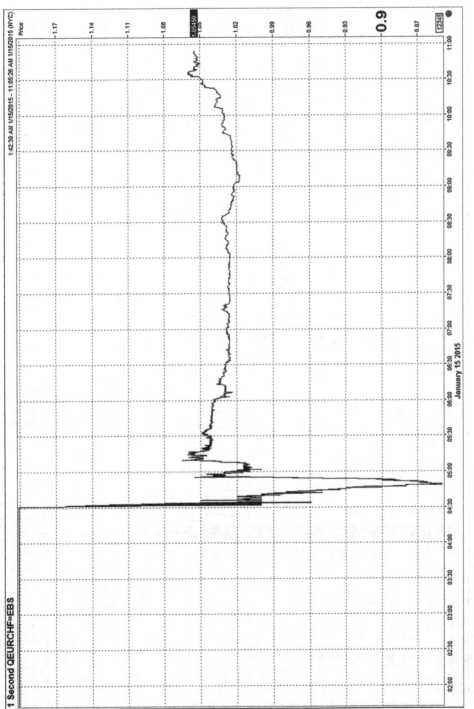

Figure 11.3 1-second EURCHF, January 15, 2015.

UNDERSTAND FREE CAPITAL

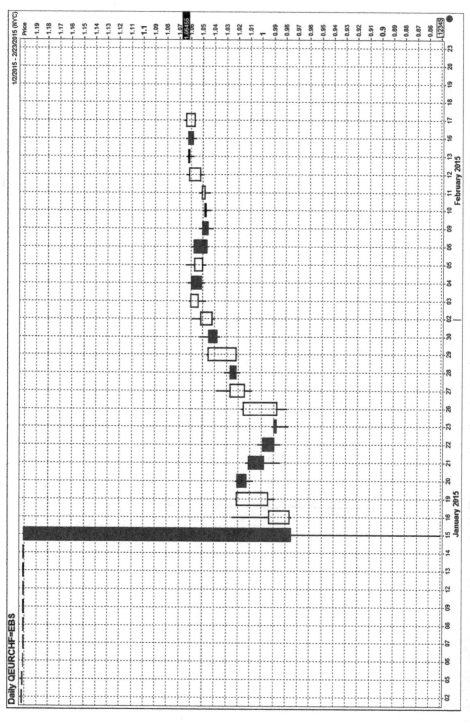

Figure 11.4 Daily EURCHF January 5, 2015, to February 22, 2015.

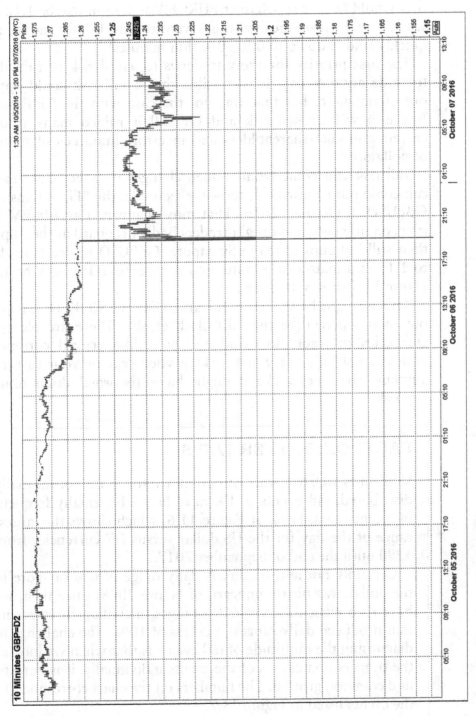

Figure 11.5 10-minute GBPUSD, the GBP Flash Crash of October 6, 2016.

Sure, there was profit to be made trading long EURCHF for several years, but the problem was that while the rewards were clear, the risks were not measurable. Many people expected that if 1.20 broke, they would be able to sell their EURCHF at 1.15 or maybe 1.12 as a worst case. Instead, the first trades were around 1.0100 and the pair quickly traded down to 0.8500 within minutes!

The first priority for every trader is to avoid risk of ruin. Live to trade another day. It is possible that a tail risk could appear out of nowhere, but that was not the case with the CHF move. It was a well-known risk and yet still it ruined many traders' careers and cost shareholders and investors hundreds of millions of dollars.

Tail risk can come from sudden changes in policy but crashes can come out of nowhere, too—for example, the "Flash Crash" in GBPUSD in October 2016. That move happened at 7:00PM NY time, on no news, and caught traders badly off guard as they sipped their still-hot cups of tea in Singapore. GBPUSD traded from 1.26 to 1.15 in a matter of minutes and soon rebounded back to 1.24. Figure 11.5 shows the chart.

Tail risks can be known in advance (like the CHF) or can come out of nowhere (like the GBP flash crash). There are plenty of currencies to trade, so avoid any pair (like pegged currencies) with tail risk; it's not worth risking your year or your career on anything that looks like it might have abnormal discontinuous gap risk.

FACTBOX: FATTER TAILS

While it is well known that currency returns are not normally distributed, tail events in FX have been abnormally frequent in recent years. Look at Figure 11.6, which shows the largest range of the day for the US dollar versus G7 currencies from 1990 until the end of September 2017.

Certainly not anti-fragile! A daily range of 6% or more in the dollar was nearly unheard of before 2008; since then, we have seen eight different 6%+ ranges, including three events that produced daily ranges in excess of 10%. The challenge in diagnosing the multitude of tail events is that when we look at the triggers and causes of the events individually, it is hard to find common ground. The numbers on the chart correspond to the events listed in Figure 11.7.

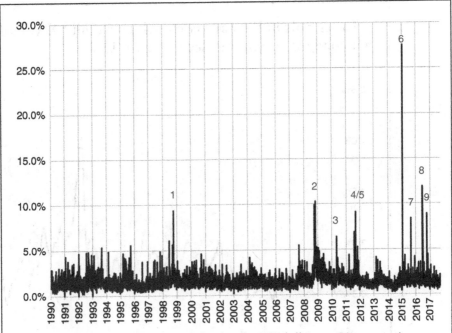

Figure 11.6 Largest range of the day for US dollar vs. G7 currencies (1990 to 2017).

Data from Bloomberg.

Event	Date	Currency	Trigger	Other Cause 1	Other Cause 2
1 Asia Crisis, LTCM unwind	October 8, 1998	NZD and USDJPY	LTCM unwind	Asian Financial Crisis	Central banks sold USDJPY
2 GFC	October 2008	AUD and NZD	Financial crisis	US politics (TARP rejected)	
3 US stock market flash crash	May 6, 2010	USDJPY	Stock market flash crash		
4 US downgraded	August 9, 2011	USDCHF	S&P downgrade of USA	Government shutdown	
5 SNB puts in the floor	Sep 6, 2011	USDCHF	SNB		
6 SNB removes the floor	January 15, 2015	USDCHF	SNB	Positioning	
7 China reval	August 24, 2015	NZDUSD	PBoC		
8 UK votes to leave EU	June 24, 2016	GBPUSD	UK voters		
9 Flash crash	October 7, 2016	GBPUSD	Stop losses	Time of day	Human error

Data from Bloomberg.

Figure 11.7 USD vs. G7 moves of 6% or more since 1990.

Fatter tails in FX have come while overall FX volatility has not changed, as you can see in Figure 11.8.

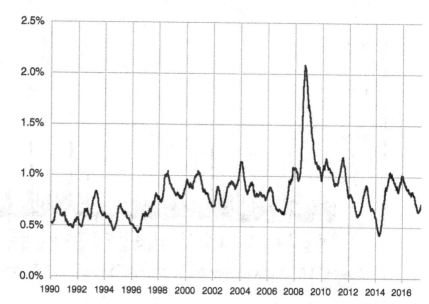

Figure 11.8 100-day rolling median daily range of USD vs. G7 currencies.

Data from Bloomberg.

There is no meaningful difference in FX volatility before and after 2008. Furthermore, global currency market volumes continue to grow, so there is no shortage of volume transacted.

Reading government reports on recent crash events in FX and other markets sheds very little extra light on causality as these reports generally cite a multitude of factors. For example, the BIS Markets Committee report "The sterling 'flash event' of 7 October 2016" says, "This analysis points to a confluence of factors catalyzing the move, rather than to a single clear driver," while the "Joint Staff Report: The US Treasury Market on October 15, 2014" says, "While no single cause is apparent in the data, the analysis thus far does point to a number of findings which, in aggregate, help explain the conditions that likely contributed to the volatility."

In other words, when tail events happen, it is often hard to nail down a single cause.

As we try to explain the rising frequency of tail events in FX since 2008, it makes sense to start with what is different about FX markets now compared to pre-2008. There are five important differences:

1. The number of senior traders in FX has dropped substantially in the past decade. This is partially because of automation and also follows the disciplinary actions resulting from multiple investigations into currency trading from 2013 to 2015.

   The BIS report on the GBP flash crash says, "The presence, outside the currency's core time zone, of staff less experienced in trading sterling, with lower risk limits and risk appetite, and with less expertise in the suitability of particular algorithms for the prevailing market conditions, appears to have further amplified the movement."

   It is sensible to think that less-experienced traders are more likely to deal off market or trigger panic moves compared to senior dealers with experience in fast markets.

2. Electronic trading is now more than 60% of the FX market. Algorithmic volumes rose throughout the second half of the 2000s (see Figure 11.9). It is possible that we hit a tipping point in human versus algorithmic participation right around 2008 and this has opened up cracks in the FX microstructure. Correlation does not always imply causation but there is plenty of evidence and logic to support a relationship here.

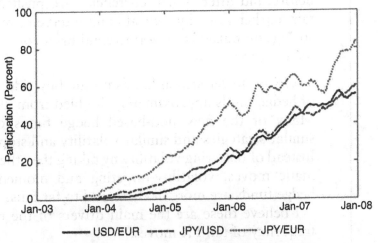

Figure 11.9 50-day moving average of the participation rate of algorithmic traders in FX markets, 2004 to 2009.

Source: US Federal Reserve (https://www.federalreserve.gov/pubs/ifdp/2009/980/ifdp980.pdf).

For example, many market-making algorithms are price makers in slow markets and price takers in fast markets. This can exacerbate feedback loops and generate negative convexity. Unlike market makers of yore, hedge funds and other non-bank electronic market makers are not obligated to maintain orderly markets. If things get crazy, VAR warnings sound and the algorithms reduce risk and turn off.

Also, the behavior of algorithms is not always perfect, adaptable, or logical. Similar to inexperienced human traders, algorithms might accidentally exacerbate large moves and flash crashes as they fail to adapt to regime shifts and fast markets.

3. Order slicing/hiding has left fewer resting orders away from top of book. Pre-2007, most orders left on ECNs showed full size and trader interest. Now, most orders are sliced into the tiniest possible increment or show nothing to the market and wait only to aggress others' liquidity. Many trading algorithms sense aggression or velocity in the market and pull back or cancel at the moment that liquidity is needed most. All this means fewer truly firm orders in the market.

4. Central bank pegs, bands, caps, and floors lead to great stability at first but extreme instability later. Stability breeds instability. While the EURCHF market was placid when the SNB supported the 1.2000 level, it was abnormally volatile before and after. When currencies are pushed away from fair market value by central bank intervention, they have a strong compulsion to revert to equilibrium once policymaker intervention stops.

5. There are fewer strong hands on the buy side. The number of hedge funds approximately doubled from 2003 to 2007. Many of the new pod-based hedge funds operate with similar strategies and similar volatility and stop loss targets. Instead of buffering volatility by taking the other side of dramatic moves, volatility-targeting and momentum-chasing hedge funds are more likely to add to fat tails.

I believe these are the main drivers of the recent rise in frequency of tail FX moves.

I am not arguing that we turn back the clock. Electronic markets are here to stay and are not a bad thing. However, in a world where many humans and algorithms are running similar strategies at higher and higher speeds, there are bound to be some accidents.

So first and foremost, my suggestion with regard to the rise in frequency of FX tail events is this: *Get used to it*. Markets populated by algorithms and inexperienced traders will have a propensity toward fatter tails. This is a fact that FX practitioners need to accept. It has important implications for the future of FX risk management, option pricing, and execution strategies.

■ Rolling Drawdown

Rolling drawdown gives you a nice visual representation of your downside volatility over time. This is in contrast to the Sharpe Ratio, which shows returns adjusted for both upside and downside volatility. There are other measures, such as the Sortino Ratio, that single out downside volatility but I have found that a combination of Sharpe Ratio and rolling drawdown gives a view of performance that is simple and easier to understand than more sophisticated metrics. Simply create a chart of your current P&L minus your YTD high P&L and this will show you rolling drawdown from peak.

■ P&L by Time of Day

An extremely useful analysis for short-term traders is P&L by time of day. The way I collected this information when I worked at a hedge fund was to manually record my P&L in a spreadsheet every 30 minutes. If you can have this done automatically, that is even better. After collecting intraday data for a while, I noticed that my P&L very consistently rose from 7:00AM and peaked around 11:00AM. It then came off gradually until the end of the day. The chart looked something like Figure 11.10.

I was unaware of this pattern until I started recording intraday P&L data. There is a strong logic to a pattern like this because the volatile and liquid period for FX markets in the New York time zone is 7:00AM until 11:00AM. After that, London goes home and things tend to die down.

Armed with the information from this chart, I started to square up much, much earlier each day. Instead of taking my risk down in the afternoon, I tried my best to reduce risk around 11:00AM. This helped me lock in more P&L and it reduced my overall stress level because once I knew that all my trading after 12 noon was net negative, I could reduce my risk and use the afternoons for research, exercise, and other more useful endeavors. An added benefit of

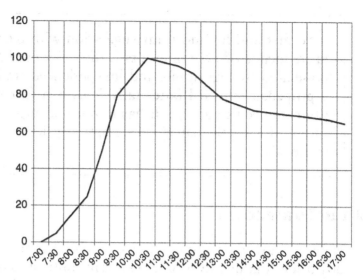

Figure 11.10   Approximate P&L by time of day when I traded at a hedge fund. The y-axis is percent of total daily P&L, on average.

squaring up earlier is that liquidity is much better at 11AM NY than it is at 4PM NY.

This is a good example of how data collection and P&L analysis can make you a better trader. Be very mindful of what data you collect, though, because the risk is that you collect so much data that you don't know what to do with it. Use data to investigate sensible hypotheses and ideas. Don't expect it to speak for itself all the time.

Be thoughtful about what data you collect so that you do not waste time dealing with a firehose of useless information. Do you think you might trade best on Mondays and worst on Fridays? Investigate it. What about the start of the month versus the end of the month? Whenever you think about your trading and performance, go back and look at your P&L data to better understand your strengths, weaknesses, and leaks.

Collecting trading performance data is extremely useful and allows you to accumulate useful quantitative data. Instead of guessing, you can go to the numbers. Armed with quantitative data, you have a good snapshot of your trading. But qualitative information is useful, too. In order to collect qualitative information, you need to maintain a trading journal.

■ Keep a Trading Journal

Every trader, regardless of experience level, should keep a trading journal. A journal helps track the evolution of your trading and captures emotions, themes, and thoughts throughout the process. Many

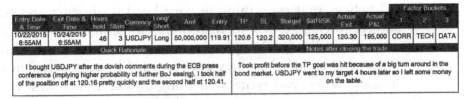

Entry Date & Time	Exit Date & Time	Hours held	Stars	Currency	Long/Short	Amt	Entry	TP	SL	Starget	SatRISK	Actual Exit	Actual P&L	Factor Buckets		
														1	2	3
10/22/2015 8:55AM	10/24/2015 6:55AM	46	3	USDJPY	Long	50,000,000	119.91	120.6	120.2	320,000	125,000	120.30	195,000	CORR	TECH	DATA
Quick Rationale							Notes after closing the trade									
I bought USDJPY after the dovish comments during the ECB press conference (implying higher probability of further BoJ easing). I took half of the position off at 120.16 pretty quickly and the second half at 120.41.							Took profit before the TP goal was hit because of a big turn around in the bond market. USDJPY went to my target 4 hours later so I left some money on the table.									

Figure 11.11 Sample entry from an Excel trading journal.

people think of a trading journal as something just for noob traders. It is not. You should use it as a professional trade strategy planning and assessment tool. There are many ways that a journal can help you.

Most of the columns in Figure 11.11 are self-explanatory, but let me explain a few that might not be:

$target = P&L if I hit my take profit
$atRISK = Loss if I hit my stop

Factor buckets are the motivation behind the trade. CORR = correlation, TECH = technical convergence, and so on. This is important because then I can see which styles and factor buckets are working and which are not.

Above all, a trading journal gives you a chance to be honest with yourself. It's one thing to think and think and think about your trading, but things become more concrete when you write them down. By writing down each trade along with a rationale and thought process, you can pick up on recurring errors, themes, and leaks in your trading.

Rule #13 of FX Trading: Keep a trading journal. Thoughts are abstract and fuzzy. Writing is concrete and solid.

A trading journal also helps you identify bias. Are you always the same way in a specific currency? Do you tend to short commodity currencies? Long the USD? You can also look at your time horizons and study whether you make more money on certain time horizons or on specific types of trades. The more you write down, the more you can go back later and investigate various hypotheses and answer questions about your trading.

A trading journal also helps you stick to your plan. If you type your plan in your journal before you do a trade (or immediately thereafter), you are much (*much!*) more likely to stick to that plan. Bad discipline often comes from having no plan whatsoever and just hitting the buy and sell keys in response to random market stimuli. A plan written down has 100 times the value of a plan loosely formulated in your head.

I believe that everything in your head is abstract and fuzzy and subject to change. It's noisy in there. Sometimes there is more than one voice talking. Thoughts become more concrete and more intelligent and lucid when they are recorded in print (written or typed is fine). When you write something down, it solidifies. It becomes much more concrete and real and firm.

I write a daily newsletter called AM/FX in which I outline my trading plan for the day and discuss the themes in focus. When I moved from an interbank trading job to a hedge fund for a few years, I stopped writing. I found that this had a major negative impact on my trading. I would walk in some mornings and just start hitting the buy and sell buttons, reacting to price action and headlines instead of trading logically according to a plan.

If you go into a trading day or into a specific trade without a written plan, it is a recipe for poor trading. If you have a written plan for every day and every trade, you will find your trading is tighter and your risk management is better. The process of writing down your plan also filters out some bad trades in advance because you realize as you write out the plan that the idea is not solid enough to deserve an allocation of risk capital.

Once trades are closed, you record the information about the trade and after a while you have enough numerical and qualitative data to go back and assess your performance. Wait until you have a few months of trades in your journal before you assess anything because otherwise you will run into sample size issues. Statistical analysis of trading and P&L is covered in the previous section, so now it's time to start asking more subjective questions such as:

Is there a mistake you make repeatedly? One of the best predictors of failure is the trader who keeps making the same mistakes over and over.

Do you stick to your plan? Or do you always take profit too early? Do you stop out at worse levels than you planned?

Do you always lose money in a specific currency? Are some times of day or days of the week or times of the month better or worse for you?

Are your high-conviction trades more profitable than your low-conviction trades? If yes, why? Are you sizing the different trades appropriately?

And so on. This type of analysis can really improve your game and reduce errors. Be creative when slicing and dicing the information and try to make an honest assessment of your performance. Always think about what is working and what is not. Do more of what works and less of what does not.

You should always work hard to understand and analyze your trading performance. This will lead to greater self-understanding and improve your chances of long-term success. Be thoughtful about your trading and about your strengths, weaknesses, and leaks. This will lead to greater self-understanding and greater profits.

This concludes our look at free capital and P&L analysis. Next, we will dig deep into two crucial topics: position sizing and stop losses. These are topics where even many experienced traders fail to optimize and therefore underperform their potential.

After reading this chapter, you should fully understand these key concepts:

- What is free capital and how do you measure it? Why is it important and how is it different from total capital under management?

- How much can you afford to lose?

- How to measure and analyze P&L

- How to set goals and track your performance

- Why a trading journal is important

Understand Position Sizing

■ Position Size as a Percentage of Capital

There are many ways to determine position size. The four primary factors that determine position size are: (1) How much free capital do you have? (2) How confident are you on this trade? (3) How volatile is the currency pair? (4) Where is your stop loss?

Over the years, by studying many risk management texts and books on professional gambling, I have come up with a very simple but effective approach. Before I do a trade, I rate it by conviction as Three-Star, Four-Star, or Five-Star. Then, I allocate approximately the following amount of adjusted free capital to the trade:

Three-Star 1%

Four-Star 3%

Five-Star 6%

Remember, when I refer to adjusted free capital, I define that as how much you can afford to lose from now until the end of the year. Adjusted just means the initial free capital adjusted for my year-to-date P&L. If my adjusted free capital is $8 million and a Five-Star trade comes along, I will risk $480,000 on it ($8 million times 6%).

It is important to note that the bar for a Five-Star trade is very high and these trades are rare. I might see 10 of them in a good year. Also note that I always calculate my risk amounts based on my adjusted free capital. If I could afford to lose $8m on January 1, but I'm up $4m on the year, I now have $12 million in adjusted free capital. If a Five-Star trade appears at that point, I will risk up to $720,000 on it ([8 million + 4 million] times 6%).

Many people will say that 6% of capital is too much for a single trade but I disagree. I believe that when you see a Five-Star setup, you need to be very aggressive. But this is only true when you are in a position to be aggressive. You cannot be extremely risky like this when you are in a weak capital position.

Understand that because of leverage available in most trading seats, you are not really allocating 6% of your total capital to a Five-Star trade. Just 6% of *free capital*. There is a big difference between free capital (amount you can afford to lose) and your total capital.

Let me explain a bit more because this concept is very important: Say you have $100m in capital but a 9% drawdown limit. You can only afford to lose $9m, not $100m. So I am saying you would be risking 6% of $9m, which is $540,000—less than 1% of your $100m capital under management. Some traders use only a trade-by-trade risk allocation system and others use only a monthly system. Some (like me) overlap the two. I am describing both methods and you can use them independently or in combination.

These numbers are starting points for risk allocation, not absolutes. I have sometimes allocated 7% or even 10% of my free capital to a trade when I believed in it very strongly and I was in a strong P&L position YTD or MTD. Obviously, you cannot be wrong many times at 10% of free capital before the hit to your equity becomes problematic. So I feel much better about taking larger risk once I am significantly profitable.

I use these per-trade risk allocations along with monthly risk limits so that I only take really big risk when I have high conviction and I am trading from strength. As I make money, my per-month and per-trade limits increase and if I'm in a slump, my per-month and per-trade risk allocations fall, ensuring that I don't blow up. If I am near my monthly stop loss and a Five-Star opportunity presents itself, too bad. I can only risk the remaining portion of my monthly risk allocation.

For example, if I start the year with $4m in free capital and have somehow lost $1m by mid-February, I probably would not be feeling very risky and would not want to put $300k (10%) of my remaining $3m on the line no matter how high my conviction on a particular trade. On the other hand, say it's June and I am up $10m so my free capital is now $14m. An extremely juicy trade idea comes along. I would probably be comfortable risking 10% of my free capital ($1.4m) on the idea knowing that if I am wrong, I am still up $8.6m on the year.

I will always trade looser when I am up and tighter when I'm down. This helps avoid risk of ruin and opens up the right tail of the distribution. Remember you want to be a call option—limited downside but unlimited upside. By trading aggressively when you are up and sticking to conservative risk percentages when you are flat or down, you maintain strong risk management in the tough times and have the potential for massive upside in your good years.

There is a time and a place to move a big stack of chips into the pot. To become the best trader possible and realize your ultimate potential, you must identify moments when you see a fantastic market opportunity and you have a big war chest of P&L. Those are the moments to go big. There is a cliché that says bulls and bears make money and pigs get slaughtered but I think that's wrong.

Rule #14 of FX Trading: There is a time and a place to go big.

Part of it comes down to personal preference and I acknowledge that some traders succeed by risking only 2% or even less on any given trade. I can only tell you what I do—I cannot guarantee it will be right for you.

Always remember: Risk of ruin is the first and biggest risk to manage. Being a pig means betting heavily on a great idea when you are already highly profitable. It does not mean risking your job or your firm on a single idea or theme. Managing risk of ruin is much more important than worrying about "risk of missing a huge opportunity." While some managers will tell you to chip away and chip away, I do not see many highly successful traders who just chip away all the time.

Most successful traders chip away until a fat opportunity comes along and then they bet big on that opportunity. This creates a right tail to the P&L distribution and acknowledges that very outsized opportunities are rare. Those superior opportunities offer very high expected value and should be met with very large bets. In poker, you are only dealt AA once in a while. You want to get paid on it.

Dynamic sizing based on capital and conviction levels automatically increases risk when you are doing well and reduces risk when you are struggling. This approach is simple to automate in a spreadsheet.

Finally, note the nonlinear jump from three-star to Five-Star. You want to keep your investment in low-conviction ideas small and save money for the big kahunas.

Rule #15 of FX Trading: Good traders vary bet size.

There is another consideration when sizing your position: Different currencies have different volatility profiles, so you need to size your position according to the volatility of the currency pair. You should take smaller positions in extremely volatile currencies and larger positions in currencies that barely move (all other things being equal). This will naturally happen if you use volatility and logic to choose your stop loss levels.

For example, if one day's range in EURUSD is 1.5% and one day's range in USDCAD is 1.0%, your stop losses should generally be closer in USDCAD and further away in EURUSD. The wider your stop, the smaller your position size if you plan to risk the same amount in $. The position sizing versus volatility dynamic should happen naturally. Don't be the person who always trades the same position size in everything, regardless of conviction or market volatility.

To find up-to-date relative volatility for different currencies, just look at 1-month implied volatility on Bloomberg, or try this link: https://www.investing.com/tools/forex-volatility-calculator.

FACTBOX: SEARCHING FOR FIVE-STARS

When multiple indicators from different branches of market analysis all point in the same direction, you have a Five-Star trade. The more indicators pointing the same way, the better. Understand that there is a difference between a Five-Star (very high-probability trade) and a perfect trade. There is no such thing as a perfect trade. No trade is guaranteed or risk-free, so be realistic. Stay ready and willing to pull the trigger. Here are the features of a Five-Star trade:

1. Fundamentals. Recent information suggests a change in fundamentals that is not fully reflected in the price. Fundamentals are improving (or getting worse) but the currency has not rallied enough to reflect the improvement (or sold off enough to reflect the deterioration).

2. Cross-market signals. Correlated variables are suggesting the currency pair is away from fair value. The more variables signaling the same thing, the better.

3. Positioning. Sentiment and positioning support the idea or at least do not hurt it.

4. Technicals. Multiple levels and patterns support the idea and allow it to be put on with good leverage. Ideally, one or two of the Seven Deadly Setups are in play. Note that sometimes all other factors are in line and technical analysis suggests patience as you wait for a better entry point. Be patient. Great trades can be ruined by terrible entry points.

5. Gut feel. The first four points are all "head." The fifth is how you feel about the trade. Do you feel extremely confident?

Good. Does everything look good on paper but you have a weird feeling about the trade? Bad. This is important because when you feel strongly about a trade, you will trade strong and if you don't feel right about the trade, you will trade weak.

In other words, you will stop out at the first sign of trouble when your gut is not on board. You will size it wrong. You will be nervous when random news hits or if the price action does not immediately go your way. Listen to your gut but treat it only as a fifth factor, not the only one in your process.

Many traders would include a sixth condition: catalyst. Is there news or an upcoming event that might push the currency pair and give it some momentum? This is a reasonable factor to look for but I find catalysts overrated. Currencies move when they want to move and sometimes there is a catalyst and sometimes there isn't. Sure, I would prefer to enter a trade when I see an upcoming catalyst, but it is not a necessary condition for me to get excited about a trade.

The percentages I describe for trade sizing are simple when you are only doing one trade. When you put on more than one trade, you need to think about the correlation between your trades and your overall P&L risk if all your trades go wrong at once. When I outline percentages to risk on a trade, sometimes that could mean dollars at risk on a theme or basket of trades as opposed to risk on a single trade.

For example, I think the dollar is going higher and it is a clear Five-Star trade. I decide to risk 6% of my free capital on that idea. I will not invest any more in anything correlated to a stronger dollar until the original trade is closed. And no matter how confident I am, I would never have three different trades on at the same time, all risking 6% (even if they appear to be uncorrelated). I prefer never to have more than 8% of my free capital at risk at any time, no matter how many trades I have on or how uncorrelated those trades might be. Something between 3% and 5% is much more reasonable most of the time.

There is a huge benefit to keeping your trading methodology as simple as possible. If you keep your methodology simple, your risk management will be simple. I rarely have more than three or four trades on at a time and often I will only have one trade on. So my sizing advice relates to distinct, individual trades executed in succession.

If you are a short-term trader or market maker who day trades, I would not think about risk on an individual trade-by-trade basis. Instead, simply allocate 1% to 6% of your capital to each day depending on the opportunity set you see for that day. Conceptually this is very similar to a trade-by-trade allocation but accounts for the fact that some short-term traders might do 20, 30, or 100 trades in a day and so it simplifies the methodology and makes it safer and easier to risk manage. Remember that your daily risk allocation has to overlap logically with your monthly risk management process if you are using one. If you are down on the month, your daily risk allocation will be driven by your monthly stop loss, not your free capital.

■ Another Simple and Effective Way for Short-Term Traders to Determine Risk

A different, safer, and simpler approach for day traders is this: Simply take your opening free capital in the morning and multiply by 0.02. Don't lose more than that much money in a given day. Each day you reset—it is all very methodical and rule based. You don't need any monthly limits under this system and it will keep you out of trouble. Every day, you risk 2% or less of your free capital. That's it. Like the other systems I describe, this system increases your risk as you accumulate profits and decreases your risk when you are losing. But this system is super-easy.

I would like to reemphasize that I am simply providing different risk management frameworks that I have used successfully at various times. You can use these as a starting point but you need to find your own methodology that is consistent with your risk appetite, volatility, and trading style. Trade at your own risk. Past performance does not guarantee future results. Etcetera.

FACTBOX: A SIMPLE AND EFFECTIVE RISK MANAGEMENT SYSTEM FOR NOVICE TRADERS

Risk 1% of capital per day. This is a simple, effective, and nearly foolproof way to manage your risk. Each day is a new day and you risk no more than 1% of your free capital. Remember to fully understand the definition of free capital (as opposed to total capital) before using this system. The system self-regulates. When you struggle, your risk allocation goes down automatically and as you make money, you risk more.

Set up a simple spreadsheet like the one shown in Figure 12.1.

	A	B	C	D	E	F	G	H	I	J
	Date	Starting Capital	Risk/trade or per day	Main Theme	Overnight	HIGH	LOW	CLOSE	MTD	YTD
21-Apr		500,000	5,000	CAD CPI + French election this weekend	3,250	8,500	(3,300)	4,400	4,400	4,400
24-Apr		504,400	5,044	French Election was Sunday	2,760	10,140	2,760	8,940	13,340	13,340
25-Apr		517,740	5,177	USDCAD breaks 1.36 on lumber tarriffs	3,440	10,600	3,000	10,160	23,500	23,500
26-Apr		541,240	5,412	Trump tax plan comes out, USDJPY rally and sell off	-	4,880	(1,200)	320	23,820	23,820
27-Apr		565,060	5,651	ECB meeting + Home Capital Group	(640)	7,560	(3,220)	520	24,340	24,340
28-Apr		589,400	5,894	Month end	(5,200)	6,600	(7,360)	5,940	30,280	30,280
1-May		619,680	6,197	London holiday, quiet	(2,340)	5,500	(4,440)	4,880	35,160	35,160
2-May		654,840	6,548	Quiet, USDCAD new highs	(3,000)	(1,600)	(4,560)	(1,700)	33,460	33,460
3-May		688,300	6,883	FOMC	(2,000)	3,500	(5,440)	2,200	35,660	35,660
4-May		723,960	7,240	Health care vote	(1,400)	5,780	(3,600)	3,900	39,560	39,560
5-May		763,520	7,635	NFP	1,200	2,280	(8,900)	(7,740)	31,820	31,820
8-May		795,340	7,953	Quiet with OPEC headlines	2,000	3,750	(280)	3,640	35,460	35,460
9-May		830,800	8,308	USD ripping	5,000	10,460	2,840	8,800	44,260	44,260
10-May		875,060	8,751	RBNZ and Comey fired	2,000	5,760	1,020	5,360	49,620	49,620
11-May		924,680	9,247	Bank of England	2,500	3,460	(5,200)	(5,200)	44,420	44,420
12-May		969,100	9,691	CPI and Retail Sales	1,400	1,420	(7,580)	(5,360)	39,060	39,060
15-May		1,008,160	10,082	OPEC Headlines	(6,080)	(5,080)	(6,080)	(5,460)	33,600	33,600
16-May		1,041,760	10,418	EUR breakout	500	600	(3,220)	(1,700)	31,900	31,900
17-May		1,073,660	10,737	Impeachment headlines	(340)	4,580	(1,180)	(220)	31,680	31,680
18-May		1,105,340	11,053	More Trump news	(2,800)	(940)	(4,980)	(4,460)	27,220	27,220
19-May		1,132,560	11,326	Canada CPI	(1,100)	(520)	(6,020)	(5,060)	22,160	22,160
22-May		1,154,720	11,547	Merkel says euro too weak	-	980	480	920	23,080	23,080
23-May		1,177,800	11,778	Schaeuble comments, EUR tops	-	4,600	(760)	4,400	27,480	27,480
24-May		1,205,280	12,053	Draghi and FOMC minutes	-	1,100	(4,040)	(1,820)	25,660	25,660
25-May		1,230,940	12,309	End of OPEC meeting	(360)	3,400	(1,660)	3,320	28,980	28,980
26-May		1,259,920	12,599	USDJPY drops as bonds rally	3,860	6,460	1,000	4,120	33,100	33,100
29-May		1,293,020	12,930	Memorial Day	2,600	3,020	1,500	2,000	35,100	35,100
30-May		1,328,120	13,281	EUR hawkish comments	2,200	5,850	-	4,620	39,720	39,720
31-May		1,367,840	13,678	Month end dollar selling	-	1,200	(8,400)	(4,700)	35,020	35,020

Figure 12.1 Sample risk management spreadsheet for a novice trader.

And follow it so that you never lose any more than 1% in a given day. This system is very simple to maintain. Let me explain how the sheet works.

Start with row 1 (21-Apr). A is the date. B is your free capital. C is Column B times 1%. D is where you record the main theme of the day just to make it easier to remember what happened if you are curious later on. E is overnight P&L. F and G are the high and low intraday. H is the closing P&L. I and J are month-to-date and year-to-date P&L.

Then in the second row (24-Apr) you simply take your starting capital (500,000) and add your YTD P&L (4,400) for a new starting capital of $504,400. So you can see as the month goes on and you make money, your risk appetite increases in linear fashion. If your capital doubles, your trade size doubles.

> *It is critical that you stick to the daily (or per-trade) risk limit.*
> You can see in the sample P&L sheet that the trader broke
> her limit twice (the highlighted cells in row G). This could be
> because of bad discipline or gap risk. Use conditional format-
> ting to color the limit breaches in red on your spreadsheet so
> that they stand out.

If you want to learn a systematic and mathematical approach to
position sizing, you should study the Kelly Criterion. While it cannot
be applied directly to trading, the theory and math behind the Kelly
Criterion are very useful when thinking about risk management. The
Kelly Criterion is a formula used to determine optimal bet size under
a few simplifying assumptions. The Kelly strategy will outperform
every other bet size strategy in the long run, so it has become an
important part of probability theory that applies to both gambling
and trading.

The Kelly strategy was described by J. L. Kelly, Jr. in 1956. Here
is a quote from the smart folks at lesswrong.com (https://www.less
wrong.com/posts/BZ6XaCwN4QGgH9CxF/the-kelly-criterion):

> It [the Kelly Criterion] is elegant, important and highly
> useful. When considering sizing wagers or investments, if
> you don't understand Kelly, *you don't know how to think
> about the problem.*

The Kelly Criterion helps gamblers determine bet size based
on known probabilities and known payouts. I encourage you to
read about the Kelly Criterion because conceptually it is highly
relevant to trading risk management. William Poundstone's book
Fortune's Formula is an entertaining and educational book about
the Kelly Criterion (and other useful topics related to gambling and
investing).

If you have a good idea of your probability of winning (either
on a specific trade or on a given day) and you know your average gain compared to your average loss, you can plug it into this
formula:

% of Capital to Risk = Win%

$$- ((1 - \text{Win\%})/(\text{AverageWin}/\text{AverageLoss}))$$

So let's say it's the first trading day of the year and I have
$4,000,000 of free capital. I make money on 50% of my trades
and my average winning trade is $370,000, while my average
losing trade is $300,000. I know this from collecting three years of

historical P&L data. The figures I am using here are realistic and approximately reflect real-life daily trading performance data for someone generating around $10 million dollars per year of P&L at a commercial bank. So, plugging these numbers into the formula we get:

$$\text{\% of Capital to Risk} = 0.50 - ((1 - 0.50)/(370,000/300,000))$$
$$= 9.4\%$$

So 9.4% times $4,000,000 would suggest this trader should risk $378,400 on their first trade of the year. The Kelly number tends to be very high relative to what you might expect because it represents the most aggressive allocation possible to maximize your upside given the parameters. Understand that the Kelly Criterion was developed for gambling scenarios where *you know the exact odds beforehand* and every bet is made in a series. Kelly assumes you are making one bet at a time, whereas in trading you might have multiple bets on at once. There are critical reasons why the Kelly Criterion is better suited to gambling games than to trading.

The main problem with a strict application of the Kelly Criterion to investing (unlike, say, blackjack) is that the probability of winning or losing on any given trade is not known beforehand. You might know, from past experience, your approximate win/loss percentage and average win versus average loss for each trade or for each trading day. But you don't have perfect knowledge of the exact future probabilities the way you do in casino gambling.

In trading, you use a past probability to estimate a future probability. To compensate for the fact that you don't know your real odds going forward (you can only estimate the future using historical odds) you should consider half-Kelly or quarter-Kelly sizing. This depends on how confident you are in your performance data and how consistent your performance has been over the years.

I used the Kelly Criterion along with my historical trading performance data over the past 10 years as a starting point for the risk allocations I described earlier for three-star, four-star, and Five-Star trades. I use less than full Kelly, even for Five-Star trades, because there is too much uncertainty in the probabilities and you can survive much longer if you err on the small side rather than the big side.

Once you find a risk percentage you are comfortable with, simply set up a spreadsheet and update your risk allocations based on YTD performance. So if I'm up $5,000,000 halfway through the year, I would add this to my original $4,000,000 and my daily or per-trade risk would be substantially more than it was on January 1.

Understand that this dynamic methodology increases risk when you are doing well and reduces it when you are doing poorly. That is the path to limited downside and huge upside and every risk management system should have this characteristic.

■ Determine Position Size

Now let's discuss how to determine appropriate position size. Say you are a junior FX trader at a bank and your maximum drawdown is $1,000,000. You have determined that your daily stop loss should be $20,000 (2% of $1M). You will treat each day as a separate bet to avoid issues around correlation or portfolios of trades. You have no positions on. You have just spent two hours conducting multifactor market analysis and you conclude that EURUSD is a screaming buy. Right here! Right now! How big a position should you take?

The first question you should ask is this: Do you want to risk your whole day on one idea? As a short-term trader there are a maximum of two or three good opportunities per day and often there is only one. Let's say the VIX is around 15 and there is not much going on—intraday opportunities are fairly limited. Usually when volatility is low, there are fewer opportunities. If it was 7:15AM and the VIX was at 40, we might want to save some of our risk capital for later because high volatility usually means more opportunity. In this case, we are going to risk the entire $20,000 on this trade.

Before determining your position size, you need to choose your entry point and stop loss. Let's assume we buy at 1.2670 and after much analysis we have determined that the ideal stop loss is 1.2622. The process for determining the position size is simple. You just back out the position size from the potential loss. The loss if the position is stopped out equals approximately (1.2670 − 1.2622) + (2 pips of slippage),[1] which equals 50 pips. How many euros can we buy so that a 50-pip loss = $20,000? The answer is 4,000,000. Calculation: (20,000 / 0.0050). Therefore, we can run a position of 4 million euros and know that if we are stopped out, we will lose approximately $20,000.

---

[1]Slippage will vary based on position size and platform. You can usually ignore slippage in many products because it will not be significant, but if there is going to be slippage, it's best to include it in your estimate of the loss if you get stopped out.

This is all fairly easy to set up in a spreadsheet and there would be a similar logic for any other product. Let's look at another example.

I think gold is going up and I decide I want to go long GC (gold futures) at $1730. My stop loss is $1680 and I expect negligible slippage. I want to risk $50,000 on the trade. How many contracts can I buy?

First, we need to know how the value of an increment in each contract. You can find this online or pull up the contract on Bloomberg and type DES {GO}. For gold, each dollar move on one contract is $100, so a $50 change in price on 10 contracts is equal to $50,000. Therefore, the correct position size is 10 contracts.

The formula is: POSITION SIZE = ($ AT RISK) / (LOSS PER UNIT IF STOP TRIGGERS).

There is no other way to choose your position size. Maintaining the same position size all the time ignores the fact that your stop could be wide on one trade and tight on another trade. Your position size should always be determined by the location of your stop, not the other way around.

Here's a good example of how incorrect position sizing can hurt you. Picture a trader who doesn't like to lose more than $100,000 in a day. Every seasoned trader knows the scenario seen in Figure 12.2.

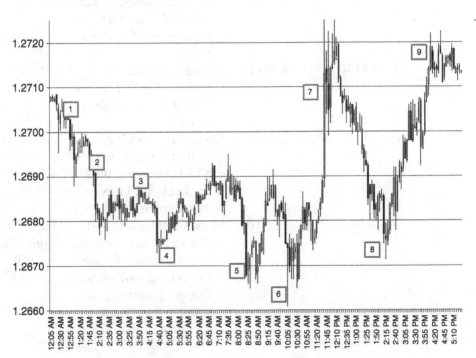

Figure 12.2 Walkthrough of how position size impacts P&L.

Undisciplined Trader with No Strong Position Sizing Process.

#	Current P&L	EURUSD spot level	Thought process	Action and position with average price
1	Flat	1.2700	OK I've been waiting for EURUSD to get to 1.2700 for three days! This is it... Here's my chance.	Buys 30 EURUSD *Long 30 @ 1.2700*
2	−$32,000	1.2690	Hmm, it trades kind of heavy.	Buys 10 more EURUSD *Long 40 @ 1.2698*
3	−$70,000	1.2680	It looks like it's basing.	Buys 10 more EURUSD *Long 50 @ 1.2694*
4	−$95,000	1.2675	Well, this isn't good; let me see what level I should be stopping out. (Sees a nice convergence of technical levels around 1.2650/55 and decides to stop out if 1.2650 breaks)	
5	−$130,000	1.2668	Ah man, I'm down $130k! That's half my P&L for the whole month.	
6	−$160,000	1.2662	Man, this is getting out of hand. I'm down $160,000 here. Why the heck did I buy so many euros?	Sells 25 EURUSD *Long 25 @ 1.2726*
7	−$40,000	1.2710	Man, I totally screwed this up, what a terrible bit of trading. At least I'm only down $40k. But my position is too small! I'll get back to 45 euros and everything will be fine when we go 1.2750 paid! I'm starving but I better not leave the desk. What a roller coaster!	Buys 20 EURUSD *Long 45 @ 1.2719*

#	Current P&L	EURUSD spot level	Thought process	Action and position with average price
8	−$211,000	1.2672	ARGHHH. I hate myself! Why the heck did I buy that spike? Am I an idiot? This thing is gone now; it's going to make a new low. I might as well stem the bleeding and get out. ARGGGHHH.	Sells out his entire position *Flat*
9	−$211,000	1.2715	I knew it was going to rally! I am so hating this market right now, it's impossible! So freaking choppy!	He reports his daily P&L of minus $211,000 and feels furious that he didn't stick with the plan. EURUSD is higher on the day and yet he just lost his whole month's P&L despite being long euros! He goes home, argues with his wife, and goes to bed early.

And here's how it works if you size the position correctly:

Disciplined Trader with Strong Position Sizing Process.

#	Current P&L	EURUSD spot level	Thought process	Action and position with average price
1	Flat	1.2700	OK I've done all my analysis and I want to be long EURUSD. I've been waiting for EURUSD to get to 1.2700! This is it… Here's my chance.	She did her technical analysis this morning and sees that 1.2644 is the optimal stop.

#	Current P&L	EURUSD spot level	Thought process	Action and position with average price
				Knowing she doesn't want to lose more than $100,000, she buys 17 million euros at 1.2700 and places her stop loss on an automated system.
2	−$17,000	1.2690	Hmm, it trades kind of heavy.	
3	−$34,000	1.2680	It looks like it's basing.	
4	−$42,500	1.2675	Well, maybe my analysis was wrong. I know if 1.2644 trades, I'm out. My historical win% is around 55% so I'm certainly not going to get emotionally involved in any single trade. If I'm wrong, I'm wrong.	
5	−$54,400	1.2668	Reads some research.	
6	−$64,600	1.2662	Finishes reading research and gets some fresh air outside for 10 minutes knowing her stop is being watched by a machine.	
7	+$17,000	1.2710	Reads some more research and prepares some ideas for tomorrow.	
8	−$47,600	1.2672	Grabs a healthy lunch and goes for a short walk to get a bit of exercise and sunshine.	
9	+$25,500	1.2715	Finishes her plan for tomorrow's trading.	Reports daily P&L of +$25k. While it's a small number for her, she feels good about sticking with the plan. She goes home and has a nice dinner and a glass of wine.

I hope these contrasting examples illustrate the dramatic difference in P&L that can result from different position sizes and different intraday behaviors. Put your trade on in the correct size and give it time to work.

Common Errors in Position Sizing

Position sizing is one of the great challenges in trading because you need to balance two countervailing realities: (1) the largest position makes the most money when you are right, but (2) smaller positions are much easier to manage and allow you to ride out the inevitable market noise. Traders of all experience levels make three common errors in position sizing:

Positions Are Too Big

Young traders and very aggressive traders tend to run positions that are too big for their P&L tolerance. They always feel like "This is the big one!" and they want to be fully leveraged for the inevitable big move. This can be problematic as the increased volatility of the P&L on a large position means that the trader is more likely to stop out at the wrong time. To get an idea of how position-sizing impacts your P&L, let's look at a regular day in EURUSD (Figure 12.3) and see how different position sizes would have generated different P&L.

Now let's say you went long right at midnight (the far left of the chart). It moved immediately against you but eventually closed the day (5:00PM, far right of chart) slightly higher. Look at Figure 12.4, which shows the running P&L (in dollars) for different-sized long EURUSD positions on this day.

Unless you have fairly deep pockets, the 50 million EURUSD position is clearly problematic as the worst drawdown is more than $200,000. On the other hand, most bank traders could ride out the P&L on the 20 million EURUSD position shown in Figure 12.4 while home traders might receive a margin call with even the 3 million EURUSD position.

You need to size the position so that you can survive the volatility if and when you are temporarily wrong. And FYI, you will be wrong a lot. The key is riding out the P&L volatility without blowing yourself up. Now let's look at the other two common position sizing errors.

Figure 12.3 5-minute price action from midnight to 5:30PM in EURUSD on November 13, 2012.

UNDERSTAND POSITION SIZING

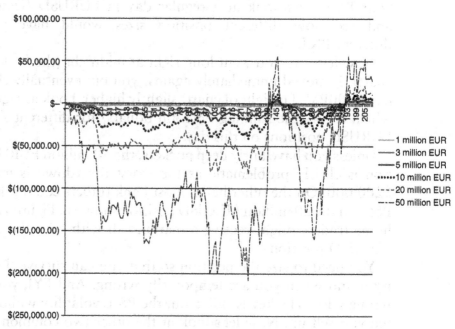

Figure 12.4 5-minute running P&L of going long EURUSD at midnight on November 13, 2012.

■ Positions Are Too Small

Many traders make the opposite mistake and trade too conservatively. If you are a bank trader and your annual budget is $10 million, can you succeed with an average position size of $5,000,000? No. You need to trade big enough that you make real money when you are right. If you need $3,000,000 of trading P&L just to cover your base salary and IT expenses at a small hedge fund, you can't be trading $2,000,000 positions back and forth.

Positioning too small won't blow you up but it can lead to a slow and inevitable death by 1000 cuts. If your positions are too big, you blow up. If they are too small you fade away. Trading too small is a problem more associated with bank traders than retail or hedge fund traders.

■ A Third Mistake Is Always Trading the Same Size of Position

If USDMXN moves 1.2% per day and AUDCAD moves 0.6% per day, does it make sense for a trader who is bullish both (with similar conviction) to be long 10 million of each? No. You need to size your positions according to the volatility of the product you are trading and the expected risk and reward of the individual trade. This is called volatility adjustment or vol-adjusting.

Sizing should relate not just to the volatility of what you are trading but also to your level of conviction. When you see a very powerful setup, you should be aggressive. This is similar to the concept that in poker you will bet much larger when you have a pair of aces than when you have a pair of threes. Remember Rule #15 of FX Trading: *Good traders vary their bet size.*

I try to size my super-high-conviction trades at least 3X or 4X my lower-conviction trades. Varying bet size is a key concept in successful gambling and there is a strong analogy to trading. When expected value of a trade is high, trade big. When you are less confident, trade small.

■ Stop Losses

Stop losses are a key feature of any good risk management system. Without a stop loss, you don't know your downside on a given trade or your downside for a given day or month of trading. This introduces risk of ruin, which is always the number-one risk to avoid. By leaving stop loss orders, you can effectively measure the risk of every trade you put on and exit risk when trades go wrong. The fundamental fact that you need to fully embrace is this: You will be wrong. A lot. So manage your risk using stop losses. Let me give you some thoughts on stop loss strategy.

Where to Put Your Stop Loss

I use the following approach, combining three techniques to come up with my stop loss levels:

1. Use technical analysis to determine the optimal stop loss level and then add about 20% of a day's range as extra room. Ideally (as discussed in Chapters 6 and 7 about understanding technical analysis), I can find an area where there is a convergence of tops, bottoms, trendlines, and other levels. Then I put the stop past those levels to give it some room.

    For example, I am short EURUSD. I see a bunch of topside levels in EURUSD at 1.1500/20 and the average range in EURUSD these days is about 100 pips. Then I would take 1.1520 and add 20 pips (20% of the 100-pip daily range) and so my stop should be 1.1540. Because of round number bias, I never leave my orders at round numbers, so in this example I would leave my stop at 1.1541.

    In an ideal world, you do not want to leave your stop loss where everyone else is leaving their stop, so some second derivative thinking is required. If you see a very obvious place to leave your stop loss or you read that many stop losses are clustered in a particular area, try to avoid getting caught up with all the other stops. Leave some extra room.

    I believe that the most useful application of technical analysis is right here. By picking the right stop loss using technical analysis, you maximize your leverage (because the closer the stop loss, the bigger position you can take) and create a firm and mechanical stop loss level.

2. The second criterion I use for setting stops is average daily range. My starting point is that I normally want to set my stop loss at least one day's range away from my entry point (but not always). Just remember there is too much noise in the market to trade profitably using super-tight stops all the time. Occasionally you might find adequate risk/reward on super micro trades but opportunities where you can risk 10 or 20 pips are rare unless you are trading a level break or a news event.

    Also note that there should be a relationship between your stop and your time horizon. For short term trades, you could use a standard formula of CURRENT PRICE + (1.2 X AVERAGE DAY RANGE) and that would be reasonable. On a medium-term trade you might take something more like CURRENT PRICE + (AVERAGE DAY RANGE X 2.5).

3. Trailing stop losses. As a trade moves further into the money, you can lock in some profit. The simplest way to do this is to move your stop up as spot moves in your favor. You can do this using a moving average or a simple, preexisting plan like: I went long at 1.1480 with a stop at 1.1397 and take profit at 1.1699. If spot gets to 1.1625, I'll move my stop up to 1.1499 to lock in a guaranteed win. This avoids a winner turning into a loser but lets the trade continue to run and make money toward 1.1699. The other way is to use a moving average such as the 100-hour MA (or another MA, depending on the time horizon of your trade).

Let's look at an example using Figure 12.5. You went short EURUSD (the black candles) at the top left of the chart (around 1.1000) with a stop at 1.1205 and a take profit at 1.0511. The 40-hour exponential moving average (the black line) has been defining the trend pretty well. So ideally you will take profit at 1.0511 but if the currency bounces significantly, it seems crazy to leave your stop way up at 1.1205 when EURUSD is now trading at 1.0585.

So you decide that on an hourly close above the moving average, you will cut the position. This is still called a stop loss even though in reality you are taking profit because you sold way higher. Any order where you are buying on the way up or selling on the way down is always called a stop loss. You don't need to update your stop on an hourly basis; you can update it once every 12 or even 24 hours by simply taking the moving average and adding 20 pips of extra space.

Understand Risk/Reward

There should be a relationship between your stop loss level and your take profit level with regard to risk/reward. As a general rule, if a trader consistently risks 100 pips on his stop loss and takes profit after 30 pips, he will not be profitable in the long run. That said, I believe that it is absolutely incorrect to insist on a fixed risk/reward ratio all the time.

Quite often it could be acceptable to risk 100 pips to make 100 if you believe the probability of making the 100-pip profit is far greater than the probability of losing the 100 pips. This boils down to expected value. If you do not understand the concept of expected value, you should Google it and do a bit of reading because it is very important. Expected value is an absolutely critical concept in many areas of finance, trading, and gambling.

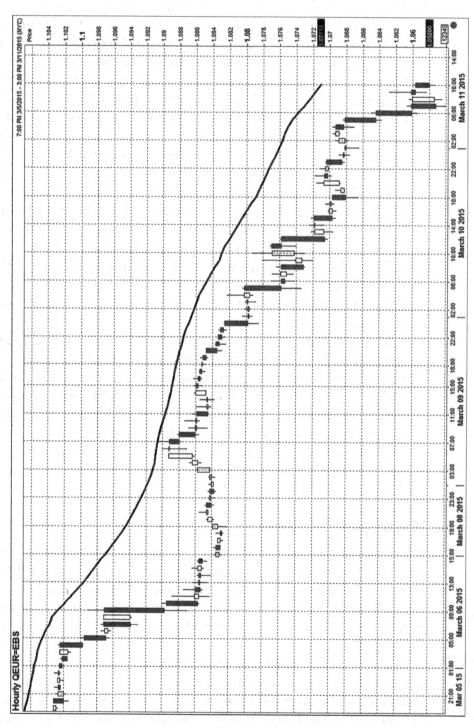

Figure 12.5 Hourly EURUSD with 40-hour EMA, March 5 to March 11, 2015.

Here is an example of a trade with great expected value where you are risking 100 pips to make 100 pips:

	RISK	REWARD
	distance in pips from entry point to stop loss (plus estimated slippage on stop loss)	distance in pips from entry point to take profit
Pips of risk and reward	(100)	(100)
multiplied by	X	X
Estimated probability of hitting stop loss or take profit (must add to 100%)	30%	70%
Total pips	= –30	= 70
	expected value of the trade (reward minus risk)	40

Don't mechanically shy away from a trade just because it's not, say, 3:1 risk/reward. If you look at only the stop loss to take profit ratio, you are taking a one-dimensional view of a two-dimensional problem. Risk/reward is calculated not just from the relationship between the stop and the take profit but also from the estimated probability of each event. Once in a while I will see a setup where the expected value looks positive even though I'm risking 70 pips to make 50. These are rare but my point is simply to keep an open mind on this topic and don't be overly rigid.

The big challenge in using an expected value framework, of course, is assessing the probability of hitting your stop loss and your take profit. These are estimates with very large potential error and so you should be conservative when estimating the probabilities. If you have a detailed trading journal, you can accumulate data that will help you assess the real-world probability of different types of trades hitting the stop loss or take profit.

You might notice that trades with 3:1 risk/reward win only 20% of the time while your trades with 1:1 risk/reward win 65% of the time. This type of observation can be very useful in improving future trading strategy. It is important to understand that in trading you deal with subjective probabilities, not objective probabilities like in a game of chance involving dice or cards. So the expected value calculation suggests more precision than it will deliver.

Here are three rules you should always follow for stop losses:

1. Write your stop loss down in your trade journal or on a scrap piece of paper in front of you before or immediately after you put on a trade. As I have discussed previously: Something written down is concrete and firm. Something in your mind is abstract and fuzzy—subject to change and manipulation.

    Always record your stop loss and treat the level with paramount importance. When you are in a losing trade, you are subject to all sorts of irrational and emotional behaviors. When you originally record the stop loss, you are acting rationally.

Don't let the emotional mind override that original, rational mind that wrote down the stop.

2. Don't keep changing your stop loss level as the market moves and you discover new technical levels or excuses to let a losing trade run. A currency chart can give you level after level as justification for losing trades, especially if you cycle between 5-minute, hourly, and daily charts. There's always another technical level to use as an excuse to change your stop. Don't do it.

   Once you have recorded your original plan, just follow it like a robot. If you are stopped out, the idea was wrong. You can always put the trade back on later but that is totally different from moving your stop over and over. If I am stopped out, I will allow myself to put the same trade back on with a different stop loss after a 4-hour cooling-off period. In theory, this is somewhat equivalent to moving the stop on an existing trade but the important difference is the cooling-off period. By staying flat for four hours I give myself the chance to cool off and to be free of confirmation bias and emotional decision making.

   Remember, the only time you are truly unbiased and unemotional is when you are flat. Any time you have a position, you are influenced by a huge range of emotions related to that position. I cannot emphasize this enough. DO NOT MOVE YOUR STOP LOSS LEVEL.

3. Automate your stop loss process, if possible. The best risk management system is one where you input your stop loss and it is automatically executed when your level hits. This prevents bad discipline and makes things automatic. Rule-based and independent risk management systems are much more robust than discretionary risk management run by the trader. The more you can outsource your risk management and stop loss execution, the better.

Reasons People Move Their Stop Losses

Good reasons:

- Upcoming event risk
- Trailing the stop loss to lock in profits
- Risk management trigger reached

Bad reasons:

- "I know if I just survive a bit longer, this will be a winner!"
- "Oh wait, I didn't notice this major technical level before. I better move my stop below it."
- "My other trades are doing well so I can let this one run against me a bit longer."

Slippage on Stop Losses

Slippage on stop losses will vary considerably depending on the liquidity of the currency pair and whether price action is gappy or continuous and fast or slow when the stop loss is executed. There are no guarantees on stop losses but as a very general rule, most stops of 20 million USD or less in liquid pairs are executed within about 2 or 3 basis points of the trigger level. So on trades under 20 million, this generally means 2 or 3 pips slippage in most G10 FX pairs or 20 or 30 pips in something like EURNOK, EURSEK, USDNOK, or USDSEK. Larger notional amounts lead to greater slippage.

In fast markets, stop loss orders will suffer from extra slippage. Sometimes this extra slippage can be significant. This is especially true through major economic data releases like nonfarm payrolls and through central bank announcements. You should make sure your positions are sized correctly if you have a position going into an event because you might end up losing more than you expected. Check out the volatility around prior releases and calculate your downside using similar slippage.

When the SNB dropped the EURCHF floor, slippage was absolutely apocalyptic with many traders losing 5X their entire trading account or even more. As discussed, this was a known tail risk and so anyone with a position at that time should have known what they were getting into.

Slippage on stop losses can be a source of great frustration for both market makers and speculators. This is because stop losses tend to be a no-win situation on both sides. The trader leaving the stop is unhappy by definition when the order is executed because he is getting taken out of his position. On the other side of the coin, market makers usually struggle to execute stops without losing money because stops are always on the weak side of the market and tend to come in clusters. This is known as "negative gamma," which means market makers become short on the way up and long on the way down when they have stop loss orders. Nobody likes negative gamma.

You will often see situations where a customer trader is stopped out on the buy side (and not happy with his fill) while on the sell side, the market maker has done his best for the customer and still lost money himself! Everybody loses. Keep this in mind when you leave stop loss orders and when grading your fills afterward.

■ Take Profits

Take profit levels should be chosen using a similar approach to stop loss selection. Do the work on the technicals and err on the conservative side of your level. So if you figure that 1.1500 is a big level, put your buy order at 1.1511 to get ahead of it. You will be happy to take profit anyway and the extra 11 pips is the price you pay for the added probability of a fill as you stay ahead of less sophisticated players who leave their buy orders at exactly 1.1500. Many traders find it very difficult to stick with their take profit plan because a trade will be doing well when it gets to the take profit level. It will often look like it has significant momentum and the trend will look strong and ready to continue.

> **Rule #16 of FX Trading: It always looks bid at the highs. It always looks heavy at the lows.**

The beauty of an advance plan is that when news comes out or a trade rips in your favor, you will take profit at the preplanned level instead of doubling down like an emotional monkey on tilt.

Here are some terrible reasons traders move their take profit orders:

- "Whoa! This thing is ripping! No point taking profit yet!"

- "Whew, I'm back to flat. I'll just get out here and forget about this stupid trade."

- "I'm deep in the money here but my take profit is still another 25 pips away and we're stalling. If it turns against me now, I'll never forgive myself!"

■ Establish a Clear, Rule-Based Risk Management Approach

Good traders have good risk management systems. You will read about superheroes who go all in and bet everything on one "can't miss" position but for every one of those who hit the jackpot there are twenty funds that you will never hear about because they went under with similar all-in bets.

If you want to rely on luck, then don't worry about risk management, but if you want to survive in the industry for a prolonged period, be vigilant. Develop a risk management process that is rule-based. If you tend to be poorly disciplined, outsource your risk management.

When I say outsource, it doesn't mean that you need an external third party. You can use an internal trader or execution person and have them monitor your risk and help manage it. This is obviously not possible for an individual trader at home but if you are at a hedge fund you can use your execution person as a risk manager to enhance your process. If you are at a bank, talk about your rules with other traders. Rules discussed out loud are more likely to be followed than rules tossed around in your head.

None of this is easy. I have been trading for more than twenty years and I still find it hard to stick to my own rules.

■ Process versus Outcome

Now that you understand the importance of developing and maintaining a proper risk management process, there is one more concept that you need to internalize: process versus outcome. This concept is extremely important in professions where short-term results are strongly influenced by chance.

Rule #17 of FX Trading: You control the process but you *do not* control the outcome.

In this section, I will explain the importance of fully internalizing the difference between process and outcome in trading. This will keep you focused on your daily process and allow you to remain unemotional when bad luck hits.

The more luck is a factor in your job, the more you need to understand the role of luck and become emotionally immune to its whims. If you are going to succeed in trading, you need to understand a few things:

- The market does not know you exist. It does not hate you. It does not like you.

- Luck is a crucial short-term factor in trading. Accept that any given day could bring good or bad luck and move on.[2] Be stoic.

- The importance of luck drops toward zero in the long run.

- God doesn't care about your trades. God will not push the market in your favor no matter how hard you pray.

Rule #18 of FX Trading: Each trade is a drop of water. The market is an ocean.

You can see how luck loses its importance over time by analyzing potential outcomes for a realistic set of assumptions. Let's say your UP DAYS and DOWN DAYS are both the same in $ terms and you are profitable on 55% of days. Your odds of making money today

---

[2]This is essentially a variation of the Serenity Prayer, which I recited quite often in 2008 as I was trading USDJPY at Lehman Brothers: *God, grant me the serenity to accept the things I cannot change, the courage to change the things I can, and the wisdom to know the difference.*

are 55%. But your odds of making money this week are closer to 60%. Your odds of making money this month are close to 75%, and your odds of making money this year are above 90%!

You just lost money today. Should you feel bad? Not really. It's part of the game. Prepare for tomorrow.

Separating process and outcome will help you find peace after your very best trade idea gets steamrolled by a random headline or you are stopped out 1 pip from the low before a trade rockets 2.5% in the money. You control the process, not the outcome.

Another way of looking at the process-versus-outcome dichotomy is to look at two poker hands. You're playing a cash poker game at the Bellagio and after grinding through bad cards for the past two hours, you are dealt a pair of aces. The player next to you is wearing a glow necklace and a $45,000 watch and he just came from a "bangin'" DJ pool party. He has been drinking vodka and soda since 11:00AM. Everyone folds to him and he raises 5X the pot. You go all in, and drunk guy calls right away. He turns over A/9 and you know you are a huge favorite (around 12:1). The dealer turns over a harmless flop and then the drunk guy is dealt runner/runner 9s. He wins the entire pot with 3-of-a-kind.

Do you feel angry and upset about your bad luck? Or do you understand there is variance in poker and you made the right decision, despite the bad outcome? A good poker player understands this is classic good decision/bad outcome and starts thinking about the next hand. Same goes for trading. This is something that is very easy to understand conceptually but very difficult to internalize. Internalize it.

PROCESS VERSUS OUTCOME IN TRADING

	GOOD OUTCOME	BAD OUTCOME
GOOD DECISION	Win. Will probably lead to more good process and more good decisions.	Disappointing, but nothing to worry about. Do not respond emotionally to these trades.
BAD DECISION	Lucky. Will probably lead to more bad process and more bad decisions. Good traders know when they get lucky despite doing the wrong thing and are willing to admit it.	Disappointing, but will probably lead to change in behavior. Learn from these trades. Are you making the same mistakes over and over? Keep a list of your mistakes and see what patterns emerge.

Understand that good decisions often lead to bad outcomes in trading but in the long run luck evens out. An amateur has a chance against pro poker players if the game goes on for only a short time. But the longer he plays with the pros, the closer his odds of going broke approach 100%. As a good trader, you know that over time your good decisions and solid risk management framework will pay off but on any given day you could win or lose.

Make sure you fully absorb this concept. When you evaluate losing trades, have a solid understanding of whether you were a victim of bad luck on a given trade or whether your process is leading to bad outcomes. The next time you're on a bad streak, take a step back. Is this just a run of bad luck, the way a roulette wheel sometimes comes up red ten times in a row? Or is this something different? Are you pressing too hard? Unable to pull the trigger? Too tired? Too angry? Too chicken?

Figure it out.

This concludes Part Three and our discussion of risk management. Now we have covered how to come up with trade ideas and how to manage risk. That's all we need to know to succeed right? Book over? Not yet.

Your biggest enemy in the market is not the central banks or other traders or hedge funds or bad luck. It's you. All the rules in the world will not mean a thing if you do not follow them. So now we go to Part Four, "Understand Yourself."

After reading this chapter, you should fully understand these key concepts:

- How to size your positions

- How position size relates to your targets

- Common mistakes in position sizing

- The importance of stop losses and how to use them

- What is the Kelly Criterion and how does it relate to trading?

- The difference between process and outcome

■ Further Reading

Duke, Annie. *Thinking in Bets: Making Smarter Decisions When You Don't Have All the Facts.* New York: Portfolio, 2018.

FACTBOX: MY FAVORITE QUOTES ON PROCESS VERSUS OUTCOME

David Sklansky, *The Theory of Poker*:

"Any time you make a bet with the best of it, where the odds are in your favor, you have earned something on that bet, whether you actually win or lose the bet. By the same token, when you make a bet with the worst of it, where the odds are not in your favor, you have lost something, whether you actually win or lose the bet."

Colm O'Shea's in Steven Drobny's *The Invisible Hands*:

"I do, actually [visualize every shot while playing golf]. I believe in visualization, and the analogies between golf and trading go beyond just visualizing the trade. With golf, you can only control your process, not the result. You can control your swing, but you cannot control where the ball goes—there are too many variables You can make a great shot but the ball could take a bad bounce and go into a bunker, or take a great bounce and go in the hole. Once the ball leaves your club after impact, you lose control and become subject to myriad imperfections on the course. Trading can be similar. You can have a great trade that loses money, or conversely a terrible trade that makes money. Regardless, the process is the only thing that you can control, never the result. My process is such that we will occasionally lose money, but over time, on average, we will make money. I try not to get too worried about good patches or bad patches in the shorter term, but rather always come back to focusing on the investment process and how we make money over time."

From a story about Brad Stevens, coach of Butler's top 10 ranked basketball team:[3]

"With his team trailing by a point in the final seconds in a Hinkle Fieldhouse cauldron of tension, Stevens watched Roosevelt Jones steal a wayward Gonzaga lob pass, drive into the frontcourt

---

[3] https://sports.yahoo.com/news/nba--forde-minutes--butler-s-flair-for-dramatic-doesn-t-excite-brad-stevens--074407732.html.

and launch a shot at the buzzer that improbably swished for a dramatic victory. Stevens observed this thrilling, stunning turn of events with his arms folded across his chest, looking more like a man watching the grass grow than his team snatching another last-second triumph. When Jones launched his shot, Stevens started to turn and walk to the Gonzaga bench, arms still folded. When it went in, he did not break stride, did not change body language, did not pump a fist or let out a howl or dance a jig. As his players dashed around the floor in celebration and the fans poured out of the stands to join them, Stevens paid no heed. He walked down and shook the hand of Gonzaga coach Mark Few...

The analytical side of his job has in many ways shut down the in-game emotions that he felt in his youth.... He is analytical enough to know that his team's performance cannot be accurately appraised on the basis of a single shot going in.... One of the reasons he was already turning to walk when Jones' shot was in the air is because it was almost irrelevant to how he viewed his team's performance. "What goes through my mind is, the hay is in the barn," Stevens said. "If a guy makes a shot like that or doesn't, it doesn't define who we are. It doesn't affect how I evaluate our team. It doesn't break our season...." As such, Stevens knows that growth comes more from the daily habits in practice and preparation, the small pieces that make up a whole body of work.

PART IV

Understand
Yourself

"90% of the game is half mental."

Yogi Berra

Learning the rules is easy. Following them is hard. Once you finish this book and feel that you have a strong understanding of how the FX market works, the hard work begins. As years pass and you gain more and more experience, you will find trading is more and more about psychology and channeling mental chaos than it is about charts and macro and behavioral analysis. You need to understand your weaknesses (and your strengths) and develop a systematic process so that you do not make the same mistakes over and over. Mistakes are how we learn in trading. Repeating mistakes is how we fail.

I know and can outline all sorts of risk management strategies in this book. Yet I have leaks. I overtrade because I'm bored. Sometimes my emotions take over and I size my positions way too big out of excitement and FOMO. After 20 years in the market, it is still a challenge for me to consistently follow my own rules. The number one determinant of a trader's success is how well he follows his own rules. All good traders need self-discipline.

Good traders share many other characteristics. We will look at the most important ones in Chapter 13.

Characteristics of a Successful Trader

■ Finds the Balance between Risky Behavior and Discipline

To be good, you need this balance. Many people are too risk averse to be good traders while others are too wild and undisciplined to succeed. The combination of mega risk appetite and disciplined personality is rare. Usually you will meet traders with heavy risk appetite who find systematic ways to manage their risk, or risk-averse traders who implement systems that allow them to take meaningful risk in a prudent way.

Over many years managing many FX traders, I have generally found that there are many more risk-averse traders than those consistently willing to take courageous risk, but both imbalances can be fixed with a solid process.

■ Thinks Independently

Don't follow the crowd, but don't be a reflexive contrarian. Think for yourself. Read everything you can but come to your own conclusions. I am going to repeat part of a quote from earlier because I think it is incredibly pertinent to trading:

> "The most contrarian thing of all is not to oppose the crowd but to think for yourself."
>
> – Peter Thiel, *Zero to One*

You should read and absorb as much as you possibly can but always trade your own view—never someone else's.

This is a concept worth emphasizing: Trade your own view. If you trade someone else's idea, you will inevitably do everything wrong. You will stop out at the wrong levels because your conviction will not be high when the trade goes against you. Also, if you are trading someone else's view, you might not know when their view changes. Frequently you will hear someone moaning about someone else's idea they followed and then have insult added to injury as they find out the original trader exited long ago or even flipped her position.

Successful traders do their own work and come to their own conclusions.

■ Knows Their Edge

Are you faster than other traders? Better at processing new information? Maybe you are really good at studying central banks and predicting what they will do. The cliché in poker is that if you don't know who the sucker at the table is, the sucker is probably you. Same goes in trading. If you can't say with a straight face that you know exactly where your edge comes from, you are in serious trouble.

Because of transaction costs, FX trading is a negative-sum game. You need an edge to win. What is your edge?

Rule #19 of FX Trading: Know your edge.

■ Trades One Time Horizon

Every trader should choose a time horizon and stick to it. Most of my trades last 3 hours to 7 days and the vast majority of my trades fall in the 1-day to 3-day bucket. The more tightly you can define your time horizon, the better. FX is the most liquid market in the world and thus it is perfectly suited to short-term trading. Whatever you do, *stick to one time horizon*. Yes, markets are fractal, but mixing time horizons is a recipe for disaster for many reasons, the main one being that you will start to notice that poorly timed short-term trades become longer-term "investments" while successful swing trades yield only tiny profits as you trade out too quickly in order to "improve your average."

I have worked with dozens of top traders over the years and I have never seen a highly successful trader take meaningful risk on multiple time horizons. To give yourself the best possible odds of sustainable success, your goal should be to master one explicitly chosen time horizon in one explicitly chosen product: foreign exchange. Forget about other time horizons and forget about trading crude, gold, and S&Ps. Jack of all markets = master of none.

Rule #20 of FX Trading: Know your time horizon.

The beauty of short-term FX trading is that there are great opportunities every single trading day. Not *almost* every day. *Every day.* This gives you great freedom and peace of mind as a trader because you know that as long as your risk management process is sound, you will always have another chance tomorrow. A big-picture macro trader might see three or four juicy opportunities per year. She can't afford to make many mistakes. Short-term currency trading is different. Each trade is like a drop of water in the ocean. There is always another trade and another opportunity right around the corner.

■ Controls Emotion/Acts Like a Robot/Self-Aware

Humans are not robots but your goal is to be as unemotional as possible. Emotion kills. If you feel yourself getting emotional, take a step back. Recognize and acknowledge the emotions. Assess where they are coming from. When you feel emotional, whether it is happiness or frustration, you should reduce your position size. Euphoria and disappointment both lead to all sorts of suboptimal decision making.

The key is to be self-aware.

Know when you are on tilt. If you high-five someone as a trade is moving your way, be aware that this high five is probably a sign of euphoria and could be signaling a turning point in the market (see Chapter 9, "Understand Behavioral Finance"). As you gain experience, you will start to see mistakes you are making *as you make them* and change course.

■ Implements a Consistent Daily Routine

Good traders are totally prepared before they start trading. They have a process and a plan before they hit any buy or sell keys. I have a daily sheet that I complete each morning before things get busy. This sheet helps me gauge where I am at emotionally and also puts numerical brackets around my day as I set a profit target and a stop loss number. This helps enforce discipline so that I know at what point I will stop myself out (how much money can I lose today?) and when I should be taking some profit (what P&L would make this a successful day? A great day?).

Rule #21 of FX Trading: Good traders have a plan. They may not always stick to the plan but they always have one.

I talked about this concept in the trading journal section but I am going to revisit it here because it is so important. Thoughts are abstract and noisy, whereas anything you write down is by definition more concrete and focused. Concrete and focused writing leads to focused trading while abstract and noisy thinking leads to noisy trading.

I encourage every trader to create at least a brief written plan before they start trading. It can be one or two paragraphs, written to yourself or sent to others. But I cannot emphasize this enough: Have a written plan every day. It can be incredibly simple. Write it on a Post-It Note if you want. But do it. This simple daily practice will make you a better FX trader.

■ Happy to Be Flat

This was touched on earlier, too, but I want to repeat it. Good short-term traders get flat. You don't always have to have a position. There are not always top-quality opportunities available. Part of your job is to show the willpower and patience to wait for good opportunities. I am not very good at this but I keep trying to improve.

■ Understands Tight/Aggressive

One of the most successful and common approaches used by good poker players is called "tight/aggressive." The concept is that you don't want to be involved in very many pots but when you are involved, be as aggressive as possible. In other words, wait until you have great cards and then go for it. While you never want to literally go all in when trading, the tight/aggressive strategy in poker is a great analogy. Wait, wait, wait... and then when everything lines up, *pounce!*

Rule #22 of FX Trading: Tight/Aggressive wins.

■ Self-Understanding and Metacognition

Good traders are self-aware and understand the importance of thinking about thinking (metacognition). This self-awareness usually develops over time but after several years of trading, you should start to hear and understand your own thoughts more clearly than you did in the past.

Know yourself. What is your edge? Understand your information processing strengths and weaknesses. Identify your biases. Do you trade poorly after fighting with your boss? Are you aggressive when selling a certain currency but full of hesitation when you go long that currency? These are questions to ask yourself. Do more of what works and less of what does not.

Assess your state of mind on an ongoing basis. Are you feeling euphoric? Depressed? Often your state of mind can provide warning ahead of potentially bad trading decisions. Whenever I find myself feeling euphoric (singing on the desk, annualizing a fast start to the year, celebrating a great trade), I know I am probably about to receive a huge kick in the pants. When I feel euphoric, I reduce risk.

■ Loves Trading

You cannot succeed at trading if you don't love it. No matter how much money you make—that's not success. Success is coming in every day and enjoying yourself and if that leads to substantial wealth, that's great. The best traders I have worked with seem like they were born to trade.

I grew up in middle-class Ottawa, Canada, and nobody in my family had any interest whatsoever in finance. Yet by the age of 14, I was already so interested in trading that I used my earnings from delivering the *Pennysaver* to subscribe to the *Financial Post*. When I was 15 I started charting stocks by hand on graph paper and taking a by-mail investment course. I worked for a stockbroker after school and opened my own trading account with $500 at the age of 16. At 18 I was the first person from my family to go to university.

I have no idea where it came from, but I was driven to become a trader from a very young age. Passion for trading is a key success factor. If you are trading just for the money, you can't win, because even if you make a ton of cash, you still lose as you miss out on whatever career should have been your true passion.

■ Learns and Adapts

Good traders keep learning. They adapt. They want to improve every day and have a growth mindset. They don't sit there and complain about how the market sucks; they identify new market regimes and try to understand whether their current process will work as the regime shifts. This ability to adapt has been especially important in recent years as market microstructure has changed dramatically with the rise of the algos.

As trading was increasingly automated during the 2000s, there were two groups of traders: One group complained every day about the algos and how they were messing up the market and changing the game in unfair ways. The other group of traders analyzed the new market structure and adapted, changing their trading style to fit the new regime. Guess which group of traders lost their jobs?

When volatility, liquidity, microstructure, and correlations change, good traders see it happening and adapt their process. Those who do not adapt are eliminated by natural selection. Remember Rule #2 of FX trading: Adapt or die.

◼ Gut versus Head: Two Very Different Decision-Making Systems

Whenever you think about a trade or potential trade idea, you run two parallel systems:

Head: This is the logic and analysis system. You analyze everything and make a decision to do a trade.

Gut: This is past experience and intuition. But it is also fear, hope, greed, and many other emotions, plus a bunch of different types of bias all boiled into one steaming, confusing pot. Your gut can signal a familiar pattern and a profitable trade idea—or it can signal you are afraid to lose money or take a risk.

Those with years of trading experience can use a combination of head and gut to their advantage. My strongest views come when my head and my gut are in sync. When strong analysis intersects with a strong gut feel, you have yourself a winner. As a general rule, the longer you have been trading, the more you can trust your gut. New traders should rely mostly on their analytical process and less on instinct. But sometimes, head and gut don't align...

All Head, No Gut

You will sometimes experience a situation where you do the analysis, come to a strong conclusion, and then find your gut is just not on board. In that case, it's time to do some deep thinking. Why is my gut not on board? Is it some sort of bias or fear? Or perhaps a pattern you subconsciously recognize that suggests the trade will not work? Maybe it's the feeling of "I've seen this movie before and I don't like how it ends!"

Or are you just afraid to lose money because you are on a cold streak? Good trading takes courage. When a good trade idea comes along, you need to do it, even if it's scary. Do your best to figure out what is troubling your gut. You will not always be able to unpack where the gut feeling is coming from but you need to try.

All Gut, No Head

The opposite situation is where you have a strong gut feel that something will happen but no logical foundation for the idea. Then you start doing analysis in an effort to confirm the gut feel. This is a tricky situation because your strong gut feel will almost certainly lead to confirmation bias as you look around for information and "logical" reasons to do the trade.

Be honest with yourself and look for information that both backs up your idea and contradicts it. Do not simply look at your main hypothesis. Think of alternative hypotheses and assess them as objectively as possible. If you find you cannot be objective, ask someone else to play devil's advocate. When you can honestly say that your logical analysis supports the gut view, go for it.

As you gain experience, you can trust your gut more and more, but the best trades happen when your gut and your head are completely aligned. Recognize those moments and allocate the maximum possible capital to those trades. When your gut and your head are in conflict, do more work or better yet: Do nothing. Wait for high-confidence setups and ignore trades that cause internal dissonance.

To learn more about instinctive versus deliberate decision making, you should read Daniel Kahneman's classic, *Thinking Fast and Slow*. He calls the two cognitive processing systems "System 1" and "System 2" and explains (with the help of supporting research) where each system can be useful or detrimental. The book is a must-read for anyone interested in trading or behavioral finance.

This chapter is all about what makes a good trader. Go through the characteristics listed and pinpoint where you are weak and where you are strong. And then get to work on your weaknesses.

After reading this chapter, you should fully understand these key characteristics of a good trader:

- Finds the balance between risky behavior and discipline
- Thinks independently
- Controls emotions and is self-aware
- Implements a consistent daily routine
- Deals from a position of strength by getting flat
- Understands tight/aggressive
- Learns and adapts

■ Further Reading

For more on the importance of analyzing alternative hypotheses I strongly suggest you read this: https://www.cia.gov/library/center-for-the-study-of-intelligence/csi-publications/books-and-monographs/psychology-of-intelligence-analysis/art11.html.

CHAPTER 14

Common Weaknesses in Trading

While it is obvious that bad traders do not display the positive qualities listed above, there is a separate list of negative qualities that often lead to failure. Here are some characteristics of traders who fail:

■ Poor Risk Management, Bad Discipline, and Negative Risk/Reward

This is the number-one reason traders fail. They run their losing trades too long, cut their winners too fast, and pile new losses onto prior losses. This is what happens when you do not have a consistent process and good discipline. Before you do a single trade, make sure you fully and completely understand the concept of risk of ruin and how it applies to your trading. How much can you lose before you are done, fired, bankrupt, blown up? How will you avoid ever getting close to that point?

■ Trading for the Wrong Reasons

People don't trade just to make money. There are all sorts of other less obvious reasons traders trade. What follows is a list of bad habits and bad psychology that lead people to trade for the wrong reasons.

1. Overtrading, gambling, entertainment, and addiction

People have many motives (some conscious, but most subconscious) for overtrading. They trade because they are bored. They trade because they can't help themselves (bad impulse control, compulsive behavior). They trade because they are somewhere on the unsafe part of the continuum between healthy risk taking and pathological gambling.

Below is a list of behaviors that DSM-VI[1] describes as signs of a pathological gambler. Do you recognize some of these traits in yourself or other traders? Substitute the word "trading" for "gambling" and see.

- Preoccupied with gambling (e.g. preoccupied with reliving past gambling experiences, handicapping, or planning the next venture, or thinking of ways to get money with which to gamble).

- Needs to gamble with increasing amounts of money in order to achieve the desired excitement.

- Repeated unsuccessful efforts to control, cut back, or stop gambling.

- Experiences restlessness or irritability when attempting to cut down or stop gambling.

- Gambles as a way of escaping from problems or of relieving dysphoric mood (e.g. feelings of helplessness, guilt, anxiety, or depression).

- After losing money gambling, often returns another day in order to get even ("chasing" one's losses).

- Lies to family members, therapists, or others to conceal the extent of involvement with gambling.

- Has committed illegal acts such as forgery, fraud, theft, or embezzlement in order to finance gambling.

- Has jeopardized or lost a significant relationship, job, or educational or career opportunity because of gambling.

- Relies on others to provide money to relieve a desperate financial situation caused by gambling.

Yes, trading is fun. There is no doubt about that. But when you read *Reminiscences of a Stock Operator* and think, "Wow, trading is

---

[1]American Psychiatric Association, *Diagnostic and Statistical Manual of Mental Disorders*, 4th ed. (Washington, DC: American Psychiatric Association, 1992), p. 616.

so fun and exciting!" just remember that despite all that excitement in the 1920s and 1930s, Jesse Livermore went bankrupt multiple times and committed suicide in the cloakroom of Manhattan's Sherry Netherland Hotel in 1940.

Trading for fun is not a recipe for long-term success or happiness. Your goal needs to be long-term success, not short-term entertainment.

■ To Feel Smarter Than Anyone Else

Contrarian traders love the feeling of being right when everyone else is wrong and this can create all sorts of bad behaviors. I had this problem a lot when I was young but have mostly plugged the leak as I got older and less arrogant.

The main risk of trying to be smart all the time is that you will miss the obvious trades because they seem too obvious or too easy. You will try to pick tops and bottoms all the time because these are the ultimate "I feel so smart!" trades when they work. And you will avoid the strong trends because you always think that everyone else is already on board.

Many, many obvious trades work; do not be afraid to jump on a trade even if it's simple. Sometimes simple is best. Remember your goal is not to be the smartest trader in the world. Your goal is to make money in a healthy and repeatable way.

■ FOMO (Fear of Missing Out)

> ...price increases generate enthusiasm among investors, who then bid up prices more, and then it feeds back again and again until prices get too high. During that period, people are motivated by envy of others who made money doing it, regret in not having participated and the gambler's excitement.
>
> – Robert Shiller, *Irrational Exuberance*

One of the most common weaknesses I see in both rookie and veteran traders is the fear of missing out. If there is a trade that makes a ton of macroeconomic sense, traders feel stupid if they miss it. So they will protect themselves from FOMO by chasing the trade whenever it starts working. If there is a strong narrative that supports a higher dollar, for example, nobody wants to miss "The Big Dollar Rally" and so whenever the dollar moves a bit higher, traders feel compelled to chase it.

If the dollar is stuck in a range, this will lead to a lot of suboptimal buying at the highs and then stopping out at the lows when the momentum and P&L turn lower.

Here is an example of how FOMO plays out: You've been bearish and short USDJPY for three weeks and it has gone nowhere. You feel like you've been banging your head against the wall. Each time it dips, you think, "This is it!" and then it recovers and goes back to the top of the range. You are not losing much money on the trade but it's been exhausting to watch the pair drop and then rally back over and over.

Your logic was very strong when you put the trade on a few weeks ago but in the last few days you have seen that the narrative is changing and the idea has become a tad stale. Some of your original reasoning no longer applies and you know in your mind and your gut the idea is at best 50/50 at this point. Can you pull the trigger and get out? Or are you afraid of missing out if the thing finally collapses? You need to be honest with yourself and exit trades that you think are wrong, while ignoring that insistent voice in your head that says, "But what if it collapses right after I cover my short?"

The worst cases of FOMO I've seen occurred in traders who were locked into the same view for a prolonged period. I knew three different traders in the mid-2000s, for example, who were always bearish USDJPY. They were bearish for so long that they couldn't bear the thought of missing "The Big One." USDJPY tended to move very asymmetrically in those days. The expression was "USDJPY goes up the escalator and down the elevator." If you were bearish USDJPY, you knew it was always possible it might completely collapse at any moment.

But what it actually did most of the time was grind slowly and painfully higher. Even when all the short-term evidence said it made no sense to be short, these traders could not help themselves because they were so afraid of missing a big selloff, they were willing to pay the cost of being wrong over and over.

In the end, all three of those traders failed to make money and lost their jobs in 2006–2007, just before USDJPY finally collapsed. One of the most dangerous mistakes you can make as a trader is to get married to a view. That is why my AM/FX signoff is: Good luck, be nimble. Always stay flexible and never get married to a view.

Rule #23 of FX trading: Be flexible. Don't get married to a view.

If you miss a move, there will be countless others.

FOMO can also lead short-term traders to chase trades. Let's say you are bullish AUD but haven't managed to pull the trigger to go long. It's 0.8010 right now and your plan is to buy near a major technical support zone at 0.7950/60. Your target is 0.8150. So if you buy here (or better yet at 0.7950/60), your profit objective is 150 to 200 points. But AUDUSD starts rallying: 0.8030, 0.8040. Darn it, 0.8065... *Grrr.* Now you're kicking yourself because you should have (obviously) just paid the offer and gone long at 0.8010. Now it's breaking out and it looks like you missed it. *Argh.*

0.8070 trades and it's taking off just like you expected. It looks like it's going to 0.8150 in a straight line. You can't control yourself. Against your better judgment, you decide you don't want to miss the move so you buy some AUDUSD at 0.8072. You were afraid of missing out but now you have a trade with poor risk reward and only 78 more pips of upside. AUDUSD peaks and turns back lower, breaking back down below 0.8000. Frustrated, you stop out of the stupid position at 0.7986, just 26 pips above your ideal 0.7950/60 buy zone.

Understand this: You will miss many, many trades. But there are infinitely more opportunities ahead. Never fear missing out on a trade. If you miss it, you miss it.

■ To Lose Money

You read that right. This is a crazy one but some people trade to lose money. Why would someone trade to lose money? Mostly subconscious reasons. The number-one reason people lose money on purpose is that they don't believe they deserve the money they have already made.

Anyone raised by hard-working parents might find it difficult to reconcile enormous profits from trading with the minimal physical exertion required to earn them. This manifests in the subconscious and leads to money-losing behavior. "I don't deserve this money and so I am going to give it back."

You need to appreciate and internalize that trading is a very difficult skill to learn and those who succeed at trading deserve to be compensated for their success. If you don't feel deserving of the money you make, you will give it back.

Another reason people lose money on purpose is that they are too tired or burnt out to care but too scared to quit trading and do something else. This is similar to the person who treats their girlfriend or boyfriend badly in the hope that the person will break up with them.

Traders will also lose money on purpose (again subconsciously) when they hit a P&L target early in the year. The feeling of reaching a destination or goal is the ultimate reward and once a dream comes true or a goal is reached, many human beings feel a strange and hard-to-explain emptiness. By losing money and falling back away from the goal, the trader gives himself a second opportunity to get that good feeling you get when you reach a goal. As Miley Cyrus says: It's the climb.

I acknowledge that this section might sound a little weird to some people, especially younger traders. But I assure you that traders who subconsciously lose money on purpose is a real thing. Think about your subconscious motivations and make sure there is nothing simmering under the surface that might lead to suboptimal trading performance.

■ Waiting for the Perfect Trade

Risk-averse traders are often paralyzed as they wait for the perfect trade. If you often feel this way, you can still be a successful trader. Force yourself to do a certain number of trades every day, week, or month (depending on your trading time horizon).

While setting a quota for number of trades goes somewhat against the tight/aggressive mantra, if you are too tight and regularly cannot pull the trigger, a trade quota system will force you to get out of your shell and take some risk. Remember: There is no such thing as a perfect trade.

■ Invincibility/Overconfidence

Traders should operate close to the middle of the emotional spectrum most of the time. If you are feeling invincible right now, I bet you are about to lose a ton of money. Many traders will feel more and more confident as they perform well and then finally blow up as the building confidence turns to a feeling of invincibility and excessive risk.

Most traders and poker players are aware of the concept of tilt. This is when you are trading very poorly or have just hit a run of bad luck and your performance goes off the rails because your emotions get the best of you. You start making stupid plays out of frustration. You are betting to recoup losses, not because the opportunity set looks good. This is the standard definition of tilt. But be aware there is another type of tilt: winner's tilt.

For me, winner's tilt is more of a problem than loser's tilt. When I am trading poorly, I have no trouble tightening up and cutting risk because I understand that controlling the left side of the P&L distribution is what lets me survive in the long run. And I want to do this job as long as I can because I freaking love it. But when I am doing very well, I get this rush of excitement and overconfidence and go on tilt the other way. I get cartoon dollar signs in my eyes.

To manage this, I have set up conditional formatting in my P&L spreadsheet to highlight when I am overearning significantly relative to budget. These orange cells light up and tell me to settle down and reduce my risk.

You are never invincible. The market wants your money and it will figure out all sorts of ways to take it. Always exercise caution if you feel the urge to cheer or high-five or celebrate or sing out loud. If you feel this way, it is very likely you are near an emotional zenith. Get flat and reset.

■ *Woulda, Coulda, Shoulda* Syndrome

Many rookie traders spend way, way too much time thinking about the past. Once you close a trade, it is literally history. It doesn't matter anymore. Yes, it is useful to analyze past trades to understand what you have done right and wrong. But careful analysis is different from banging your head against the desk over past trades or missed trades. Once you get flat, it doesn't matter what the price does afterward. Move on.

Picture each trade that you do as a single drop in an infinite ocean. When one trade is over, there will be another. Then another. Quickly extract the lessons from failed trades and then flush them from your memory.

■ Directional Bias

Bad traders stick with the same view for way too long. This depends partly on your time horizon because if you are a long-term trader you are much more likely to be successful maintaining the same view for a long period. If you are a short-term trader, you should be flexible and able to trade every currency from both the long and the short side.

Identify currencies where you have a bias and get used to trading them from both sides. For example, if you can't stand being long AUD, try a tiny long position one day, just to see how it feels. The best short-term traders can flip from long to short and back to long as new information comes in. Sticking with a core view too long is like wearing trading handcuffs. You can waste a month or even a year committed to a faulty core view and watch dozens of great opportunities come and go. Again: Don't get married to a view.

This concludes my list of characteristics of a bad trader. Check this list and find where you match up. Write down a short list of ways you can improve in these areas. And ask yourself once in a while: Why am I trading?

The obvious answer is "to make money" but if you are honest with yourself, you might slowly pick out some other more complex reasons. Boredom, gambling, fear, to show off what big risk appetite you have, for entertainment, and so on. There are many non-economic reasons people trade and if you recognize yours, you will instantly become a better trader.

After reading this chapter, you should fully understand these key characteristics to avoid:

- Poor risk management, no consistent process, bad discipline

- Trading for the wrong reasons

- Waiting for the perfect trade

- Invincibility/overconfidence

- Directional bias (always wanting to be long or short a specific currency)

■ Further Reading

Baumeister, Roy. *Willpower: Rediscovering the Greatest Human Strength*. New York: Penguin, 2011.

CHAPTER 15

The Voice of Experience

This chapter is a collection of other thoughts, tips, and advice I can offer after 20-plus years of trading experience. I have learned a lot from all the success, mistakes, joy, pain, slumps, hills, and valleys. Remember: Take the advice that resonates with you and ignore the advice that does not. Develop your own process and find a trading style that suits your personality. Do not copy someone else's methodology. Learn and gain experience and develop your own way of doing things.

Without further ado . . . a few more tips.

■ Don't Let Random Trades Bleed You

Do you believe in the trades you have on? If yes, great. If no, get out. If you are not sure, set a clear stop loss level and stick to it. Too many random trades done out of boredom or poor discipline can drown out the P&L from your good ideas.

Quite often when I am trading poorly, my primary, well-thought-out ideas are still good but the P&L from these trades is wiped out by losses on spontaneous, knee-jerk trades. This type of overtrading can be very discouraging as you are forced to cut good ideas to cover losses in stupid ding-dong trades.

> Rule #24 of FX trading: Do not let random, low-conviction
> trades kill you.

The human brain loves novelty. It is always looking for something new to do and a new trade to consider or add to the portfolio. Resist this constant need to adjust your positions. Let your trades breathe.

■ How to Avoid Overtrading

The simplest way to avoid overtrading is to be extremely disciplined. This is obvious and self-explanatory. But what if you are not a very well-disciplined person or have poor impulse control? You need to understand yourself and be honest about your strengths *and your weaknesses*. The x-factor skills that make good traders (risk appetite, strong instincts, rapid decision making, courage, decisiveness, confidence) can also be the trader's worst enemy as the flipside of those positive traits can be: too much risk, overtrading, overconfidence, and impulsive, addictive, reactionary behavior that deviates from plan.

If you have a severe problem with overtrading, set a trade quota or specific time windows to trade. Use stop loss and take profit orders to manage your positions the rest of the time. A quota system means simply allowing yourself only a certain number of trades per day or per week. Maybe three. Maybe five. Set the quota based on your trading history. When you are trading well, how many trades do you average per day?

If you don't like the quota approach, another trick is to allow yourself to trade only at specific times. For example, it often makes sense to put new trades on or take trades off at 7AM NY and then leave everything until at least 11:00AM NY. This allows your trades a full NY/LDN overlap session to play out and avoids the need for instant gratification and constant fine-tuning. It also saves mental energy because you are not constantly analyzing and reevaluating everything on a second-to-second basis. Finally, it avoids the very high transaction costs and P&L drain associated with frequent unnecessary intraday trading in and out of the same position.

Under this time of day method, you do as many trades as you like but only at the designated times of day. This could be the equity open, end of day, the 11:00AM fixing (when FX volumes peak), or any other time related to your trading style. When I am trading well, I tend to put new trades on in the morning (7/8AM) and reduce them or take them off at either 11:00AM or 4:00PM. This is because I feel like the good moves tend to happen during the NY/LDN overlap and because I tend to have more risk during the day than overnight.

The quota or time-based approaches are effective because they are very clear and rule-based. *Write down your rules and follow them.* Set yourself a trade quota or set specific times of day when you are allowed to trade and then stick to your rules. A major side benefit of this approach is that it gives you more time to concentrate, read, and do research, undistracted by flickering price action on the screen and free of the need to constantly reevaluate and make new decisions.

In my early years of trading, it was always a huge struggle to solve my overtrading problem. I would write myself Post-It Notes and stick them all over my desk: "Don't trade until 9AM!" or "WAIT! WAIT!" and so on, but nothing worked. I wouldn't follow my own rules. Then finally (after a great cost) I had a breakthrough.

Recognizing that I have the sort of personality that makes me frequently trade out of boredom, I found a new technique. Instead of trying to abstain completely from trading, I decided to vary my position size dramatically. Now I trade all the time, but when I'm dabbling and messing around, I trade 1 unit of risk compared to 5 or 10 or 20 units of risk on a high-conviction trade. This is riskier and more open-ended than the rule-based approach outlined above but sometimes you have to be realistic and make your approach fit your personality, style, and job description.

The benefit of this extremely flexible position sizing strategy is that I remain involved in the market all the time. That helps keep me in the zone and gives me a feel for the market while I wait for high-conviction trades to emerge. If I can break even or lose small on my 1-unit trades and they help me be in the right place at the right time for the Five-Star, 20-unit trades, that's a win. This method of managing my overtrading has improved my profitability and reduced my frustration level dramatically. It acknowledges the faults in my personality and deals with them in an honest way.

Try to design rules, systems, and processes that fit your personality and allow you to function with as little mental friction as possible. Overtrading is one of the main issues that ruins traders. If you are prone to overtrading, get serious about it and fix the problem before you churn away your trading career.

■ Trading Slumps

There is nothing more gut-wrenching than a major trading slump. No matter how many losing streaks you have experienced, each slump brings with it the same array of negative emotions. Self-hate, frustration, self-doubt, physical nausea, a lump in the throat, the urge to smash keyboards, sadness, confusion, and vertigo are all normal symptoms of a trading slump.

Slumps can come completely out of the blue. One day you seem to know what will happen before it happens. The next day, you have fat fingers, you hesitate, you miss the great opportunities and double down on the bad ones. Suddenly, you've lost money eight days in a row and you feel like you might never make money again. FX is hard.

The first thing to understand is that there are probabilities at work. A trader with 55% winning days will average two or three 5-day losing streaks per year and probably one 6-day losing streak. A 6-day losing streak is enough to make the best trader feel like a complete moron. But he isn't. It's just probability.

It is easy to say this, and a totally different thing to embrace and accept it. That is why slumps can be very dangerous. They can morph from a simple run of good decision/bad outcome into something much more nefarious. If the run of bad outcomes leads to process breakdown and bad decisions, what was initially just bad luck becomes a negative feedback loop. If you are normally a 55% winner and you came in this morning angry, frustrated, and a bit hopeless, what do you think your odds of making money are going to be today? 40%? 35%?

The first key to dealing with slumps is good self-awareness. Recognize physical signs of frustration and acknowledge them. You cannot deal with a trading slump if you are not aware of it or you are in denial.

Once you realize that you are in a slump, the first thing to do is slow down. Breathe. Take a day off or cut your positions down dramatically. If I usually trade 100 million USD positions, I might cut myself down to 20 million. If I lose money again, I'll drop to 10 million.

Why not stop trading completely?

This is a matter of personal preference but I rarely stop trading completely. I might take one day off to reset mentally but if I am at work I keep trading, just in smaller size. Short-term trading has a rhythm and you are apt to lose that rhythm if you stop trading completely. Instead, cut yourself down to something small enough that it will not matter if you are right or wrong. The object at this point is not to make money but to reset your emotions while still maintaining a connection to the market.

If things are going really, really badly, and I feel really dejected or down, I will stop trading altogether for one or two days and jump into a research project. I keep a file of ideas and projects so that when I hit a very rough patch, I can step away from the market and still feel like I am doing something useful. It's hard to do research when you are in the zone trading so I try to see bad slumps as blessings that finally let me get to that backtesting or correlation research project I have not had time for.

Some traders prefer to disconnect from the market completely by pulling out temporarily, but as Jared Dillian once said, the markets are like a story. You can't just flip ahead 10 pages and know what is going on.

My view on taking scheduled time off is different. Vacations are a necessary part of a healthy trading process. Your brain cannot process billions of bits of market information efficiently 52 weeks a year. You need to turn off the noise now and then.

Three or four days away from the market should be enough to clear your brain and allow you to come back fresh. The only way to achieve this is to go on vacation and *stay flat while on vacation*; otherwise your brain will be running all the scenarios about possible EURUSD outcomes instead of just digging holes with your kid on the beach or enjoying the music at Ibiza or whatever it is you do to unwind.

Go on vacation flat at least once per year. Any positive P&L you might generate with your holiday positions is more than offset by the mental damage you do to your brain when you refuse to let it disconnect from the matrix.

With experience, you will know when a slump is over. Things will seem easier again. Each losing trade will not trigger an emotional or physical reaction (tight throat, white knuckles). Given my belief that trading is very much about probabilities and process, I don't stay in defensive mode for very long. Once I feel okay, I go back to my normal size. The best cure for a trading slump is a perfectly executed Five-Star trade.

A different type of slump is one precipitated not by a run of bad luck but by a concrete externality. This type of slump is totally different from a normal slump and is triggered by something outside the market, not just random variance: your health, financial security, marriage, mental well-being, an addiction, or something of that sort. If a slump like this comes along, get flat right away and figure things out before you come back.

Trading is not an escape and there are cheaper ways to forget about your worries. Until the issue is resolved or dealt with in a way that will not interrupt your train of thought at work, stay flat. Trading is stressful enough; if you are shaking with anger as you just hung up the phone after a fight with your sibling about who will take care of your sick mother, take the rest of the day off.

Next-level trading is when you know yourself and you consistently put that knowledge to use. Don't let externalities ruin you. You will never know what kind of trader you have the potential to become unless you give yourself the opportunity to succeed. Part of this is knowing when to trade and when not to trade.

FACTBOX: HOW I HANDLE SLUMPS

Here is my step-by-step strategy for handling slumps.

Square Up

First, I cut all existing positions so that any residual frustration related to those losing views can dissipate.

Trade Smaller

Next, I cut my position size for new ideas to about 20% of normal for a few days (or more) until I get a strong feeling and high-conviction idea. Some people recommend not trading at all for a bit but I find this disconnects me too much from the market and I lose my feel. I would rather trade small, wait for a Five-Star idea, then fully reengage. If I am feeling extremely frustrated (angry lump in throat) or recognize my state of mind is poor (bad health, external real-life issues), I'll stop completely, but this is rare.

Talk about the Slump

I find just talking about a slump makes me feel better about it. Frustration boils inside but releases when you open up. Some firms have trading psychologists around but you can also just talk to your peers or friends or boss. When you discuss your trading out loud, it helps crystallize your thoughts and leads to forward progress and a calmer state of mind.

Read and Do Research

When I'm trading well, my entire focus is on the market and on staying in the zone. When things are not going well, it's a chance to catch up on reading, do some cool research projects I haven't had time for, and get back to basics by rereading stuff like the Market Wizards books.

Get Some Perspective

I am one of 7.6 billion people sitting on a huge, spinning rock hurtling around a spherical ball of hot plasma in an infinitely large universe. Meanwhile, this is the safest time in human history to be alive. My wife and kids are healthy. It's sunny and warm outside. No matter what happens in G10 FX today, the sun will still come up tomorrow. Markets always get better; you just have to ride out the tough times and stay resilient and optimistic.

■ Tips for a Happy Life

Believe it or not, there is more to life than FX trading. Think about the long game and your entire career. While it is fun to trade all night and live a fast and exciting life, you cannot do that forever. FX does not provide a path to happiness, no matter how much money you make. Financial freedom is one small part of happiness, but most research shows true happiness comes from other areas: health, relationships, family, friends, and a feeling of purpose.

In fact, the relationship between money and happiness becomes very weak once you break above around $75,000 in the United States. A variety of research[1] shows that once you can comfortably provide food, clothing, and shelter plus a bit more, money doesn't make you any happier.

■ Get Some Perspective

While it might feel like your P&L ups and down are a matter of life and death, they are not. Traders spend way too much time thinking about P&L and money and all the things it might mean to them. The reality is that money is a small input into overall happiness. Focus on trading when you are at work and focus on relationships and activities you love when you are not.

A life of trading is a life full of hills and valleys. Every time you lose more money than you ever have before, it hurts. Right in the gut. And every time you make a new "best day" or hit your lifetime high-water mark, there is a giddy sensation that is hard to regulate. If you are a good trader, you will trade with more and more capital and bigger and bigger positions as the years go by and therefore by definition your biggest up and down days will get bigger and bigger over time.

Some traders (including myself up until about 5 or 6 years ago) are afraid to feel happy or admit their satisfaction after a great day or a great trade because they don't want to jinx themselves. This creates an asymmetry where you feel bad after bad days but you don't give yourself the right to feel good after good days. Over the years, this can be incredibly draining because you only let yourself feel the bad emotions. *If you have a good day, feel good about it.* Be happy. Go celebrate. Buy the better bottle of wine. But don't celebrate until you have taken profit! Celebrating while in a winning position is a recipe for upcoming disaster. Take profit, then go be happy.

So again, it is fine to feel good about your trading. It is fine to give yourself credit where credit is due. Don't dissect your great days to find the tiny thing you could have done better. Just be happy for one day.

Make lower highs and higher lows emotionally as time goes on. Avoid euphoria but give yourself permission to be happy and to feel fulfilled when you are trading well. A life of hating yourself when

---

[1]This is a good example: http://www.pnas.org/content/107/38/16489.full.pdf.

you're down and fearing the next drawdown when you're up is not healthy. When you do a good job, it's okay to be proud of yourself.

As time goes on, you should be able to figure out how to manage your emotions so that while your P&L is making higher highs, your emotions become less volatile. You recognize after a while that no matter how bad the day, or how bad the loss, you don't die. It might feel like you are going to die, but you don't. The only way to learn this is to experience mind-numbing losses. As my boss once told me after a particularly bad day of trading: You don't learn anything when you win. Every loss is a lesson. Every gain is a blessing. Stay positive.

A major requirement for staying positive is that you must have a risk management system that you trust. If you know you can trust yourself and your risk management, the sick feeling of having blown through your stop loss can be avoided. Many world-class traders are only right 50% or 55% of the time. There is no reason to feel bad on days you lose money. Imagine if Michael Jordan got down on himself every time he missed a shot. He would be a sad person, full of self-loathing.

The time you *should* feel bad is when you planned to risk $200,000 on a trade and you lost a million dollars. These are the cases when you should feel bad because deep down inside these days make you wonder if you can really trust yourself and if you are truly in control of the process. This is the worst possible feeling. It's scary.

You need to have clear risk management rules and then treat every day as a separate unit and compartmentalize your feelings. You run into problems when your risk management is bad and it spills into the next day and the next because it puts you under pressure or forces you to change your process or abandon your plan.

Don't break the rules.

Simple right?

No. It is very, very difficult. Everyone knows that if you eat too much and don't exercise, you will gain weight. But there are still plenty of overweight people around. Knowing the rules is easy. Following them is hard.

Always remember though: hills and valleys, hills and valleys. Don't let yourself get too high or too low. Regardless of your P&L, the sun will still rise tomorrow, your kids will still love you, and even in the most extreme situation where you end up losing your job as a trader, life *still* goes on.

■ Don't Constantly Check the Market

Spend time with your family. Stop checking the market every two seconds for no reason when you have a one-week view! Exercise, play with your kids, and get a solid block of sleep every night.

■ Turn off Your Phone at Night

It sounds cool to tell people at parties that you wake up at 2:00AM every night to check the market and do some FX trades, but it is counterproductive. You will burn yourself out. The net result of getting up to trade in the middle of the night will be that your career will be shorter and your lifetime earning potential will be lower. You will also trade poorly the next day because of fatigue. I have a strict policy: I turn my phone off at 10:00PM and turn it back on when I wake up at 4:00AM. Phone calls in the middle of the night don't have enough upside to justify the downside. You make poor trading decisions when you are half-asleep.

■ Read Nonfinancial Books

I like to alternate between finance/math books and "other." There is nothing more boring than a person who reads only finance books.

■ Eat Properly and Exercise

I know I'm starting to sound like your mom, but she was right. Bank traders tend to eat fatty restaurant food every day because the desk analyst takes one bulk order and picks up lunch for everyone. It is easier just to add your order to the list than to get off the trading floor and get your own lunch. Don't be lazy.

A secondary benefit to getting your own lunch is that there is value in getting away from the market intraday to collect your thoughts. Many traders report moments of clarity and trade ideas that came to the surface on the way to or from the bathroom. It won't hurt you to go for a quick walk once or twice a day. Sure, there is a chance you might miss a great headline trade but in the long run you will be better off. Take care of yourself and think about the long game.

■ Have Fun

This is a tough one because most traders beat themselves up when they lose and are afraid to be happy when they win. But remember that FX trading is a fun job compared to most—you are lucky to be a trader. When I was day trading the NASDAQ with my own money during the tech bubble, the firm where I rented a seat had a huge banner hung above the trading floor that read: THANK GOD IT'S MONDAY. If you don't feel like that most of the time, find another job.

To succeed, you need to absolutely love FX trading. Smile, have fun, and be thankful you get to enjoy such an intellectually challenging and heart-pounding pursuit.

When people used to ask me why I chose trading as a career, I would answer:

> "Because I am not good enough to play major league baseball."

Trading is the second-best job in the world.
I am thankful.

> **Rule #25 of FX trading: Have fun. If you don't enjoy it, what's the point?**

After reading this chapter, you should fully understand these key concepts:

- Do not let random trades bleed your capital

- How to deal with trading slumps

- How to maintain a healthy perspective on life and trading

- Why it's important to have fun

■ Further Reading

Coates, John. *The Hour Between Dog and Wolf: Risk Taking, Gut Feelings and the Biology of Boom and Bust.* New York: Penguin Press, 2012.

Douglas, Mark. *The Disciplined Trader: Developing Winning Attitudes.* New York Institute of Finance, 1990.

———. *Trading in the Zone: Master the Market with Confidence, Discipline and a Winning Attitude.* Upper Saddle River, NJ: Prentice Hall Press, 2000.

Gardner, Dan. *Risk: The Science of Politics and Fear.* London: Virgin Books, 2008.

Krakauer, Jon. *Into the Wild.* New York: Anchor Books, 1996.

Pirsig, Robert. *Zen and the Art of Motorcycle Maintenance: An Inquiry into Values.* New York: William Morrow, 1974.

Thoreau, Henry David. *Walden.* Boston: Ticknor and Fields, 1854.

CHAPTER 16

Conclusion

When I started trading at a commercial bank in 1995, my boss said to me, "Burl,[1] you're in the right place at the wrong time. Everything is going electronic and there will be no such thing as human FX traders in the next 10 years. Sorry about your luck!"

Needless to say, the guy was blunt. To the point. And to be fair, his overall thesis was accurate. Major spot FX trading desks that employed 20 or 30 traders in 1995 now employ 3 or 4. But those who survived this attrition (like me, thankfully, so far) continue to prosper and the job has become much, much more intellectually stimulating.

When it was busy in the 1990s, you spent your whole day acting like a broker, executing client trades with no regard for any macro or fundamental stories. All you wanted was to keep your position straight and survive the waves of insanity and yelling. Now, electronic platforms handle the majority of client flow and human traders are left to manage the big tickets and think about how to stay one step ahead of the market. Instead of pushing through client tickets all day like an agent, FX traders today spend most of their time thinking about how to beat the market.

With electronification comes other new opportunities. Retail FX technology has gone from 0 to 100 in two short decades and now individual traders can buy and sell currencies from home on spreads as narrow as one basis point. They can access almost all the same research that was once available only to interbank and buy-side traders. Quant and research jobs are no longer niche; they are a big part of every FX business. As transaction costs tumble, high-frequency strategies and electronic market making have gained a foothold and opened the door for a whole new generation of mathletes.

---

[1]He claims to this day that I look like Burl Ives.

Things will always change. Rangebound markets will range and range until they break and finally trend. Trending markets will grind through painful consolidations and eventually fail. Correlation traders will clean up one year and get rinsed the next. Momentum rules, until it doesn't.

There is a world of money to be made in the FX markets. Those with skill who do the work and have the discipline to stick to a plan will win. Those without skill, those with poor self-control, and those who are lazy or cannot adapt will go extinct via natural selection.

Do the work. Have courage. Follow your own rules. Enjoy yourself, and be thankful.

Thank you so much for taking the time to read my book. I hope it has given you a new perspective on trading along with new strategies, tools, and ideas that you can put to work right away. I hope it makes you a better currency trader and helps you generate profitable trade ideas. I hope you have enjoyed *The Art of Currency Trading*.

Good luck ↕ Be nimble

www.theartofcurrencytrading.com

Brent Donnelly's 25 Rules of FX Trading

Rule #1 of FX Trading: Don't blow up. Avoid risk of ruin above all else.

Rule #2 of FX Trading: Adapt or die.

Rule #3 of FX Trading: Do the work. Read the speeches. Analyze, read, and study.

Rule #4 of FX trading: If you look hard enough, you can always a find a tech level to justify a bad trade!

Rule #5 of FX trading: "It's a big level" is not a good enough reason to put on a trade.

Rule #6 of FX Trading: No mo' FOMO. Never worry about missing it. There will always be another trade.

Rule #7 of FX Trading: Flat is the strongest position. When in doubt, get out.

Rule #8 of FX Trading: It doesn't always have to make sense.

Rule #9 of FX Trading: Never fade unexpected central bank moves. Jump on them!

Rule #10 of FX Trading: Making money is hard. Keeping it is harder.

Rule #11 of FX Trading: Successful traders make more money on up days than they lose on down days.

Rule #12 of FX Trading: Anything can happen.

Rule #13 of FX Trading: Keep a trading journal. Thoughts are abstract and fuzzy. Writing is concrete and solid.

Rule #14 of FX Trading: There is a time and a place to go big.

Rule #15 of FX Trading: Good traders vary bet size.

Rule #16 of FX Trading: It always looks bid at the highs. It always looks heavy at the lows.

Rule #17 of FX Trading: You control the process but you *do not* control the outcome.

Rule #18 of FX Trading: Each trade is a drop of water. The market is an ocean.

Rule #19 of FX Trading: Know your edge.

Rule #20 of FX Trading: Know your time horizon.

Rule #21 of FX Trading: Good traders have a plan. They may not always stick to the plan but they always have one.

Rule #22 of FX Trading: Tight/aggressive wins.

Rule #23 of FX trading: Be flexible. Don't get married to a view.

Rule #24 of FX trading: Do not let random, low-conviction trades kill you.

Rule #25 of FX trading: Have fun. If you don't enjoy it, what's the point?

Brent Donnelly has been trading currencies since 1995 and is currently a senior FX trader at HSBC New York. He writes a widely read and highly respected macro and FX daily called AM/FX. Over the course of his career, he has been a market maker, trader, and senior manager at some of the top banks in foreign exchange. He has extensive experience trading spot FX, interest rate products, FX options, stock index futures, single name equities, and commodities.

Brent is a respected macroeconomic and currency analyst with the unique perspective of a senior risk taker. His work has been quoted by the *Economist,* the *Wall Street Journal, Financial Times,* Bloomberg, and CNBC.

Before joining HSBC, Brent was head of G10 Spot Trading at Citi New York and global head of G10 FX Trading at Nomura New York. He was also a portfolio manager at a major hedge fund in Connecticut for three years. He created and wrote a cartoon called "Daft Planet," which aired on TV in Canada, and he dreams of one day winning the Man Booker Prize.